THE EAGLE IN ITS FLIGHT

Being The Memoir Of
The Hon. Sir Udo Udoma, CFR

Unless, we do things -
that have never been done
the Law stands still.

In Church On February 1, 1998

Order placed: May 12th
Delivered: May 14th 2021.
National Anthem. Nigeria
O GOD... Help us to Build a Nation

THE EAGLE IN ITS FLIGHT

A Disciple of Justice.
Where Peace and Justice shall Reign.
Where Being the Memoir of The no man
is Hon. Sir Udo Udoma, CFR oppressed.
Matthew. 12:20.
"A Battered Reed HE will - not break, and a smoldering Wick HE will not quench, till HE Bring Justice and a Just Cause to Victory."

Amazing Grace Publishers

USA • Nigeria • UK

IEI

Published by Amazing Grace Publishers, an Ikemesit Enterprise

Ikemesit Enterprises, Inc.,
P. O. Box 42, West Haven, CT 06516, USA
8 Dr. Udoma Street, Ikot Abasi, Akwa Ibom State, NIGERIA

Copyright©2008 by Estate of Sir Udo Udoma
All rights reserved

ISBN 978-0-9819192-1-8
ISBN 978-1-7342415-4-9

Printed in the UK and the USA
Designed by Ayanti Udo Udoma

THE LAW OF PERIODICITY

"There is a tide to the affairs of men, which, taken at the flood, leads on to fortune". – **SHAKESPEARE**

"To every thing there is a season, and a time to every purpose under the heaven; a time to be born, and a time to die; a time to plant, and a time to pluck up that which is planted". – **KING SOLOMON**

"And is not time even as love is, undivided and paceless? But if in your thought you must measure time into seasons, let every season encircle all the other seasons, And let today embrace the past with remembrance and the future with longing". – **KHALIL GIBRAN**

IN MEMORIAM

The Hon Sir Udo Udoma passed through transition in the morning of February 2, 1998 and was buried among the bones of his ancestors, as he wished, on March 27, 1998 in his pre-designed chamber at MFUT ITIAT ENIN (in the shelter of the Elephant Rock), his family home in Ikot Abasi, Akwa Ibom State of Nigeria.

Proceeds from sales will benefit the SIR UDO UDOMA LIBRARY and the SIR UDO UDOMA CHAPEL projects.

TABLE OF CONTENTS

Table of Contents

Preface

"Be ashamed to die until you have won some victory for humanity".
- Horace Mann

Growing up as kids at Aba, we hardly saw our dad since he was always away making the name that the world has come to recognise. We would get home from school to hear that he had come back from one trip but then had left again on another. When he was at home, nobody would go near him since he would be working in his Chambers, located in the premises, entertaining guests in the living room or perhaps having his meal. Unless we ran into him as he was walking somewhere at which time we would greet him, we did not have cause to speak with him. When occasion arose, of course, he would call for us, usually individually, to discuss our school report or maybe to give us chocolate, or grapes or the like which he had brought back for us from a trip. When we were noisy playing around the house, we would hear his "roar" and instantaneously perform the disappearing act. So, essentially, our mum passed on his marching orders to us and delivered to him whatever requests we had. Mum paid our school fees and bought our clothes although the money came from dad.

After we moved to Lagos and I grew into my teen years, my perception of dad began to take form. As I got more aware of the political, economic and moralistic goings on in the country, I began to appreciate the narrow road my dad was taking vis-à-vis these happenings and began to identify with his stand on various issues. I even understood his stand that if his children's fees were paid to their boarding school, which fees included their allowance – albeit all of three pounds ten (£3.10s) for an entire term - there was no reason to give them any "pocket money" as they called it. Of course, then the onus of trying to explain this to my younger brothers who, like me, could not do much with their allowance, a little of which they would have to line up on Saturdays in front of the bursar's office to withdraw, and sign for, fell upon me. People perceived our family as bourgeoisie and we the children as *aje butter* – butter eaters. But little did they know that we were *aje butter* with no money in our pockets to buy butter!

How many people in their twenties would get invited to the Royal Empire Hotel in London to meet with Lord Frederick Dealtry Lugard, the man who amalgamated Nigeria? What are the chances that a young colony native would get to confront a predecessor of the Governor General of their country whose soldiers mowed down their mother along with other defenceless women over a civil protest against the imposition of toll tax on women after they merely respectfully accepted a meeting invitation from the Colonial Divisional Officer? And how many people in their twenties would dare to write a Society Presidency installation address at a United Kingdom College as a critique of British colonial policy? Further, how many who perchance do would have one of the greatest British colonial administrators request for their autograph on his personal copy of that same Presidential Address that criticises him? Well, my dad had the rare combination of intelligence, industry, conviction, guts, opportunity and honour to accomplish all of the above feats at a time that there was ongoing debate on British colonial policy, particularly Indirect Rule of which Lord Lugard was reputedly the authority and originator. If, before that, the authorities did not realise what a rare breed dad was, you can say that they had started noticing. In contrast to him, what did I accomplish in my twenties? Well, I played cricket for Lagos state, Nigeria and West Africa and left behind an enviable record. Some cricket enthusiasts even say that I revolutionised wicket keeping in West Africa. I got to shake hands with the presidents of several African countries, too. I may even have been the ladies' best friend. Well, that compares to my dad's feat; does it not? Yeah, right; think again.

By the age of 39, "the Man" had a thriving law practice going and was the Vice-President of the Nigerian Bar Association; he had formed a political party along with some people of like mind; he was the President of the Ibibio Union; he was the proprietor of a newspaper; he was the founder of a secondary school; he was the recognised champion of the COR State Movement - the first agitators for the creation of states in Nigeria - and he had paid for several students abroad to be able to complete their studies and return home. He financed most of these endeavours himself. Yes, by 39! In contrast, what did I accomplish at 39? Well, you get my drift …

Dad was so visionary and such a pioneering spirit; but he was also, oh, so traditional. But, he did not just wallow in the simple security of traditional assumptions but rather handed down to us only the tested statements, beliefs, legends, customs, etc. that came from his father's generation to his. He found initiation into and therefore membership of traditional societies, like the "Ekpe", "Attat" and "Ekpo Nyoho" titled societies not incompatible with being a Christian (being like Christ) because he realised that symbolism is actually the boon of spirituality. He quoted from the *Ibibio Book of Wisdom* in all his books and in this one explains how he named his family home and his children the Ibibio way. So flexible was dad though, in spite of his adherence to tradition, that when at fifteen I wrote to him to enquire as to the meaning of my name, realising that "Anyanti" was an Igbo name (see "My Odyssey – An Autobiography" by Nnamdi Azikiwe; ref. P. 261, 441), he agreed with me in his reply and directed that it should be changed from "Anyanti" to "Ayanti", which has Ibibio connotation. My great, great grandfather whose name I bear must have whispered into his ears. My enquiry was made notwithstanding the fact that "Anyanti" ("the ear's eyes" in Ibo) had a certain appeal to me as it connoted something in the realm of "psychic". Anyway, being a traditionalist, dad not surprisingly uses the old spelling in the earlier chapters of this book but the new spelling in Chapter 25.

I am extremely proud of my father – proud of all his accomplishments but more than anything else, I am most proud of who he was. He was a man of integrity and the utmost honesty and he was driven by the need to give of himself and to do the utmost good. I admire his relentless pursuit of the truth and of progress for his people, be they Ibibios, Nigerians or Africans. I feel immensely privileged and proud to be able to get his autobiography published even if over ten years after the fact. It was unfinished when he left us and I knew as soon as I was made aware of the manuscript of this book that this was part of his legacy to you and us. I know that he, the traditional person that he was, wanted me to finish this book and he would have been most unhappy had we used a ghost-writer to do it. I have written the last two chapters as I saw him during that period before his death and I believe that those two chapters in addition to this preface will give you an added perspective often absent from an autobiography such as this.

The chapters of this book are, in the main, in the same order that my dad had them in the manuscript even though I could see that there were one or two of them that he reordered at one time or another. I took the liberty of moving the lengthy report of the landmark case *Uganda vs. The Commissioner of Prisons Ex parte Matovu* to the end of the book as an appendix to enhance the readability of the book. The case generated interest among legal practitioners and those in the legal system in Nigeria, primarily because of the parallels as well as the contrasts drawn between it and *Lakanmi vs. Attorney-General, West*, a case that was heard by the Supreme Court of Nigeria in 1970 with dad, who later referred to the court's judgment as nonsense, being one of the sitting judges. I believe that moving it to the end of the book allows those not particularly interested in constitutional law or coupe jurisprudence to read the book unburdened while those who are can skip to the appendices at their leisure to peruse the details of the case. I have also included as an appendix his much celebrated Presidential Address at his installation as President of the Philosophical Society (the Phil) at Trinity College, Dublin. It is titled "The Lion & The Oil Palm". Also appendices are his silver medal essay at the Phil, which essay is titled "The Clash of Cultures", and his address on how the states movements started in Nigeria. I have "cut and pasted" a couple of paragraphs in order to conform to the chronological approach that dad seems to have adopted. The only thematic chapter is Chapter 25 which was positioned to correspond with the year that his family was consummated, i.e., the year his last child, Enoabasi, was born. I have also inserted, under "Fair Use" protection, a selection from dad's treasury of *quotable quotes* at the beginning of each chapter of this book.

I have written what I know to be the truth and nothing but the truth and am publishing what my dad wrote from his first hand knowledge, all for posterity. Like him who lived "Law and Order", I have absolute faith in the Law and Justice of the land and more importantly in the Laws and Justice of nature. I take full responsibility for publishing this my loving dad's memoir and any objections, questions, criticisms or actions should be directed at or to me. As Khalil Gibran says in "The Prophet":

What man's law shall bind you if you break your yoke but upon no man's prison door? What laws shall you fear if you dance but stumble against no man's iron chains? And who is he that shall bring you to judgment if you tear your garment yet leave it in no man's path?

Dad was a man of peace, a man of faith and a man of action. He believed in the practice of "teaching to fish" rather than "giving fish". He played the cards that Providence dealt him in the unwavering belief that that was his destiny. That destiny is the legacy handed us by him. Let us use it for our own edification and progress so that his vision for us all will be perpetuated. That was his hope. On behalf of my siblings Inam, Udoma, Ebong, Ekpo, and Enoabasi, and my humble self I sincerely hope that you derive the utmost pleasure and benefit from reading this book. Our mother, Lady Grace Udoma, joins us in wishing you all well. Please, feel free to send me comments. God bless you.

Ayanti Udo Udoma   June 21, 2008 (dad's 91st birth anniversary day)

Mfut Itiat Enin,
No. 8 Dr. Udoma Street,
Ikot Abasi, Akwa Ibom State, NIGERIA.
ikemesit.inc@gmail.com

CHAPTER ONE

The Eagle Flaps Its Wings And Flies Off

"A family has at its core the agnatic lineage. A lineage is a group of people coming or who are descended from a common ancestor. An agnatic or patrilineal lineage is a group of people descended from a common ancestor through males".

I was born on 21 June 1917 at Ete town of Oduk Ukpuum, that is Ukpuum clan, on the auspicious occasion of the staging and performance of *Mbre Abakpa*, which means Abakpa Masquerade display, by the young men of Ikot Abasi town of Ikpa Ibekwe Ntanaran Akama Obio Offiong (Ikpa Ibekwe for short) clan under the distinguished leadership of my beloved father of blessed memory, who was also the grand patron and head of the Abakpa Masquerade Club. The occasion of my birth was unique and significant in that both my parents were visitors to Ete town primarily in connection with the staging and performing of the Abakpa masquerade dance, my father being accompanied, as was the practice in those days, by my mother, his younger wife, then under pregnancy.

As was well known in the area, both my father, Obong Udoma Inam Anyanti Umo Idonho Abasi Akpan Enin (Udoma Inam for short) and my mother, Madam Adiaha Edem, whose Christian name was Mary, were indigenes of Ikot Abasi Akpan Enin (Ikot Abasi for short) village, the former being a prominent member of Otung Anyanti (that is, Anyanti quarter) and the latter a member of Otung Ima (Ima quarter) both of which quarters were units within Ikot Abasi village in Ikpa Ibekwe clan. My father, Obong Udoma Inam, was the younger brother of Obong Akpan Inam Anyanti Umo Idonho Abasi Akpan Enin (Akpan Inam for short) who, as my natural uncle, was famous as the President of the old native court known as Qua Court, which was the first native court converted from an equity court, in Ikot Abasi river, established by the British Administration. The court was called Qua Court because the people of Bonny usually then referred to the Ibibio inhabitants of Ibekwe clan as Qua (Kwa) people. The Qua (Kwa) people of Ikot Abasi and Ibekwe clan must not be confused with the Qua people of Calabar division.

As the first court established by the British administration for the local people of Ikot Abasi in those days, Qua Court later had to serve the people of Andoni, Ogoni and Ibibio areas then regarded as the same and related peoples in the administrative division, which came to be called Opobo following the foundation of Opobo Town on December 25, 1870 by refugees from Bonny under the leadership of Jaja (Chief Jack Jojo Annie Pepple) and there after the establishment of the Oil Rivers protectorate in 1891 by Sir Claude MacDonald, Commissioner and Consul General of the Oil Rivers protectorate of which Calabar was constituted headquarters or capital.

The story of my birth, as told, was that at the material time my father, being the leader of the young men in Ikot Abasi, was selected by elders to take charge of the staging of Abakpa masquerade display. As a result, my father was in charge of all the dancers and drummers and had to lead them as a team to Ete town for the staging of the masquerade display in response to the invitation extended to the club, of which my father was head, by the Obongs and the people of Ete town. The masquerade display and dance were staged at the public square in Ete town for the entertainment of the people. My father, when leaving for Ete town, had to take his younger wife, my mother, with him, as was the practice in those days even though my mother was at an advanced stage of pregnancy.

My father along with the dancers, drummers, masquerades and all those who accompanied them had to spend over one week in Ete town so as to satisfy the demands of the Obongs and people of Ete who admired the masquerades and also enjoyed their dances. Indeed, it was reported that the Obongs and people were so thrilled and excited by the dances as performed by the visitors that, like Oliver Twist, they had to ask for more. Consequently, the masquerades and the dancers had to extend the period of their stay in Ete town in order to satisfy the wishes of the Obongs and people. It was during the extension of their stay at Ete town beyond the original planned period, and indeed because of it, that I had to be born there. Had the period not been extended, it might have been possible for my mother to have returned home in normal circumstances to give birth to me at Ikot Abasi. Therefore, my birth at Ete was purely accidental and circumstantial.

By reason of my having been born at Ete during the staging and display of *Mbre Abakpa* and to commemorate the occasion, which was considered significant in the life of my father, I was named "Abakpa" and the first young woman engaged to serve my mother as my nanny was an indigene of Ete named Emma. My mother brought the young woman to Ikot Abasi during the evacuation of Ete by the players for the purpose of returning to Ikot Abasi after their rewarding performance. According to the story, five months after the return of the team of dancers engaged in staging *Mbre Abakpa* at Ete, "Armistice" in connection with the First World War was declared on November II, 1917 by the booming of guns at the Consulate beach at Ikot Abasi (then known as Opobo).

Curiously enough, shortly after my birth and immediately my parents returned with the team of dancers to Ikot Abasi, my father made special arrangements for my initiation and I, even though a child, was initiated into the Attat and the Ekpo Nyoho titled societies, having previously on my birth at Ete been initiated into the Ekong titled society by the usual ceremony known as the tying of *ejei* (young palm fronds) round the wrist of my left hand. Before my initiation into the titled societies, I was given the name of Inam according to tradition and as a result of which my beloved father used to call me *Ete,* meaning father, since I was named after his father, Inam. From then on, my father used to address me as *Ete* up till the time of his death in 1936. I was his beloved son - the image of his father.

Miss Emma, having served my mother for over three years as my nanny, was herself engaged to be married to Mr. Johnson Ukpa, a famous carpenter in Ikot Abasi who had his training at Bonny Government School. On her marriage to Mr. Johnson Ukpa, she was succeeded by another young woman known as Ukwa, a native of Ikot Ekop in Mkpat Enin local government area.

Having taken on the job of being my nanny, Miss Ukwa was very fond of me and devoted a good deal of her time, while living with and serving my mother, to teaching me some Ibibio folklore. She also taught me how to swim in both fresh water streams and salt-water creeks, which then abounded in Ikot Abasi. She used to take me with her every Sunday afternoon after morning service in the company of other young men and women to Esuk Akpan Akrasi (Akpan Akrasi creek) for swimming. I used to enjoy it very much.

Unhappily for me, after staying with my mother as my nanny for a period of three years, Miss Ukwa Ikot Ekop was engaged to be married to, and indeed married, one Mr. Briggs who was Her Majesty's prison's warder at Ikot Abasi. Even though married, Miss Ukwa Ikot Ekop found it difficult to part with me. She used to visit my mother's house regularly to assist in looking after me although I had then started primary school. She later had two children by the names of Rebecca Briggs and Hanna Briggs who turned out to be brilliant girls at school and great sports women in Egwanga Methodist School during Empire day performances. In particular, Miss Rebecca Briggs was always regularly a prizewinner at races.

My Primary Education

*"Our gifts freely given are for the work of God in this our beautiful
church and the extension of His Kingdom on earth. For us Methodists, in
the words of John Wesley, the world is our parish. We must therefore give
and give until it hurts".*

I started school at the age of 5 years at the Ebenezer Methodist
School, Ibekwe. Indeed, I combined attending school during weekdays from Monday to Friday inclusive every week with attending Sunday school every Sunday afternoon after the morning Christian religious worship. The Sunday school used to be held from 2 p.m. to 4
p.m. every Sunday and thereafter there was held the Sunday evening
religious service or worship as from 7 p.m. to 9 p.m.

As regards the Sunday school, I was very fortunate in that I had a
very close and trustworthy friend in the person of the late Mr. Robinson
Ukofia, who was the late Mr. Abel Ukofia's junior brother. Both Mr.
Robinson Ukofia and I were rivals. We were both competitors in the
educational field in that we always seized the least opportunity to
educate ourselves. Both of us were registered in the Sunday school
class the same day to read A B C alphabets in the Efik dialect. We were
both promoted after two months as being conversant with the Efik
alphabets to join the Efik *Ikpat-Ke-Ikpat* (Step by Step) class. We were
also both promoted the same day from the Efik *Ikpat-Ke-Ikpat* class,
having been tested and found able to read the book from cover to
cover, to *Udian Edikot Nwet Iba* (that is, the second book). Again we
both had only to spend two months studying the Efik *Udian Edikot
Nwet Iba*. Thereafter, having passed the prescribed test we were both
promoted to the Efik Bible class. And it was after we had spent some

time studying the Efik Bible and memorising certain passages in the Psalms of David that it was approved that we both be baptised as Methodist Christians. It was at baptism that I was given the Christian name of "Egbert", being the name of the first Christian king of England. After baptism, we were both classified in the Church as Catechumen and continued to study the Efik Bible and were able to read and sing hymns written in the Efik dialect of the Ibibio language. We were both passed on to our class leader and had to attend Sunday morning class meetings where we were registered as Catechumen.

I then had to turn my attention to my education in the primary school where we were taught everything in the English language. I was then attending Ebenezer (Church) School; the school was conducted in the same building as the Sunday church service, the school being conducted in the building during weekdays from Monday to Friday. The school was unapproved by the government of the day for grants-in-aid. We were taught Arithmetic, Reading and Writing in the English language. For writing, we used slates and slate pencil, which we brought with us to school every school day and also returned from school with. For the purpose of writing at school we were provided with desks and benches.

I was very fond of attending school every day of the week, except on Saturdays; and on Sundays I still had to attend the Sunday school for the study of the Bible. Nevertheless, I used to be delighted during vacation time, when school was out and we were on holidays. During my primary school days I used to be considered a hard worker. I loved my work at school and because of my having done very well I was promoted from Primary 1 to Primary 3 without having to read Primary 2. Because of such jumping of classes, I had only to spend 3 years in the Infant department of Ebenezer School, before I was promoted to Standard 1 in the school.

Having been promoted to Standard 1, I then changed schools and had to attend Egwanga Methodist School in Mensah Town as Ebenezer School then consisted of the Infant Department only. So, any one who had read up to Standard 1 had to continue his education in those days at Egwanga Methodist School which was recognised as a Standard 4 school.

In Standard 1, our teacher at Egwanga Methodist School was Mr. Edmund Okponoeyen, a native of Ikot Etetuk. As from Standard 1 we were taught English grammar tenses, analysis and parsing, using "Alcock's Grammar" as our textbook. We were also taught Arithmetic using "Pendelbury Arithmetic" extensively up to mensuration.

It was when I was in Standard 3 and living with my mother, who was a prosperous and wealthy trader, that the Revd. A. W. Hodgetts approached me. The Reverend A. W. Hodgetts, on seeing me playing with his small boy, who was my personal friend, at the Mission House that was the Manse, enquired whether, like his small boy, James, I would be prepared to offer my services to his friend, Mr. N. H. Cox, the then Collector of Customs, to be carrying for him the latter's golf-bag containing his golf-clubs. The idea was that, if I was willing to do so, it would only mean my going with him, Revd. A. W. Hodgetts, to the golf course, or the link, every 4 o'clock in the afternoon after my schooling period. I would then be introduced to Mr. N. H. Cox, the Collector of Customs. I accepted the invitation subject to approval by my mother.

On the appointed day, with the approval of my mother, I, with James, joined Revd. A. W. Hodgetts in his car and we drove with his golf clubs to the golf club there to meet the Collector of Customs, Mr. N. H. Cox. On arrival, having alighted from the car, I was promptly introduced to Mr. N. H. Cox who immediately handed over to me his golf-bag and directed me to accompany them as they both were playing the game of golf. While carrying the golf-bag, I also had to make a tee with a small quantity of mud for resting the golf ball for driving off at the start of each hole. For doing this and carrying the golf-bag, I used to earn ten shillings (10/-) every month as my pocket money.

Having served satisfactorily for over three months, the Collector of Customs offered to house me in his compound at the Consulate beach and on terms that I continued my schooling daily and subject to the consent of my parents. After consultation with my father, who most reluctantly gave his consent, I moved house into the Collector of Customs' compound.

Having served as a golf caddy for some six months, the Collector of Customs offered to pay me one pound, ten (£1.10s) per month provided, in addition to carrying the golf-bag, I also served as his domestic servant by assisting his steward and cook, but particularly his steward boy, Daniel, in performing his domestic chores and at the same time attending school during the week days and provided my father would accept such an arrangement. I accepted the offer, having obtained the consent of my father, who insisted that on no account must I absent myself from school without reasonable justification.

While at Egwanga Methodist School, I was invited to sing in the choir as a chorister every Sunday during the morning and evening services. The invitation was extended to me through the headmaster, Mr. H. B. Sambo, who was a native of Brass. I most willingly accepted the invitation and thereby became a choirboy. It was therefore part of my duty to attend church services every Sunday as a chorister in addition to attending school regularly.

In those days it was part of Mr. H. B. Sambo's practice, as Headmaster, to ascertain from the pupils every Monday morning at school all those who were absent from church service and to inflict severe punishment on all such absentees. In this connection, I remember that as soon as Mr. H. B. Sambo had ascertained that I was absent from church service on a particular Sunday, I was given 12 strokes of the cane on my bareback as my due punishment. The caning left wheels on my back.

On my return to my residence at the Collector of Customs premises, I developed a chill, and on enquiry, I reported to Mrs. N. H. Cox the accident of my having been caned for being absent from church service the previous Sunday. Mrs. N. H. Cox appeared somewhat upset. She was at a loss to appreciate my having been so severely punished for merely being absent from church service on a Sunday. She took up the matter with her husband, Mr. N. H Cox, the Collector of Customs, who was very fond of me.

On receiving the information, Mr. N. H. Cox, the Collector of Customs, appeared very angry and by mutual consent they both composed a letter addressed to the then Superintendent of the Methodist Church, the Revd. Jas A. Sollitt, complaining about the incident and demanding that the headmaster who had so violently treated me be disciplined as such caning amounted to criminal assault and battery on my person. I eventually delivered the letter to Revd. Jas A. Sollitt, who, after discussing the matter with Mrs. Jas A. Sollitt, his wife, sent for Mr. H. B. Sambo, the headmaster and, in my presence, queried him for his explanation of why he should have subjected me to such an undignified, violent treatment.

In extenuation of his action, the headmaster explained that as far back as when the Revd. Superintendent A. W. Hodgetts introduced me to the Collector of Customs, after the consent of my father had been obtained, I was earmarked by the Mission that, after having obtained my first school leaving certificate, I would be awarded a scholarship by the Mission to undergo teacher training at Wesley College, Ibadan, Western Nigeria and on qualifying by passing my final examination as a certificated teacher would return to Egwanga Methodist School to serve the Mission as a certificated teacher. In preparation for this, I was to be watched carefully to see that I developed both in character and knowledge in an excellent manner befitting the high responsibility to be imposed on me. In that connection, it became his duty to see that, as choirboy, I attended both choir practices and Sunday services regularly as a way of building up my character.

All the same, Mr. H. B. Sambo appeared very badly shaken and apologised for his action in this regard. In reporting back to the Collector of Custom, the Revd. Jas A. Sollitt mentioned that the headmaster, Mr. H. B. Sambo, regretted his action. From then on, no pupil was again caned in the manner in which I had been caned in the school.

Later, Mr. N. H. Cox, having been transferred to Lagos, was succeeded by Mr. C. F. C. Everest as Collector of Customs. I was then handed over to him by Mr. & Mrs. N. H. Cox. I continued my service in the same manner to Mr. & Mrs. C. F. C. Everest. After a while, I decided, at the request of my father, to return home and concentrate on my education. For that purpose, I also left Egwanga Methodist School and returned to Ebenezer School, that is, Ibekwe Methodist School. I decided to leave the service of Mr. & Mrs. C. F .C. Everest and to return to Ikot Abasi village and there to continue schooling in Ebenezer School because of the untimely death of my beloved mother in the circumstances to be narrated in the next two chapters.

CHAPTER THREE

My Mother Obtains Divorce And Is Married Again

"Heaven has no rage like love to hatred turn'd; Nor Hell a fury like a woman scorned" – *William Congreve's "The Mourning Bride"*

Before taking up residence at Ibekwe, I was invited by my mother to live with her at her residence at Mensah Town and there to continue my schooling because she was anxious to see that I did not stop schooling at all. As a result and in consequence of my acceptance of the invitation, I took up residence with her as from January 1929. That being so, I decided to continue schooling for a while at Egwanga Methodist School since I was living very close to the school.

My mother was then seriously engaged in her trade. In that connection and in furtherance of her trade, she used to deposit large sums of money with Messrs G. B. Ollivant Limited, Messrs African Oil Nuts and Messrs African Traders Corporation Limited (ATC) for goods like stock fish (then sold in bales), kerosene (then sold in tins), bar soaps, bags of salt, salted beef and pork, as well as detergents. She used to buy these goods wholesale for retailing in her big market stall. She also had a sewing machine for dressmaking, as she was also a seamstress. She was a hardworking and prosperous trader. She used to transport some of the consumer goods to her agents and representatives at Ikot Ekpene, Eket and Etinan. She used to visit these areas regularly and from time to time.

My mother was well known among Ibibio women of the area as well as Ogoni and Opobo Town's women, and occupied a prominent position as a leader in her own right. She was highly respected. Unlike my father, my mother was Christian and her Christian name was Mary while her indigenous name was Adiaha Edem, that is, the first daughter of Edem. Originally, of course, she was a member of the *Ebre* titled society, the head of which was my grand mother by name Adiaha Ekpo Abia. My grand mother used to preside over all ceremonies concerning the celebration of the "feast of new yams" which usually presaged the harvesting of *Ebre* yams, being the type of yam usually cultivated exclusively by women, as well as the ceremony of *Ubio Owonwan Ino*, that is the symbolical killing of a woman who had committed the offence of praedial larceny. Once the ceremony had been successfully performed on any woman culprit then such a woman would stand ostracised from society. *Ebre* titled society, on the death of the ostracised woman, would refuse to bury her. For having been symbolically destroyed, she would be considered an empty shell so long as she lived to be shunned by members of *Ebre* society.

After my birth and while I was still a child, my mother was converted to Christianity. Hence my mother brought me up a Christian even though my father did not accept Christianity as a true religion. Indeed, my father treated Christianity as the last refuge of the scoundrel and most Christians with contempt. My father was a leading figure in the *Ekpo Nyoho* titled society and the *Attat* and *Idiong* titled societies. Being a member of high rank in all these ancient societies, he was entrusted with the custody of the principal talking drum known as *Akpan Ibiit Ekpo Nyoho* of the *Ekpo Nyoho* titled society. This signified that, without the approval of my father, no one could stage *Ekpo Nyoho* masquerade.

As a result of my mother having been converted Christian, baptised and confirmed a full member of the Wesleyan Methodist Church, Nigeria, she considered it her duty to convert my father to the Christian faith. All her efforts in that regard proved futile. She failed woefully to have my father converted to Christianity. She then felt that it was incompatible for her to continue to be married to my father however distinguished and powerful my father was in society. Hence she took a firm decision and filed an action under customary law in the customary court of Qua Court against my father praying the court that her marriage to my father be dissolved as she found it difficult and un-Christian to be still identified with my father as his wife.

My father on his part, to add insult to injury, quickly got married under customary law to another woman known as and called

Unwa Ama, in Ete town. Apparently, Unwa Ama had picked on my father as her boy friend during the time of the staging of the masquerade play and dances at Ete. She thus became, by customary marriage, the third wife of my father as sanctioned by a polygamous society while my mother was the second wife, the first wife of my father being known and called Ekwere Uko Inyang Etuk of Ikot Etetuk. The father of Ekwere Uko was the village head of Ikot Etetuk and a court-sitting member. He was known as and called Obong Uko Inyang Etuk of Ikot Etetuk in Ikpa Ibekwe clan. On the death of Chief Uko Inyang Etuk, the next court-sitting member for Ikot Etetuk was Chief Umani.

My mother's action against my father in Qua Court was in due course heard. The petition for divorce was granted on the ground of incompatibility. The court held that my father, being a distinguished and venerated leader in *Attat* and *Ekpo Nyoho* titled societies, could not tolerate a Christian wife in his compound. Such a situation could not be sanctioned by society. The petition was therefore granted on terms, according to custom in a polygamous society, that my father's dowry, paid when my mother was married, be refunded in full since it was my mother who sought to be divorced. In addition, both Adiaha'ma, my sister, and myself be handed over to my father and thence to remain and be fully recognised as the lawful children of my father, Obong Udoma Inam, and that my mother be thenceforth released as a free woman to practice her Christian religion and worship her chosen God. While my mother had naturally rejoiced over her success, both my sister, Adiaha'ma, who was older than I, and myself were sorry of the separation of our parents.

Having been granted divorce, even before the expiration of the period fixed by court, there were many men who sought my mother's hand in marriage. All of them were members of the Wesleyan Methodist Church in Ikot Abasi. Of all of them, one man naturally was successful. The only person who succeeded and whose hand was accepted in marriage by my mother in due time was a famous and wealthy Efik man who was a Civil Engineering contractor and a Christian leader in the Wesleyan Methodist Church, Egwanga by the name of Mr. Fenton Ambiet. In due course my mother was married to Mr. Fenton Ambiet, a prosperous contractor. After the consummation of the marriage, which could not be described as a particularly happy one, both my mother and Mr. Fenton Ambiet lived together as Christians at the overside of Mensah Town known as *Oto Ambiet*, meaning Ambiet's settlement, for a number of years apparently happily and there was only one son of the marriage who was given the name of Archibong Fenton Ambiet. At the overside of Mensah Town across the bridge constructed by Mr. Fenton Ambiet there lived another Efik man of distinction with his own family. The Efik man was a veteran military officer who had seen service as a member of the West African Frontier Force stationed at Enugu and later at Calabar and who, in 1902, took part in the British military expedition to Arochuku for the destruction of the notorious *long juju*. The veteran military officer was known as Okon Ibuot. He was also a devout Christian.

Veteran Okon Ibuot was always in the habit of regaling people of his exploits as a sergeant in the West African Frontier Force. His compound was very close to *Oto Ambiet* and both families lived happily together, each family in its respective separate compound. Veteran Okon Ibuot, as it happened, survived Mr. Fenton Ambiet, and used to assist in looking after Archibong Fenton Ambiet, my uterine brother, even to the extent that on the death of Mr. Fenton Ambiet it was Veteran Okon Ibuot who assisted Mr. Archibong Fenton Ambiet, then a boy still at school, in the arrangement for administration of the estate of Mr. Fenton Ambiet. For that purpose, the services of Lawyer Ebitto of Calabar had to be retained. Another Efik man who rendered immense services in connection with the administration of the estate was the late Mr. Otudor of the then His Majesty's Customs Department, Opobo division.

All told, my mother had only three children namely, Adiaha'ma, my sister and the eldest of us, Archibong Fenton Ambiet and myself. This was unlike my maternal grand mother, Madam Adiaha Ekpo Abia of Ata Ekong family of Ikot Aba, who had six children, five of whom were male - my mother being the only female child. Of the six, only two children survived to adulthood, the two being Nathaniel Akpan Enin and my mother, Adiaha Edem. After the death of Mr. Fenton Ambiet, my mother turned her attention to the development of trade and soon became a highly respected and respectable prosperous trader whose fame spread far and wide. She had agents and representatives stationed at Abak, Eket, Ikot Ekpene, Etinan and Uyo.

Then early in 1929, there was a persistent rumour circulating throughout what was known as Eastern Nigeria that the women at Aba Ngwa, now in Abia state, were planning to rise in rebellion against the British administration generally for maladministration and particularly for having decided to impose poll tax on women. I was then living with my mother in her home in Mensah Town and attending Egwanga Methodist School. I was then in Standard IV and one of our teachers then was Mr. Adolphus S. Jaja. My mother did not appear to be particularly disturbed regarding the rumour relating to the plan by the women for rebellion at Aba Ngwa. She was then rather busily engaged in her trading business which she was anxious to develop by conveying her merchandise to her market stalls in Egwanga market and there disposing her wares for sale. She was also concerned with having a big turnover.

In November 1929, my mother received a message from the senior divisional officer, Opobo division, Mr. A. R. Whitman, inviting her as a prominent and leading woman to attend a meeting to be held at the divisional office, which meeting was to be addressed by the senior divisional officer, himself. My mother was to appeal to other women and prevail upon them to accompany her to the meeting, which the senior divisional officer described as a very important meeting concerning the future of women and taxation. The invitation was in writing. The meeting was scheduled to take place on 16 December 1929.

Early in December 1929 a large number of women assembled at the rear garden of my mother's house, which had a large compound. My mother addressed the assembly and at the same time showed to the assembled women the invitation from the senior divisional officer. The contents of the invitation were fully discussed. In the course of the discussion, it was disclosed that there had been rioting by women at Aba Ngwa. It was unanimously agreed that the senior divisional officer's invitation be accepted and that no efforts should be spared on prevailing upon many more women to attend the meeting.

CHAPTER FOUR

My First Bereavement - The Death Of My Mother

"If we cannot grumble when we feel like it, what's the use of living at all?". - Anonymous

Accordingly, on 16 December 1929, I woke up early and, after elaborate preparation, conscious of the fact that my mother had to attend the meeting to be held at the Divisional Office, I left for school after bidding my mother good bye in the usual manner. At school we were told that there was a large assembly of women from the different regions of the division, that is to say from Andoni, Opobo Town, Ogoni and Ibibio areas at the divisional office. In addition, there was a large contingent of soldiers who had arrived from Enugu and Calabar, and which had arranged itself in front of the divisional office under the command of one Captain J. Hill. The soldiers were fully armed.

Then just about mid-day while still at school we heard a loud report in the form of volleys being the sound of a discharge of rounds of gunfire by soldiers. It then came as a shock to all of us at school when we were told that the soldiers had shot some of the women who held a meeting with the divisional officer. I was even more shocked when at the school I was visited by some police officers who disclosed that I was required to accompany them to the mortuary for the purpose of identifying my mother who apparently was one of the women who had been shot dead by the soldiers. It sounded rather incredible that a divisional officer could have invited women to the divisional office only for them to be mown down by British soldiers.

In response to the invitation and with the approval of the headmaster, I went with the police officers to the mortuary. There I met several corpses of dead women apparently victims of British soldiers' gun fire. I was able to identify the corpse of my dead mother among the corpses. Subsequently with the permission of the police officers we succeeded in removing the corpse of my mother, which was taken home for the purpose of according her a befitting burial as a heroine. My mother was fittingly buried as a heroine at Atan Ndon after a Christian religious service. At the meeting, the women had raised objection to the imposition of poll tax by government. The senior divisional officer apparently did not like that; hence soldiers mowed down the women.

After the shooting of the women, the whole atmosphere in the entire division of Opobo was tense for several months. There was also the imposition of curfew from sunset to dawn. Two gunboats were immediately dispatched from Lagos and had to rest at anchor in Opobo river (now Ikot Abasi river) which every night displayed searchlights in the sky. I was personally disconcerted, not knowing to whom to turn and, after oscillating between my paternal grandmother and my maternal grandmother, I had finally to rest on my maternal grandmother, Madam Adiaha Ekpo Abia.

The death of my mother so suddenly also affected the course and progress of my education. I had to change schools. I had to move from Egwanga Methodist School to Ebenezer Methodist School, Ibekwe, which meant loss of old friends and acquaintances. At Egwanga Methodist School I had many friends like Matthew F. Pepple, Moses Dappa, Gordon Fah Cookey, Gordon Opusunju, Nathan S. Pepple, Monday Bruce Jaja, Phillip Leg Jack, Nathan Pepple, and Nelson Toby, to name just a few. I was also a leading figure both in the school band in which I was a fifer and in the church choir as a treble singer. I had to make new friends in Ebenezer School. As an indigene of Ibekwe this was not difficult. Indeed, during my first year at the school I had to associate with important personalities like

Marcus Mbat, Peter George Atauba, John Okpoho Udodong, Frankson Iwatt, William Udo Enang, John A. Usen, and Davies Akpan Abaikpa to name only few. The headmaster of Ebenezer School was Willie A. Young, alias Okon Edem, a man of great distinction, a well-known academician and a product of Hope Waddel Institute of Calabar.

At Ebenezer School I was in Standard V. It was the responsibility of Mr. Young himself to take charge of Standards V and VI. He taught us the classics which are Latin, Hebrew, and Greek and commercial subjects including shorthand and typewriting, bookkeeping and accountancy, and music (staff notation). I also learned how to play the piano. As already mentioned, I was a fifer in the school band and a treble singer in the church choir as a chorister. Ebenezer School became very popular and was patronized by many parents because of the teaching of commercial subjects. I soon became absorbed in my studies. I worked hard on my subjects, which I found most interesting. Although it was rather difficult to overcome my sorrow over the death of my beloved mother in such circumstances as have been narrated herein, I was somehow consoled by activities of many friends and relations around me along with the assistance rendered to me by my dear father since the death of my beloved mother.

Then, subsequently, Mr. E. E. Ekpenyong was posted from Banham Memorial Methodist School, Port Harcourt to head Ebenezer Methodist School, Ibekwe in succession to Mr. Willie A. Young, who then became the catechist in charge of the church and the organ. In 1931 I took my Standard VI examination, that is the first school leaving certificate examination, and passed. I should have mentioned before that, on my return to Ebenezer School, I found that there had been erected up the hill beyond the church hall used for Sunday religious worship a new well designed and properly constructed school hall, which housed all the classes up to Standard VI. The Standard VI class occupied a quasi-rectangular section of the building on the right side of the headmaster's table quite open to the view of the headmaster.

CHAPTER FIVE

Uzuakoli Institute Or Methodist College

*"Education should have three objectives: education should aim at
The raising of the general cultural level of the people,
The linking of education and employment, and
The greater participation of teachers in the social life of the country".*

In 1932 I took the entrance examination to the Methodist Institute, later known as the Methodist College, Uzuakoli, and passed with flying colours. There were altogether 300 of us students who sat the entrance examination at the time seeking admission into Class III Middle. Out of the 300, only 50 of us passed the examination and I scored the highest marks and secured first place, having obtained distinction in English and Mathematics. I was admitted along with others into Class III Middle. In our class there were also Matthew Nwosu, Mfon Afahaene Eyo, Ibebulem, Ebong and Udo Akang. At the time Uzuakoli was at the height of academic achievement. That was because of a record created by one Dick Ogan who, in his teacher's certificate examination that was held through out Nigeria, successfully occupied First Class and first place nation wide. In any case, Uzuakoli College consisted of two distinct Institutions, namely the Teachers Training Institute and the Middle School.

At the end of 1932, I sat and passed two examinations namely, the Class III Middle Annual and the Methodist scholarship for teachers for admission into the Teachers' Training Institute. I was very pleased with myself and was congratulated by everyone who wished me well. I was awarded the scholarship for teachers training to commence in 1933. The agreement, to be executed by me and the Methodist Mission and covering the scholarship, was forwarded by the Principal, Methodist Institute Uzuakoli, to the Revd. Superintendent-in-Charge of the Methodist Mission, Opobo division, now Ikot Abasi local government area (LGA). On invitation, I reported at the manse in the company of Mr. Richard Udoma, then a teacher at Ebenezer School, and there both the Revd. Superintendent-in-Charge of the mission, the Revd. Jas A. Sollitt, as a representative of the Methodist Mission, and I, on my personal behalf, executed the agreement in the presence of Richard Udoma as a witness to the signatures. The agreement was thus signed, sealed and delivered. Mr. Richard Udoma, Revd. Jas A. Sollitt and Mrs. Sollitt then enthusiastically congratulated me. That was in December 1932.

After the agreement had been properly executed and I, having been informed that the sealed document would be dispatched to the Principal, Uzuakoli Institute in Bende Division of Owerri province, now Abia state, departed from the manse in the company of Mr. Richard Udoma glorifying God for His generosity to His creature. But, the last word, of course, had not been heard of the scholarship awarded to me by the mission. For, in January 1933, I went with my father to the manse to receive from the Superintendent-in-Charge of the Methodist Mission annual rent in respect of the land occupied by the manse which was then due to be paid to my father, Obong Udoma Inam. The land of which the mission was tenant was the property of Anyanti family of which my father was then head in succession to Obong Akpan Inam.

On our arrival at the manse, the Revd. Jas A. Sollitt greeted my father enthusiastically and excitedly and thereafter congratulated my father for my having been awarded the mission's scholarship which would enable me to continue my education at Uzuakoli without my father being called upon to pay for my education, the Methodist Mission having accepted the burden of financing my education and maintenance at school in Uzuakoli. According to the Revd. Jas A. Sollitt, I was to be trained as a certificated teacher by the Methodist Mission. My father listened most attentively to the Superintendent of the Methodist Mission, Opobo division without blinking his eyes.

After having been paid the land rent, my father and I left the manse for home in the village. At home, my father asked me to explain what was meant by my being awarded scholarship which would enable me to be trained as a certificated teacher by the Methodist Mission and whether I had applied to the mission for aid. I took time to explain to my father that I was awarded the scholarship because I had done well in the scholarship examination which I had sat and which was a competitive examination usually conducted by the mission every year for the purpose of selecting young students in the school who had done well in their class work and had been considered to be of excellent character for training as certificated teachers; and that, on completion of the prescribed course of study and passing all necessary examinations, the successful students would then be posted to the mission field as certified teachers to teach in the various mission schools. I explained further that, in my case, I would be sent back to Ikot Abasi on successfully completing the course of study and passing the prescribed examinations, in which event I would always be close to him at home.

My father then informed me, rather quietly, that I must refuse the scholarship, as he did not wish me to accept any work as an employee of the mission. I was stunned. I then pleaded with my father to overlook his disapproval of the Christian Church as a foreign religion. I made bold to point out that I was not unaware of his standing in society as a leader of the *Attat* and the *Ekpo Nyoho* titled societies as well as a distinguished president of the customary court in succession to his brother, Obong Akpan Inam, of blessed memory. I mentioned that I was very proud of my father having regard to his achievements in life and his high reputation in the community. My father then turned to me and said with a smile "then you must obey my command". I then turned and looked at my father. I noticed that he was in a pensive and serious mood.

My father then said to me: "For years I have been wishing you well and have been full of hope that you would take your studies seriously and would pass your examinations regularly and well with credits so that, when you passed out of Uzuakoli, I would then send you overseas there to continue your education in the field of law returning home to Ikot Abasi as a qualified lawyer of distinction to practise in our courts in Nigeria like other lawyers from foreign lands. Therefore, that conception on my part is utterly incompatible with your accepting a job from the mission as a school teacher. The scholarship must be rejected by you in obedience to my command".

Having heard this observation and command from my father, I became worried. In vain I endeavoured to explain the position to my father. I then sought the assistance of his intimate friend, the now late Chief King Usoro, who was then the divisional officer's interpreter. But the latter refused to intervene on the ground that he supported my father up to the hilt and shared his views that I should refuse the scholarship. Both Mr. Wilcox A. Meyen and Mr. Richard Udoma, certificated teachers and employees of the Methodist Mission and highly respected members of the community, intervened at my request. Their appeal to my father was treated with levity and proved of no avail. In the end it was my father who won the day by prevailing upon the two of them to draft for his signature a letter addressed to Mr. H. L. O. Williams, Principal, Uzuakoli Institute, rejecting the scholarship awarded me by the mission and repudiating the agreement already executed by me and directing that the scholarship be awarded to another student in real need whose parents could not maintain them at the institute. As regards my education, my father gave a solemn undertaking to continue to finance it to the end until I was fully qualified to attend a university overseas. All the same I was personally dissatisfied. I was in deep sorrow.

Later, at the commencement of term at the institute, I duly appeared before the principal at his request and, on enquiry as to the status of my father in Ikot Abasi community, I explained that my father was a highly respected member of the community being a leader in his own right and following the footsteps of his ancestors who were the founders of Ikot Abasi village; that my father was not only a title holder in *Attat* and *Ekpo Nyoho* titled societies but also the president of Ibekwe Native Court and therefore was in close association with the senior divisional officer, Opobo division; and that he was not a Christian. The principal, Revd. H. L. O. Williams, received the information with astonishment. He said he was at a loss to understand why my father should have rejected the mission scholarship for teacher training, which is usually much sought for by others. All the same, he confessed that he was somewhat impressed although he considered my father's reaction to the scholarship awarded me purely by merit after appropriate examination as extraordinary and somewhat incredible. The principal maintained that I was entitled to continue my education at my father's expense at the institute. Thus ended that episode which, in the end, enhanced my reputation and that of my father's although my father was illiterate but honest and sincere.

Thereafter, I pursued my prescribed course of study in peace and harmony under the direct sponsorship of my beloved father and at his sole expense. I was then in Class IV Middle and used to be asked from time to time by the principal to teach Classes I and II in Mathematics, particularly Algebra, in the absence of the master assigned for the subject who was then Mr. Georgewill, an expert in Arts, Science and Mathematics. I was very happy with my progress and reputation as always securing Excellent in English and Mathematics, including English Grammar and Science.

At the College, Uzuakoli, being a Middle School in so far as secondary education was concerned, we were not taught the Classics like Latin, Greek or Hebrew. What knowledge I had of the Classics I had acquired at Ebenezer Methodist School, Ibekwe, which later became a Central School for the area. Being considered an outstanding student, I was able to make many friends at the college. Most of the senior students in the upper classes who were mostly on scholarship constituted what was known as the Normal College, engaged in teacher training. I considered them as personal friends. They included Amakwo, Matthew Okorie, S. N. Okorocha, J. K. Usuah, A. J. U. Ema, Edet Okon Unanaowo, Mfon Afahaene Eyo, Jacob Akpan Adiaha, Okon Okpo, J. C. Achara, Dick Okorie, Ndem Abam, R. W. Iteke and Chikwendu, to name only a few. There were also others who were not necessarily scholarship holders like Gideon James Atai, Matthew Ude, Gordon Opusunju, Banigo, Sunday Obiago and G. C. Mborogwu (later G. C. M. Akomass) who were close friends.

When I entered the college in 1932, the first friend to whom I was introduced was Udo Udo Okure who was then in his final year. Mr. Richard Udoma who was then teaching in Ebenezer Methodist School, Ibekwe, introduced me to Udo Udo Okure. But Udo Udo Okure left the college at the end of that year, after having completed his course of studies and taken his final Teachers' Certificate examination.

Uzuakoli College of the period with which I am concerned was very well staffed, the majority of the staff being expatriate consisting of the Revd. H. L. O. Williams, Principal, the Revd. A. S. Fenby, the Revd. C. E. Wiles, the Revd. R. S. D. Williams, the Revd. W. J. Wood, Mrs. Williams and Mrs. A. S. Fenby. African masters on the staff included Mr. E. E. Nkana, Mr. G. Hart, Mr. R. A. Georgewill, Mr. Otu, the Carpenter, and Revd. Nwanna. In the campus of the college there were some other tutors like Mr. R. Okoro who were concerned with the lower classes of the institution. There was also Mr. Dick Ogan who was preparing for the London Matriculation examination even though on the staff of the College.

In January 1934, it was announced that the common entrance examination into the government civil service had been suspended owing to the general recession or depression, which was being experienced worldwide. In those days it was the practice for students of the Secondary Education Department of the college to be prepared for public examination, including the common entrance into the civil service of the government of Nigeria.

CHAPTER SIX

The First Scandal Involving Me

"I discovered that there was a fine practical wisdom, which owed nothing to books and academics". – Lord Tweedsmuir in "Biography and Autobiography"

The announcement of the suspension of the common entrance examination into the civil service of the British government in Nigeria came as a bolt from the blue. Every secondary school student in Uzuakoli College received the announcement with shock and trepidation having spent a good deal of time in the preparation for the examination. It was not then clear for how long the suspension might last nor were we aware for how long the depression or recession might also continue. The feeling was that perhaps the suspension might last so long as the depression persisted. The future then appeared gloomy and uncertain and the only aspect of life that was still full of hope was the realisation that, in this world of mortal beings, certainty is but an illusion and repose is not the destiny of man. The announcement meant that some of us secondary school students would have to spend an extra year in the hope that things might turn out right.

At the end of the year, I took my final Class IV Middle examination and passed with flying colours as usual. Early in 1935, Sunday Obiago and I went to Aba Ngwa to sit an entrance examination for admission into Government School of Agriculture at Umudike. This was by an arrangement between the Principal, Methodist College, Uzuakoli and the Departments of Public Works and Agriculture. At Aba Ngwa we noticed that only the two of us from Uzuakoli were the candidates taking part in the examination. Later we were both advised through the principal that there were no vacancies to which we could be appointed. At Uzuakoli we both continued in our studies in the usual away.

Then, towards the end of the school year in 1935, there broke out a scandal in which I was involved. At the time I was very friendly with both Mr. & Mrs. Remi Okoro and used to visit them at their residence within the campus of the college and would spend my leisure hours with both of them. Some times we used to dine together on the invitation of the husband. But my friendship with Mrs. Okoro was purely platonic.

The scandal occurred in the following way. During the continuation of our friendship, Mr. Okoro was in the habit of telling me that he trusted me whole heartedly because he was a colleague of my relation, Mr. Richard Udoma, who was also his friend and with whom he used to dine together when Mr. Richard Udoma was undergoing his training and later as a qualified certificated teacher. He intimated that my association with him was a constant reminder of the kindness shown him by my relation. Subsequently, Mr. Okoro left on a visit to another station in the hope of being absent from the college campus for about one week. He advised me to do him the favour of keeping Mrs. Okoro company. In the house, besides Mrs. Okoro, there were two young boys, one of whom was known as Wachuku Abengowe.

During the absence of Mr. Okoro, I visited Mrs. Okoro from time to time and there would spend some time with her playing *ludo* in the belief that I was keeping her company. Then, on a Friday at the request of Mrs. Okoro, I visited her in the evening. As soon as Wachuku Abengowe saw me enter the house he raised an alarm. I suspected there was something in the offing as that was an unexpected behaviour on the part of Wachuku Abengowe. I thereupon retreated.

The next morning, Mr. Okoro returned from his journey. I visited him and his wife in the house on the Sunday. We had a meal together. Mr. Okoro did not question me as to the incident of Friday evening in which I was involved. We played board games together as usual. Then, the following day being a Monday, I was sent for by the principal. I reported at his office. He interrogated me as to my relationship with Mr. & Mrs. Okoro. I assured him that my relationship with Mr. & Mrs. Okoro was cordial. He questioned me as to whether I had sexual intercourse with Mrs. Okoro. I denied any such association and assured him that I had never entertained any such feeling towards Mrs. Okoro.

The principal then told me that Mr. Okoro was seriously suspecting me of having sex with his wife. I maintained that I was rather astonished to hear that from the principal because Mr. Okoro had never mentioned any such matter to me. The principal then informed me that Mr. Okoro had reported my suspected conduct towards his wife during his absence to him and he had decided to investigate the report. That being so, the Principal maintained that it would be necessary for me to leave the college to enable him to investigate the matter thoroughly. I, in the circumstances, decided to return home to Ikot Abasi in the hope that, after investigation, I might be recalled.

To make sure that I had left the college, Mr. Gabriel C. Mborogwu was ordered to see me to the railway station and on board the train en route to Aba Ngwa. This was done. I accordingly left for home. Later I ran into Mr. George Hart, one of the tutors at Uzuakoli. He informed me that the principal was full of regrets for having sent me away from the college at all. He explained that, after my departure, it was discovered that I was innocent and that it was someone else, a tutor in the college, who had had sexual intercourse with Mrs. Okoro and that Mrs. Okoro was not particularly happy with her marriage because, since her marriage to Mr. Okoro, there had been no issue of the marriage and that she was anxious to have a child.

As a result of the information, I applied, having been so prompted by my father, for my school leaving certificate. In return I received the certificate for Class IV Middle, which was signed by Mr. A. S. Fenby, the acting principal. I acknowledged the receipt of the certificate. Later, also at the request of my father, I applied to King's College, Lagos for admission. I was informed that I should avail myself of the entrance examination to be held in January 1935.

In the meantime, my father took me to Messrs G. B. Ollivant Ltd., Ikot Abasi, Egwanga, Opobo and after the payment of security in my name, I was employed as a shopkeeper in charge of the shop subject to my being trained at Port Harcourt as a bookkeeper for the company. Following upon the employment on the appointed day, Mr. A. C. Butler, Agent-in-Charge, Messrs G. B. Ollivant Ltd., conveyed my beloved father and myself in his car to Port Harcourt. There I was introduced to the Agent-in-Charge, Messrs G. B. Ollivant Ltd., Mr. Skinner, as the new employee of the company to be there trained on the job as a book-keeper and after having qualified and been found competent to return to take charge of the company's shop at Ikot Abasi branch as a secured employee of the company. My father remained at Port Harcourt with me for one whole week to make certain that I was properly settled before returning to Ikot Abasi.

At Messrs G. B. Ollivant Ltd., Port Harcourt, I assumed duty in the Accounts department, which was a building situated behind the Haberdashery and Sundries department. I was posted to take charge of clients' accounts ledger, working directly under the supervision of the Chief Bookkeeper, Mr. A. A. Simon Hart. The keeping of clients' accounts involved the recording of the activities of credit customers in the ledger as regards their purchases in the course of each month on credit with a view to the liquidation of the debt thus incurred at the end of each month. There was a ledger kept by me especially for that purpose.

The credit customers' ledger contained the names of all credit customers and each such customer had an account opened for him. In the course of each month all credit purchases by the customer were debited to his account in the ledger and whatever payment was made also credited to the account. In the event of any customer failing,at the end of the relevant month, to liquidate his debt then it was the duty of the bookkeeper in charge of the clients' ledger to demand payment failing which an action in court to recover the amount due would follow after due warnings. It was my duty also to send to each customer the statement of his account at the end of each month and such statement of account was known as a bill. A bill was a statement of account sent to a customer to remind him of his indebtedness to the company.

Having done the work successfully for three months without any blemish, the agent sent me a congratulatory letter and all the staff in the Accounts department marvelled at the way and manner I had discharged my duty. They asked in wonderment whether I had been taught bookkeeping elsewhere before joining the company. I had no alternative but to confess that at Ebenezer School, Ibekwe, we were taught commercial subjects, which included bookkeeping, accountancy, shorthand and typewriting and that I was a typist or stenographer as we were taught to call it. The staff of Messrs G. B. Ollivant Ltd. was astonished.

The following month, to my delight and surprise, I received a letter promoting me to the post of Assistant Chief Bookkeeper for the company. My field of operation was also expanded. I had also to take charge of the company's stations outside Port Harcourt. Being at the port, I was responsible for railing goods imported by the company to our branches and out stations at Imo, Aba, Umuahia, Uzuakoli, Enugu as well as loading similar goods on lorries or mammy wagons to Onitsha and thereafter to debit the accounts of the out stations and call upon them to pay for such goods. I then had to work in cooperation with the main storekeeper and our customs clerk because the goods were usually railed to out stations ex the Customs warehouse.

At the special request of Mr. Evans Stanley Evans, who succeeded Mr. Skinner as the agent-in-charge, Messrs G. B. Ollivant Ltd., Port Harcourt headquarters, I had to maintain a special graph register showing the rise and fall of trade every month so that, at a glance, one could see whether the company was doing well in business. In spite of the fact that I was kept rather busy daily, yet I felt unhappy considering that working for a commercial house like Messrs G. B. Ollivant Ltd. was like entering a blind alley for a young man of my status especially having regard to my ambition to go overseas to acquire education in the field of law. My employment in Messrs G. B. Ollivant Ltd. was regarded by my father as a mere conduit pipe to greater achievement. I felt I had no future in the company or, rather, to put it in another way, the company held no prospect of a bright future for me.

In the circumstances, after consultation with my father, I decided to resign from the company, which I did. But, before doing so, I forwarded my application to the Customs Department, Port Harcourt seeking employment and in return I received an acknowledgement of the receipt of the application and an advice that the application on account of the financial stringency had been forwarded to Lagos for approval and instruction that I be employed and that, in the event such an approval was given, I would be informed in due course. I next applied to the Electricity Corporation of Nigeria (ECN for short), for employment on the advice of Mr. E. E. Adam, the then electrician in the employ of the ECN, which was a section in the Public Works Department (PWD), Nigeria. In response I was invited for interview and thereafter I was employed as a bookkeeper and timekeeper in the Accounts department of the ECN.

I assumed appointment at once. Then, after three months, my name was forwarded with my application to the Public Works Department, Ijora, Lagos Headquarters, requesting that I be there accepted to be there trained on government scholarship as an electrician. The application was approved and I was invited to Ijora, Lagos to undergo training as an electrician the following year. Having communicated to my father the decision of my going to Lagos for training as an electrician under government auspices as a scholar and receiving the latter's disapproval, I had in turn to inform the electrical engineer under whom I was serving that I had changed my mind and was no longer enamoured with the idea of becoming an electrician. I therefore continued in my post as bookkeeper and timekeeper in the Accounts Department of the Electricity Corporation of Nigeria, Port Harcourt.

My Second Bereavement

"Be patient, my soul: thou hast suffered more than this." – Homer c 800 BC

Then, in June 1936, I received information that my beloved father was very ill. I decided to go home so as to assist as regards his treatment. Unfortunately, on arrival at Ikot Abasi, I was greeted with the sorrowful information that my father was dead. It was indeed a sad day for me. I could not believe my ears. I went to my father's residence. Instead of finding my beloved father alive, I found, to my grief, only the corpse being guarded by members of the *Ekpo Nyoho* and *Attat* titled societies. *Ekpo Nyoho* drums were already talking and singing praises of my beloved father. I was at a loss what to do except to cry aloud and pray to God to give me the fortitude to bear such an irreparable loss. I was rather confused by the wailing voices.

I spent one whole week engaged in the usual customary burial rites and ceremonies befitting my father's status as a leader in his own right, president of the native court in Ibekwe clan and head of the *Ekponyoho*, *Attat* and *Ekong* titled societies. The talking drums as well as *Ekponyoho* masquerades were busy through out the week. For the burial ceremonies, the principal person, as the chief mourner, was Martin A. Inam, my cousin, who, immediately on the death of my beloved father, was proclaimed, according to custom, his successor and therefore head of Ayanti Umo Idonho Abasi Akpan Enin family. He was in charge just as my beloved father was responsible for all obsequies at the time of the burial of Chief Akpan Inam, his senior brother and father of Martin A. Inam.

At the end of the week, I returned to Port Harcourt to report for work at the Electricity Corporation of Nigeria (ECN). I arrived in Port Harcourt on Sunday afternoon. In front of my residence I observed quite a large crowd. The teeming crowd took me aback. I was emboldened to approach the front door of my residence in the belief that perhaps the crowd there assembled were those who had paid me a visit with a view to conveying to me their condolences and being entertained by reason of the death of my father who was until his death a well known philanthropist and a famous leader. In front of my residence, familiar voices and faces greeted me. The first persons I took notice of were my former colleagues in Messrs G. B. Ollivant and Mr. Gage Odwyer, the typist. They greeted me on behalf of the crowd and informed me that the crowd had assembled there to rejoice with me because of the news then widely in circulation in the township of Port Harcourt that I was wanted by the Collector of Customs on the instruction from Lagos that I should be employed. I was astonished and listened to the tale with my mouth ajar.

I was flabbergasted. I could not understand how an official instruction from Lagos should have become public property. Nevertheless, I was delighted to receive the news. I greeted the crowd, which returned the greetings with an ovation, as I passed through the main gate into my residence. The people there assembled were rejoicing. I immediately arranged for the people to be entertained as best I could. The people were very cheerful. It was then explained to me that the day before my arrival was a busy day at Port Harcourt and that it was also on that day the Senior Collector of Customs, Port Harcourt, Mr. L. G. Perkins was engaged on telephoning both Mr. Evans Stanley Evans, Agent Messrs G. B. Ollivant Limited, Port Harcourt and Mr. L. A. Gordon, Provincial Engineer, Public Works Department, Port Harcourt enquiring about my whereabouts in the township.

In the course of their conversation, Mr. Evans Stanley Evans was reported to have recommended me very highly to the Senior Collector of Customs, Mr. L. G. Perkins, to the extent of asserting that he, in his experience of working with me, had found me most efficient as a bookkeeper for the company and that since my resignation and departure he had to employ three clerks to do the work which used to be done by me alone. I was very pleased to hear what my previous employers had said of me.

The crowd eventually dispersed in the evening. The following morning, being a Monday, I reported normally for work at the offices of the ECN. I met the Senior Clerk and we exchanged greetings. I engaged myself in bringing my books up to date. Shortly thereafter, I asked for leave to be absent for a couple of days. The Senior Clerk, Mr. Fakulajo, granted permission, somewhat reluctantly. In the course of the day I reported at the Customs Department.

CHAPTER EIGHT

I become A Customs Officer In June 1936

*"The World is a bridge to pass over, not to build on. He revered the forti-
tude of human nature, the courage with which men stumbled up the
steep ascent of life. It was the business of a leader not so much to put
quality into his following as to elicit it since the quality is already there".*

At His Majesty's Customs office at Port Harcourt, I was directed
to the Correspondence department on the first floor of the storey building in charge of which there was Mr. Dennis Osadebay, then a second-
class officer of the Customs Department. I introduced myself to Mr.
Dennis Osadebay as directed. He was delighted to see me and told me
that the Collector of Customs, Mr. L. G. Perkins, was anxious to see
me. He then took me across to the collector's office and there introduced me to the Collector who in turn asked me if I was the young
man, E. Udo Udoma, about whom Mr. Evans Stanley Evans, agent of
Messrs G. B. Ollivant Limited, had spoken so highly. In reply, I said, "I
believe so, Sir". The Collector of Customs in return said, "If you are,
you are sure to be employed by the Customs Department of Nigeria".

On the instructions of the Collector of Customs, Mr. Dennis
Osadebay, the Correspondence Officer, supplied me with certain forms
and advised me to complete them. One of the forms was an application to the senior medical officer-in-charge, Hospitals, Port Harcourt
that I be medically examined and a certificate be issued to me indicating that I was fit to be employed as an officer in the Customs Department, Nigeria. Having completed the forms, the Senior Collector of

Customs instructed me to report to the senior medical officer for medical examination, which I did.

After the medical examination, I was accordingly issued with a certificate of fitness. The following day, I reported to the Senior Collector of Customs who was delighted with the results of the examination. I was immediately appointed a customs officer on probation and assigned to a section in the long room down stairs. I had to serve directly under Mr. S. L. John in the Invoice section. Mr. Archibong, the principal customs officer-in-charge of the long room, did the assignment.

Then, in November 1936, I was transferred and posted to Bonny, which was then regarded as a customs preventive station against smuggling. I then had to serve under Mr. J. B. Monnie who was the officer in charge of the station. At Bonny the bulk of our engagement as customs officers was known as *Tide-waiting* and consisted of boarding a ship as she entered Bonny port from the Atlantic Ocean from overseas and remaining aboard and serving the government as an officer of customs to prevent smuggling and travelling with the ship to her destination which was either Degema port or the port of Port Harcourt. It involved working and living on board the ship and being served all meals on board and remaining throughout the period on the ship and also working ashore on the port discharging and loading cargo until the ship returned to Bonny and there to discharge the Customs officer. During the period, an officer was paid over time if the ship had to work over time while at the port.

At Bonny at the period under consideration, there were other officers serving with me under the supervision of the officer-in-charge of the station, which was at first Mr. J. B. Monnie and later Mr. Mc Jaja Amakiri (sometime Amachree). The customs officers then included Mr. Albert Babatunde Philips, Mr. T. A. E. Spiff, Mr. B. O. Igwebe and Mr. E. T. Ngeri. We were like a happy family at the station.

In November 1937, as a result of the visit by the Senior Collector of Customs to Bonny, I was ordered to leave Bonny and return to Port

Harcourt. The Senior Collector of Customs, then Mr. W. John E. Rodwell, thought it was not right that someone of my qualification and intellectual ability should be posted from Headquarters at Port Harcourt to an outstation like Bonny. I thereupon returned to Port Harcourt by December 1937. At Port Harcourt, I was posted to the Correspondence branch to serve this time under Mr. B. A. Okokon who was then officer-in-charge, Correspondence section.

Having resumed at Port Harcourt, I also had to engage myself in extra mural activities such as membership of the Ibibio Union of which I used to be General Secretary in succession to Mr. W. U. Nsuk, also of the Customs Department, Port Harcourt. I enjoyed both my work at the Customs Department and my extra mural activities during the period. Shortly after my resumption of work, Mr. B. A. Okokon was certified sick and admitted into the General Hospital, Port Harcourt. I had to take charge of the Correspondence section alone. This was not a problem as far as I was concerned as I was a qualified stenographer and a competent typist. For three months, I was alone at the Correspondence branch. Thereafter, Mr. J. B. Monnie was posted to take charge of the Correspondence section, he being a senior officer. As soon as he took over from me, Mr. W. John E. Rodwell, the Senior Collector of Customs forwarded a recommendation to Lagos to the effect that I be granted increment on the ground that I had acted at a post which should have been filled by a senior officer. The recommendation was disapproved by Lagos on the ground that I was still a probationer since my appointment had not then yet been confirmed.

Before hearing from Lagos, the Senior Collector of Customs decided to rearrange the office and the office was rearranged. I was then posted to the Harbour Dues section of the Customs Department, there to relieve Mr. I. O. Dina who was then able to proceed on leave of absence, while Mr. P. B. Mfon was posted from the long room upstairs to relieve me from the Correspondence branch and then to serve as assistant officer to Mr. J. B. Monnie in the Correspondence branch.

CHAPTER NINE

I Become An Ibibio Scholar

"The function of a University is to expand wherever possible the boundaries of knowledge and information in all fields. Not only is knowledge pursued for its own sake but also for its practical effects".

Early in 1938, on the advice of the executive committee of the Ibibio Union, Opobo division, I applied for scholarship to study overseas along with others who were indigenes of the Ibibio area of Opobo division. To the application I attached, as was requested, the original of my Class IV Middle school leaving certificate. Shortly thereafter, I received a letter informing me that my application had been approved and that I had been awarded the scholarship to proceed overseas to read Law, and that I must resign my appointment as a customs officer at once. I did as I was bid. In spite of my having resigned my appointment, I discovered to my horror that my notice of resignation was not forwarded to Lagos by the senior collector of customs, Mr. W. John E. Rodwell, who incidentally felt that he might successfully prevail upon me to withdraw the resignation. In the attempt to persuade me to withdraw my resignation on the ground that my future progress in the Customs Department was assured and that there was no guarantee that my sponsors, Ibibio Union, which was then an unknown organisation, would be able to maintain me throughout the period of my reading Law in the United Kingdom, the senior collector of customs failed woefully. I was adamant and could not be so persuaded. At my specific request, the resignation letter was at last forwarded to the authorities in Lagos. I left Port Harcourt in March 1938 for home at Ikot Abasi.

At home, I was able to discover that it was my beloved father's old intimate friend, Chief John King Usoro, then district interpreter in the Divisional Officer's office, himself an activist of the Ibibio Union, who was responsible for inducing Ibibio Union, Opobo division branch to call for my application for the scholarship. He, it was, had to advise Mr. Gabriel Ufford, the General President, Ibibio Union, Opobo division branch that it would be unwise and contrary to the policy of the central office at Uyo of the Ibibio Union, Opobo division branch to award its scholarship to Mr. Obot Essien Antia-Obong since he was an indigene of Itu division. Mr. Antia-Obong was then a clerk in the Divisional Officer's office, Opobo division, a keen and active member of the Ibibio Union, and a local preacher in the Wesleyan Methodist Church, Egwanga, Opobo. He had applied to the Ibibio Union, Opobo division for award of the scholarship to study overseas even though he was not an indigene of that division. Chief Usoro was able to influence the chiefs, officers and members of the executive committee of Ibibio Union, Opobo division to desist from awarding the scholarship then available and tenable in an institution of higher learning overseas to a non-indigene of the Ibibio area of Opobo division. He then pressed that I be invited to apply for the scholarship.

Consequent upon such compelling submission and explanation of the policy of the Ibibio Union at its central office in Uyo, coupled with extensive prompting, the chiefs, officers and members of the executive committee of the Ibibio Union, Opobo division had no alternative but to press that I be requested to apply directly for the award of the scholarship. In my application in response to the request of the home union at Ikot Akan, Opobo division, I considered it necessary to submit that I would be extremely grateful if my application could be considered along with the applications put in by others. In other words, that the application should be considered on its merit. As already mentioned, I was successful and I was awarded the scholarship. Thus I came to regard Chief John King Usoro as my godfather.

At home in Ikot Abasi, I was engaged in making arrangements for my overseas journey. I had also to attend several meetings of the Ibibio Union, Opobo division after I had reported to the chiefs, officers and members of the executive committee of the union. At the very first meeting of the union, which I attended, I was received with a standing ovation and I was constantly referred to as "our future lawyer" whenever I was mentioned by anyone in the course of his speech at the meeting. I gained the impression that I was a popular recipient of the scholarship. Throughout the period of my stay at home I felt I was well received by the majority of the people.

I also discovered during the period that the most influential individuals in the union included Chief Ntuenibok of Nunasang, Chief Jonah Ukpe of Ikpetim Ibekwe, Chief Gabriel Ufford, the General President of the Union, Chief Harry Ekanem of Ikot Akpaden, Chief Umoeren Akpanta of Minya, Chief Akpan Akpan Udo of Ikpa Ikono, Chief Martin A. Inam also of Ibekwe and Chief John King Usoro. It was also most consoling and satisfactory to find that, eventually, with the help of the leading figures in Opobo division, Mr. Obot Essien Antia-Obong was awarded scholarship by Itu division branch of the Ibibio Union and that he had chosen to read Medicine in Scotland.

In the course of my preparations, I visited Mr. A. C. Butler, agent of Messrs G. B. Ollivant Limited, Opobo branch and demanded the refund to me of the security deposit, which my beloved father had paid to enable me to be employed by the company as a shopkeeper. For the purpose, I had to tender to him the very receipt that he, as the agent of Messrs G. B. Ollivant Limited, had issued in my name for the amount at the request of my beloved father. The receipt was for the sum of two hundred and fifty pounds (£250). I was very happy to receive the same amount without any interest due thereon when it was tendered to me. This was because, after the death of my father, Abraham, my senior paternal brother, had applied to Mr. A. C. Butler for the refund of the security deposit on the ground that the same was part of my father's estate to which he had succeeded as heir. Before payment, the matter had to be referred to me while I was still serving at Port Harcourt as a Custom's officer. Because of my resistance on the ground that the amount was nothing more than an endowment or permanent gift by way of advancement made to me by my beloved father in his life time and that, in the event of his death, the money should belong to me personally, on the advice of the Divisional Officer, Opobo, to whom Mr. A. C. Butler had referred the matter, Abraham failed in his bid to recover the amount from Messrs G. B. Ollivant Limited, Opobo Branch.

Towards the end of July, 1938, all but one of the recipients of the scholarship awarded, that is Asuquo Udo Idiong of Abak for Medicine in Canada, Ibanga Udo Akpabio of Ikot Ekpene for Education in the United States of America, Bassey Udo Adiaha Attah of Uyo for Agriculture in the United States of America, Obot Essien Antia-Obong of Itu for Medicine in Scotland, United Kingdom and Egbert Udo Udoma of Opobo (now Ikot Abasi) for Law in Dublin, Eire assembled at Uyo for a general meeting with their sponsors and a farewell party given by the Central Executive of the Ibibio Union at which function each scholarship holder was given a sealed envelope (the contents of which were not disclosed but turned out to be sand from the soil of Ibibio land) with instructions that, on the return of each of the students from overseas on completion of his course of study, the envelope be also delivered back to the Central Executive Committee members of the Ibibio Union or their successors.

On 31 July 1938, we left Uyo and went in a procession to Ikot Ekpene for a divine service which was conducted by the Revd. Groves, the then superintendent minister of the Methodist Church, Ikot Ekpene at the request of the Central Executive Committee of the Ibibio Union of which Sampson Udo Etuk, government supervisor of education, was General President. After the service, it was decided that it was necessary the next day for us to leave for Port Harcourt via Aba, there to make final arrangement for our embarkation via Lagos to Liverpool, the port of our disembarkation in the United Kingdom.

Accordingly, after leaving Ikot Ekpene, we stopped at Aba that day for a reception by the Ibibio Union, Aba branch, which reception was a very grand affair. At Aba all the scholars but one (and that one being James Lawson Nsima of Eket whose case was later resolved as a result of which he had to join us later) under the leadership of Sampson Udo Etuk and the whole entourage from Ikot Ekpene proceeded to Port Harcourt arriving there on 1 August 1938. At Port Harcourt members of the entourage were lodged at different homes but my companions and I were lodged together at the home of Edet Effiong Edo Okon, then a clerk in the Medical Department there.

On 2 August 1938, the whole entourage under the leadership of Sampson Udo Etuk had, according to a prearranged programme, to meet the solicitor for the Ibibio Union, F. O. Lucas, Esq., at his office at Port Harcourt. There all the scholars were made to execute (witnessed by their respective sponsors) the scholarship agreement made by and between the Ibibio Union (then represented by its trustees) and each and every recipient of the scholarship binding himself to be of good behaviour while overseas and undergoing his prescribed course of studies in an approved institution of learning and thereafter to return home to Nigeria without entering into any marriage arrangement or getting engaged to be married to any girl or woman, whether European or otherwise, and, in any event and in so far as marriage

was concerned, each and every recipient of the scholarship was to return, on completion of his chosen course of study and obtaining the
necessary qualification, to Nigeria singly and uncommitted to any
form of marriage to anyone overseas.

On completion of the ceremony of the execution of the agreement, the whole entourage then wended its way to the then Messrs
Barclays Bank & Company Limited in the government reservation
area, Port Harcourt, and there, on behalf of each scholarship holder,
was paid a deposit in favour of the then government of Nigeria sufficient to cover the cost of repatriation of any of the scholarship holders
who might, peradventure, fall fowl of the British government in the
United Kingdom or the government elsewhere and thereby merited
repatriation. Funds were also withdrawn and paid to each student to
cover the cost of his keep and maintenance, and university expenses
for one year while overseas. Then all the scholarship holders had in
the evening to attend a reception and farewell party organised in their
honour by the Ibibio Union, Port Harcourt branch.

On 3 August 1938 all the scholars afore-named in the company
of their well wishers, mostly members of the Ibibio Union, having first
undergone medical immunisation according to law, assembled in the
morning at the Port Harcourt customs wharf, and thereafter boarded
M/V Calabar in the course of their embarkation en route to Lagos
after having bade farewell to their well wishers.

Our ship, M/V Calabar, having arrived at Lagos and berthed at
Apapa Harbour, we, that is, I together with the other scholars under
the leadership of Sampson Udo Etuk, who was then travelling with us
on his own to the United Kingdom on study leave granted to him as
supervisory education officer by the government of Nigeria, disembarked as transit passengers. I then parted company with the other
scholars and boarded an outboard engine canoe on the assistance and
advice of emissaries from the executive committee of the Ibibio Union, Opobo division branch, in the city of Lagos and landed on the
Customs Wharf, Marina, Lagos. I thereupon informed the emissaries
that it was necessary that I should call at the Customs Department
long room to report my arrival to Mr. William Udo Nsuk, a customs
officer and a former colleague and a personal intimate friend with
whom I was to lodge until my departure to the United Kingdom as I
had also to arrange for my passport at the Immigration Department. I
discharged the emissaries after thanking them for their wonderful serv-

ice in assisting me during disembarkation and ferrying me across to Lagos from Apapa. There was no information given to me concerning any arrangements as regards where I was to be lodged during the period of my stay in Lagos pending my departure to the United Kingdom nor as to any reception or farewell function arranged in my honour by the Ibibio Union, Opobo division branch in Lagos.

Fortunately for me, I was successful in meeting Mr. William Udo Nsuk who, immediately on seeing me, rushed enthusiastically to welcome me to Lagos. He embraced me and thereafter took permission to leave the office with me. Outside the Customs Department, we were able to pick a taxicab and, having loaded my luggage there on, we both boarded the car and headed for his residence in Lagos. Thereafter, Mr. William Udo Nsuk accompanied me to the Immigration Department to see about my passport.

The following morning I alone reported at the Immigration Department and my passport was handed over to me after I had paid the usual fees. Those who were still at the office and had seen me the previous day marvelled at the speed with which my passport was issued to me without realising that, in fact, I had applied for the passport for which I was recommended by the senior collector of customs, Mr. John E. Rodwell, while still in His Majesty's Customs Department some six months previously and that I was advised to collect the same on arrival in Lagos en route for the United Kingdom.

After collecting my passport, I returned to the residence of Mr. William Udo Nsuk to relax until the latter returned from work and joined me in the house. In the evening we were both joined by Efiong Akpan Okon, who was then a medical student at Yaba Higher College, and we had a jolly good time together. I did not then realise nor was I informed that the executive committee members of the Ibibio Union, Opobo division branch in Lagos, had organised a reception and farewell party in my honour. It was late that night that information was received by me that there was organised in my honour a reception cum farewell by the Ibibio Union, Opobo division branch in Lagos, which was attended by Sampson Udo Etuk and a couple of the other scholars who were astonished to find that I was not at the function. On learning of the situation, both Mr. William Udo Nsuk and I visited the address given to me where the function was taking place. There, to my sorrow, I discovered that in fact and in truth the function had taken place without my being present and it was now rounding up. I was so full of mortification that I could no longer contain myself.

I and Mr. William Udo Nsuk together there and then tendered to the remnant of the people there present profuse apologies for my absence from the function which was not deliberate. I then explained that, since my arrival in Lagos, no one had informed me either officially or unofficially, verbally or in writing, that a function of the kind was to be organised in my honour anywhere in Lagos. I pointed out further that, since my arrival, I had been engaged in arranging for my passport without which I could not travel to the United Kingdom, as they all knew. In the course of my explanation, more people began to gather at the spot. In the end I was able to show to them that I was not at fault and that the fault was theirs. The assembled persons there and then turned against members of the executive committee of the Ibibio Union, Opobo division branch in Lagos and, particularly, the secretary whose duty it was disclosed it was to have got in touch with me and who had failed to do so. In turn, those members present that night tendered to me on behalf of the union an unreserved apology for the abuses that had been poured on me for having been absent at such an important function. I thereafter retired with Mr. William Udo Nsuk with a free conscience.

The following day, I attended a reception cum farewell function organised by the central executive committee members of the Ibibio Union, Lagos branch in honour of all the recipients of the scholarships awarded by the Ibibio Union at home in Ibibio Country, Calabar province, Nigeria. The function was held at Aroloya Church hall under the chairmanship of the General President, Ibibio Union, Lagos branch. The function was followed by traditional and cultural dances in the open field at Campus Square, Lagos.

Then on 5 August 1938 we all, under the leadership of Sampson Udo Etuk, boarded the Elder Dempster mail boat M/V Apapa at the Apapa harbour as passengers on our journey or voyage to Liverpool. On board M/V Apapa but before the completion of embarkation formalities, I received a delegation from the Ibibio Union, Opobo division branch in Lagos who, after a repetition of the apology tendered to me the previous night, presented to me a gift comprising of a Parker fountain pen with a golden nib and a purse containing ten guineas (£10.10s) as a token to remind me of my voyage from Lagos to Liverpool in the United Kingdom. It was a delightful gift and I was extremely delighted to receive it. I was full of gratitude to the Almighty God who had most speedily effected reconciliation between members of the Ibibio Union, Opobo division branch in Lagos and my good self. I thereafter undertook my voyage with a clear conscience as a free man without any burden or chip on his shoulders.

All passengers having embarked upon the ship, we steamed off for Liverpool. En route, the ship called at Takoradi in Ghana, Freetown in Sierra Leone and Las Palmas, a Spanish island settlement. It was a relief to be able to go ashore for sight seeing on the island of Las Palmas after having been on board the ship for over one week. Ashore, we were greeted by a large contingent of troops, which brought forcefully to our attention the fact that Spain was at war - a civil war caused by General Franco in his bid as a dictator to usurp the power of the King of Spain after having overthrown the latter.[FN] At Las Palmas, also, we had the first taste of being in a country predominantly white in population. It was indeed a spectacle to see a large number of people bathing in the sunshine at the seashore - most of whom were swimming in the open sea. It was very attractive.

Having arrived at Las Palmas in the morning, we did not take off again till the evening. Moreover, while at Las Palmas, we were able to see the storey building that was said to have been occupied by Christopher Columbus during his voyage of discovery of America in 1492. It was explained to us that Christopher Columbus, during the voyage and after having departed from Spain, had to spend his first night at Las Palmas before proceeding to what turned out to be America on his way, as an explorer, in search of the route leading to the Far East. On the whole, we found Las Palmas very peaceful and enjoyable in spite of the Spanish civil war and the presence of a large number of soldiers apparently guarding that important island.

FOOTNOTE (FN)

A military dictatorship embraced by King Alfonso XIII governed Spain from 1923 to 1930, but municipal elections held in April 1931 deposed the king and ushered in the so-called Second Republic. On the night of 17 July 1936, the Spanish army, inspired most of all by General Francisco Franco, started the Spanish Civil War by rebelling against the Second Republic. General Franco went on to rule over Spain as a military dictator from 1939, after the Nationalist victory in the Civil War, until his death in 1975.

On taking off from Las Palmas, we set off for the high seas and after several days in turbulent and heavy seas at the Bay of Biscay, we finally berthed in the port of Liverpool calling only at Plymouth en route. On the Mersey side, emissaries or representatives of the Saintly Pastor Ekarte, the head and founder of the African Churches Mission of Liverpool fame, met us on arrival. They assisted all of us through the customs and immigration authorities of the United Kingdom. In my own case, because of the contract made on my behalf by the Revd. Alfred W Hodgetts, the Wesleyan Methodist expatriate superintendent in charge of Egwanga-Opobo (now Ikot Abasi) circuit of the Wesleyan Methodist Church, the superintendent minister of the Wesleyan Methodist Church, Liverpool also visited me personally and assisted immeasurably in facilitating my discharge by His Majesty's Customs and Immigration much sooner than I would have been. Thereafter, the Wesleyan Methodist minister invited me to drive with him in his car to his residence in Liverpool. I most politely declined the invitation promising to visit him after I and the other Ibibio Union scholars had settled in at the African Churches Mission as we were then guests of the Saintly Pastor Ekarte - a Nigerian settler in Liverpool.

After having been through the formalities usually associated with new arrivals at the Liverpool harbour, all of us scholars, under the leadership of Sampson Udo Etuk, were driven in a big bus to the residence of the Saintly Pastor Ekarte within the precinct of the African Churches Mission, Liverpool. There we were all given a very warm reception commencing with a Christian church thanksgiving service in praise of God for happy deliverance of all of us through the vicissitudes of heavy and sometimes stormy seas until we were able to set our feet once more on *firma terra* and ending in general entertainment. Thereafter, the scholars for America departed, under the leadership of Sampson Udo Etuk, as transit passengers to London for the procurement of visas at the American Embassy for their onward journey to the United States of America. In the evening of the same day, which, as far as I can remember was a Saturday, the Wesleyan Churches Methodist superintendent minister collected me from the African Churches Mission and took me to his residence where I was lavishly entertained to tea. After tea, I was conveyed back in his car to the African Churches Mission where I spent the weekend.

Matriculation And Admission Into TCD In 1938

"The function of a University is not simply to respond to social needs but to transform society".

On Saturday, 27 August 1938, Mr. Obot Essien Antia-Obong, the scholar who was to study medicine in Glasgow, boarded his train en route for Scotland and I boarded a passenger ship on the Mersey side for Dublin, arriving at North Wall harbour in the River Liffey in Dublin. From there, having disembarked, I took a taxicab early in the summer morning, at about 10 a. m., for the Methodist Centenary Church, St. Stephen's Green in search of the superintendent minister of the Wesleyan Methodist Church for whom I had with me a letter of introduction which was given to me by the Revd. Alfred W. Hodgetts and the Revd. Paul Kingston of Egwanga circuit of Opobo division, Calabar province, Nigeria, before my departure from Nigeria.

On arrival at the Wesleyan Methodist Centenary Church, St. Stephen's Green, I met the caretaker in charge of the church who was kind enough to inform me, on enquiry, that the Revd. R. Lee Cole, the superintendent minister in charge of the church, was resident at No. 2 Arranmore Road, Herbert Park, Dublin and that he would be glad to receive me and the letter. On his advice and direction, the driver of the taxicab thereupon drove me to the Herbert Park, Dublin address supplied to us in writing, and there, fortunately for me, having pressed the door bell, there came forth a lady who, on opening the door, introduced herself to me as the wife of the Revd. The lady then informed me that her husband was still resting in bed and that I should not offload my luggage from the taxicab at the premises. She then directed the driver of the taxicab to convey me to No. 81 Upper Leeson Street where, she said, I would find a Nigerian medical student whose name was Soyode Franklin who would be prepared and willing to receive and accommodate me. I thereupon handed over to her the letter addressed to her husband.

There and then the driver of the taxicab and I left for the new address. On arriving there, unfortunately for me, the young lady who answered the door bell informed me that Soyode Franklin, although a lodger there, was away to Great Britain on holiday, that being the period of long vacation for university institutions. The young lady was also kind enough to direct me to No. 74 Lower Leeson Street where, she informed me, was the habitat of a number of Nigerian students.

At this point the taxicab driver pretentiously appeared somewhat upset and weary of wandering round and round and so informed me. I pacified him and we left for No. 74 Lower Leeson Street which, fortunately for me, was not too far distant. Once more, I pressed the door bell and there came forth, truly enough, a Nigerian student who introduced himself to me as Olu Johnson and who appeared alarmed after having heard the story of my wandering from one end of the city of Dublin to another since I disembarked from the mail boat at Northwall at 10 a. m. that day. He therefore ordered the driver to offload my luggage from the taxicab after discovering on examination that the taximeter had registered a large sum of money to be paid by me for the hiring of the taxicab. I immediately settled my bill and discharged the driver and his taxicab from my service.

Olu Johnson and I then went upstairs with my luggage to the living room, and, like a good Samaritan, Olu Johnson was more concerned in a typical African hospitality fashion with feeding me than with anything else for it was then 2.30 p. m., realising, as he did, that I had disembarked from the mail boat at 10 a. m. Consequently he at once engaged himself in arranging for my feeding. He served me with tea and some sandwiches and cakes, hurriedly prepared, before even asking to know about the part of Nigeria to which I belonged. I soon settled down and, having rested for a while, engaged myself in meaningful conversation with Olu Johnson. After I had told him frankly all about myself and the purpose of my journey to the city of Dublin, Olu Johnson then disclosed that he was himself a law student at Trinity College, Dublin in the University of Dublin, Eire, that all the flats at No. 74 Lower Leeson Street were in the occupation of Nigerian students engaged in reading Law and Medicine in the University of Dublin, Eire, and that some of the students were spending their vacation in Great Britain while others were also on holiday at a place outside the city of Dublin known as Dalkey.

At the conclusion of our exchanges, Mr. Olu Johnson decided that we both boarded an omni-bus for Dalkey. On arrival, Olu Johnson gracefully and delightfully introduced me to two of his flat mates. The two students were John A. Kester, a law student, and O. Sasegbon, a medical student, both of whom were delighted to see me and received me rather warmly to my delight and satisfaction. Later in the evening of that day, all of us, that is Mr. John A. Kester, Mr. O. Sasegbon,

Olu Johnson and I, returned and resumed possession of No. 74 Lower Leeson Street. Furthermore, not very long after our return to No. 74 Lower Leeson Street, to my surprise and astonishment, I was visited by the Revd. Superintendent R. Lee Cole who voluntarily conveyed me in his car to different addresses in the city of Dublin in an attempt to see whether he could secure an accommodation for me as a lodger. The attempt ended in utter failure and I was discharged from the car at No. 74 Lower Leeson Street, Dublin. Thereafter, I spent about one week at No. 74 Lower Leeson Street, Dublin with Mr. John A. Kester, Mr. O. Sasegbon and Olu Johnson, all three of whom proved of immense help to me, after which I joined Mr. Soyode Franklin at No. 81 Upper Leeson Street, Dublin, the latter having returned to Dublin from Great Britain after his summer holiday.

At No. 81 Upper Leeson Street, by special arrangement effected on my behalf with the landlady, Mrs Trench, by Mr. Soyode Franklin, I was accommodated temporarily in a spare room as a lodger entitled to bed and breakfast, my lunch and high tea or supper to be had outside in a restaurant. I was delighted with the room occupied by me. It was quite spacious and warm since it had a fireplace. It then became necessary for me to prepare for my matriculation examination into Trinity College, Dublin (TCD). Having procured the syllabus with the kind assistance of Mr. Sasegbon, I had also to engage the services of a coach or grinder, especially as I discovered that in addition to Latin, Trinity College being a classical University, I had also to be examined in French, considered a modern language. The subjects to be taken by me for matriculation included Mathematics (Arithmetic and Algebra), Geometry (or Euclid), Trigonometry, English, French, Latin, Geography and History, and some of the subjects had to be taken both written and oral or viva voce.

It should be mentioned that, while in Nigeria since leaving school, I had taken postal tuition from Great Britain in preparation for the London Matriculation Examination, which was then considered a public examination. Therefore, on arrival in Dublin and after thorough scrutiny of the syllabus, I was satisfied that it would be possible for me to pass with ease the matriculation examination which was scheduled to be held in the autumn during the first week of October, 1938. With the help of the grinder, I was then engaged in a revision of the subjects of the examination except French, which I had to study afresh. I was regarded at school as naturally very good in Mathematics, Geometry and Trigonometry as well as English. As far as Latin was concerned, I believe, I had adequate knowledge of the subject even when I was in elementary school at Ibekwe. I therefore decided that I must take the examination in October 1938 without delay.

Subsequent to my arrival in Dublin, there also arrived one Mr. Jaja Anucha Wachuku, a Nigerian who informed me during discussion that he was formerly a student of Higher College, Yaba and later of a French School in Togoland on the boarder of the Gold Coast (now Ghana) where he had studied French far in excess of the standard required for the matriculation examination at Trinity College, Dublin. The result was that, according to him, he was exempted from taking some of the subjects, including French, prescribed for the matriculation examination. After having studied the syllabus, he proclaimed that he was also to register to take the matriculation examination scheduled for the autumn so as to save him time.

Then during the first week of October, 1938 I took the matriculation examination and had a bare pass, not doing very well, in Geography and History, both of which dealt with the Irish situation, while obtaining excellent in Mathematics, Geometry and Trigonometry, English, French and Latin. I was said to be entitled to a small certificate that, in effect, meant that I was entitled to be admitted into the university as a student to pursue my chosen course of study but not entitled to be issued with any certificate at all. Having thus been accepted as a student of the university, I chose to pursue a course of study in Moderatorship in Legal Science in the Honours School.

On the other hand, Mr. Jaja Wachuku delayed his matriculation examination until January 1939 and, after having taken it and been successful, he chose to read for the Moderatorship in Legal Science as well in the Honours School. We were thus both in the same class, the University session having commenced in October 1938 that is, since Michaelmas term. From then on I was engaged in my studies in earnest as a university student. When the news of the success was received in Ibibio Country, most people at home were very pleased and I received congratulatory messages from all and sundry and from unexpected quarters. The news of my having matriculated and been admitted into Trinity College, Dublin so soon after arrival caused considerable excitement at home. There was jubilation in the streets and villages in Opobo division. This was because the branch union at home, having realised that I had not taken the matriculation examination at the time I left school but thereafter had been preparing for the examination, had given me one year of grace, while in the United Kingdom, to prepare for the matriculation examination. I was therefore expected to matriculate for admission into any university of my choice on the expiration of one year after my arrival in the United Kingdom. I was elated and had a general sense of satisfaction over my achievement. I felt it was a sign of the things to come.

CHAPTER ELEVEN

Life At Trinity College, Dublin

"To be wholly devoted to some intellectual exercise is to have succeeded in life, and perhaps only in law and the higher mathematics may this devotion be maintained, suffice it itself without reaction, and find continuous rewards without aid". – Robert Louis Stevenson

During my first year at College, I lived outside the university campus as a lodger in approved digs, first at No. 81 Upper Leeson Street and latterly at No. 53 Lower Leeson Street where I lived on the invitation of Mr. Emmanuel Tete Osong Annan, a Ghanaian student who took a liking to me. He was a medical student and I shared double digs with him. While I was at No. 81 Upper Leeson Street as a lodger, I was fortunate enough to be accompanying Mr. Soyode Franklin, on his invitation, to attend every Sunday with him a Bible class meeting under the leadership of a distinguished Christian and merchant, Mr. Fannin, who was the proprietor and manager of a famous medical store in which medical appliances were sold at Grafton Street in Dublin. As a result of the association, Mr. Fannin developed an interest in me. Moreover, again on the invitation of Mr. Soyode Franklin, I used to worship with him every Sunday after the Bible class at the Centenary Methodist Church, St. Stephen's Green, Dublin, of which Mr. Fannin was also a very important member. Within the short time I was at No. 81 Upper Leeson Street, I was able to form the impression that Mr. Soyode Franklin, unlike many other African students in Dublin, was a keen and honest churchman. His conduct was unimpeachable and exemplary and worthy of emulation particularly in relation to his relationship with white people. He was also reasonably thrifty.

Consequent upon my regular attendance at the Bible class meetings and thereafter participating in Sunday services of religious worship, it was possible for Mr. Fannin to listen attentively to the manner in which I used to sing the church hymns, especially at the class meetings and, being obviously impressed with the manner of my singing the church hymns at the class meetings and, particularly with my personal tenor voice, recommended me to the choir mistress of the Methodist Centenary Church, St. Stephen's Green, Miss Sylvia Fannin, who incidentally happened to be his daughter. In his recommendation, Mr. Fannin suggested that I might prove useful as a tenor singer in the choir of the church. To my surprise, after having been attending the class meeting for some six months, I received an invitation from Miss Sylvia Fannin to join the Methodist Centenary Church choir as she understood that I was a good tenor singer. I was delighted to accept the invitation. I was thus promoted from being an occupier of one of the pews of the galleries of the church to a singer in the choir occupying a seat in the chancery of the church. I was very pleased with my good fortune since, at home in Nigeria, I was a member of the choir in both Ebenezer Church, Ibekwe, now the Methodist Cathedral, and Egwanga Methodist Church Urban. I was pleased to be able to maintain the tradition. From then on I became a member of the Methodist Centenary Church choir - a chorister; and throughout the period of my sojourn in Dublin remained a member of, and continued to sing regularly without any intermission in, the choir of Centenary Methodist Church, St. Stephen's Green, Dublin.

In my last year, however, in addition to singing in the choir I was appointed Chairman of the Missionary Overseas Council, which was considered an unprecedented record. Furthermore, to show how benevolent Mr. Fannin was towards me all the time, I quite clearly remember that, during my second year at College, it was Mr. Fannin who, at my request, most willingly and readily signed my application form for admission into Gray's Inn in London as a student still undergoing education at Trinity College, Dublin, Eire. In addition to signing the form as my guardian he also recommended me as a fit and proper person to be admitted to the Inns of Court in London. I was delighted and indeed felt myself extremely fortunate to have had such a well-known Christian leader to accept to be my guardian for the purpose of the Inns of Court, which is a very important and learned institution.

It was most interesting to observe that while I was a tenor singer in the choir of the Centenary Church, there was also Dr. Eustace Fannin - a medical doctor and the son of the highly respected Mr. Fannin - who was singing bass in the same choir. Dr. Eustace Fannin was also a well-known and world famous Irish international tennis star that had won several prizes as a first class tennis player. He was very good company and somewhat on the quiet side. He was simple but by no means a simpleton. The organist of the church was Mr. Nelson.

As soon as I was admitted into Trinity College, Dublin, I was advised by my tutor in college, Professor W. B. Stanford, FTCD to seek admission also into the Law School of the university, which I did. The registrar of the Law School there was Dr. G. A. Duncan, with whom I had previously been in communication when I was in Nigeria planning to enter Trinity College, Dublin. I remember writing to inform Dr. G. A. Duncan, as the registrar of the Law School, that I was about to leave Nigeria for Dublin to seek admission into the University of Dublin to read Law, that, according to my information, on boarding my ship on the Mersey side in Liverpool I would arrive in the Liffey on the Northwall and that I would appreciate it very much if the university authorities could send someone to meet me at Northwall and thence to escort me to the university as I had never been to Southern Ireland before.

In his most generous reply, Dr. G. A. Duncan had indicated that, although he appreciated my predicament as a complete stranger to Ireland, he regretted to have to inform me that it was not the practice for universities to send out emissaries to escort new entrants or would be students. Dr. G. A. Duncan then went out of his way to enclose, in his letter to me, a sketch map showing the way to the University of Dublin from the harbour known as Northwall in the river Liffey in Dublin, Eire. On receiving Dr. G. A. Duncan's letter and noting the contents thereof, I felt ashamed of myself.

In the Law School at Trinity, in addition to the registrar, there were then the Professor of Laws, Professor Frances Moran, MA, LLD, who was the specialist in Irish Law of Real Property and lectured on that subject and Conveyancing as well as The Law of Contract and Tort; Dr. A. Mackenna, MA, LLD, lecturer on Roman Law, Advanced Roman Law and Roman in Modern Practice; Professor J. Archibald Coutts, MA, LLD, FTCD, lecturer in Legal History, Jurisprudence, International Law and Public Administration and Professor Baker, Reid's Professor and lecturer in Constitutional Law and History, Criminal Law and Procedure and the Law of Evidence. When, later, Professor Frances Moran retired, it was Professor Archibald Coutts, MA, LLB, FTCD, who succeeded as the Professor of Laws. Attending all these lectures was for me a duty, which had to be done, and proved a remarkable experience and most rewarding.

According to the arrangement in the university, all Honour School students were expected to take their terminal examinations not immediately at the end of term nor at the close of lectures for the term but at the commencement of the following term so that in the case of, for instance, Michaelmas term examinations, all Honour students, that is, all students pursuing the Moderatorship course, were expected to sit for their Michaelmas term Honour examination just before the commencement of lectures for the Hilary term. This meant, in effect, that Honours students were expected to spend their vacations working and preparing for examinations to be conducted at commencement of the ensuing term. Bearing that situation in mind, at the end of Michaelmas term, that is, my first term in college, to test the extent to which I had followed the lectures delivered by Dr. Mackenna on Roman Law based on Leige's Roman Law, I ventured to take the examination intended for non-Honours students who were engaged in working for Pass degrees. To my great surprise, I did not do well at all. That experience stimulated me to engage myself in very serious work indeed, preparing during the vacation for the Honours term examination, which was held just before the commencement of Hilary term and which I took and passed very well, obtaining Second Class honours. After that examination, I was encouraged to work even still harder so as to maintain my position in the class.

CHAPTER TWELVE

I Go Into Residence At College

"Learning is like riding a bicycle; if you stop pedalling you are bound to fall". Albert Einstein

I must confess that, throughout my career at college, I had always considered myself a very lucky man, if there is anything called "luck". Now, during my second year in college, I received an invitation from a young student - a Methodist member of the Centenary Church, St. Stephen's Green - who was reading Philosophy, which course was known at College as Mental and Moral Science Moderatorship or Moderatorship in Mental and Moral Science, to share his double rooms in college with him. I mentioned to him in confidence that I was told by African students lodging in digs outside the campus of the university that African students were never allowed to live in rooms in the campus of the university when I first mooted at the idea of living in rooms in the college. He was shocked to hear of such a tale. He immediately assured me that such a tale could not be true and that he would take up the matter with his tutor, as he honestly believed that the tale had no foundation in fact.

Now that bold and courageous student was no other person than Mr. Thomas Alfred Bradshaw who later graduated from Trinity College with a first class degree in Moderatorship in Mental and Moral Science and subsequently volunteered for service in the Methodist Church. The matter concerning his application for approval by the university authorities that I should share his double rooms with him which was boldly transmitted by his amiable tutor, Dr. F. La Touche Godfrey, FTCD, having been favourably considered and approved, was communicated to me by Mr. Thomas Alfred Bradshaw with the greatest of pleasure, and gave a lie to the wicked rumour which was being wrongly spread among African students. I immediately, with a heart full of gratitude, moved house and joined the angelic Thomas Alfred Bradshaw and shared with him No. 2 T.C.D. at the front square of cobbled stones next door to the Examination Hall and opposite the College Chapel and not far from the Campanille. It was a unique position indeed and the rooms were well appointed. Thus, in living memory, I became the first Nigerian, if not African, student to live in rooms in college at Trinity.

Having successfully moved into rooms in college and thereby enjoyed all amenities available therein, I then that same year became an active member of the University Philosophical Society based in the Graduates Memorial Building which also housed another important student's society known as the Historical Society. The Historical Society became very famous because it was reputed to be the society which had produced the famous Edmund Burke, Nationalist Politician, who rose to become Member of Parliament at Westminster, Great Britain. Those two societies, the University Philosophical Society and the Historical Society were at the time the two most important students' societies in college and dominated the social activities and affairs of students at the time. They were not organised on the basis of trade unionism. They were not specifically dining clubs. While the University Philosophical Society was organised on the basis that, during term at its meetings, any member might volunteer to read a well prepared paper on any subject of his choice under the sun, the delivery of such paper to be followed by a debate by the whole house on the topic of the paper, the Historical Society was purely a debating society and its debates on a variety of subjects were open to those members of the society who desired to participate therein actively. In the case of the University Philosophical Society, at the close of each meeting all members present thereat were entitled to award marks to the readers of the papers that provided the topics of the debate as regards their literary style, as well as to speakers who participated in the general debates ensuing, the papers upon which such marks were indicated being distributed in the course of the proceedings. So too, in the Historical Society, speakers who participated in debates were also awarded marks for their oratory. Such marks were collated at the end of the university year or session at Trinity term and it was then determined the orders of merit for the award of medals which consisted of gold or silver. In the case of the University Philosophical Society, two gold medals and two silver medals were usually awarded in a good and prosperous year, the best prepared paper delivered attracting a gold medal and the second in rank receiving the silver medal and similar awards being made in respect to oratory. But, in the Historical Society, the best speaker would receive a gold medal and the next in command would be entitled to a silver medal. Medals were awarded only for oratory.

Furthermore, in the case of the University Philosophical Society, apart from the marks awarded at the time of the delivery of each paper, the papers carrying the highest marks given by members of the society were then sent to outside examiners, not necessarily members of the society, who then would assess the merits of such papers as prized essays and award marks accordingly, the paper carrying the highest mark awarded receiving a gold medal and the next in rank fetching a silver medal, the papers delivered being judged severely according to the material contents and literary style.

It should also be observed that, while the head or presiding official at all meetings of the University Philosophical Society was styled "President", that of the Historical Society was known as the "Auditor" - a unique name or title to be borne by the head of a students' organisation. Needless to state, the two students' institutions were rivals. They often competed for membership. All the same they were both housed in the Graduates Memorial Building and shared a common debating hall which was situated on the ground floor of the building practically next door to the well appointed common room of the University Philosophical Society where daily papers and weekly magazines were usually exhibited for reading by all members and which had an ornate fire place.

The common room for members of the Historical Society was situated on the second floor upstairs of the same building. Each society had an executive committee known as Council that was responsible for the management of the apartments and the affairs of the society within the building subject to the overall control of the trustees of the Graduates Memorial Building.

In my second year as a member of the University Philosophical Society, during the tenure in office of Mr. R. J. Harvey as President, I was elected to the office of Librarian of the society, that being the second to the lowest office in the society, the lowest office being the Registrar of the society. In my third year, as a reward for efficient service, I was fortunate enough to be elected to the high office of General Secretary of the society, that being the office next to the office of President thereby skipping the office of Treasurer of the society. In my final year during which I had to sit for my Moderatorship in Legal Science examination, I was the official nominee for the office of the President of the society, that being the highest office available to be filled by the process of election by any student duly qualified as member of the society of good standing. I was nominated in accordance with the established norm of the society to contest the office in succession to Mr. W. John White, the outgoing President, under whom I had served the society most diligently as Hon. General Secretary. The contest was a rather serious one, which I propose to deal with elsewhere in some detail.

CHAPTER THIRTEEN

In The Pursuit Of My Education In The University

"The war had shown that our mastery over physical forces might end in a nightmare, that mankind was becoming like an overgrown child armed with deadly weapons, a child with immense limbs and tiny head".

In my first year in college, I had devoted a great deal of my time to reading in the college library - Biblotheque - and of course attending lectures prescribed for my course of study which, as already stated, was Moderatorship in Legal Science as well as Law Simpliciter. At the same time, I had also to prepare myself for taking my "Littlego" examination, which is known in other universities, like the University of London, as Intermediate Bachelor of Arts Degree examination. As I was entitled to as an honours student, I took full advantage of the privilege of taking the examination in two parts provided I could complete the whole examination within the period of two years from the date of my admission into the university.

Accordingly, I was able to take the first part of my "Littlego" examination comprising English, French and Latin in my first year since I had obtained a second class honour during the Michaelmas term Honour examination. Happily I did very well in the examination as I passed with credit in all the subjects. I then turned, after lectures had ended for the Trinity term, to prepare quite hard for the Honour examination, which I took successfully, obtaining a first class honour and prize money of four pounds (£4) as the examination was treated as a prize examination as well.

Having come into residence in college and sharing rooms with Thomas Alfred Bradshaw, whose parents I later learned were domiciled in Australia, my work in college was facilitated and improved considerably. For, living in college and having the assistance of a "skip", which means a porter - invariably an ex-service man, as I did, made a world of difference. In addition to being a member of the University Philosophical Society, I also joined the Students' Christian Movement in college. Thus, apart from being a chorister in the Centenary Church, St. Stephen's Green, I was an active member of the University Philosophical Society and the Student's Christian Movement in college and by reason of which I was able to make many friends both inside and outside college. With the help of such friends I also became a member of the Laymen's Association of the Methodist Church, which was a powerful group associated with the management of the affairs of the Methodist Church in Ireland.

Being placed in such a position, I was able to make the contacts that would enable me to also become a member of the Methodist Church Summer School, which throughout the period of my studentship I enjoyed attending every year whether it was organised in the South or in the North of Ireland. Incidentally, the first Summer School that I attended was held at the Portora Royal School, Enniskillen in Northern Ireland. It was very well organised and turned out to be most enjoyable. There were also well organised sports including both lawn and table tennis.

It was because I was a member of the Centenary Church, St Stephen's Green that I was able to associate with a number of young men who were, themselves, Christians under the leadership of the Revd. Jack Kells who became famous because of his work among the youth. In this connection, I was happy and proud to be associated with a large number of young men such as David Rowe, Bertie Onie, Reginald Crowe, Kenneth Crowe, Basil Booth, Lionel Booth, Ian Browne, George Parker, S. W. Wolfe and Thomas Alfred Bradshaw, to name only a few. I also was in the happy position of being invited from time to time by important Christian families such as the Hannahs, the Baskins, the Reas, the Booths and the Brownes to have tea with their families. I was always happy to accept such invitations as I had regarded dining out among families as forming part of my education. I really felt that as a student in Trinity College, Dublin my life was a joy to me and I discovered that one learned a great deal by associating with good Christian men and women. For that reason, I attached very great importance and value to my membership of the University Philosophical Society and of the Students' Christian Movement in the university, and more particularly that I ultimately rose to the office of President of the University Philosophical Society in my last year at college. I found my association with such institutions most rewarding. I was also a member of the Co-operative Society in college and, ultimately,

I became a member of the Management Committee of the Society, which ran the only grocery store in the college.

I completed my "Littlego" examination in my second year in college by taking the remaining subjects consisting of Higher Mathematics, including Euclid and Trigonometry, Mechanics and Logic. I passed the examination with flying colours and was featured in the University Gazette implying that I was thereafter entitled to proceed unhampered with my normal course of study in the Honours School. In my third year, I was free to take my Intermediate LLB examination and I did and passed obtaining first class honours and it was so gazetted. I took that examination during Hilary term. During as well as at the end of Trinity and during the ensuing Michaelmas term, I sat for the Honours examination and passed obtaining first class honours and a prize of £4, which I used to buy relevant books for my use.

In my third year in college, I was invited by a generous friend of mine, Michael Booth, an Engineering student who, having completed his final examination, was leaving college preparatory to joining voluntarily the British Army in defence of democracy and the world against Nazism and Hitlerite Germany after the fall of France in 1940 during World War II of 1939-45, to move from my rooms at No. 2 Front Square to No. 17 Botany Bay, his well appointed and superbly furnished double rooms. Incidentally, the rooms at No. 17 Botany Bay were furnished under the personal supervision of his highly respected mother in expectation that the son would continue with his education in college by supplicating for a higher degree on graduation but, by reason of the war, the son, Michael, decided otherwise in the interest of democracy and of the peace of the world.

Michael was of course a staunch Methodist Christian and son of one of the Booths who were keenly interested in me. In my time in Dublin there were two Booths - one Edwin and the other Robert - both of whom were interested and engaged in the automobile industry. They dealt in cars. The two Booths were also members of the Centenary Church, St Stephen's Green, Dublin. Michael was not alone in volunteering for the army. Indeed, in 1940 after the fall of France as a result of German invasion, there were several graduates as well as undergraduates in universities in the British Isles who volunteered for the army for the purpose of defending Europe against Nazism.

I was happy to accept the invitation. I immediately moved house on receiving the approval of the university authorities communicated to me through the Junior Dean, Dr. K. C. Bailey, the Senior Dean then being Sir Robert (popularly known as Babi) Tate. Both deans were responsible for the maintenance of discipline in college. I took possession of No. 17 Botany Bay, which I found to be well furnished, attractive and neat and fitted with an excellent fireplace. Michael Booth, my friend, confided in me that from the time he entered college he had always occupied the rooms alone.

In those days, Botany Bay, according to tradition, was regarded as the area or part of the college in the occupation usually of students who took special delight and derived considerable pleasure in the entertainment of themselves and their friends at any time of the day or night. There was always entertainment of one form or another. Many of the occupants of the rooms at Botany Bay were members of the Boat Club and Michael Booth was himself a member of the Boat Club. In any case, I did not need to be told that because as I entered the sitting room there was hanging along the wall an oar.

My rooms at No.17 TCD or Botany Bay I found exceedingly useful at the time of my presidency of the University Philosophical Society, as it was part of the duty of my office as President to entertain members of the society to supper after meetings of the society every Thursday evening during term. The rooms, which were situated behind the Graduates Memorial Buildings in which the society was accommodated, were well equipped for the purpose. There was plenty of room to manoeuvre. In particular, the rooms served me extremely well, being on the second floor, on the night when the results of my election to the office of President of the society were announced and I was successful, despite the pressure exerted on members of the society by my opponents. All members of the society were lavishly entertained in my rooms that night. It was a wonderful night and a tremendous experience for me. There was rejoicing generally and the celebrations following my success at the polls continued till the small hours of the morning. The spectacle was really incredible.

In my fourth year in college, that is in the year 1942 in the midst of World War II, I had to sit for my final Moderatorship in Legal Science examination which I did and passed in October 1942 obtaining, in the absence of first class, a second class honour and second place in the examination. There were only three of us in the class to be awarded second class honour, the rest were awarded third class honour. Then in December 1942 I obtained first class honour in my LLB final degree examination. In January 1943 I was permitted to supplicate for the PhD degree as a post-graduate student. By special arrangement, it was approved that I should conduct research and produce a thesis for the PhD degree partly in England within the prescribed period of two years for which reason I had to work during the long vacation after Trinity term of 1943. The highly respected Professor J. A. Coutts, FTCD, Professor of Laws, supervised my work as my tutor for the post-graduate degree. While at Oxford, my work was supervised by Professor Daryll Forde of the University of Oxford. The topic for research and preparation of my thesis was "Law and Administration in South Eastern Nigeria".

Before sitting for my final Moderatorship in Legal Science examination, I, having been nominated as the official candidate for the office of President of the University Philosophical Society, had to enter the contest for the office of President. There were five other candidates who opposed my candidature and had themselves been nominated as candidates to contest the office with me. The contest was indeed a serious one particularly as I was the first African student at Trinity College to be nominated to contest the office. I was personally determined to win and to make history in the college. There were many of the students who were fond of me and they wished me well.

Some of the students who professed friendship with me advised me to withdraw my candidature for the election to the office of President. I personally ignored their advice. For instance, Mr. Jaja A. Wachuku was of the view that I would not be returned as President and therefore I should withdraw from the contest. On the other hand, there was a friend of mine, Mr. Emmanuel Tete Osong Annan, who pressed hard on me to contest the election to the office since it was the first time that an African student was being considered worthy of being nominated for such a high office. He was very strongly of the view that on no account should I yield to those who were advising me to withdraw from the contest. As a man of his word, on the night when the results of the election were to be announced, he voluntarily joined me in my rooms awaiting the announcement of the results and only left me after having received the report that I was successful and that I had been returned President of the society, and I was so declared. Soon thereafter it was disclosed to me by the committee in charge of the conduct of the election that my greatest opponent among the five students who contested the election against me was Mr. Dennis R. Godfrey, a student in the School of Modern Languages specialising in English Literature.

As soon as the results were announced and I was declared the winner there followed entertainment galore. I was myself thankful to God for my success at the poll. Some of the candidates who contested as my opponents on learning of the results came forward and congratulated me on the occasion and we shook hands in reconciliation. For me, it was a glorious victory. I felt myself on top of the world and therefore could not afford to entertain animosity towards any one. My motto was: **In victory, generosity**.

The results of the election to the office of President having been announced on Thursday evening, the following Saturday I entertained members of the executive council of the University Philosophical Society and members of the election committee to dinner at the Metropole hotel, which all who attended enjoyed very much and were apparently appreciative of the gesture. I then set out at once to plan for my inauguration as the President of the University Philosophical Society in October 1942.

My winning the election was sensational and attracted press comments worldwide. For instance, the Irish Christian Advocate of 3rd July 1942 wrote:

> *"His numerous friends in Irish Methodism, including members of the Young Laymen's League and the Missionary Summer School, desire to congratulate most heartily Mr. Egbert Udo Udoma on his election as President of the Philosophical Society at Trinity College Dublin, for the Session 1942-43."*

The writer of "TCD Notes" said –

> *"Mr. Udoma is a law student, and has the distinction of being the first African to be elected President of a major society at College. He will bring to his office as President a considerable working knowledge of the Society, as he was elected Secretary last year, and before that held the post of Librarian."*

"Quidnunc" also wrote in "An Irish Man's Diary" –

> *"Mr. Udoma is a Nigerian Student and has been an active member of the "Phil" for the last three years. I believe that his unfailing good humour and sound personal qualities had earned him the widest popularity. He has been a staunch supporter of the Methodist Centenary Church, Stephen's Green, for some time, and sings in the choir. This is the first time that an African student has reached the principal office in a major Trinity Society and I feel sure that the precedent will be welcomed in all quarters".*

Then in October 1942 came the opening meeting of the Philosophical Society for my installation as the President of the society for the 1942-1943 session in accordance with the university academic session. The opening meeting, which was scheduled to take place on 30th October 1942, did take place accordingly. But before that, as member of the Fabian Society and of the Labour Party of Great Britain, I was able through my contacts to secure the presence of Dr. Julian Huxley, FRS and Secretary of the Biological Society of Great Britain, then a Brains trust of Britain, and Professor W. N. McMillan, author and head of the Imperial Intelligence Service of the BBC, at the opening meeting. Both of them had to come from London in England to participate in the ceremony of my installation as President of the University Philosophical Society, Dublin, Southern Ireland.

According to tradition, the provost of the University had to be invited by me to preside over the opening meeting of the society. Others whom I invited and who were generous in accepting my invitation as special guests to take part in the discussion of my presidential address on the occasion of my installation included Sir John Kean, senator and chairman of the Board of Directors of the Bank of Ireland and Sean O'Faolain, the editor of the famous magazine known as the "Bell". My presidential address on the occasion was titled: "The Lion and the Oil Palm" (see Appendix A), being a dissertation on British colonial policy in West Africa. The opening meeting, which was presided over by the provost of the University, Dr. E. H. Alton, took place as scheduled at 9 p. m. after coffee had been served to the numerous guests who attended, and was most sensational and attracted the world press.

In order to demonstrate how sensational the meeting was and the great importance attached not only to the occasion but also to the subject which constituted the topic for discussion, I can do no better than reproduce the report of the event in at least two newspapers of the day. In the "Irish Times" of October 30, 1942, the address was displayed in its banner headline as "**Vision of Colonial Future - Dr. Julian Huxley's Forecast**". The report ran as follows: -

> *"Julian Huxley, writer, lecturer, doctor of science and member of the BBC Brains Trust speaking in Trinity College last night envisaged a new world in which no country would be completely independent.*
>
> *An African, E. Udo Udoma, President of the University Philosophical Society in an address on "The Lion and the Oil*

Palm" tugged at the few remaining hairs on the lion's tail by way of criticism of Britain's administration of his native country.

When the large dining hall had filled to overflowing for the opening meeting of the Philosophical Society, many had to go to the Graduates' Memorial Hall and listen to the speeches coming through amplifiers.

AFRICA

Mr. E. Udo Udoma dealt with the development and present position of Africa. The Treaty of Versailles, he said, had tried in a rather vague utopian way to protect African interests. The native people were deprived of their natural wealth and were compelled to work for a bare subsistence. Was it any wonder that there were occasional outbursts against the Government? West Africa now hungered, as never before, for education. He envisaged an education that would teach the people not what, but how, to think for themselves. Africans needed not emotional pity but sympathetic and intelligent thought.

MAJOR PROBLEM

Dr. Julian Huxley said that the world was passing through a revolution of basic ideas. The trend was towards conscious planning with maximum health, nutrition, and education for the people, which could be implemented in a totalitarian or democratic way. "The major problem," he said, "was how to enable the colonies to develop as quickly as possible towards fullness of life and self government." The great bulk of the colonies were in an economically backward state. There was enormous amount of leeway to be made up before the desirable standard of living for the native people would be attained.

He could not imagine that after the war a completely independent major power would exist and minor powers probably would be absorbed by the larger. Self-government was best achieved by enlisting more and more of the native people in administrative and executive positions. The real "have notes" were the colonial people who would not be as backward if they had not been exploited.

He was in favour of setting up planning authorities with adequate funds who would work in cooperation with the na-

tive peoples to develop the more backward colonies. There should be international effort, in which he hoped the United States would join, to develop all backward areas. This was the only possible substitute that democrats could envisage for the old imperialism.

TOO CUT-OFF

Professor MacMillan said that the trouble with Africa was not its contact with civilisation, but its lack of contact - it was too cut off. They would not know what Africa was capable of until the African had a chance of being a normal healthy being and in few parts was he ever that. There was a new vision of things that was not seen, perhaps, on this side of the channel. Africans and Indians were thinking in British terms; they had "cooperative differences", but there was little danger of those differences resulting in the bondage that is seen in some parts of the world today.

Mr. Sean O'Faolain related his speech to the situation in Ireland and so too did Senator Sir John Kean."

Then the Irish Press printed its report of the proceedings under the banner headline thus: - "**Dr. Huxley on Post War World**", and went on to report as follows: -

"Hundreds queued four-deep at Trinity College Dublin last night to hear a West African plead for the people of his native place, and to hear Dr. Julian Huxley, writer, lecturer and zoologist speak on the same subject. Mr. E. Udo Udoma, new President of the University Philosophical Society, lectured on Britain's rule in West Africa in his paper: The Lion and the Oil Palm.

Dr. Huxley, who proposed the vote of thanks, said they were passing through a world revolution. There was a tendency towards planning of better social conditions. This tendency could be implemented by a totalitarian or democratic idea. The colonies could only be considered in view of these trends. The great bulk of them were in a backward state. Improvements would come only as a part of a general movement.

AFTER THE WAR

In future there would be few politically independent or economically independent powers. Few nations would stand economically on their own. He could not imagine after the war even a completely independent major power; minor powers would be absorbed probably willingly by the larger. He did not agree with international administration of colonies. Self-government of colonies could be completed within a few generations.

Professor MacMillan said that the trouble with Africa was not its contact with civilisation but the lack of it. Out of Africa came little light, and worse, into it went very little light.

FOR AND WITH THE PEOPLE

Mr. E. Udo Udoma said that the solution to the West African problem was a planning for and with the people instead of against them. It would amount to an assurance that within a limited number of years the colonial people would be entitled to take their place as equals within the British Commonwealth of Nations. Separation, he said, was not only undesirable, it was unthinkable."

After the opening meeting there was held a dinner party at the hotel Metropole for the purpose of entertaining the special guests at the meeting that night. Then on 31 October 1942 there appeared this Editorial in "The Irish Press"; it was titled: **Colonial Rule**.

"The interesting discussion which took place at Trinity College, Dublin the other night evoked some new comments on an old problem. The theme of debate may have been the future of Britain's West African colonies, but as might have been expected, the speeches ranged much farther afield. The problem of West Africa is not an isolated one.

Most of the speakers appeared to be agreed on two points: that colonial rule, as it exists at present, is far from satisfactory; and secondly, that in the post war era a new and more enlightened attitude of mind must be brought to bear upon it. Africa or, at any rate, that part of it which is still the Dark Continent is admittedly a difficult problem. Where the light of civilisation has hardly begun to penetrate the approach to any thing in the nature of self-government must be a gradual process. But, meanwhile, is there no alternative to the administrative and economic system that permitted the ruthless exploitation, which thirty years ago kindled a white flame of anger in the soul of

Roger Casement? Only a hidebound imperialist would answer the question in the affirmative. Today Rudyard Kipling's idea of the "white man's burden" is utterly discredited. Nobody now is so hypocritical as to assert that European colonisers went into the lands of the coloured races from motives of duty or that they looked upon their conquests as a sacred trust. History has had its say upon that and the picture that survives is not one of crusading armies bent on a noble mission, but of an unholy scramble for regions rich in the precious things of the earth. Out of it all has sprung great wealth, great misery, international jealousies and the seeds of war.

If re-planning in the colonial sphere is to take place in the post war era, what form will it take? If it is actuated by just and Christian principles, it will in the words of the West African lecturer, be 'a planning for and with the people and not against them'.

In the long run, and viewing it even on the lowest plane, no other form of colonisation will be successful. Colonising must be accompanied with civilising. To give the natives of regions where civilisation is still in a primitive stage their share of God's sunshine, to prevent their exploitation at the hands of big business, to better living conditions in the lands of which they were the first inhabitants - purposes such as these should shape the administrative policy of all colonial rule".

After my installation as President, University Philosophical Society, Dublin, Eire, I settled down to face my research work and to manage the society. During the session, I conducted many meetings of the society with remarkable success, after which meetings members were customarily liberally entertained to their satisfaction.

Then to commemorate the opening meeting and my installation, the Council of the University Philosophical Society decided to publish, in a booklet, my inaugural address together with my prize essay, that is to say, an essay entitled "The Clash of Cultures" (see Appendix B) for which I was awarded a prize by the University Philosophical Society. The prize was a silver medal. The two essays were published together in a booklet: "The Lion & the Oil Palm and another essay". The event was publicised by "The Irish Times" of Monday, July19, 1943 just when I was ready to leave Dublin for Oxford.

The publication assumed the form of "TCD Notes" by our correspondent and read:

> *"Today the Library opens again, and the Dulles period of the summer vacation in College will be over.*
>
> *A recent publication of note was that of "The Lion and the Oil Palm" being the inaugural address delivered by E. Udo Udoma at the opening meeting of the Philosophical Society for the session 1942-43 when Dr. Julian Huxley, Professor MacMillan, Sean O. Faolin and Senator Sir John Kean addressed an audience that filled the large hall to capacity and when hundreds were unable to gain admission. The essay is preceded by a foreword by A. Creech Jones M.P.*
>
> *Mr. Udoma is well qualified to write on the colonial problem, for he is in the position of uniting the subjective sympathy of an African born and bred with the more objective outlook of the European familiar with the problems that confront both sides. His essay is subjective enough to make interesting reading, and objective enough to be intelligent.*
>
> *Also included in the booklet is a prize essay, "The Clash of Cultures", which was delivered some years ago before a general public meeting of the Philosophical Society. It is printed at the University Press, Dublin, by Ponsonby and Gibbs and costs one shilling".*

In the summer of 1943 during the long vacation, I left Dublin for Oxford via London where I also checked on my position as regards Gray's Inn and the then current requirements. This was particularly important because during the war years students of the Council of Legal Education who were undergoing university education outside London were granted exemption from dinners in the Inns of Court in London because of constant air raids.

On the way to London via Liverpool, I spent some days on the Merseyside with Pastor Daniel Ekarte at the African Churches Mission. On arrival in London, I was accepted as a lodger at WASU at 1 South Villa off Cantillowes Road purely on temporary terms. There were many West African students at WASU. They were all delighted to see me. The General Secretary of WASU and the proprietor and landlord of 1 South Villa, Chief Solanke, and his wife, Olu, who was the matron of the hostel which catered primarily for students, were most delighted to receive me. For me it was an eye opener to find so many West African students clubbing and lodging together and being able to hold regular meetings at some premises that they could regard as their own exclusive property. I threw myself into the activities of WASU. It was a most exciting experience. But then soon I was on my way to Oxford since I was required to be there before the commencement of Michaelmas term 1943.

While still in London, I had the good fortune of being introduced to several members of Parliament. In the course of conversation with some of them, I mentioned the fact that I was on my way to Oxford to complete my thesis for a post graduate degree during the academic session and that I was not sure that my sponsors, the Ibibio Union in Nigeria, would still be in funds. Thereupon, through the instrumentality of Chief Solanke, I was advised to apply to the British Council for sponsorship during my studentship in Oxford, which I did. As a result, I was awarded scholarship for one academic session at Oxford which amounted to three hundred pounds (£300). I was very happy to be the recipient of such a scholarship.

In the meantime, in London I had the privilege and honour of meeting with Sir Hans Vicsher of the African and Eastern Institute, formerly of the colonial administration of Nigeria, and Lord Lugard at the Royal Empire Society through the good offices of the Colonial Office - Sir G. G. Shute of the Colonial Office and Sir Hoskyns Abrahall, the Chief Secretary to the Government of Nigeria who was in London on vacation leave. In those days, the Royal Empire Society tearooms constituted a common meeting place for those interested in the affairs of the colonies. And, by special arrangements by the Colonial Office, I had the honour of having tea on a number of occasions with distinguished retired colonial administrators who happened to be available. This happened to be so, I later discovered, because my booklet published by the University Press in Dublin had been quickly distributed among experts on British colonial policy with particular reference to Indirect Rule of which Lord Lugard was reputedly the authority and originator. The booklet was of course titled "The Lion & the Oil Palm and another essay". Thus the booklet contained my inaugural address delivered at my installation as President, University Philosophical Society and the other essay entitled "The Clash of Cultures" being a prize essay for which I was awarded a silver medal by the Society. "The Lion and the Oil Palm" being a critique of British Colonial Policy had to be referred to various experts, for them to take note of the emergence of African thought on the problem.

CHAPTER FOURTEEN

In The Pursuit Of My Studies At Oxford

"Even if I had taken a doctorate in business technique magna cum laude, it would have made no difference".

Eventually I arrived in Oxford and, matriculation exercises having been completed, I was admitted into St. Catherine's Society, which was then a non-collegiate institution. I reported to Miss (later Dame) Margery Perham, an outstanding lecturer in History. I served under her for three months. Thereafter things fell apart. She accused me of extreme nationalism that was likely to colour my work as a scholar. I apologised to her profusely and pointed out that my views were genuine, formulated as they were from documents studied and, of course, on matters peculiarly within my knowledge as an indigene of the places concerned. Miss (later Dame) Margery Perham then felt that our views were irreconcilable even though, on her suggestion, I had to narrow the field of my inquiry. She felt that she was a liberal and I a nationalist and that the two were incompatible. The university authorities thereupon decided to assign me to another lecturer who agreed to supervise my work. At Oxford I lived at No. 245 Iffley Road - a flat, the property of one Mrs. Cranston, whose son was a student at the University of Bristol.

After due consultation, I was assigned to Professor Daryll Forde, a Geographer and an Anthropologist. On the advice of the authorities concerned, I reported to Professor Daryll Forde as my new supervisor. The latter was delighted to see me and, without much ado, set about examining the work I had done so far and enquired as to my plan for the future. I unfolded the plan of my work to him and he listened at every stage with absorbing interest. He made no comment. He was anxious that I should at once set out to work according to my plan by committing my ideas into writing.

Acting on his instruction, I engaged myself in written work. I committed my ideas into writing in accordance with my plan commencing from where I had suddenly stopped while working under the supervision of Miss (later Dame) Margery Perham. On completion of each whole chapter, I would submit the work for approval. After about one week, I would receive the work back together with some criticisms and some important suggestions as to the mode of improving presentation. I felt happy and satisfied with the criticisms, which I then considered reasonable and constructive. What was even more important was that the atmosphere existing between us was relaxed, friendly and helpful. There was complete absence of tension and the atmosphere was peaceful.

It was thus possible for me to continue my research and complete the work within the stipulated period without any obstruction. I was able to complete my thesis and have work typewritten and bound in five copies. When the work was submitted to Professor Daryll Forde, he was full of praises for me. He was delighted that I was able to get the work so well together. He congratulated me on such an achievement. That was during Trinity term at Oxford; it was in the summer of 1944.

I then left Oxford for London and was temporally lodged at WASU at 1 South Villa off Cantillowes Road. Later I was able to secure a flat for myself somewhere in North London. I became active in the affairs of WASU and was elected vice-president. I was also elected editor-in-chief of WASU Magazine and chairman of the editorial board. The magazine was a quarterly publication. Other members of the board included Mr. S. O. Awokoya, Charles Ekere, Ako Adjei - WASU study group leader, and Kamkam Boadu.

In the midst of all my WASU involvement, there was also my final Bar examination for which I had to prepare in earnest since by then I was notified that I was exempted from taking Part I of the examination by reason of my having obtained BA (Moderator) in Legal Science as well as first class Honours in the final LLB examination in Trinity College, Dublin, Eire. In the course of the long vacation, I received a letter from the board of examiners to the effect that I was exempted from being called upon to be examined viva voce in regard to my thesis. With that out of the way it was possible for me to concentrate on the preparation for my final Bar examination and to tackle the problem of satisfying the council of Legal Education.

Although by then I felt rather exhausted, having worked so hard on my thesis for the PhD degree in that I had to complete the work within the stipulated time despite having lost a whole term seemingly working but in fact disputing with Miss (later Dame) Margery Perham. It came as a relief to be informed that I was exempted from the viva voce. Finally, while still occupied with preparation for my final Bar examination, I received a letter from the Board of Examiners to the effect that I was successful in my doctorate degree in that I had been recommended to the Board of the University of Dublin, Eire, that I be awarded the degree. Shortly thereafter, I received another letter from the Board of the University of Dublin - Trinity College, Dublin, informing me that my thesis had been accepted and that it had been approved that I be awarded the degree of Doctor of Philosophy i.e., *doctoratus in Philosopia*, on the basis of my thesis. On receiving the letter, I jumped for joy and many of my friends at WASU joined me in celebrating the occasion. It came as a relief to me.

On that account, I seemingly lost interest temporarily in my Bar final even though, on all accounts, I could not practice at the bar as a qualified lawyer without being able to produce for inspection the certificate of my having been called to the bar by one of the Inns of Court in London, and in my particular case, Grays Inn, London, of which I was registered as a student. On reflection, I felt that it was absolutely necessary that I should take my final Bar examination and pass it creditably. On the other hand, I found myself in a dilemma in that, in actual fact, I tended to belittle the Bar final examination as of no consequence. In consequence, I felt within me that the spirit was willing but the flesh was weak. In the end, I took the examination and found to my surprise that I did sufficiently well to pass the examination but not well enough to earn a second class Honour because I did not seem to have done very well in respect to the English Law of Real Property which I had to take as an extra subject since it was different from the Irish Law of Real Property of the time.

As a result, in the summer of 1945 I was called to the bar by Gray's Inn, London. Thereafter, I spent most of my time at WASU, 1 South Villas when I was not in my newly furnished flat in North London. During the summer time I was also free to campaign for the Labour Party of which I was a member. I was engaged to lecture to a group of Labour Party supporters at Beaconsfield and in Manchester and the Lake District. I then moved house. Soon after my call to the bar, I found that my flat in North London was somewhat inadequate for my purposes. I therefore acquired, by the payment of rent, another property known as and situated at No. 52 Belsize Road, Swiss Cottage, London. It was a well-maintained property by the Swiss Cottage underground railway. I lived there very happily.

Incidentally, just at that time Mr. (later Dr.) Kwame Nkrumah arrived from the United States of America. He also visited us at WASU, 1 South Villas. Later he used to come to WASU occasionally for discussions as to the future of West Africa with the conclusion of the war. On arrival from the United States of America, Mr. (later Dr.) Nkrumah offered to share my flat with me temporarily. I most willingly agreed to accommodate him. He left me after six months and after having secured for himself a flat elsewhere, and quickly established his office at Gray's Inn Road, London where he maintained a register for the registration of all West Africans who volunteered to support him in his struggles for the independence of West Africa from colonial imperialism.

Mr. (later Dr.) Nkrumah, having rested in London after a well orchestrated welcome which he received on arrival and which was organised by a group of communists apparently on advice from the United States of America, applied to the London School of Economics, then headed by Professor Harold Laski for admission to supplicate for a doctorate degree. He was refused admission and quietly told that the primary degree that he had obtained in the United States of America did not measure up to the required standard of excellence by the University of London. Mr. (later Dr) Nkrumah was rather upset by being refused admission in such a shabby manner and mentioned the matter to me. He then confessed as well as confided in me to the effect that, while in the United States, he had spent a great deal of his time in the study of communism as a means of liberating West Africa. For that purpose, he had studied with great care the technique of communist organisation and of religious intolerance.

In confirmation of his assertion, he produced for my inspection a bundle of typewritten manuscripts the contents whereof consisting of a collection of communist doctrines and techniques of mass organisation. He assured me that he had prepared the bound volume of manuscripts for use in Ghana and that I was the only African sufficiently trusted by him to warrant his discussion of such a delicate and sensitive matter with for fear of betrayal. I tried but in vain to prevail upon him to take to the study of law as a profession in one of the Inns of Court in London under the auspices of the Council of Legal Education. In vain I endeavoured to explain to him that returning home back to Accra in the Gold Coast as a fully qualified Barrister-at Law licensed to practice would place him on a sound footing with tremendous advantages for he would then be entering politics as a fully insured person against a possible difficult period if it should fall to his lot to be arrested for insurrection. He was adamant and treated any mention of Law or Legal studies with contempt, maintaining that he was a professional politician. Mr. (later Dr.) Kwame Nkrumah was unusually odd in his ways. During the period I was with him in London he never once accepted an invitation by WASU to participate in any public lecture. He avoided attending such a lecture like the plague. For instance, immediately after the war in 1945, there was organised a general strike by the Railways Workers Union led by Mr. Imoudu in Nigeria for increase of wages at the rate of seven shillings and six pence (7s.6d) per week. The information was relayed to WASU in London. Thereupon WASU organised a protest meeting to replay the grievances of the Nigerian Railway workers to the people of Great Britain. The protest meeting was held at Caxton Hall, London. Many distinguished West Africans and people of African descent including Mr. George Padmore, a distinguished journalist, addressed the meeting. But Mr. (later Dr.) Kwame Nkrumah refused to attend the meeting even though duly invited. Funds raised at the meeting were transmitted to the Nigerian Railway Workers Union of which Mr. Imoudu became president for life.

During the summer of 1945 there were held elections of officers at WASU and I was returned president, having been the previous year, vice-president. I declined to accept the new office of president and declared that I was content to continue as vice-president provided some one from either Sierra Leone or the Gold Coast could be returned as president and that I would be prepared to serve under such a person. Thereupon, Mr. Abeoku Betts of Freetown, Sierra Leone was elected president of WASU. He was reading for the Bar and was then engaged in working for his final Bar examinations. I accepted to serve under Mr. Abeoku Betts as vice-president. I then also began to prepare for the publication of WASU magazine after a decision to do so had been taken by the editorial committee or board. I accepted the office of vice-president because, at the time, there was the tendency for Nigerians to overplay their predominance at WASU.

Mr. J. L. Keith, as the head of the Welfare Department of the Colonial Office, wrote to enquire when I would be prepared to return by ship to Nigeria as ocean liners were then very scarce. In reply, I indicated that I would like to return to Nigeria at the first available opportunity preferably at the end of August 1945. I then together with members of the editorial board embarked upon the publication of the WASU magazine, the last issue to be edited by me. On production it was hailed as a wonderful, glossy magazine. It constituted a class by itself. The most outstanding contribution in the magazine was my article on the missionary work being done then on the Merseyside by Pastor Daniel Ekarte of the "African Saint".

While working on the WASU magazine, I also joined with Mr. (later Dr.) Kwame Nkrumah, Mr. Jomo Kenyatta of Kenya, Dr. Banda of then Nyassaland and now Malawi, and Dr. Moody of London to arrange for the holding of Pan African Congress, which was then scheduled to take place in Manchester in August 1945. The major part of the WASU magazine was devoted to a petition issued by WASU and directed to all the colonial governments of the Gambia, Sierra Leone, the Gold Coast and Nigeria and the Cameroons, introducing Chief Solanke as the general secretary in charge of WASU and appealing passionately to each and every one of them to contribute funds towards the building of a permanent structure for WASU in London, which would serve as a home from home for West African students in the British Isles and Southern Ireland. The magazine was well produced. It was splendid. It was attractive.

Incidentally, I should have mentioned before that in addition to having been called to the bar by Gray's Inn, London, in obedience to Nigerian requirements for the purpose of enrolment by the Supreme Court, Nigeria which would enable me to be admitted to practice as a Solicitor of the Supreme Court, Nigeria, I had also to read in the chambers of a practising Barrister in London for a period of not less than one year for which I was issued with a certificate on the payment of one hundred guineas (£105).

As Hon. Librarian of the Council of the University Philosophical Society at
Trinity College, Dublin for the 1940-41 session

With Alfred Chukwu Nwapa (center) and another member of the Nigerian
House of Representatives

My 50s look

With Chief Judge de Lestang and Judges Onyeama, Sowemimo and Lambo of
the Lagos High Court in 1962

My wife and I as guests of the US Ambassador to Uganda, William Clyde Trueheart and his wife

Inspecting the Chief Justice's Chambers in Kampala, Uganda

Touring the High Court precincts in Kampala, Uganda

Grace and I with the Ambassador of the Socialist Republic of Yugoslavia, Mr.
Aleksandar Bozovic and his wife In Kampala

My wife and I at Beginning of Law Year Service in Kampala, Uganda

Being "toasted" by comrades in Kampala, Uganda

With some other attendees of the July 1965 Commonwealth and Empire Law
Conference in Sydney, Australia

Chief Justices of the Commonwealth at the Canberra, Australia Conference of
September 2 and 3, 1965

Grace and I with the Chief Justice of Ghana at the World Peace Through Law Conference in Washington, DC in late September 1965

At the World Peace Through Law conference dinner in Washington, DC with Nigerian Minister, Jaja Anucha Wachuku, sitting at extreme right

Donating to the Federal Troops Comfort and the Rehabilitation of Refugees funds with Colonel U. J. Esuene, Military Governor of SE state, looking on

Grace and I with Sir Louis Edet, Justice P. Bassey and another guest

CHAPTER FIFTEEN

My Return Voyage To Africa

"In Europe a hiss in public is a form of salutation of endearment but in Africa it is an obscenity".

Since I was preparing very hard towards my return to Nigeria, it was necessary for me to move from London to Liverpool. On arrival at Liverpool, I decided to travel midlands in Lancashire to visit Dr. Obot Essien Antia-Obong in fulfillment of my promise to him since, before then, I had visited Dr. David J. Amah at Barrow-in Furness, where the latter was serving as a house surgeon in residence. That was in the summer of 1943 on my way to Oxford. In the midlands, having reserved accommodation for myself in a local hotel, on arrival I checked in without difficulty. I later contacted Dr. Obot Essien Antia-Obong who visited me at the hotel. He was able to explain to me that he was doing *locum tenens* for an Indian doctor who had an attack of chicken pox. Because of that, he explained that he would be unable, much to his regret, to spend a great deal of his time with me. I was, of course, in sympathy with him in the circumstances and was prepared to take care of myself, which I did. The result was that Dr. Antia-Obong used to visit me every morning before going to work.

On 24 August 1945, I received an urgent telegram from the Welfare department of the Colonial Office informing me that it was imperative that I should embark at Liverpool on a South African mail boat en route to South Africa via Freetown, Sierra Leone, where I must be transhipped into a West African naval vessel heading for Lagos, Nigeria via Accra. The mail boat was to sail from Liverpool on 29 August for South Africa via Freetown, Sierra Leone. In the event I should miss the South African mail boat then it would be impossible for me to secure a passage on any boat within the next six months for Lagos, Nigeria - hence the hurried arrangement. On receiving the telegram, I decided to leave after lunch the next day for Liverpool for embarkation.

On 25 August 1945, therefore, by special arrangement, I had to lunch with the sick Indian doctor and Dr. Antia-Obong, sharing the same dining table on the advice of both doctors that the incubation period – the dangerous period during which I might have been expected to be contaminated with the disease of chicken-pox - had expired, and that I should have nothing to fear. After lunch, I refused to shake hands with the Indian doctor for fear of contamination. I left my hotel in sufficient time as to be able to embark on board the South African mail boat on 29 August 1945. On arrival at the Merseyside, I was surprised to find there waiting for me some agents from the Colonial Office in London. It was there and then delivered to me my tickets, which enabled me to board the ship with ease. I was then led to my berth and bunk, which I was to occupy alone for the voyage to Freetown, Sierra Leone. We set sail for our destination the same day. I was sorry to leave Merseyside and all my friends behind. This was like everything else - all straight roads must have a bend; all good things must have an end, as the saying goes. The accommodation occupied by me on the ship was for a first class passenger, which I was.

On leaving the Mersey, the ship steamed into the Bay of Biscay, home to some of the Atlantic Ocean's fiercest weather. The sailing was rough owing to heavy waves in the ocean. From the Mersey it took us a fortnight to get to Freetown, Sierra Leone. There was the quasi-naval ship at anchor mid-stream waiting to have all passengers meant for West Africa transhipped into her. Transhipment, which was done in a hurry so as to enable the South African mail boat to sail off without delay, was arranged in such a way that luggage was first discharged into the waiting boat and thereafter transit passengers were discharged to enable them board the waiting boat. When it was the turn for transit passengers for the West Coast of Africa to embark upon the waiting boat under the control of the Navy, I was informed that I must disembark at Freetown because there were no extra berths for me and another African from Accra, Gold Coast. We both therefore were landed at Freetown, Sierra Leone and could not go beyond Freetown, Sierra Leone, while the mail boat that had brought us thus far had to steam off to South Africa.

Having landed on Freetown harbour, my first duty was to visit the customs warehouse in order to ascertain whether my personal luggage had been discharged there for warehousing. To my astonishment there was not a single piece of luggage of mine to be found there. What was worse, I had carried nothing with me on landing at the wharf. I was then wearing a pair of slacks, no tie and a blazer carrying only my brief case with me. I was alarmed and did not know what to do. Ashore I was housed in a hotel whose manageress was Mrs. Davies. Other occupants of the hotel at the time in Freetown, Sierra Leone consisted of some naval officers and other transit passengers.

I immediately took up my case with Messrs Elder Dempster & Co Ltd at Freetown, Sierra Leone, they being the most important shipping agents in West Africa at the time. The local agents immediately disclaimed responsibility, emphasising that, it being war time, all shipping by law were under the control of His Majesty's Navy. Then within the week of my arrival and living in Freetown, Sierra Leone, I was ill with chicken pox. Fortunately for me Dr. Taylor Cummings, the medical officer of health in-charge Freetown, Sierra Leone was well known. He had served as a member of Sir Walter-Elliott's Commission on Higher Education in West Africa before which, as a member and representative of WASU, I together with others had submitted a memorandum for consideration by the commission. Furthermore, the medical officer-in-charge, Government General Hospital, Freetown, Dr. Johnson, and the sister-in-charge, Miss Olive Johnson, were well known to me. After a thorough examination, the medical officer of health declared that on no account must I be sent to the Infectious Disease Hospital but that my hotel room would have to be declared out-of-bounds and there I be isolated in the hotel and be regularly treated twice a day by the hospital authorities. One of the maids in the hotel who had before had chickenpox was assigned and directed to take care of me. It was a miserable time for me.

The medical officer of health, Dr. Taylor Cummings, also diagnosed that I had caught chicken pox in Lancashire, Midlands during my visit to Dr. Antia-Obong and that the period of the voyage from Liverpool to Freetown, Sierra Leone which had taken us practically a fortnight was precisely the period of incubation. I was completely flabbergasted having regard to the assurances the two doctors had given me that it was safe for me to join both of them at lunch, which I did. I therefore had to be detained in Freetown, Sierra Leone until I was completely cured of the disease. While at Freetown, Sierra Leone, I had to spend a lot of money in buying plenty of tropical wear, as I had no change of clothes when I landed at the harbour.

During my unhappy sojourn at Freetown, Sierra Leone, I had to make contact with Lagos from time to time, communicating with them and explaining to them the reason for the delay occasioned on my way to Lagos and the confusion caused. Then from the General President of the Ibibio Union, Lagos, I received a query as to whether it was true that I was returning to Nigeria as an administrative officer of the colonial government as was alleged to have been published in the passengers list exhibited by the South African mail boat which brought us to Freetown, Sierra Leone from Liverpool. I immediately in return denied the allegation. I explained further that, on boarding the ship at Liverpool, some colonial office agents, who delivered to me a first class ticket which enabled me to board the ship preparatory to embarkation, had instructed me that, on arrival in Lagos, it was expected as my duty to report to the Chief Secretary to the Government of Nigeria, Sir Hoskyns Abrahall, for further instruction and posting and that at no time in London did I accept any appointment offered me by the colonial government of Nigeria. I was ill undergoing treatment for 3 weeks. I was discharged completely cured at the end of September 1945.

CHAPTER SIXTEEN

I Embark On The M/V Mary Kingsley For Lagos

"Conscience is but a dispensable item of social equipment". – John Buchan

On the first week of October 1945, I embarked on M/V Mary Kingsley, an Elder Dempster twin cargo and mail boat converted during the war years, for Lagos at last. We sailed the same day and by the end of the week we were able to drop anchor at the waterfront at Accra, the ship being worked mid-stream by means of tugboats and lighters. The ship spent two weeks loading and discharging mid-stream. I seized the opportunity of the lull thus created to go ashore, and after having seen Ollenu, Esqr., Barrister-at-Law and Advocate of the Supreme Court of the Gold Coast, I decided to remain ashore so as to be able to visit places of interest in Accra and the environs, including Achimota, particularly the University section. Accordingly, in due course, I visited the University section of Achimota College (now University of Ghana, Legon). I was struck by the absence of relevant books in the library. I formed a very poor impression about the establishment despite its worldwide fame.

Afterwards, I visited the Supreme Court and its library under the kind guidance of Dr. Dankwa. I was very impressed with a fine collection of law reports. I browsed through some of them especially the House of Lords law reports including Privy Council reports and West African Court of Appeal reports. I also visited other places of interest but had to stop when I received information that the ship had completed her assignment and was engaged in arranging her departure. I returned to and boarded the ship that day in the afternoon.

In the evening, the ship set sail on her way to Nigeria, after having been kept very busy daily at Accra during the best part of 2 weeks. Eventually, we arrived at the Lagos harbour. There, the ship was anchored and berthed alongside the harbour. I disembarked from the ship on October 30, 1945 with the assistance of delegates designated by the Ibibio Union, Lagos branch to facilitate my disembarkation and to also arrange my lodging. On disembarkation, I was driven by car straight to the residence of Chief R. E. Effiong of the Government Treasury Department. To my utter dismay, on enquiry, I was informed that my luggage discharged from the South African boat at Freetown, Sierra Leone was not delivered in Lagos. I was completely flabbergasted.

I took up the matter of my missing luggage with Messrs Elder Dempster Lines & Co Ltd, Lagos. The company herself received the news with great shock and promised to take up the matter with her head office in Liverpool. In the mean time, I gathered, while lodging with Chief R. E. Effiong, that the Ibibio Union, Lagos branch was no longer a united body. It was split down the middle in that, as a result of a dispute, the Opobo (now Ikot Abasi) district branch in Lagos had walked out of a general meeting and had since then boycotted the main Lagos branch of the union. The dispute had still remained unresolved. It was therefore pointed out to me that it was inappropriate for me to accept the hospitality of the main Lagos branch of the Ibibio Union as a putative member of the Opobo district branch since I belonged there by birth. Consequent upon persistent representation made to me in that connection, I decided after considerable reflection and remembering the saying *Vox populi vox Dei*, to move from Chief R. E. Effiong's bungalow to Chief D. E. Usen's quarters at No. 42 Wakeman Street, Yaba, Lagos there to remain during the period of my sojourn in Lagos.

I then took it upon myself to see that the dispute was settled. Luckily for me, the man who had brought the trouble about, Prince Eket Inyang Udoh, was still in Lagos awaiting my arrival from overseas as a very important reception was planned for me in Lagos. The dispute was amicably settled by Prince Eket Inyang Udoh - *agent provocateur* - offering voluntarily to apologise to Chief D. E. Usen and all members of the then Opobo district union of the Lagos branch of the Ibibio Union. Incidentally, Chief D. E. Usen was, at the time of the dispute resulting from abuse by word of mouth issued by Prince Eket Inyang Udoh to the entire members of Opobo district union of the Lagos branch of Ibibio Union, the President of the Ibibio Union, Lagos branch. The apology was there and then tendered and accepted, and that was the end of the matter. Reconciliation was effected and remained effective.

Thereafter, the Ibibio Union, Lagos branch set about arranging my reception, which was held at the Glover Memorial Hall, Marina at the end of the second full week of November 1945. The chairman at the reception was Mr. Herbert Macaulay while Mr. Sam Akpabot entertained the assembly with his xylophone. The speakers at the reception included Mr. Anthony Enahoro, then Editor of "The Comet", which was one of the papers within the Zik's group of newspapers published in Nigeria. It was indeed a grand reception. After the reception I had to turn my attention to my missing luggage. For, as might be expected, all my certificates and testimonials obtained from the universities and inns of court under the supervision of the Council of Legal Education which must be produced for inspection for the purpose of my admission to practice as an Advocate and Solicitor of the Supreme Court of Nigeria were all locked up in my luggage and personal effects. Until the luggage was traced it would be impossible for me to be admitted by the Supreme Court under the control of the Chief Justice of Nigeria. It was therefore my duty to put pressure on Messrs Elder Dempster Lines all the time.

In the meantime, I had to arrange for a Barrister-at-Law of long standing who had been in practice before the Supreme Court for many years to sponsor my candidature. I succeeded in obtaining the services of Jubril Martin, Esqr, a devout Muslim and an experienced Advocate and Solicitor of the Supreme Court of Nigeria who was, himself, interested in the affairs of the Ibibio Union, nation wide. Soon thereafter, I was informed by Messrs Elder Dempster Lines that the company had received a cablegram informing her that the luggage had been traced to Takoradi where they had been discharged into the warehouse there by a quasi-naval boat on her way to Lagos and that the luggage would be shipped to Lagos by the first available boat coming to Lagos. It was pleasant news indeed, and I thank God for His small mercies for that piece of useful information. It was good news indeed. God's name must be praised.

Within one week of receiving the information, the luggage arrived and was discharged at the Lagos harbour to the delight of most members of the Ibibio Union and their supporters. I personally took delivery of my luggage and personal effects. Most members of the Ibibio Union, Lagos branch were jubilant. On examination, however, I discovered that some of the luggage was broached and some personal effects and books were stolen. I had to put in my claims to Messrs Elder Dempster Lines Limited who, this time, could not dispute the claims nor disclaim responsibility unlike their branch office at Freetown, Sierra Leone. My claims were immediately met by the payment of cash, which I was glad to receive, having been out of pocket for so long.

During the fourth week of November 1945, at a brief ceremony, I was admitted to practice before the Supreme Court as an Advocate and Solicitor of the Supreme Court of Nigeria.

CHAPTER SEVENTEEN

I Depart Lagos For The Eastern Provinces And Ibibio State College Is Born

"Failure is the foundation of success and success is the lurking place of failure but who can tell when the turning point will come?" – Sommerset Maugham in "The Painted Veil".

At the end of the fourth week of November 1945, after breakfast in the morning, I boarded the Nigerian railway passenger train at Iddo, Lagos as a first class passenger en route for Aba in the Eastern provinces. By midday at lunchtime, I resorted to the catering coach for lunch. Sitting at the table with me for lunch there was the famous Chief (James, I believe) Majekodunmi, the Otun of Egba land. He introduced himself to me as the father of a lawyer and of a doctor too, both of whom, according to him, were trained in Great Britain. He spoke in contemptuous tone about Yaba Higher College which he contended was an institution established by the white man as a means of preventing Nigerians from going to the British Isles for sound education. He pointed out that the British government was deceiving Nigerians when it maintained that there was no difference between a graduate from any University in the British Isles and a graduate of Yaba Higher College; because a graduate doctor from Yaba Higher College was paid only £98 per annum while a graduate doctor from any University in the British Isles was paid £200 per annum and yet the British government maintained that there was no difference between the two. Having said that he laughed to his hearts content and said, "See how Nigerians are made fools of by the British?"

At Abeokuta railway station, Chief Majekodumi departed and I missed a good companion and a conversationist. At the railway station in Ilorin, to my surprise, there boarded the train one Effiong Akpan Okon, a medical officer and, incidentally, a product of Yaba Higher College employed in the British government Hospital, Jos, Plateau. He introduced himself as one of the students in the faculty of medicine specially trained to look after the health of European miners settled in Jos, Plateau, in the Northern provinces. He stated that, on graduation, he was one of a team posted to the General Hospital, Jos where most of the patients were Europeans. Dr. Effiong Akpan Okon also informed me that he was married to an Efik lady and that he was a native of Ikot Offiong in Itu district and had boarded the train at Ilorin for the purpose of catching a glimpse of me. At the next station after Ilorin, Dr. Effiong Akpan Okon alighted from the train and I bade him farewell. Thereafter I was alone in my accommodation on the train.

All along the journey to Kaduna, thence to Kafanchan, thence to Enugu and finally to the Aba railway station, I found myself alone in my apartment. I had no one with whom to exchange ideas until I arrived at the railway station, Aba where the now late Mr. Harry A. Ekanem of Ikot Akpaden in Opobo division met me together with his entourage and some prominent members of the Ibibio Union, Aba branch. I was received at the Aba railway station with great ovation and enthusiasm. Mr. Harry A. Ekanem, the road overseer, had arrived at the railway station early in the morning in a Chevrolet kit car. The train arrived Aba at noon and I immediately disembarked, after necessary introductions, and then boarded the kit car ready for take off after my luggage had been loaded thereon on being discharged from the train. We left Aba railway station for Aba township and stopped at a prearranged rendezvous there to be greeted by a great concourse of people already there assembled. That was on a Sunday.

The kit car then hit the high road out of Aba township on its way to Azumini on the way to Opobo division in the Eastern provinces, Opobo division being then part of Calabar province. The kit car driven on a very smooth murram road arrived at Ikot Abasi village in Ibekwe clan at 5 p.m. It was a relief to be at home at last. I met Chief Martin A. Inam, the then head of the compound who took over from my father, Chief Udoma Inam. My dad, before his death in June 1936, was the head of the compound in succession to Chief Akpan Inam, a distinguished court sitting member and Vice-President of Qua Court, headed by the expatriate district officer who used to be President ex-officio. At Ikot Abasi village, I was the recipient of the warm embrace of most members of the family and compound and, indeed, of the whole village. Everyone appeared delighted. There was rejoicing everywhere and the big bell belonging to the Methodist Church was rung almost incessantly. I was at once reunited with my people. It was a happy re-union.

Three days after my arrival at Ikot Abasi, Mr. James Udo Affia, General President, and Mr. Robert U. Umoinyang, Vice General President, Ibibio Union visited me there from Central Office, Uyo. Again, it was a pleasant reunion. Just before their arrival, I had received an invitation from Chief Albert Affia to visit him in his house as my brother-in-law as he was then married to my half sister, Adiaha Equere. At my request, Mr. James Udo Affia and Mr. R. U. Umoinyang accompanied me to the residence of Chief Albert Affia and there we were all treated to some rare hospitality of being served old and left over palm wine, which I could not consume. We then returned to Chief Martin A. Inam's where I stayed and enjoyed myself very well in a well maintained surrounding. While there, Mr. James Udo Affia then informed me that I had been selected to lead a team of Ibibio Union representatives to the Provincial Education Officer, Calabar in connection with the affairs of the proposed Ibibio State College, Ikot Ekpene, the establishment of which had been hanging fire. He narrated the background story leading to the decision to establish the Ibibio State College at Ikot Ekpene with the return from the United States of America of both Mr. Ibanga Udo Akpabio and Mr. James Lawson Nsima, both of whom were designated Principal and Vice-Principal of the college respectively. Invitation having in such circumstances been extended to me, I willingly accepted to join the team as its spokesman under the leadership of Mr. James Udo Affia as the General President. As both Mr. James Udo Affia and Mr. R. U. Umoinyang were government supervisors of education, I appreciated the official position occupied by them. I also appreciated that, to either of them, it would be a source of embarrassment for them to lead a team of protesters to their superior officers in the same department. It had been represented to me by both of them that officers of the union were alarmed on learning that the previous Provincial Education Officer, one Mr. B. Adam, on proceeding on vacation leave, had minuted in his handing over notes to his successor, Mr. Smith, that on

no account must approval be granted to the Ibibio Union sanction-
ing the commencement by way of opening of the projected Ibibio
State College, Ikot Ekpene in 1946.

On the appointed day, I arrived Uyo early enough to join the
team selected to constitute the delegation to meet the Provincial Officer, Education Department at Calabar. We then set off for Calabar
where we were joined by others. At Calabar, the delegation consisted
of Mr. James Udo Affia, General President, Ibibio Union, Mr. Ibanga
Udo Akpabio, Principal-designate, Ibibio State College, Ikot Ekpene,
Mr. Akpan Akpakpan representing the land owners of the Ibibio State
College site at Ikot Ekpene, Chief the Honourable Nyong Essien, formerly member, Legislative Council, Lagos representing Ibibio division, Paul Bassey Okon, President, Ibibio Union, Calabar branch, Mr.
Mbrey Bassey Mbrey, General Secretary, Ibibio Union, and Dr. Egbert
Udo Udoma, spokesman for the team. On meeting the Provincial Edu-
cation Officer, Mr. Smith, who was successor to Mr. B. Adam, in his
office at Calabar, I, as the official principal spokesman for the Ibibio
Union, raised the issue by observing that we were there as a team to
enquire into the circumstances of the delay occasioned in connection with the opening of and commencement of work in the projected
Ibibio State College, Ikot Ekpene for the impression abroad in the
Ibibio country was that instead of the government, as represented by
the provincial education office, Calabar, assisting the Ibibio Union in
its efforts to provide education for its people in the practice of self
help as taught by Samuel Smiles, the government was engaged in
obstructing such efforts contrary to its profession.

I then pointed out, quite unequivocally, that the Ibibio people
were alarmed that government should have refused to grant Ibibio
Union approval for the commencement of the Ibibio State College
already sited at Ikot Ekpene with the consent of the local people, themselves members of the Ibibio Union. The college as planned was to be
a coeducational secondary grammar school, already built at Ikot Ekpene at the sole expense of the Ibibio people without the aid of government, and yet no approval from government was forth coming even
though application for such approval had been submitted to government through the provincial education office, Calabar since 1943. I
submitted further that, already, there were available to man the insti-

tution two graduates duly trained overseas and qualified and already designated Principal and Vice-Principal of the institution. In elaboration, I repeated with emphasis that our delegation was there to ascertain the reason for the untoward delay so far occasioned and the problem confronting government, which has made it difficult for the grant of approval as requested. Thereafter, Chief the Honourable Nyong Essien also spoke in support of the points already made and cited references in a book published on British policy of education in the colonies.

Thereupon, the Provincial Education Officer, Mr. Smith, in reply explained that whatever delay had been occasioned so far had been caused by the Principal-designate of the Ibibio State College, Ikot Ekpene, Mr. Ibanga Udo Akpabio, whom his predecessor, Mr. B. Adam had found wanting and that instead of the Principal-designate concentrating on the requirements of the projected college, he had dissipated his efforts in writing and attacking the government on the pages of the West African Pilot newspaper. As an example of the misplaced efforts on the part of the Principal-designate, he mentioned and, in confirmation, produced for our inspection a sketch plan of the school which had no dimensions and which the Principal-designate had submitted to the provincial education department in support of the application for approval. He maintained that on no account would the government have approved such an application, supported, as it was, by a dimensionless sketch plan of a secondary grammar school, whether the school was to be established by a community or by an individual. He affirmed emphatically that all stipulations and conditions imposed by the government had been fulfilled by the Ibibio Union save and except the sketch plan submitted by the Principal-designate which must be rectified.

On that score, I asked for permission which was there and then granted, to have the dimensionless sketch plan withdrawn with an undertaking and assurance to submit a fresh appropriately drawn sketch plan with accurate dimensions to the office the following Monday, the meeting having taken place on a Friday. Accordingly, the requisite sketch plan was on Monday, December 17, 1946, delivered by me personally to Mr. Smith, the Provincial Education Officer who, after proper scrutiny, accepted the same. And, two weeks later, a telegram was received by the General Secretary, Ibibio Union, conveying to the Ibibio Union approval by the government to the effect that the Ibibio State College, Ikot Ekpene should commence functioning as from the first week of January 1946. The contents of the telegram were subsequently confirmed in a letter signed by the Provincial Education Officer, Calabar. Therefore, Ibibio State College, Ikot Ekpene started operation with Mr. Ibanga Udo Akpabio as the first Principal.

While I was at Calabar in connection with the representation by Ibibio Union to the provincial education office concerning Ibibio State College, members of the Ibibio Union, Calabar branch seized the opportunity to hold a reception for me during the weekend of my visit thereby stealing the show from the Ibibio Union central office at Uyo. Thus, since my arrival from the United Kingdom, the Ibibio Union, Calabar branch was the first to organise a reception for me.

The reception which was held in the evening of Saturday, December 15, 1946, in the African Club hall was well organised under the distinguished chairmanship of Professor Eyo Ita, Principal and proprietor of the West African Peoples Institute (WAPI for short), Calabar. The reception was grand and well attended and dancing was introduced during periods of intermission. Speakers at the reception included Mr. James Udo Affia, General President, Ibibio Union, Uyo, Mr. Paul Bassey Okon, President, Ibibio Union, Calabar branch and Chief the Honourable Nyong Essien, formerly member representing Ibibio division in the Legislative Council.

After the formal reception, there was also a banquet that was organised by the Ibibio Union, Calabar branch at the residence of Mr. Paul Bassey Okon, President, Ibibio Union, Calabar branch. Attendance at the banquet was restricted to members of the Executive Committee of the union and specially invited guests. On the whole, the reception at Calabar was very warm indeed and enjoyable and I felt personally grateful and heavily indebted to Mr. Paul Bassey Okon, President, Ibibio Union, Calabar branch for having worked so well as a team and being able to organise such an elaborate and grand reception at such short notice. I seemed to have taken the ancient city of Calabar by storm for my reception successfully left an indelible impression in the minds of the populace and constituted the topic of conversation many years thereafter. It therefore facilitated my practice as a Barrister-at-Law in the then Supreme Court, Calabar.

CHAPTER EIGHTEEN

My Election As Ibibio Union President And Some Of My Sensational Cases

"When I examine my political faith, I find that my stronger belief was in democracy according to my own definition. Democracy – the essential thing is distinguished from this or that democratic government – was primarily an attitude of mind, a spiritual testament and not an economic structure or a political machinery. The testament involved certain basic beliefs – that the personality was sacrosanct, that policy should be settled by free discussion; that normally a minority should be ready to yield to a majority which in turn should respect a minority's sacred things".

As soon as I returned from Calabar to the mainland of the Ibibio country of the then Calabar province, and arriving home at Ikot Abasi in the then Opobo division, I received invitations to attend receptions arranged in my honour by the Ibibio people of Opobo, Ikot Ekpene and Aba under the auspices of the respective branches of the Ibibio Union and scheduled for December 29, January 4 and January 12, respectively. The Opobo reception took place at Ikot Akan, then the headquarters of Opobo division's Ibibio native administration and also the seat of Ibibio Union, Opobo division branch. It was a very grand reception interspersed with traditional dances by various groups in the division. The reception started at midday and continued till the evening. It was wonderful entertainment. The reception was attended by most, if not all, of the prominent chiefs of the area at the head of whom was Chief Ime Ntuenibok of Nunasang, then the paramount ruler of the area. Among the chiefs and title holders who were present at the function, mention must be made of Chief Jonah Ukpe of Ikpetim, Ibekwe, Chief Umoeren Akpanta of Ukpum Minya, Chief Sampson Ayara Akpabio of Abak Midim, Chief William Umo of Ibesit Nung Ikot, Chief Japhet Akpan Udo of Ikot Ekpaw, Ikpa Ikono, Chief Tom Usen of Ikot Akpaden, Ikpa Ibom, Chief Wilson Akpan Nya of Ibekwe Akpan Nya, Ikpa Ibiaku, Chief Sambo Uku of Ikot Obong, Ikpa Ibekwe and Chief Martin A. Inam of Ikot Abasi, Ikpa Ibekwe.

After the receptions, I received a circular letter from the Ibibio Union central office at Uyo directing that all future receptions for me should be staggered so as to enable me to establish my practice as a Barrister-at-Law at Aba, being the town of my choice. Thereafter, the next reception I attended was the official Ibibio Union reception that was held at Uyo at the end of January 1946. The Ibibio Union central office, that is to say, the Executive Committee of the Ibibio Union, organised it. It was very well attended by representatives of the various districts and branches. In the course of the proceedings, I surrendered the envelope containing sand, being the soil from Ibibio land, which was given to me at the farewell party organised in honour of all of us student beneficiaries of the Ibibio Union scholarships before our departure to Great Britain, Canada and the United States of America, back to the Executive Committee of the union. When the envelopes were delivered to us we were each instructed to take great care of the envelope because, on our return from overseas, the envelope would be demanded from each of us, and we were told that to surrender the envelopes back to the union on our return would be regarded as rendering a true account of our stewardships as university graduates. From that point of view, the ceremony concerning the envelopes was significant.

After the reception at Uyo, I was declared a free man and I therefore considered myself free to establish my law practice at Aba township. In those days, Aba township, now in Abia state, had considerable advantages. In particular Aba was so well situated as to be equidistant to many important commercial townships in Rivers, Owerri and Calabar provinces. For instance, the distance from Aba to Port Harcourt was equal to the distance from Aba to Owerri township as well as the distance from Aba to Uyo, and each distance was only 40 miles. Furthermore, Aba was situated along the railway line, which facilitated travelling by train to Enugu and the northern provinces - hence my decision to establish the headquarters of my practice at Aba where I was also happy to be associated with Dr. John Udo Ekpo, a distinguished medical practitioner in those days.

As soon as I was settled at Aba, I was able to make many friends. Then I received an invitation to join the Aba Community League, which was then an organisation catering to the welfare of the people of Aba township in the absence of a municipal council or any local government council of any sort. For, most astonishingly, Aba was then ruled by an expatriate official called a Local Authority who was as-sisted by a small African advisory body. Having had the opportunity to study the organisation, I was satisfied that the Aba Community League was serving a real need. I therefore decided to accept and did accept the invitation that was extended to me. Within six months of my becoming a member of the Aba Community League, there was held a general election for the election of officers of the league. I contested the election for the office of President of Aba Community League. As I was not opposed by anyone, I was declared as having been returned unopposed as President, Aba Community League. Mr. J. J. Onyia, who was then headmaster of Government School, Aba was elected Vice-President; Chief Marcus W. Ubani was elected General Secretary; Mr. J. A. Iwunah was elected Treasurer and Mr. A. Nwoke was elected Auditor. After the elections, we all settled down to hard work.

In the mean time, I had also once a month to attend receptions organised in my honour at Eket, Abak and Itu divisions, which, as already stated, were staggered. All the receptions were very well or-ganised and equally well attended. In particular, the reception held for me at Eket was superb. It was organised in a grand style and it was possible for me also to pay my humble respect to Chief King Usoro, a trusted friend of my father and my Godfather, so regarded because, probably, without his intervention, I might not have been awarded the Ibibio Union scholarship in 1938.

All the while, I was engaged in my law practice, which by the end of 1946 had become well established and extensive and had cov-ered the whole of the Eastern province. The practice was also very lucrative. My Chief Clerk who was in charge of my head office at Aba was Mr. E. E. Ewa of Henshaw Town. He was formerly law clerk to Mr. Asuquo Okon who that year, 1946, was appointed Magistrate Grade I. Mr. Ewa was a clerk who served me faithfully with enthusiasm and pride. During the early stage of my practice, he constituted a useful link between the Efik people of Henshaw Town, Calabar and my good self. I enjoyed my practice in Calabar both before the Magistrate Grade I, Eveyln Brown, Esqr. and the Supreme Court, Calabar, presided over by the Honourable Mr. Justice A. G. B. Manson and it was then a pleasant spectacle to watch my practice grow in leaps and bounds. I was encouraged to work still harder since it was seldom that I lost any case in court. I was regarded in high esteem by judges as well as members of the public and therefore acquired a high reputation as a successful legal practitioner.

Then, towards the end of 1946, an organisation known as the National Council of Nigeria and the Cameroons (NCNC), under the leadership of Herbert Macaulay as its General President with Dr. Nnamdi Azikiwe as its General Secretary, was engaged in touring Nigeria for the purpose of raising funds for leading a delegation to the Colonial Office in London to protest against the regionalisation of Nigeria by Sir Arthur Richard (later Lord Milverton) in his constitution prepared and imposed on Nigeria (called the Nigerian Constitution 1945). In the course of the tour, Herbert Macaulay died in the Northern province of Nigeria and was brought back to Lagos for burial as a national hero. Thereupon, the mantle of leadership of the National Council of Nigeria and the Cameroons (NCNC) fell upon Dr. Nnamdi Azikiwe who was declared the General President of the council.

Under the leadership of Dr. Nnamdi Azikiwe, the tour was continued and concluded. A large sum of money was raised for financing the delegation to London. During the tour of the Eastern province, a warm reception was accorded the NCNC team under the auspices of the Aba Community League. At the conclusion of the reception, Dr. Nnamdi Azikiwe, as the General President of the NCNC, invited me to join the delegation that was selected to visit London for the purpose of lodging a protest to the Secretary of State for the Colonies, Mr. Creech M. P. Jones, who was at the time an acknowledged friend of mine. I most reluctantly declined the offer. Instead, I suggested that the Honourable Chief Nyong Essien be selected from Calabar province to join the delegation. The suggestion was accepted.

In October 1946, Mr. James Udo Affia, General President, Ibibio Union suddenly announced his intention to proceed overseas for higher and professional education in the field of law and thereupon resigned his office as General President, Ibibio Union. I was consequently invited to accept the office of General President, Ibibio Union in succession to Mr. James Udo Affia. I was at first reluctant to fill the vacancy. I had then felt that, having just then engaged in the establishment of my practice as a lawyer, it would be unwise to accept such an important assignment which might have the tendency to distract me from the concentration which I desired in building up my practice. My first impulse was to avoid getting entangled in national and political affairs at such an early stage in my career.

Somehow, however, in order to circumvent my anticipated refusal, at a general conference of the Ibibio Union held at Ikot Akan in Opobo division in February 1947, I was elected General President, Ibibio Union in absentia and a delegation was detailed to meet me at Aba, my residence, and to convey me willy-nilly to Ikot Akan there to be sworn in and installed General President of the union. In the circumstances, having been informed of the result of the election and inflexible determination of the chiefs and people there assembled, I had no alternative but to bow to the popular will of the people for, as the saying goes, "the voice of the people is the voice of God".

At Ikot Akan, I accepted the result of the election and agreed to serve the Ibibio nation as General President, Ibibio Union. Thereupon, having thus openly signified my assent, I was carried shoulder-high and installed General President, Ibibio Union on the throne of King Solomon, so-called, and in accordance with ancient rites and tradition. At the request of the concourse of people there assembled, I addressed the conference in all humility promising to serve the people with sincerity and a sense of dedication. I acknowledged the wisdom of the union in investing funds in the education of its leadership by the award of scholarships for specialised studies overseas in Europe and America. I congratulated the union on its wonderful achievement of having had the foresight and God given inspiration of awarding scholarship to six of its stalwart and deserving students endowed with determination to realise their ambitions in their specialised fields of study overseas. It did not necessarily follow that all the students who went overseas would necessarily do well to the satisfaction of the union nor would such students always appear grateful. I urged that the union should not feel disappointed because some of the scholars might fall by the wayside. The union should remain satisfied that it had done its duty. I pointed out that I considered myself fortunate to have been one of the union's scholars, and that I was grateful to God that the union had considered me worthy of its scholarship and then also worthy of its leadership in the difficult years ahead, and that words failed me with which to express my gratitude to the union. My address was punctuated with applause and at its conclusion I was greeted with a standing ovation. I there and then assumed the office of General President and adjourned the conference in accordance with ancient tradition and the exchange of greetings.

Thereafter, it fell to my lot to examine some records of proceedings of the union at conferences and at its general and executive committee meetings. I discovered to my amazement that the union had no constitution even though it had been actively in existence for over two decades. This was most astonishing. I therefore decided to provide the union with a written constitution which would proclaim to the whole world its aims and objectives. I felt very strongly that the union ought not to continue to operate as if in a blind alley. It was also necessary to proclaim as if on a housetop that the union was not a trade or industrial union but a national institution for the avoidance of misunderstanding. For the purpose of receiving a constitution already prepared by me, an important and special conference of the Ibibio Union was held at Uyo in August 1948. It was an elaborate conference with representatives from branches far and wide, including branches as distant as Lagos, Enugu and Kano, attending.

At the conference in session, a scrutinising committee was set up with Mr. O. Bassey of the Government Treasury, Enugu as chairman. To the committee was assigned the duty of scrutinising the constitution and submitting the same back to the Executive Committee that, within the context of the proposed constitution, was to be known as the National Executive Committee. There were other vital alterations introduced by way of nomenclature by the proposed constitution. For instance, the name "Ibibio Union" was changed to "the Ibibio State Union", the "General President" was changed to the "National President" and "Vice General President" to "National Vice President". Indeed, the titles of the officers manning and responsible for the administration of the main union at the Central Office at Uyo were entitled with the prefix "National". Thus the General Secretary now bore the nomenclature of the National Chief Secretary, the Treasurer that of the National Treasurer etc. while the Presidents and Secretaries responsible for administering the branches were known as General Presidents and General Secretaries etc. There were two National Vice Presidents; the first National Vice President was elected among the Chiefs and the Second National Vice President was a man of education elected among the commoners.

Of the changes introduced, the most important was of course the new name assigned to the union, which was no longer to be known as the Ibibio Union but the Ibibio State Union. This was significant and was prompted by the changes introduced by Sir Arthur Richards' Constitution of 1945. In that constitution, Nigeria was decentralised into three regions of Northern, Western and Eastern regions each with its headquarters thereby proclaiming to the whole world that the system of administration hitherto in vogue and known as Unitarianism had been abandoned in preference to Federalism. On that assumption it was also necessary that the Ibibio people should serve notice to the whole of Nigeria and indeed the world that Ibibio land deserved to be located a place in the scheme of things as a separate state. Hence the nomenclature of Ibibio State Union.

It is interesting to note that following in the footsteps of the Ibibio State Union, in 1949 the Ibo Union conference which was held at Asaba also changed its name to the Ibo State Union, which goes to show that, even then, the Ibo people were also desirous that the Ibo nation be constituted a state for the Ibo people. Thus the conversion of a unitary Nigeria into a federation of states became imperative and a desiratum almost universally. While engaged in planning for the Ibibio people, subject to the advice of the chiefs and elders, it was also necessary for me to push forward with my law practice.

Starting from 1946, that being the year when I first set up my practice as a Barrister-at-Law and Solicitor of the Supreme Court of Nigeria at the township of Aba, now in Abia state of Nigeria, up to and including the year 1950, I can recall at random four important and sensational cases which I had to handle successfully.

The first was the case of *Okon Ekpenyong, being the Village head of Nwaniba for himself and on behalf of the people of Nwaniba vs. Chief Udo Ekong and 6 other Chiefs of Mbiakong.* This was an application by motion in a civil suit, which was brought by Mr. E. E. E. Anwan, counsel for the applicants, the people of Nwaniba, seeking that the respondents, the Chiefs of Mbiakong, be committed for contempt of court. My services were retained by the Chiefs of Mbiakong to oppose the motion. This was the first case in which my services were retained. The people of Mbiakong were introduced to me by Chief Okon Udo Ndok of Uruan clan in Uyo division - the people of Mbiakong being also of Uruan clan.

On the facts, the application, which sought that the Chiefs of Mbiakong named on the motion be committed for contempt of court and be incarcerated in prison for disobedience, arose in this way. The applicants, known as the people of Nwaniba in Uyo, regarded themselves as descendants of the Efik community of Creek Town, Calabar.

Originally, the people of Mbiakong, as represented by Chief Okon Ekpenyong, had instituted an action in the Supreme Court at Uyo seeking a declaration that the piece or parcel of land known as Nwaniba had been granted to their ancestors of Creek Town, Calabar by the ancestors or predecessors in title of the people of Mbiakong, there to settle and to carry out their business as traders.

But subsequently, on the arrival of the other traders and business men in the area, the present descendants, as represented by Chief Udo Ekong and 6 other Chiefs of Mbiakong, had encroached upon the land in dispute and had granted portions of the said land to these alien traders. With the claim for declaration was coupled the claim for account and perpetual injunction.

At the hearing of the suit, Mr. E. E. E. Anwan of Counsel appeared for and represented the people of Nwaniba while Mr. Asuquo Okon of Counsel appeared and conducted the case for the defendants, the people of Mbiakong. In the course of the hearing, the Plaintiffs therein sought and, with the leave of the court, withdrew their claims for accounts and for injunction. In the end, they won the case and were granted a declaration that the land in dispute known as Nwaniba was originally the property of Mbiakong but that, the ancestors of the defendants, that is the people of Mbiakong, had granted permission to the people of Nwaniba to make use of the land for the purpose of their trade and business. And to that extent the Plaintiffs succeeded in their claim for a declaration of title.

On appeal by Chief Udo Ekong and 6 other chiefs of Mbiakong, for themselves and on behalf of the people of Mbiakong, the appeal was dismissed by the West African Court of Appeal sitting in Lagos.

Thereafter, Mr. E. E. E. Anwan of Counsel, acting for the people of Nwaniba, brought this application requesting that Chief Udo Ekong and the 6 other chiefs of Mbiakong be committed for contempt and incarcerated for having committed a breach of the order of court.

At the hearing of the application during a call over day in the Supreme Court of Calabar, presided over by the Honourable Mr. Justice A. G. B. Manson, and when the court was particularly full and it being the first day of my appearance in the Supreme Court, I had to appear and act for the respondents, the people of Mbiakong, and in particular for Chief Udo Ekong and the 6 other chiefs of Mbiakong.

On the motion being called I, having announced that I was appearing for Chief Udo Ekong and the 6 other Chiefs of Mbiakong, raised an objection on point of law. I submitted that the application was misconceived and must be dismissed. I then referred to the affidavit filed and pointed out that, on the face of the application, there was no disclosure that, since the decision granting the applicants a declaration of title to the land in dispute, the court had made any other order demanding that the respondents should engage themselves in the performance of any act or the carrying out of any instructions which the respondents had disobeyed. It was clear that, in the absence of any act or performance apart from the declaration on title, then the application must be dismissed as disclosing no cause of action. It was misconceived. The objection was upheld and the application was dismissed with costs after Mr. E. E. E. Anwan of Counsel had made his reply to the submissions.

Then came the case of <u>*Rex vs. Akpanitang*</u> that was tried by Mr. Justice Pollard, PJ at Ikot Ekpene Assizes. It was a murder case. The man who was murdered was a big trader. In addition to trading by himself, he had engaged two other trade boys who used to report to him at the end of every month to render account of their sales as retailers. Accordingly, at the end of the month concerned, both of them reported in the evening to their master for the purpose of rendering account of their sales for the month. In the course of the exercise of accounting, they broke off and pertook of dinner served at the request of their master. After dinner, they resumed their accounting exercise, which continued till practically midnight at an area of the town without electricity. They had to work with the aid of lanterns in the parlour of the master's residence. While engaged in the accounting exercise, the master got up from his seat and walked towards the adjacent bedroom. Just at that moment in the dark night, a gun shot was heard fired apparently by someone outside the house in hiding among the banana trees that constituted an orchard in front of the house at an angle. The master was shot and fell headlong on the floor. The man who shot the gun could not be seen as the night was dark. The two trade boys and others in the parlour were terror-stricken and immediately shut the main door of the parlour, which door until then was left ajar.

The following morning, the two boys went to the police station at Ikot Ekpene township to report the incident. At the police station, they reported the matter and it was recorded in the station diary. As recorded in the station diary, the dead man was shot by an unknown person. Thereupon, the police entered into the investigation of the matter. In the course of the investigation of the case, the two trade boys made written statements to the police, disclosing that they were able in the dark night not only to see but also to identify the man who had shot the gun that killed their master. They identified the man who shot their master with a gun as Akpan Itang. The statement was reared before the magistrate at the Preliminary Investigation. Akpan Itang, the accused, was thereupon committed to be tried at the Assizes to be conducted by Mr. Justice C. N. S. Pollard, Acting Judge. In the course of the trial of the accused, Akpan Itang, for the defence of whom I had to appear, the police testified that in their conduct of a search of the houses in the neighbourhood of the deceased's house in the outskirts of Ikot Ekpene township, they had recovered a gun in the house of Akpan Itang even though they found him in bed complaining of illness, and that that was the only gun they could find in the whole neighbourhood. The gun was tendered and admitted and marked as an exhibit.

Under cross-examination by me, the police witness admitted that the report lodged with the police by the two trade boys in the morning succeeding the event was to the effect that an unknown and unidentifiable person shot the deceased. But, at the trial, the two trade boys had denied that statement. At the close of the case for the prosecution, without any submission of "**no case to answer**", I decided to take the bull by the horns. I therefore called the police station diary keeper as a witness, and he produced and tendered the station diary and identified his own hand writing as having recorded the statement of the two trade boys at the time. I then put the accused, Akpan Itang, in the witness box. He testified as to his condition of health that had confined him to bed for over one month. He identified the gun produced by the police as his personal property, which had never been fired by him during the then past six months. I next called his wife to corroborate the story of his illness. I then addressed the court after which the crown counsel also addressed the court. Subsequently, in a reserved judgment, Akpan Itang was acquitted and discharged. His story as to his ill condition was accepted by the court in preference to the lies told by the two trade boys.

The next case concerned private prosecution. It was the case of <u>R. vs. Chief Bob-Manuel</u> - the head of the Bob-Manuel's house at Abonnema in Degema division. It was a private prosecution that originated from a civil suit that was tried in the Degema Native Court. What happened was that, in the course of the hearing of a civil suit between two parties, Chief Walter Bob-Manuel, having been called as witness, testified in the witness box that the piece of land then in dispute belonged to the party who had called him as a witness. He was held for perjury because, in a suit some 10 years previously, he had given evidence to the effect that the same piece of land was the property of some one else. He refused to be tried by the Native Court of Degema division. Thereupon, he was brought before the magistrate in Degema and preliminary investigation was conducted. Thereafter, Chief Bob-Manuel was committed to the Assizes.

As the police at that stage refused to continue to prosecute the case, it became necessary for the services of a counsel to be retained for the purpose of prosecuting the case before the judge at the Assizes as a private prosecution. Thereupon, the services of Lambert Bellgam, Esqr., Barrister-at-Law were retained. He handled the prosecution and I appeared at the Assizes to defend Chief Bob-Manuel. Chief Bob-Manuel being an old man of over 70 years of age and the head of one of the most important houses in Abonnema town and the prosecution being private and handled by a lawyer of distinction during the Assizes, all added colour to the case and made it sensational.

At the trial before the Judge of the Supreme Court, learned counsel, having opened his case for the prosecution by addressing the court, called witnesses to substantiate the case for the prosecution by their testimonies and sought to tender documents some of which were objected to, which objections were sustained where appropriate, and subsequently closed his case. Thereupon, as counsel for the accused, I indicated that I did not propose to call the accused person as a witness but to rest the defence on my submission that **no case had been made out for the accused to answer.** I accordingly addressed the court and submitted that, in a case of perjury, it was not sufficient proof of the perjury for the prosecution to tender and be admitted in evidence two contradictory statements purported to have been made by the accused person without going further to prove which of the contradictory statements was true because, for all the court knew, the two statements might be false or true depending upon the circumstances. The court having heard Bellgam of Counsel in reply, reserved its ruling and judgment over the weekend, the trial of the case having lasted for three weeks and ending on a Friday afternoon. The presiding judge at the trial of the case was no other than the famous and scholarly the Honourable Mr. Justice Hallinan, who had to travel from Port Harcourt to conduct the Assizes at Degema.

The following Monday, the court reassembled. Both the counsel for the prosecution, Mr. Lambert Bellgam, and I, counsel for the defence, together with the accused person, Chief Walter Bob-Manuel, the head of Bob-Manuel house of Abonnema, who was on bail throughout the trial, appeared for judgment. The court delivered its long awaited judgment, upheld the submission of "no case" for the accused person to answer, and found the accused person not guilty. The judge accordingly acquitted and discharged the accused person and also awarded three hundred and fifty guineas (£367.10s) costs to the accused person. The accused person, throughout the delivery of the judgment by the judge, stood dazed in the dock and appeared confused not knowing what was happening until I advised him that he should leave the dock because it was all over. The accused person, as if in a dream, then walked out of the court a free man amidst the jubilation of the crowd then assembled at the precincts of the court. As I also walked out of the court, I was carried shoulder high by the supporters of the accused person. It was sensational. The church bells at Abonnema began to toll and kept on ringing throughout the day at intervals. There was general rejoicing in the great commercial emporium known as Abonnema, in which there were established famous commercial houses and banks as well as the Bulk-oil plant, which served as a refinery for vegetable oil from palm fruits.

From then on, I came to be regarded as the principal lawyer for Kalabari people and Chief Bishop Davies-Manuel became my bosom friend and admirer. Consequently, when there broke out a serious land and fishery rights dispute between the Kalabari people and Okrika people for the determination of which a Commission of Inquiry, headed by the Honourable Justice G. G. Robinson, was set up, I alone appeared as counsel for the Kalabari people while Mr. Louis N. Mbanefo and Mr. J. T. Nelson Williams had to appear for the people of Okrika.

Finally, there was the case of *Rex vs. H. E. Antia and another*. Mr. Hogan E. Antia was a Registrar of the Supreme Court at Aba. He and his house servant, an Igbo man, were charged with being in possession of counterfeit currency notes. Mr. Hogan E. Antia was an Ibibio man. He had a reputation of being honest and not allowing the other staff of the Court at Aba to indulge in corruption which earned him hatred and contempt from the rest of the staff among whom was one Nwosu from Nnewi.

The case for <u>the prosecution</u> was that on a day certain, some counterfeiters, pretending to be honest businessmen, visited him and after some discussion delivered to him a bundle of counterfeit currency notes, pretending they were genuine notes, for his inspection. After a cursory examination, Mr. Hogan E. Antia asked for permission to keep the currency notes for a thorough examination to which request the counterfeiters consented and departed. Subsequently, the notes were secreted in the ceiling of the verandah of the house to the knowledge of the house servant, who had participated in the discussion.

Later in the evening, a Police officer came and stood where the currency notes were said to have been secreted at the back verandah of the house, the policeman having entered the compound from the rear entrance unbeknownst to the occupiers of the house who were then in the kitchen. When the Police officer asked for Mr. Hogan E. Antia, the boys in the kitchen informed him that their master had gone out. The Police officer remained at the verandah and later, at his own leisure, walked out of the compound by the backyard gate.

The following morning, being a Saturday, the Police Inspector in-charge of crimes, armed with a search warrant, went with a team and conducted a search of the house of Mr. Hogan E. Antia for some counterfeit currency notes. During the search, some counterfeit currency notes were recovered from the ceiling at the back verandah of the house directly opposite the kitchen. Thereupon, Mr. Hogan E. Antia and one of his domestic servants were arrested and charged with conspiracy and being in an unlawful possession of counterfeit currency notes. My services were retained by the 1st accused, Mr. Hogan E. Antia.

For the first time in the Supreme Court, Aba, a criminal case was tried before a Judge of the Supreme Court, Aba, without a preliminary investigation of the case having been conducted by a Magistrate. Rather, Mr. Hogan E. Antia and his domestic servant were tried before the Honourable Mr. Justice Desalu, Acting Judge, summarily, a summary of the facts and evidence to be relied upon being supplied to the Judge alone by the police despite my protest as counsel for the defendants.

At the commencement of the trial, when charges were read over to the accused persons, while Mr. Hogan E. Antia pleaded not guilty to the charges, his domestic servant pleaded guilty to the charges. The

2nd accused was, accordingly, convicted and sentenced according to law, while the trial had to be conducted against Mr. Hogan E. Antia alone. In the course of the trial, the Judge had to visit the *locus in quo* after the conclusion of the trial. Apart from the visit, it was quite clear that the locus in quo, where the false currency notes were secreted, was accessible to any visitor to the house entering therein from the backyard gate. After the visit, the trial judge had made no notes of the scenery nor did he put the identification witness, that is the Police officer, into the witness box for cross examination.

Throughout the trial, the 1st accused, that is Mr. Hogan E. Antia, had denied any knowledge of the counterfeit currency notes.

At the conclusion of the trial, I repeated my protest that the judge had no right to be supplied with the summary of evidence, copies of which were not available to the accused, when in fact there was no preliminary investigation. As counsel for the 1st accused, I also objected to the 1st accused being tried together or jointly with the 2nd accused. I then submitted that it was quite obvious that the *locus in quo* was accessible to any member of the public out for mischief.

In a reserved judgment, which reserved for a whole week, the Honourable Mr. Desalu, Acting judge, convicted the 1st accused and sentenced him to three years imprisonment with hard labour. On appeal, the West African Court of Appeal allowed the appeal and acquitted and discharged the 1st accused on several grounds, among which were:

(i).   The *locus in quo* was accessible to any member of the public.

(ii).   It was wrong to have tried the 1st accused jointly with the 2nd accused who had pleaded guilty.

(iii).   It was wrong for the trial judge to have been supplied with a summary of evidence when there was no preliminary investigation.

(iv).   There was no record of the purpose of the visit to the *locus in quo*; there was no record of proceedings of and observations made during the visit to the *locus in quo*; and there was no record of the description of the scenery of the *locus in quo*.

(v).   It was wrong to have convicted on such flimsy evidence as was provided.

Ibibio Union Expels Its General Secretary

"Liberty is the only thing you can never have unless you are prepared or willing to give it to others". - William Allen White

In 1948, an incident occurred which nearly affected my reputation and from which I learnt a great lesson concerning the organisation of my practice. The incident occurred in the following way. During the man-leopard menace in Ibibio land, with the approval of the government of the day, the Ibibio Union selected a team of prominent chiefs and some other highly respected Ibibio leaders of thought to tour the whole area affected by the menace and perform traditional rites and rituals for the purpose of terminating the menace, which was causing considerable havoc in the affected area, involving the loss of human lives. At the conclusion of the tour, the team, having performed its tasks well to the satisfaction of all concerned, was congratulated by me. Shortly thereafter, Mr. Usen Udo Usen, who was the General Secretary, Ibibio Union and therefore ex-officio secretary to the Ibibio Union touring team, informed me that he was engaged in writing a report of the tour, and the experience gained there from, for submission to the Ibibio Union for consideration at its annual conference and that, for the purpose of assisting him in the typing of the report, I should be graciously pleased to grant permission to Mr. W. J. Ekanem, the Assistant-Secretary at the Head-office, Uyo to move from Uyo and join him at his office at Abak. I did so without hesitation. Accordingly, at the appointed time, Mr. W. J. Ekanem, the Assistant Secretary, joined Mr. Usen Udo Usen at his office at Abak, Mr. Usen Udo Usen being then officially the chief clerk in charge of the district office in Abak working under the direction of the expatriate district officer in charge of Abak division.

In due course, I travelled from my station, Aba, to Lagos to attend a session of the West African Court of Appeal. While at Lagos, as was my custom in those days of the crisis relating to the man-leopard menace, I, in the company of Mr. Dick E. Usen, then General President of the Ibibio Union, Lagos branch visited the Chief Secretary to the government of Nigeria in the Nigerian Secretariat. I found the Chief Secretary at his desk. He was unusually delighted to see me and told me so. Rising up he extended his hand to shake my own with exceeding joy and enthusiasm. He said that he was especially delighted to see me that morning because, according to him, he had the previous day received an official report in writing concerning the man-leopard tour, which had been conducted by a selected team of leaders of the Ibibio Union of which I was the President. He told me that he was very pleased with the report, which he considered fair and frank, and without any inhibition. He thought the report excellent and most revealing and informative and of considerable assistance to the government. Thereafter, we left the Secretariat and, on the way in my car, Mr. Dick E. Usen asked to know what report of the Ibibio Union was sent to the Chief Secretary to the government of Nigeria. In reply, I told him quite frankly that I was not aware of any official report concerning the man-leopard menace that had been sent to the Chief Secretary with the approval of the Ibibio Union and that I was taken aback by the disclosure made to me by the Chief Secretary to the government of Nigeria. I promised to enquire into the matter as soon as I was back at home as I could not expect the Ibibio Union to dispatch an official report of any kind to the Chief Secretary to the government of Nigeria without my prior approval. As an act of diplomacy, I had to pretend before the Chief Secretary as if I knew all about it especially as the latter had regarded the report as containing helpful information, which might be of assistance to the government of Nigeria in tackling the menace.

On my return home to Aba, before I could set in motion the instrument constituting the enquiry, I received a parcel sent to me by post from Enugu by some Ibibio patriots. On opening the parcel, to my astonishment, I found a bound volume bearing the inscription "An official report relating to the tour of the man-leopard area of the Ibibio country by delegates of the Ibibio Union". The report bore the signature of Usen Udo Usen as the General Secretary, Ibibio Union.

In the meantime, there appeared a publication in a local paper to the effect that, at a meeting of the Legislative Assembly held at Enugu, Chief the Honourable Nyong Essien was attacked by the Chief Commissioner, Eastern region when he criticised the government of Nigeria for the banning of *Idiong* cult because of its association with the man-leopard menace. In particular, it was alleged that the Chief Commissioner, Eastern region had pointed out that Chief the Honourable Nyong Essien was out of touch with the affairs of the Ibibio people in that, whereas the Ibibio Union in its latest report had congratulated the government for having banned *Idiong*, the Chief was criticising the government for having done the same thing. In saying so, the Chief Commissioner had waved the report about in his hand. The report, a copy of which was sent to me, happened to be a copy of the report about which the Chief Secretary to the government of Nigeria had mentioned to me. The report was sensational and attracted my attention. I spent a great deal of my time reading it. It was revealing. It purported to have been issued with the approval of the Ibibio Union. What was more, it contained the names of Annang and Ibibio chiefs alleged to have been members of the man-leopard society - all of whom were also members of the *Idiong* society. I was dumbfounded. I could not understand why Mr. Usen Udo Usen should have prepared such a report and dispatched copies to government officials secretly purporting the same to have been prepared with the authority and approval of the Ibibio Union. The information contained in the report was most damaging to the Ibibio people as a whole, as it was contradictory to the official report submitted to me by the Ibibio Union and which was also signed by the General Secretary, Mr. Usen Udo Usen.

I immediately tried unsuccessfully to contact Mr. Usen Udo Usen at the District Office, Abak. I was informed that Mr. Usen Udo Usen was no longer in the District Office, Abak, but was permanently attached to and was resident at Ikot Okoro, then the headquarters of the police officers assigned for duty concerned with the man-leopard menace. He was then designated Acting Senior Superintendent of Police engaged in the investigation of cases arising from man-leopard activities. I was stunned. I, thereupon, arranged for an emergency meeting of the Ibibio Union to be held at Ikot Okoro in the Native Court hall by the police station. I then wrote to the Commissioner of Police in charge Ikot Okoro man-leopard area informing him of the scheduled meeting of the Ibibio Union and requesting him to grant to Mr. Usen Udo Usen, his new Senior Superintendent of Police, leave of absence to attend and be present throughout the proceedings of the meeting of the Ibibio Union as the meeting had been convened for the sole purpose of discussing Mr. Usen Udo Usen's report circulated to the Chief Secretary to the government of Nigeria and the Chief Commissioner, Eastern province. I pointed out that he would be required to justify his allegation that certain chiefs in the Ibibio country were members of the man-leopard society. In a flash, as it were, I received a letter from the commissioner informing me that Mr. Usen

Udo Usen had been granted leave of absence and had also been instructed to attend the meeting and that there would be other police officers in attendance at the meeting as a matter of duty.

While preparing for the meeting, I was met by some men of goodwill advising me not to attend the meeting personally because Mr. Usen Udo Usen, who was seen cleaning his rifle, had sworn that if I attended the meeting and disclosed to the gathering his secret report to the people there assembled that he was going to shoot me down dead with his rifle. I made light of the report and ignored the advice. In defiance of such cowardly report, I attended the meeting at Ikot Okoro in the Native Court hall. Indeed the meeting was well attended. All those who received my special invitation attended the meeting. There was not a single absentee. I had two interpreters in attendance at the meeting - one Mr. Akpaso who later became the first National Chief Secretary of the Ibibio State Union and Mr. Hezekiah, then field Secretary of Ibibio Union. Mr. Usen Udo Usen also attended. There were police officers at the meeting who rendered essential services and assisted in the maintenance of order. Mr. Usen Udo Usen's secret report was read and interpreted where necessary to the audience and Mr. Usen Udo Usen was cross-examined on his allegations against some of the chiefs present at the meeting. The proceedings were adjourned to be continued at Uyo at the annual conference of the union scheduled for August 1948. There was no rifle shooting incident.

During the interval, I received information that Mr. Usen Udo Usen had been posted to the District Office, Ikot Ekpene again as District Clerk. Consequently, on the eve of the Ibibio Union conference to be held at Uyo, I again addressed a letter to the Senior District Officer, Ikot Ekpene informing him of the resumed hearing of the complaint against Mr. Usen Udo Usen and requesting that permission be granted to Mr. Usen Udo Usen which would enable him to attend the annual conference of the Ibibio Union to justify his allegations against certain chiefs, members of the Ibibio Union, in his secret report to government relating to the man-leopard menace. Subsequently, the Senior District Officer in his letter addressed to me as General President, Ibibio Union informed me that, as requested, permission had been granted to Mr. Usen Udo Usen with instructions that he should feel quite free to attend the annual conference of the Ibibio Union to be held at Uyo, at the appropriate time. Based on that information, I then addressed a special letter inviting Mr. Usen Udo Usen, as General Secretary, to attend the annual conference of the union to be held at Uyo as the adjourned session of the emergency meeting of the Ibibio Union that was held at Ikot Okoro. The letter was dispatched to Mr. Usen Udo Usen by special hand delivery. Needless to state that, on the appointed day, Mr. Usen Udo Usen failed to attend the conference at Uyo. It therefore became necessary to summon his presence at the conference. For that purpose a high-powered team under the leadership of the Vice General President, Mr. R. U. Umoinyang, had to be dispatched with adequate transport to fetch him at Ikot Ekpene. On arrival at Ikot Ekpene the team pleaded with him but in vain to join them in their return journey to Uyo. Mr. Usen Udo Usen was adamant in his refusal to come to Uyo for the purpose of attending the conference.

In the circumstances, the conference had no alternative but to proceed to the hearing of the complaint against Mr. Usen Udo Usen and came to the conclusion that he was guilty beyond redemption. He was found guilty and consequently expelled from the Ibibio Union as a traitor to the national cause and therefore was ostracised for life as a person unworthy of trust as an Ibibio man. The expulsion was communicated to Mr. Usen Udo Usen and copies of the communication were sent to the relevant authorities responsible for the government of Nigeria for their information in connection with his report circulated to them. The order of expulsion was also published in the press.

In consequence of the expulsion and the prominent part I, as President of the union, had played in exposing Mr. Usen Udo Usen's false allegations against some prominent chiefs in Ibibio land, Mr. Usen Udo Usen decided to wreck vengeance on me. He got hold of Chief Akpan Nkanta, the head Chief of Afaha Obong in Abak division who had consulted me and sought unsuccessfully to retain my services as counsel in their land dispute with the people of Adiasim in Ikot Ekpene division and induced him to make a false allegation against me that I was their counsel. In doing this, Mr. Usen Udo Usen acted in collaboration with lawyer Coco-Bassey who was himself responsible for my refusing to act for Chief Akpan Nkanta's people of Afaha Obong, in that he, having been in the case long before my arrival in Nigeria from the United Kingdom, had disapproved when he was informed by the Chief that his people wanted to retain my services to handle their case. Mr. Coco-Bassey was afraid that I might displace him. When therefore I declined the retainer, Mr. Usen Udo Usen having heard that I had agreed to act for the people of Adiasim prevailed upon Chief Akpan Nkanta to claim that I was also their lawyer and thereupon raised objection before the judge at the hearing of the case that, having been their lawyer, it was improper for me to have accepted to act also for the people of Adiasim. In order to make the objection effective, Chief Akpan Nkanta, on the advice of Mr. Usen Udo Usen, had to pay some fees at Uyo to my clerk, Mr. Okon Essien Okon, who, on receiving the fees, had issued to him a temporary receipt. In doing this, Chief Akpan Nkanta avoided going to Aba to pay the fees to my office, knowing that the fees would be refused. This was arranged as a strategy for keeping me out of the case altogether. In other words, since I had refused their case, I ought not also to act for the people of Adiasim according to them.

At the hearing of the case, the judge, Mr. Justice Wells Palmer, endeavoured to make a mountain out of a molehill by dramatising the incident. He, instead of disposing of the matter there and then, declared in open court that he was reporting the matter to the Chief Justice in Lagos for necessary action against me. Once more, the judge took this step in retaliation for my having reported him to the Chief Justice of Nigeria in Lagos because of his conduct towards Mr. Rhodes-Vivour, then a junior member of the Bar, for which he was rebuked. By reporting this matter to the Chief Justice, the judge exposed himself to being regarded as ignorant of the law of procedure. However, in the end I had to hand over my brief of the case of the people of Adiasim to Mr. L. N. Mbanefo to dispose of the matter as I felt embarrassed by the incident. That, in effect, meant that Mr. Usen Udo Usen, assisted by Mr. Coco-Bassey, successfully placed me in an embarrassing position.

Mr. Usen Udo Usen was eventually transferred away from the Ibibio country to Enugu and promoted Assistant Administrative Officer and issued with a certificate of merit. In the result and finally as an act of retributive justice, Chief Akpan Nkanta of Afaha Obong caught small pox and died in default of proper medical treatment. Mr. Coco-Bassey got drunk on illicit gin and developed an attack of pneumonia from which he died on admission in hospital. Mr. Lambert Bellgam, who assisted in spreading the false rumour that I had been debarred from practice as a lawyer by reason of the report to the judge, developed a heart attack and died shortly thereafter. Mr. Justice Wells Palmer at Kano, where he was on transfer, also developed a heart attack and died suddenly. Mr. Usen Udo Usen also died of a heart attack. Thus the episode ended, within six months of its inception, with the death of the conspirators - one after another in succession.

The Establishment Of A Newspaper And Seminar On Nigerian Constitution

"Our politics in this country with tribalism and sectarianism at its centre appears to be an ulcerous wastage of material – mankind and intellect. It is counterproductive".

In 1950 I decided to enter into politics as part time member of parliament. As an adjunct to that decision, I founded the Eastern States Express newspaper at Aba township for which I had been engaged in planning since 1948. The system of election then in vogue was not encouraging being one of electoral colleges according to the constitution promulgated at Ibadan. The first election took place finally in December 1951. There was of course the question of organising a warming ceremony for my newly built house at Aba, which, thereafter, served as my residence at No. 22 Park Road, Aba. For the warming ceremony and the unveiling of the Eastern States Express newspaper at Aba, the services of the Anglican Bishop of the Niger Delta, Bishop Dimeari (formerly Jumbo) of Bonny were retained and he performed both ceremonies at No. 22 and No. 34 Park Road, Aba with diligence and religious thoroughness and enthusiasm. It was a great occasion. The Resident, Calabar province, Mr. C. J. Mayne and the Resident, Rivers province, Major Allen, both attended the celebrations as special guests in the unavoidable absence of the Resident, Owerri province, Mr. J. S. Smith, with his new headquarters at Umuahia-Ibeku. The latter extended to me regrets for his absence.

By special invitations, prominent chiefs like Chief Ntuenibok of Nunasang, Chief Ekpenyong Udo Ekong, Oduongo Nkanga of Oku and J. D. Imeh of Ndon Utin all of Uyo, Chiefs Udo Ekong and Sampson Udo Idiong of Abak, Chief Sampson Ayara Akpabio of Abak Midim, Chief Nathaniel Umoh of Ibesit Nung Ikot, Chief John King Usoro, Chief J. I. Amah all of Eket, Chief Thompson Udo Nsuk of Itam, Chief and Revd Effiong Utit of Ibiono, Chief & Revd Uya of Ibiono all of Itu, Chief Benjamin Umo of Nyara Enyin, Chief Jimmy Etuk

Udo Ukpanah of Nsekhe, Chief R. U. Umoinyang and Chief Joseph M. Ito both of Ikot Ekpene, and Chief Akpan Nkanta of Afaha Obong, Abak, to name only a few, also attended the celebrations at Aba. It was a red-letter day. The chiefs and people of Aba joined in the celebrations. Those who participated actively included Chief Marcus W. Ubani, Mr. J. I. J. Onyia, Mr. J. A. Iwunah, Mr. A. Nwoke, Mr. S. W. Ubani-Ukoma and Mr. C. N. Obioha.

The foundation editor of the Eastern States Express newspaper was Mr. Abiodun Aloba, formerly of the Daily Times and the West African Pilot newspapers both of which were published in Lagos, Nigeria. The people of Aba also rallied round the Eastern States Express newspaper, which the majority of the inhabitants of Aba metropolis regarded as their pioneer newspaper. Incidentally, the technical manager of the machines for the production of the paper was Mr. Coulson Labor, a famous and experienced newspaper producer and an expert on printing machines. For establishing the newspaper at Aba, I was the recipient of congratulatory messages and messages of goodwill from far and near. Curiously enough, it was only Dr. Nnamdi Azikiwe at Lagos who failed to congratulate me on the occasion by reason of the fact, according to him, that I did not consult him before embarking upon the field of Journalism as a publisher and proprietor.

In this connection, it may be interesting to note that Dr. Nnamdi Azikiwe's reaction to my failure to consult him before embarking upon the project was to indicate to me that I was mistaken in my enterprise because it was likely that all my wealth realised from my lucrative practice in court as an utter Barrister would be wasted on newspaper publication, and that in any event, the Eastern States Express newspaper was likely to expire within six months of its foundation. I most humbly disclosed to him that rather than allow the Eastern States newspaper to be in liquidation within six months of its foundation, I would be prepared to sell the last suit in my wardrobe to make sure that the newspaper survived. In other words, that I would prefer to be considered a bankrupt to standing by and allowing the Ikemesit Company Limited, publishers of the Eastern States Express newspaper, to go into liquidation. From the onset of the publication of the newspaper, its greatest opponent was a personal friend of mine by name Nwachukwu Abengowe, who, incidentally, died within three years of the successful publication of the newspaper by motor accident. It was a violent death.

While still on the story of the foundation of the Eastern States Express newspaper, it may be worth mentioning that, contrary to Dr.

Nnamdi Azikiwe's prognostication, within three months of the debut of the newspaper, its office flooded with advertisements through the good offices of the West African Publicity Limited and, indeed, the government of the then Eastern region of Nigeria. Also, after one year of its existence, its editor, Mr. Abiodun Aloba, with my approval, was awarded a scholarship for one year which enabled him to proceed to the United Kingdom for a conducted tour of newspaper establishments for the purpose of gaining experience in respect to newspaper management. All these were indicators to the fact that the newspaper had come to stay and to compete with other newspapers in Nigeria. The newspaper was prosperous.

The year 1950 also witnessed my marriage to my beloved wife, Grace, who was then known as Miss Grace Bassey of Queens College, Lagos. I was a very happy man for that same year also witnessed the birth of my first son, to whom I gave the name Anyanti, being the name of my great grand father whose ancestor founded Ikot Abasi village and was known as Abasi Akpan Enin - Ikot Abasi Akpan Enin meaning followers or the people of the God of Akpan Enin - the maker of heaven and earth. And Akpan Enin, strictly interpreted, meaning the first son of an elephant. Similarly Nkpat Enin may be interpreted to mean the footprints left in the sands of time by Akpan Enin in the course of his journey from the home of his origin to Ikot Abasi, via Ikot Obio Nkwaha. In other words it means the footprints left in the sands of time by the elephant. Extensive details of my family are given in Chapter 25.

In 1951, I contested election to the House of Assembly at Enugu, being the headquarters of the Eastern region. My election was sponsored by the Ibibio Union in the absence of any properly organised political party in the region. I therefore contested the election as an independent. As the president of the National Council of Nigeria and the Cameroons (NCNC for short) in succession to the late Mr. Herbert McCauley, Dr. Nnamdi Azikiwe converted the remnant of the NCNC to a political party with himself as its leader and the party confined itself to Lagos and the Western region, Lagos then being part of Western region. The deputy leader of the NCNC party was Dr. Ibiyinka Olorun-Nimbe and its general secretary was Prince Adedoyin. Indeed most of the politicians who contested the election in the Eastern region contested as independents. For instance, Mr. Louis N. Mbanefo in Onitsha constituency, Mr. Enoch I. Oli of Oba also in Onitsha constituency, Mr. Rueben I. Uzomah of Orlu constituency, Mr. Alfred Chukwu Nwapa of Owerri constituency and Chief Ezerioha of Orlu constituency who contested in partnership and cooperation with Mr. K. O. Mbadiwe to the detriment of Mr. Mbonu Ojike - all contested and won the elections as independents.

Every one of us in Calabar province who contested as independents won our seats. It was only Professor Eyo Ita and Mr. E. Eniang Essien in the whole of Calabar province that contested as NCNC supporters and both also won their seats even though they both contested on the NCNC platform. In Calabar province it was only Mr. O. O. Ita and Mr. Alvan Ikokwu who were not sponsored by the Ibibio Union directly. After the elections in the divisions, R. U. Umoinyang, Akpan Udo Akpan Inyang and Ibanga Udo Akpabio, all of Ikot Ekpene constituency, Mr. D. U. Assam of Eket constituency, Mr. Anthony George Umoh of Itu constituency, Mr. J. E. Ubom and Mr. I. U. Imeh of Abak constituency and Akpan Jack Ekpe and my good self of Opobo constituency, at a meeting of the Ibibio State Union gave a solemn undertaking to remain united under the umbrella of the union as members of the regional assembly. That meeting was held under the auspices of the Ibibio State Union prior to our departure to Enugu. In addition to Chief Ntuenibok who presided, ably assisted by Chief Udo Ekong of Abak and Chief Ekpenyong Udo Ekong of Uyo, there were present several paramount rulers according to tradition including particularly Chief Ikpeme Akpan of the then Eastern Ibibio Ikono and James Udo Ibok of Eket, who usually played prominent roles in the affairs of the Ibibio State Union.

It was therefore not difficult for all of us to remain united under my leadership at Enugu at the early stages of the proceedings. Hence on arrival and finding that Professor Eyo Ita of Calabar had been selected by the Lieutenant Governor, Col. J. G. Pykenot, as the leader of government business in the House of Assembly and Nigerian head of the regional executive council of which the Lieutenant Governor was president and chairman, it took little persuasion for the team to rally round Professor Eyo Ita and his executive council and, incidentally, the Eastern regional government. Having learnt that the Northern regional government and their supporters had declared themselves as constituted by the Northern People's Congress (NPC for short) under the leadership of the Sardauna of Sokoto and the Western regional government and their supporters had also declared themselves as constituted by the Action Group under the leadership of Chief Obafemi Awolowo, it was considered expedient that the Eastern regional government and their supporters should also declare themselves constituted by the NCNC party under the leadership of Professor Eyo Ita of

Calabar, in due conformity with the spirit of the time. It should be pointed out that in each region the government was formed by the Lieutenant Governor of the region. In *stricti sensu*, no regional government was a party government having regard to the provisions of the constitution. For the purpose of selecting members of the executive committee of the region, the Lieutenant Governor set up a special committee called Selection Committee. In the Eastern region, I was a member of the Selection Committee but refused to accept appointment as a minister, either of the region or of the central government at Lagos. The government of each region consisting of the executive committee was constituted in January, 1952.

This partly accounted for the reason Dr. Nnamdi Azikiwe who, having failed to achieve his ambition of becoming the first premier of the Western region at Ibadan in 1952, had abandoned his principal seat in Lagos and had come to the Eastern region to overthrow Professor Eyo Ita by a civilian coup d'état in 1953. What really happened was that after the election of 1951 during which Dr. Nnamdi Azikiwe had contested in the Western region as the leader of the NCNC party and had won as the first member for the municipality of Lagos, Dr. Nnamdi Azikiwe had set out for Ibadan with the full expectation of the NCNC party forming the first government of the Western region of Nigeria and he being installed the first premier of the region, the NCNC party there having ostensibly won the majority of the seats contested during the election. Unfortunately for Dr. Nnamdi Azikiwe, when the Western regional house of assembly assembled, to the astonishment of everyone, it was the Action Group party which had captured the majority of seats and therefore had to form the government and Chief Obafemi Awolowo was installed the first premier of the region to the delight of Yoruba people. Not only that, as the Western regional house of assembly constituted the electoral college for election to the House of Representatives in Lagos, Dr. Nnamdi Azikiwe also was squeezed out of the House of Representatives and his place was taken by Prince Adedoyin, another NCNC party man from Lagos. Dr. Nnamdi Azikiwe's political activities as a parliamentarian had perforce to be restricted to the Western House of Assembly where he was least effective or harmful.

It therefore became necessary to oppose Dr. Nnamdi Azikiwe when, as a voluntary exile, he staged a return back to the Eastern region of Nigeria because, during the entire election of 1951 he had turned his back to the region and had never once campaigned there.

It was wrong of him to have taken the region for granted. I, along with others of like mind, had to resign from the NCNC party and thereby formed another political party, which we named National Independence Party of Nigeria. After the amalgamation of the United National Party with the National Independence Party, the party was known as United National Independence Party (UNIP for short). Thus, those of us who broke away from the NCNC party joined with a small minority party under the leadership of Mr. Alvan Ikoku to form the United National Independence Party under the leadership of Professor Eyo Ita. It was a powerful political party and embraced the cross-section of the peoples of the Eastern region.

In 1952, as a serving member of the Eastern regional house of assembly, I was also elected a member of the Nigerian House of Representatives located in Lagos as one of the representatives of the Eastern region for which election to the Eastern regional house of assembly was appropriately constituted an electoral college, according to the constitution. Thus I was a member of both the Eastern regional house of assembly and the Nigerian House of Representatives at one and the same time. Furthermore, as a member of the Eastern regional house of assembly, I was appointed by the government of the Eastern region under the leadership of Professor Eyo Ita, as Leader of Government Business in the regional House of Assembly, a member of the Nigerian Produce Marketing Board and *ipso facto* a director of the Nigerian Produce Marketing Company Limited Board; a member of the Managing Committee of the West African Institute for Oil Palm Research (WAIFOR for short) situated off Benin City in the present Edo state of Nigeria; a member of the Eastern Regional Production Development Board; and director of the Oban Rubber Development Corporation with rubber estates in the Oban area of Calabar administrative division of the Old Calabar province, Eastern region of Nigeria.

For the proper appreciation of the functions of the Nigerian Produce Marketing Board and the Nigerian Produce Marketing Company Limited, it is necessary to explain that it was the duty of the Nigerian Produce Marketing Board to arrange for the purchase of and, in fact, to purchase produce in bulk from persons or organisations to whom it had already granted licenses and who were known as licensed buying agents. The produce were, in the case of the Eastern region, palm oil and palm kernels; in the case of the Western region, cocoa; and in the case of the Northern region, ground nuts and cotton seeds; for shipment to the United Kingdom for sale in the world market. The selling aspect of the produce in the world market was the responsibility of the Nigerian Produce Marketing Company Limited with headquarters in London. For the Nigerian Produce Marketing Company Limited there was appointed a managing agent resident in London in the United Kingdom. The duty of the agent included the convening of the annual general meeting of the Nigerian Produce Marketing Company Limited, which was usually held in London presided over by the chairman of the Nigerian Produce Marketing Board who was also ipso facto chairman of the Nigerian Produce Marketing Company Limited. It was also the special duty of the managing agent to take full charge of the sale of Nigerian produce shipped to London in the world market at a reasonably good price prevailing in the world market and to transmit the proceeds of such sales immediately on realisation to each of the three regional organisations in Nigeria which had shipped the said produce to the United Kingdom. It was thereafter the duty of each regional organisation to distribute such proceeds in such a way as to ensure that part of the proceeds of the sales was preserved for the event and, at the time of depression, in local prices while the balance of such proceeds would be disbursed in the development of the area of production in each region by the Regional Production Development Board which in the Eastern region was known as the Eastern Regional Production Development Board. It was the duty of members of the Nigerian Produce Marketing Company Limited to attend every year the annual general meeting of the company in London.

Members of the Eastern Regional Production Development Board were held responsible for the development of the region classified as the area of production of the palm oil and palm kernel from funds made available to them by the Nigerian Produce Marketing Board from the proceeds of the sale of palm oil and palm kernel shipped to the United Kingdom in the world market according to the ruling or prevailing world market prices. On the other hand, it was the duty of members of the managing committee of the West African Institute for Oil Palm Research to establish oil palm plantations in suitable areas of Nigeria, treat and develop the oil palm seedlings and have the young palms cultivated in suitable areas and distribute such seedlings to other parts of West Africa like the Gold Coast, Sierra Leone and the Gambia for proper cultivation. It was in the course of executing its duty that the managing committee of the West African Institute for Oil Palm Research had to establish oil palm plantations at

Abak in the administrative division of Abak of the Old Calabar province by clearing areas of land and cultivating young oil palms and seedlings transplanted from the research headquarters near Benin and classifying the Abak oil palm plantations as a sub-station of the West African Institute for Oil Palm Research. At Benin, there were large oil palm plantations as well as areas of land reserved for the seedlings. There was also installed a stock mill or machine for the purpose of boiling palm fruits and extracting oil and kernel there from and the kernel extracted from such a process would then be developed in the nursery as seedlings and young palms ready for cultivation in suitable areas approved by the technologists attached to the Institute.

In 1953, due to concatenation of events, the House of Representatives at Lagos and the Eastern Regional House of Assembly had to be dissolved. There was then convened a conference for the drawing up of a new constitution for Nigeria to be held in London under the chairmanship of the Secretary of States for the colonies. The UNIP was represented in full force at the conference and also at the final conference held in 1957 preceding the independence of Nigeria in 1960.

In 1954, before the direct election to the House of Representatives at Lagos in which I was successful, as a member of the Eastern Regional Development Board, I was able to arrange for the Eastern Regional Development Board to establish its boat building yard at Ikot Abasi river front for the purpose of building creek crafts intended to replace the ancient carved or dug up canoes for the conveyance of passengers and produce as well as goods to other parts of the creeks, for instance to Ogoni and Andoni. The Eastern Regional Production Development Board boatyard was commissioned in 1954 by the government of the Eastern region of Nigeria. Later, however, during the premiership of Dr. Nnamdi Azikiwe in the Eastern region, the name of the Eastern Regional Production Development Board was changed to the Eastern Regional Production Corporation.

In 1957, as a result of the grant of independence to Ghana by the British Imperial power, Ghana pulled out of the West African Institute for Oil Palm Research in consequence of which the name of the West African Institute for Oil Palm Research was changed to the Nigerian Institute for Oil Palm Research (NIFOR for short). In 1959 I failed to win my seat into the House of Representatives despite the fact that I was the leader of the COR State Movement which advocated the creation of states throughout Nigeria (COR being an acronym for

Calabar, Ogoja, Rivers; for further details, please, refer to my book "The Story of the Ibibio Union").

In May 1960, there was held in Lagos a seminar on the Nigerian independence constitution under the auspices of the Supreme Court of Nigeria and the sponsorship of the Ford Foundation of the United States of America. I attended the seminar as a representative of the Bar Association of Nigeria of which I was then Vice-President. In the course of the conduct of the proceedings of the seminar and towards the termination thereof, I was interviewed and thereafter offered the post of a Justice of the Supreme Court of Nigeria, which was to be inaugurated on October 1, 1960, and I was also given up to November 1960 to signify my acceptance of the offer. I had there and then felt the necessity to consult my people and supporters since I was then not only a legal practitioner but also a politician of some standing as I was the principal leader of the COR State Movement and its outstanding and recognised champion. I was then also National President of the Ibibio State Union.

For the purpose of consultation, a special meeting of the various segments of the organisations of which I was a member had to be arranged. The meeting, which was convened by Obong Ime Ntuenibok, paramount ruler of Nunasang, and Obong Udo Ekong, paramount ruler of Abak division, was held at Abak. Those who attended the meeting came from far and wide. There were the representatives of the Obong of Calabar which included Etubom Henshaw of Henshaw Town, the Revd. Okon Efiong and Mrs. Hannah Otudor. There were also the various clan heads in the Ibibio mainland territory of the then Calabar province that attended in full force. There were also the representatives of the non-Ibo section of Ogoja province consisting then of Obubra, Ikom, Ogoja and Obudu divisions as well as the representatives of the Rivers province. The issue as to whether or not I should regard myself as having been released from my responsibility to the people of the COR State Movement merely because I had failed to be elected a member of the House of Representatives during the general election of December 1959 was fully debated. The issue was decided in the negative. It was held unanimously that I was still under obligation to the whole of the people of the COR State area and therefore that it was not open to me to accept the offer of the appointment as a Justice of the Supreme Court at that time. Quite reluctantly I had to convey the message back to the authorities concerned and, in effect, I had to decline the offer.

CHAPTER TWENTY-ONE

I Am Appointed A Judge In 1961

"I left the Bar with sincere regrets. There is no more honourable and expert profession, none in which the sinews of the mind are kept in better trim, as there is no more loyal and kindly fraternity. And I believe that there are few callings in which success is more certain for anyone with reasonable talents and the requisite industry and patience".- John Buchan in "Memory Holds the Door".

In May 1961, on my return from Calabar where I had attended a session of the High Court that was presided over by the Honourable Mr. Justice Horace Palmer, I received a message that my presence was required urgently in Lagos. I had spent two weeks in Calabar and returned to Aba, my station and residence, on a Friday when the session ended. Then, to my surprise, I received Mr. Tom Mbanefo from Onitsha with a message from the Honourable Mr. Justice L. N. Mbanefo, Chief Justice of Eastern Nigeria at Enugu, that I was wanted in Lagos and that it was very important that I must be in Lagos the following Monday. I received that message on the same Friday I returned from Calabar. On delivering the message, Mr. Tom Mbanefo emphasised that his brother, the Honourable Mr. Justice L. N. Mbanefo, had requested him to contact me as the last resort because every effort to get me on the telephone had failed and that it was his brother's desire that I should call to see him at Onitsha on the Sunday on my way to Lagos as he would then be engaged in the affairs of the Anglican Church which was having its synod there, he being the Chancellor of the church. The request for me to visit Lagos was rather vague as the purpose for which my presence was required in Lagos was not stated. Still I felt that it was my duty to oblige.

I discussed the matter with my wife, Grace, who advised that it was necessary for me to travel to Lagos to find out the reason my presence was considered necessary especially as the request to visit Lagos had come from the Prime Minister of Nigeria, the Honourable Sir. Tafawa Balewa. Then, on Sunday morning, I left for Lagos via Onitsha where I had to cross the river Niger by a ferryboat. At Onitsha, I called on the Honourable Mr. Justice Louis N. Mbanefo who received me most warmly. He said he was delighted I could make it. He wished me good luck but could not say why I was wanted so urgently. On being questioned, he advised me not to worry and that everything would soon reveal itself. With such good words of encouragement I left for Lagos.

Soon thereafter, I was able to be ferried across to Asaba on the opposite side of the river Niger. I drove all the way throughout the night and arrived in Lagos about 7.30 a. m. on Monday. I met the Prime Minister at 8.30 a. m. that morning in his office. He welcomed me to Lagos with a glint of pleasure in his eyes. He congratulated me for responding without unwarranted delay to the invitation and then directed me to see the Honourable the Chief Justice of Nigeria, Sir Adetokunbo Ademola, K. B. E.. I thereupon immediately called on the Honourable the Chief Justice of Nigeria who in turn directed me to see the Honourable the Chief Justice of the High Court of the federal territory of Lagos, Sir Clement de Lestang, which I did. Immediately on receiving me at about 10 a. m., Sir Clement exclaimed with excitement "thank God you are here at last!" And without having any discussion with me at once sent for his chief registrar. On the arrival of the chief registrar, he instructed him to get in touch at once with the Governor-General's office and arrange for the swearing in of judges as he understood that the Governor-General, then Dr. Nnamdi Azikiwe, was planning to visit the University of Nigeria, Nsukka that week. Then turning to me, he expressed the hope that I was ready and prepared to be sworn in as Judge of the High Court of the federal territory of Lagos. I was dumfounded. I could not understand why I should have been brought to Lagos with out any previous arrangement between me and the "powers that be". Out of curiosity, I then asked to know who were to be sworn in as judges. The answer came back in a flash. "Surely you know that you are to be sworn in today". In answering back, I pointed out that those concerned had not been fair to me at all because there was never a time I had ever been interviewed relating to the post of Judge of the High Court of the federal territory of Lagos. He then turned around to me and asked: "What specific interview did you expect apart from the several conversations that had taken place between you and some members of the authorities concerned?"

Then just at that stage, the chief registrar of the High Court reported that everything had been arranged with the Governor-General's office for the swearing in of the judges and that it was the wish of the Governor-General to receive the judges that morning. Thereupon on the invitation of the Honourable the Chief Justice of the High Court of the federal territory of Lagos, I boarded the latter's car while Mr. Sowemimo drove in his own car and we left for the State House, Marina, the residence of the Governor-General. In the course of the journey, the Honourable the Chief Justice, Sir Clement de Lestang, in conversation, asked to know my relationship with Dr. Nnamdi Azikiwe, the Governor-General. In answer I said "somewhat cordial". I then pointed out to Sir Clement, however, that Dr. Nnamdi Azikiwe (Zik for short) had a high opinion of me, just as I had of him but that often times we agreed to disagree on issues and that was all.

On arrival at the State House, the Governor-General greeted us with a smile and, turning to Mr. A. K. Blankson, the General Manager of the African Continental Bank Limited of Zik's fame, shook his head and winked at me. Shortly thereafter we were sworn in, the Honourable Mr. Justice G. S. Sowemimo, who was at the time an Acting Judge of the High Court of the federal territory of Lagos being sworn in after me thereby making me senior to him in the hierarchy of the judges of the High Court of the federal territory of Lagos. This was on the direction of the Honourable the Chief Justice of the High Court of the federal territory of Lagos. On completion of the swearing in, we were treated to a sherry party as guests of the Governor-General in celebration of the historic event as we were said to be the first judges to be sworn in by the Governor-General since his assumption of office. During the entertainment, the Governor-General in conversation with me asked what it felt like to be a judge. Without hesitation, I answered that having just then been sworn in I did not consider myself a judge as yet since I had then not tried a single case. We both laughed it off but I believe that, in his heart of hearts, Dr. Nnamdi Azikiwe, the Governor-General was saying "thank God they have caught this man at last". That must have been so because, even when Zik was premier of the Eastern region, it was his desire that I should abandon politics and accept a judgeship. He would have preferred to see me a judge then than a politician in Parliament in the opposition.

We then took leave of the Governor-General and returned to the High Court of the federal territory of Lagos. On arrival, the Honourable the Chief Justice instructed the chief registrar to have Court

No. 1 prepared for me to sit in commencement of work as a judge. I immediately protested. I pointed out that my chambers at Aba were still open and functioning with all my staff discharging each his assignment, that even my family had no idea I was coming to Lagos to be sworn in as a judge, that I did not even bring with me my gown and a change of dress, and that it would be impossible as well as unfair for me to be expected to be able to discharge my duties properly. I, thereupon, requested that I be granted leave of absence of about one month to enable me to return to Aba to put my office in order and that, in any case, consideration should be given of the fact that I had fixtures in various courts for the next six months since it was not within my contemplation that I was likely to be appointed a judge so soon. In reply, the Honourable the Chief Justice stated that, in any case since I had already been sworn in as a judge, which event was broadcast to the world, it would be inappropriate for me to continue my practice as a Barrister or to appear in any court as counsel from then on; but that, considering my representation, he most reluctantly granted me leave of absence of 14 days within which I must wind up my practice and assume duty as a judge of the High Court of Lagos as there was considerable shortage of judges to man the courts.

Having been granted permission, I left for Aba and arrived there the following day to a tumultuous welcome by members of the Nigerian Bar Association, Aba branch. Apparently having heard of the announcement of my having been appointed a judge over the radio and television, members of the Bar Association, Aba branch had set up a committee to make plans concerning my reception on my return from Lagos to Aba and subsequently a farewell party to be organised in my honour as a well known and active member of the association nation wide. On my arrival at Aba therefore, I found myself in the warm embrace of receptions and farewell parties. In particular, during the week of my departure from Aba to Lagos, I was the guest of honour at a farewell party consisting of ballroom dancing and a sumptuous banquet. It was wonderful entertainment that continued till the small hours of the morning in the hall and premises of the Recreation Club, Aba.

While at Aba, I found it difficult to contact my clients because the period of leave granted me was too short. I therefore decided to and did handover my chambers and the offices attached thereto to a consortium comprising Dan A. Eno, Esqr., Dr Okoi Arikpo, B. L. and A. J. Aseme, Esq., the latter also occupying my house, No. 22 Park Road,

Aba as my tenant. Indeed Barrister Aseme was also principally and ostensibly virtually in charge of my chambers. I returned to Lagos and assumed the office of a judge of the High Court of the federal territory of Lagos on or about 1st June, 1961. It was a remarkable change, nay, a transformation. It took some time for me to be able to adjust to the situation and the new environment.

Thinking aloud and on reflection, I must confess that I left the Nigerian Bar as a legal practitioner with reluctance and profound regret. I have since found that there is no more honourable and expert profession, none in which "the sinews", to borrow an expression from "Memory Holds the Door" by John Buchan, "of the mind are kept in better trim, as there is no more loyal and kindly fraternity". I personally share in the belief that there are few callings in which success is more certain for any one with reasonable talents and the requisite industry and patience. Incidentally, I think it may be in order to mention here that I was at the time preparing to apply to be granted the rank of the then equivalent of "SAN" (Q.C.) when I was appointed a Judge of the High Court of the federal territory of Lagos.

Having settled down as a judge, I found the work quite interesting. I was also full of determination to enjoy the work. During the period of my judgeship at Lagos, I sought and was granted interview by the Honourable the Chief Justice of Nigeria, Sir Adetokunbo Ademola, in connection with my having been appointed a judge of the High Court of the federal territory of Lagos in 1961 whereas in May 1960 I was in actual fact offered the post of a justice of the Supreme Court of Nigeria. The Honourable the Chief Justice of Nigeria explained that, since I had declined the offer of the post of the justice of the Supreme Court of Nigeria in 1961, that post was offered to the then Attorney-General of Nigeria, Mr. Unsworth who, incidentally, was to serve in the court for one year only after which he was to proceed to Malawi, then known as Nyassaland, there to assume the post of Chief Justice. The reason why the post was offered to him was to enable him to gain experience of the system of administration of justice in court and the maintenance of court records. In the meantime, I was to serve in the High Court of Lagos pending his departure to Malawi when it would then be easier for me to be elevated to the Supreme Court bench. My being in Lagos, according to the Honourable the Chief Justice, would facilitate the process of my elevation to the higher bench.

Perhaps, at this juncture, it may be of interest to mention that during my tenure of the office of Judge of the High Court of the federal territory of Lagos, one of the most important cases that I had to deal with was the constitutional case involving Chief Obafemi Awolowo and some of his supporters. It was the case of Chief Obafemi Awolowo and others vs. The Federal Minister of Internal Affairs and the Attorney-General of the Federation, which arose out of the fact of Chief Obafemi Awolowo and some of his supporters having been charged with treasonable felony in that they had plotted the overthrow, by force, of the government of Nigeria of which Alhaji Sir Tafawa Balewa was prime minister.

There were altogether three separate cases - suits Nos. LD/ 595/ 1962, LD/598/1962, and LD/599/1962 - which were consolidated by order of court and heard together. The suits were instituted in the High Court of the federal territory of Lagos by Chief Obafemi Awolowo and two out of his 24 supporters - all of whom were together charged with the criminal offences of treasonable felony contrary to Section 4 (b) and conspiracy contrary to Section 518(6) of the criminal code and arraigned before Sowemimo J. and thereafter remanded in custody to await trial. At the material time, the Action Group - a political party - was the official opposition party in the Federal Parliament of Nigeria and Chief Obafemi Awolowo being its leader was also the leader of the official opposition and all the 24 supporters of Chief Obafemi Awolowo charged jointly with him were members of the Action Group. On the other hand, the first defendant, the Federal Minister of Internal Affairs, was a member of the Northern People's Congress - a political party - while the second defendant, the Attorney General of the Federation was a member of the National Conference of Nigerian Citizens – yet another political party; both the Northern People's Congress and the National Conference of Nigerian Citizens being in alliance had formed a coalition government of the federation of Nigeria at the material time. The Federal Minister of Internal Affairs was by law charged with the responsibility for immigration, which was a subject on the exclusive federal legislative list.

While in custody, Chief Obafemi Awolowo and the two of his supporters aforesaid, hereinafter to be referred to as the plaintiffs in the three consolidated cases, arranged and successfully retained, as counsel, the services of one E. F. N. Gratiaen, Esqr., Q. C. who was normally resident in the United Kingdom to come over to Nigeria for the purpose of defending them in court at the trial of the criminal charges. Mr. Gratiaen was not a Nigerian citizen but a British subject though a member of the Nigerian Bar who was enrolled in 1959 as a legal practitioner in Nigerian courts. Having accepted the retainer, Mr. Gratiaen arrived in Nigeria for the purpose of appearing before the High Court as leading counsel for the defence of the plaintiffs in the criminal charges. Mr. Efueye, who was to act as one of the junior counsel to Mr. Gratiaen, met him at the Lagos Airport, Ikeja. At the airport, an immigration officer acting on the direction of the first defendant as the Federal Minister for Internal Affairs refused Mr. Gratiaen entry into Nigeria even though all his papers were in order. Mr. Gratiaen was thus treated as persona non grata *in Nigeria. By reason of that refusal, the first plaintiff, Chief Obafemi Awolowo, in particular, had to defend himself in person without a counsel and the other two were defended by counsel not of their own choice at the trial of the criminal charges.*

In consequence of their predicament, Chief Obafemi Awolowo and his two supporters instituted the three suits, the claim in each case comprising two main headings:-

1. (a). **The Plaintiff is entitled under the (Nigerian Constitution) order in council to be defended in the criminal charge in which he is an accused person by Mr. E. F. N. Gratiaen, Q. C. or any other counsel of the Plaintiff's choice, whether British or indigenous;**

   (b). The order of the defendants prohibiting the entry of the said Mr. E. F. N. Gratiaen, Q. C. into Nigeria for the purpose of defending the Plaintiff in the aforementioned charge is ultra vires the said (Nigerian Constitution) order in council and is therefore null and void.

2. An injunction restraining the defendants from preventing the said Mr. E. F.N. Gratiaen, Q. C. or any other British counsel who might be counsel of the Plaintiff's choice from entering into Nigeria for the purpose of defending the Plaintiff on the said charge.

At the hearing of the consolidated suits, it was contended on behalf of the plaintiffs that the refusal to admit Mr. Gratiaen into Nigeria for the purpose of defending the plaintiffs during the trial of the criminal charges was prejudicial to their best interest as their liberty was in jeopardy and that the refusal had deprived them of their fundamental right to be defended in the circumstances by a counsel of their choice. It was further submitted that the refusal was a denial to them of their constitutional right as provided in Section 21(5) (c) of the second schedule to the Nigerian (constitutional) order in council 1960 and therefore unconstitutional and ultra vires. It was also the complaint of the plaintiffs that the refusal was malicious and without just cause having regard to the fact that, on three different occasions between 1961 and 1962, non-Nigerian counsel from the United Kingdom had been allowed entry into Nigeria for the sole purpose of appearing and conducting cases in court for the persons who were involved in such cases. Hence the claim for a declaration and an injunction. On the other hand, it was admitted on behalf of the defendants that Mr. E. F. N. Gratiaen was refused entry into Nigeria on the authority vested in the first defendant under Section 13 of the Immigration Act because Mr. E. F. N. Gratiaen was not a Nigerian citizen. It was the case of the defendants that it was competent for the first defendant to have refused Mr. Gratiaen entry into Nigeria in the exercise of the absolute discretion vested in him and that Section 13 of the Immigration Act was not in any way inconsistent with Section 21(5) (c) of the Nigerian constitution.

In his address, learned counsel for the defendants submitted that the right secured under Sect 21 (5) (c) was not an absolute one. It was subject to at least two limitations, the first limitation being that the legal representative chosen must be a qualified person entitled to a right of audience in Nigerian courts. The second limitation was that he must be available to take up the case, and therefore must be able to enter Nigeria as of right and therefore must be a Nigerian.

It was also contended that Section 13 of the Immigration Act was consistent with the rights guaranteed to Nigerian citizens by Sect 26 (1) of the constitution as the provisions of Sect 13 of the Immigration Act only affected the right of aliens or non Nigerians. Finally, it was submitted that there was no evidence of malice and that, having regard to the wording of Sect 13 of the Immigration Act, the motive for the refusal of Mr. E. F. N. Gratiaen entry into Nigerian was irrelevant.

In reply to the submissions of learned counsel for the defendants, counsel for the plaintiffs submitted that all exercise of executive power must be subject to, and be directed towards, the maintenance of the constitution, and therefore directed towards securing for the benefit of the citizens the rights enshrined therein. Any exercise of ministerial power which made it difficult for the citizen to benefit to the fullest extent from any of the provisions of the constitution must be considered ultra vires and therefore inconsistent with the constitution having regard to the provisions of Sections 78 and 79 of the constitution. It was the plaintiffs' submission that the direction given by the first defendant was ultra vires the provisions of Section 21(5) (c) of the constitution, which had placed no limitations on the legal practitioner, or representative whose services should be retained by the citizen. It was therefore not necessary that such a legal representative should be a Nigerian or should be able to enter Nigeria as of right so long as he had a right of audience in Nigerian courts.

In my judgement it was necessary first to consider the provisions of Sect 13 of the Immigration Act which read:-

> "13. Notwithstanding anything in this ordinance contained, the Governor-General may, in his absolute discretion, prohibit the entry into Nigeria of any person, not being a native of Nigeria".

This power, which was originally vested in the Governor-General as the Head of State and the representative of the Sovereign, was by legal Notice No 258 of 1959 and by the authority of the Transfer of Functions (Federation) order 1959 transferred to the minister charged with the responsibility for immigration. Since then, the power was only exercisable by the Federal Minister of Internal Affairs, that it to say, the first defendant. Accordingly, the Federal Minister of Internal Affairs had been empowered by parliament to prohibit the entry into Nigeria of a non-Nigerian and that in the exercise of his absolute discretion, which meant <u>even without reference to the cabinet</u> or probably in spite of such reference, or regardless of what might be the opinion of his colleagues. It was not contended that the minister had not the power to have directed as he did. There could be no question that, in giving the direction, the first defendant acted within the scope of the power conferred on him by parliament. I therefore held that in refusing the counsel, Mr. E. F. N. Gratiaen, entry into Nigeria, he did so within the ambit of the power conferred on him by parliament since Mr. E. F. N. Gratiaen was a non-Nigerian. He therefore acted intra vires his powers.

The exercise of the power under Section 13 of the Immigration Act had been seriously challenged on two main grounds, namely, (1) malice and (2) the principle of ultra vires and inconsistency. On the issue of malice, the first plaintiff gave evidence to the effect that because he was a member and the leader of the official opposition in the

Federal Parliament while the two defendants belonged to the parties which formed the coalition government, he believed that the two defendants concerned were hostile to him and his party men and supporters including the second and third plaintiffs and that indeed both defendants hated him. Since some non-Nigerian counsel from the United Kingdom between 1961 and 1962 had been permitted to enter into Nigeria and to practice in Nigerian courts it was the hatred entertained against him and his party men that had motivated the first defendant in refusing Mr. Gratiaen entry into Nigeria. I was however not satisfied that there was sufficient evidence which should entitle me to hold that plaintiffs had discharged the onus on them of establishing malice. I was also of the view that, in a matter of the kind where the first defendant had been given absolute discretionary power by parliament, very strong evidence of malice was required. For, in my view as I held then, an ill motive would not convert a lawful act like the present one to an unlawful one.

As was said by Lord Halsbury, although in different circumstances in <u>Mayor of Bradford vs. Pickles (1895) AC HL 587 at p594</u> "This is not a case in which the state of the mind of the person doing the act can affect the right to do it. If it was a lawful act, however ill the motive might be, he had a right to do it. If it was an unlawful act, however good his motive might be, he would have no right to do it". It appeared that the legislature having enacted that it was lawful for the first defendant in his absolute discretion to prohibit certain class of persons from entering Nigeria, it could not be said that what the legislature had authorised was unlawful and therefore an actionable wrong unless it could be shown that the Act was inconsistent with the constitution.

Then turning to the consideration of the provisions of section 21 (5) (c) of the Nigerian constitution on which the claims of the plaintiffs were based and which read as follows:-

> "21 (5) (c) Every person who is charged with a criminal offence shall be entitled to defend himself in person or by legal representatives of his own choice".

Now learned counsel for the plaintiffs had contended that the provision as contained in section 21 (5) (c) of the constitution as set out above entitled every person charged with a criminal offence as of right to bring into Nigeria from the United Kingdom any non-Nigerian counsel for the purpose of defending him. It was submitted that liberally interpreted the provision admitted of no limitation whatsoever. It was not necessary, it was submitted, that the legal representative should be a Nigerian. All that was required was that the legal representative should be the choice of the person concerned in the criminal charge, and should have a right of audience in Nigerian courts.

I did not accept as a sound proposition the submission that the provision as contained in section 21 (5) (c) of the constitution as set out above liberally interpreted could be construed to entitle anyone to bring a counsel from the United Kingdom for the purpose of defending him in a criminal charge. To accept that submission would be to strain language. The constitution, I held, was a Nigerian constitution meant for Nigerians in Nigeria. It only ran in Nigeria. The natural consequence of that was the legal representative contemplated in section 21 (5) (c) of the constitution ought to be someone in Nigeria; not outside it. I then observed that nothing which had been urged before me had suggested that the framers of the constitution ever had any special reason to contemplate, at the time of the framing of the constitution, that in the ordinary course of events, Nigerians involved in criminal charges would normally engage legal representatives outside Nigeria. I did not think that that particular provision of the constitution was ever intended to be invoked in support of the expensive undertaking of importing lawyers whether British or otherwise into Nigeria.

I then went on to state that it seemed to me that the probable reason why it was considered necessary to include the provision in Section 21 of the constitution was because of the tendency, which was at one time prevalent in certain parts of Nigeria, to legislate for the exclusion of legal practitioners in certain courts of the land. When the provision was included it was necessary to add an escape clause in the form of a proviso thereby saving some native courts in which legal practitioners had no right of audience.

Having examined the provisions very carefully, I was inclined to accept the submission of the learned counsel of the defendants that the provisions of section 21 (5) (c) of the constitution were subject to certain limitations. It was clear that any legal representative chosen must not be under disability of any kind. Such legal representative must be someone who, if outside Nigeria, could enter the country as of right; and he must be someone enrolled to practice as a lawyer in Nigeria. For if the legal representative chosen could not enter Nigeria as of right, and if he had no right of audience in Nigerian courts then he would be under a disability. In both such cases the legal representative chosen would run the risk of being refused entry into Nigeria by the immigration authority, and of being refused enrolment by the Chief Justice of the federation of Nigeria. For, in the latter case, by the authority of Legal Notice No. 1 of 1956, it was only the Chief Justice of the federation who might, in his discretion, admit any person who satisfied him to practice as a solicitor in the Federal Supreme Court.

In the former case, questions of immigration involved matters of Foreign and Commonwealth Relations Policy, both of which were matters for government. Foreigners, whether British or otherwise, could not enter into Nigeria as of right. They all had conditional right of entry, which was then regulated by sections 20, 21 and 23 of the Immigration Act.

All this was to say in plain language that the choice open to the person contemplated under section 21 (5) (c) of the constitution was limited, and indeed, limited to legal representatives in Nigeria, not outside it. If it was desired that a person charged with criminal offence should be at liberty to choose legal representatives not only in Nigeria but also from elsewhere, it was my considered view then that the words: "whether in Nigeria or elsewhere" would have been added to subsection (c) of Sect 21 (5) after the word "choice". The essential protection offered to an accused person by the provision of section 21 (5) (c) was, entitled by law, to be represented at his trial by a legal representative who must not be someone chosen for him by the prosecutor or government or someone else not approved by him.

From this it followed that, after a most careful consideration, I had reached the conclusion that section 13 of the Immigration Act, the provisions of which were designed to control the immigration into Nigeria of foreign nationals, was not inconsistent with the provisions of section 21 (5) (c) of the Nigerian constitution. I was also clearly satisfied that it was not in any way ultra vires the said section 21 (5) (c) of the constitution. In the result, and finding as I did, that it was both competent and lawful for the first defendant in the exercise of his power under section 13 of the Immigration Act to have refused Mr. Gratiaen entry into Nigeria, I must refuse, and did refuse, the plaintiffs the declaration and the injunction which they had sought and dismiss the actions. ***Order: Suits Nos. LD/595/62; Ld/598/62 and LD/599/62 accordingly dismissed.***

CHAPTER TWENTY-TWO

I Am Promoted Chief Justice In 1963

"This was not the first time – or indeed the last – that I have received a blessing in what was at the time a very effective disguise".

In 1962, I was informed by the Prime Minister of Nigeria, Alhaji Sir Abubakar Tafawa Balewa, that the Council of Ministers had decided that I be promoted and posted to Uganda, Eastern Africa on secondment as Chief Justice in satisfaction of the request by the government of Uganda, which request had been made to Nigeria by the Prime Minister of Uganda, Dr. Milton Obote. The Prime Minister then told me that he did not, there and then, require my assent as to whether or not I would accept the offer of the appointment and that he was therefore prepared to give me a period of one month within which to ponder over the matter before responding as to whether or not I would accept the offer and be prepared to be posted to Uganda as Chief Justice; and that, as Chief Justice of Uganda, I would be entitled to a knighthood after one year's service, as a prerequisite. I thanked the Prime Minister and assured him that I was going to give very serious consideration to the matter. I also expressed my gratitude to him for the opportunity he was offering to me.

Shortly thereafter, I made it a point of duty to call upon the Chief Justice of Nigeria, the Honourable Sir Adetokunbo Ademola, to discuss the matter with him. On meeting him, I immediately broached upon the subject of the possibility of my being transferred to Uganda, Eastern Africa on promotion and as to whether he was aware of the proposal, and, if so, whether that was not inconsistent with his promise that I would be elevated to the Supreme Court bench in a year's time after the departure of Mr. Justice Unsworth. In reply, the Honourable the Chief Justice of Nigeria assured me that being the Chief Justice of Uganda, Eastern Africa was still an act in the process of my eventual elevation to the Supreme Court of Nigeria, in that after my service in Uganda, Eastern Africa, I would, on my return to Nigeria, proceed straight away to the Supreme Court, since I would only be in

Uganda, Eastern Africa for a limited period, Uganda having only become independent in 1962.

Two weeks thereafter, I travelled to Enugu in response to an invitation by the Honourable Mr. Justice Louis N. Mbanefo, Chief Justice of the Eastern region of Nigeria. At Enugu I, also, called at the secretariat and went straight to the Legal Department, to the office of the Solicitor General, and there I met the Solicitor General, who was then Mr. Ajegbo, and the Director of Public Prosecutions, Mr. Gabriel Onyuike. Both of them were excited to see me. They both congratulated me as the new Chief Justice of Uganda. They both spoke to me in wonderment. They wondered what I had done to the Federal Government of Nigeria which made them feel that I deserved all the important appointments given to me at the time and felt that I was being pampered. They asked me when I would be leaving for Uganda to assume my new office and said that I should appreciate the fact that to be appointed to such an important office was an honour conferred on me. I, of course, ignored the question and the observation. I was more interested in getting to know what they were doing and how they were performing their respective duties and so started conversation along those lines. Shortly thereafter, when my presence there appeared to be attracting attention, I left the secretariat. I felt embarrassed to be congratulated by such a large number of people in respect of an appointment yet in an embryo, so to speak. I, therefore, made myself scarce. I found my way home and had consultations with some friends and relatives and was the recipient of encouragement from all and sundry with the exception of one individual who made the fantastic suggestion that it might be a means of getting me out of Nigeria so as to deprive me of the opportunity of continuing to fight for my people especially in connection with the creation of states.

I returned to Lagos within a fortnight and immediately reported to the Honourable, the Prime Minister, Alhaji Sir Abubakar Tafawa Balewa, positively that I was prepared to accept the appointment as Chief Justice of Uganda on terms proposed by him. There and then, the Prime Minister was delighted. He then said that, since I had accepted the offer, he would then communicate with the Prime Minister of Uganda and advise him to invite me to accept the offer of the post of Chief Justice of Uganda as the first African to be appointed to the post. Subsequently that same year, I received an invitation from Mr. Milton Obote, Prime Minister of Uganda, to fill the vacant post of Chief Justice of Uganda in succession to the European holder of the post who had then retired on terms offered by him as to salary, period and conditions of service. After having discussed the terms with the Honourable, the Prime Minister of Nigeria, I dispatched my acceptance of the offer of the office of Chief Justice of Uganda, Eastern Africa, to the Prime Minister of Uganda, Dr. Milton Obote. I accepted to serve for 5 years in Uganda. The Honourable, the Prime Minister of Nigeria, Alhaji Sir Abubakar Tafawa Balewa, accepted on behalf of the Nigerian Government to pay me, during the period of my absence from Nigeria, an expatriation allowance and on my return to Nigeria to have me absorbed in the Supreme Court of Nigeria as a Justice of the Supreme Court of Nigeria. I was quite happy and satisfied with the terms of my appointment. Before my departure, I received another letter from the Prime Minister of Uganda that I would act as Governor-General on my arrival.

I flew by an Ethiopian Airlines plane on 1st May, 1963 to Entebbe Airport in Uganda. I was seen off by a number of friends and well-wishers, including Dr. Chike Obi, the famous mathematician and leader of the then Dynamic Party of Nigeria. At the Lagos airport where I bade farewell to all my friends, Dr. Chike Obi assured me that even though I would be away in Eastern Africa, he would still be thinking of me and that he had earmarked me for the post of his legal adviser as soon as he achieved his ambition of becoming a dictator of Nigeria after a successful coup d'état in consequence of which Gbenekaka forest at Benin would be developed as a detention camp for obstinates and counter *coup d'état* plotters. We together laughed that off. Still he assured me that what he told me was his plan of action and that he would surprise Nigerians as to what he was capable of doing. *En route* for Entebbe we broke our flight at Addis Ababa in Ethiopia and then headed to Nairobi in Kenya where I had to change my plane by boarding a DC 3 belonging to the Eastern African Airways - a local flight. But, before boarding the plane at Nairobi Airport, I had two surprises in connection with my arrival at the airport - one very pleasant, the other not so pleasant but rather ominous. The very pleasant one was that, to my greatest surprise, on arrival at the airport at Nairobi and on alighting from the plane, I was quite unexpectedly met by the Honourable Sir John Ainley who, then unknown to me, was the Honourable the Chief Justice of Kenya, Eastern Africa. Apparently prepared to welcome me, the Honourable Sir John Ainley, already waiting for me at the airport, on seeing me alight from the plane drew near and embraced me and immediately after welcoming me informed me that it was purely by chance that he heard over Radio Kenya that I would be passing to Uganda as the new Chief Justice appointed by the Ugandan government from Nigeria. He, thereupon, had come to the airport in order to satisfy his curiosity because, as the first Chief Justice of the Eastern region of Nigeria under the premiership of Dr Nnamdi Azikiwe, he had wished in vain to have had me made a judge of the High Court of the Eastern Region of Nigeria. He said he was full of delight to find me at last fulfil his expectation in that I was then not only a judge but a Chief Justice. To celebrate and commemorate the occasion, he had arranged, he said, for both of us to have lunch together at the airport before my departure to Entebbe in Uganda.

Accordingly, we lunched together at the airport and promised mutually to keep in touch. After lunch, I expressed my appreciation to him for his kindness to me and explained, rather apologetically, that since his sudden departure from the Eastern region of Nigeria where he was the first Chief Justice, I feared that I had not kept in touch with him and therefore had no idea that he was then the Chief Justice of Kenya, otherwise I would have written to inform him first of my appointment as a judge of the High Court of the federal territory of Lagos and then of my appointment as the Chief Justice of Uganda. The other surprise occurred just when I was about to board my plane at the airport for Entebbe in Uganda. The then wife of the British High Commissioner for Tanganyika (now Tanzania) arrived and was met at the airport by her husband, the High Commissioner who had come to the airport to receive her on arrival. On seeing me, the husband, that is, the British High Commissioner to whom I had already been introduced previously, there and then introduced me to his wife as the new Nigerian Chief Justice for Uganda. Thereupon the wife, in great astonishment, exclaimed quite unconsciously: "Darling, this is a complete takeover"! The reason for such an exclamation was that there were then already a significant number of Nigerian magistrates serving in Tanganyika.

Thereafter, I boarded my plane, a DC 3, and took off on our flight from Nairobi airport to Entebbe in Uganda. On arrival at Entebbe, a government agent and representatives of the Prime Minister of Uganda, Dr. Milton Obote, received me. That was on 8th May, 1963. Then, by a special arrangement, I was at once sworn in by the acting Chief Justice, the Honourable Mr. Justice Sheridan, at the Government House, Entebbe, witnessed by some judges of the High Court of Uganda and the Principal Private Secretary of the Governor-General, first, as the Chief Justice of Uganda, and thereafter as the acting Governor-General of Uganda, the incumbent Governor-General, Sir. Walter Coutts, KCMG having already departed to the United Kingdom on a three months leave of absence. I was then informed that, on leaving for the United Kingdom, the Governor-General, Sir Walter Coutts, had arranged for me, while acting as Governor-General, to occupy the Governor-General's residence annexed in Kampala township instead of occupying the government house at Entebbe, then the capital of Uganda and that both his Principal Private Secretary, Mr. Steward, and his house-keeper should serve me during the period until his return to Uganda as Governor-General in resumption of his duty. I felt that it was most generous of the Governor-General to have made such an arrangement in my favour and in anticipation of my arrival.

Consequently, Mr. Steward, the Principal Private Secretary directed me to the Governor-General's residence annexed in Kampala township that I found to have been properly prepared for my occupation by the housekeeper and some other government officials. I was very delighted and thanked Heaven for my good fortune. As acting Governor-General, I was therefore quartered at the Governor-General's residence annexed in Kampala Township under the kind direction, advice and guidance of Mr. Steward, the Principal Private Secretary. There, the Prime Minister, Dr. Milton Obote, the Principal Agent of the Government, the Minister of Justice, Mrs. Grace Ibingira, the Attorney General, Mr. Godfrey Binaisa and other guests visited me. My first duty apart from visiting the court was to be taken round to visit some important places of interest in Entebbe, where the headquarters of the Army and the Royal Hotel, situated near the airport, were located and in Kampala, the main capital city in which there was established an interesting and important museum. I also visited Her Majesty's Prison and the army barracks. When I visited the court, I seized the opportunity to advise on necessary alterations to be made in the precincts of the High Court of Uganda which include the provision of a robing room for the Chief Justice, which room I found missing. On visiting the official residence of the Chief Justice of Uganda in the city of Kampala, I was told that the previous Chief Justice of Uganda was Sir Audley Mackisack who was, at one time during the colonial era, the Attorney General of Nigeria. I knew Sir Audley Mackisack personally.

Precisely one week after my arrival and having had a feel of the place by familiarising myself with Entebbe and Kampala as the principal towns of Uganda, I was accorded an official reception by the government of Uganda. It was a very warm and enthusiastic reception at which all the judges available in the country were present. The Law Society of Uganda, as the equivalent of the Bar Association, participated fully in the reception, which was given the widest possible publicity. It was a glorious and delightful occasion. Thereafter, I had to serve the country in a dual capacity. I had to officiate both as the acting Governor-General and as the substantive Chief Justice of Uganda. As Chief Justice, I used to sit in court to deal with cases. As already stated, for some time I combined the two functions but reverted to my substantive office of Chief Justice when the incumbent Governor-General returned to Uganda and resumed his office.

As is well known, Uganda became independent from Great Britain on 9th October, 1962 and was described as quasi-federal because of the belief then that, under the constitution, there was a distribution of functions between the four kingdoms of Uganda consisting of Buganda, Bunyoro, Ankole and Toro and the various district administrations scattered over the remaining parts of the country on the one hand and the central government of Uganda on the other. In my view, it was not appropriate to have described the 1962 constitution as quasi-federal. In any case, it was only the kingdom of Buganda, presided over by the Kabaka (then his Highness, Sir Edward Mutesa), with its Lukiko (Parliament) that had any distinctive functions from those of the central government especially in respect to revenue. However, since the constitution of 1962 was since abrogated and replaced by another one, namely, the Constitution of Uganda of 1967, speculation as to the structure of the system of political administration or dispensation under the constitution of 1962 would now be an unprofitable academic exercise.

Uganda, like any other African country to achieve independence under British rule, prides itself as belonging to that great current of the British system of administration of justice according to law, a tradition enshrined in and exemplified by the doctrine of the rule of law and the independence of the judiciary - the latter deriving its origin from the doctrine of the separation of powers propounded by Baron de Montesquieu in his "The Spirit of the Laws".

A fortnight before the return of the Governor-General from furlough, I moved house - I moved into and took possession of the residence of the Chief Justice at Kampala. It was a very interesting building situated on a hill. I also visited the Namiberembe Cathedral, the Anglican Church Cathedral, and met both the dean in charge of the cathedral and the Arch Bishop of Uganda - an expatriate. During the absence of the Governor-General, I found the Principal Private Secretary and the housekeeper very helpful to me. I was satisfied with their services and grew quite fond of them both. But as soon as the

Governor-General, Sir Walter Coutts, returned from furlough both the Principal Private Secretary and the house-keeper returned and resumed their relationships with him after bidding me farewell. Even so, our personal relationship was still maintained but in a low key. Both of them continued to render me assistance from time to time. For instance, before I could move into the official residence of the Chief Justice, the house-keeper on her initiative arranged with the government and successfully got the residence properly furnished with soft furnishings and a large quantity of assorted crockery and cutlery were supplied and the residence itself was properly decorated. I was more than satisfied with that performance especially having regard to the fact that, under the terms of my appointment, I was entitled to a residence with hard furnishings only.

Having reverted back fully to my office as Chief Justice of Uganda, I found the job most interesting and I therefore concentrated on developing and planning to establish an enduring system of the administration of justice throughout Uganda.

At the time of my arrival in Uganda to assume appointment as Chief Justice on May 8, 1963, there were altogether five judges and one acting judge of the High Court of Uganda, namely, the Honourable Mr. Justice K. G. Bennet, the most senior judge then on furlough, the Honourable Mr. Justice Sheridan, the Acting Chief Justice, the Honourable Mr. Justice Slade, the Honourable Mr. Justice D. Jeffreys-Jones, the Honourable Mr. Justice Keating, then posted to take charge of Jinja Station, and the Honourable Mr. Justice Baerleen, Ag Judge. As Chief Justice, I was also ex-officio chairman of the Judicial Service Commission, which commission had the responsibility for the recruitment and selection of qualified personnel for appointment as judges of the High Court of Uganda. I was also, at the time of arrival, by law an ex-officio member of the Court of Appeal for Eastern Africa. The registrar of the High Court was an expatriate - a solicitor from Scotland. In anticipation of my arrival from Nigeria and having learnt that I was an African from Nigeria, he had given notice of his retirement effective on my arrival, apparently as a precautionary measure. But on my assumption of office, he sought to retract the notice after having observed that I was given a very enthusiastic reception and that things might not be as bad as he had imagined. He made a representation to me to that effect and sought my permission to withdraw his notice of retirement but I declined to communicate the fact to government and advised him to stick to his previous decision since he did not originally wish to risk his fortune and his future, as I felt that he should have known at the time that life itself was a risk and that anyone unable to stick to his decision was untrustworthy.

Having commenced work in full force as Chief Justice, I considered it necessary to concentrate on the job and, after a careful study, I introduced reforms into the system of the administration of justice. There were then, in fact, two parallel systems of administration of justice, one system being known as the African Court system and the other the High Court system. Whenever there was a dispute between two or more Africans, such disputes were confined to the African Court since no Africans involved in civil disputes had any access into the Magistrate's or the High Court, the Magistrate's and the High Court being available only to expatriates, that is, Europeans and Asians - the latter being Indians and Pakistanis. On the other hand, any African involved in a criminal case must be tried either in the Magistrate's or the High Court. In civil matters, all appeals lay to the African Court of Appeal. All criminal trials in the High Court of heinous offences like murder were tried with the aid of assessors instead of a jury.

In the reform of the system introduced by me with the approval of the government, I abolished the parallelism. I considered that all the courts in the country were African Courts since Uganda was an African country. What was also remarkable under the old system was that in the whole judiciary there was not a single African judge even though there were some qualified African legal practitioners. There were only two African magistrates and, in the registry of the High Court, the majority of the executive staff was European and Asian. On the departure of the registrar, I decided at once to have the senior of the two African magistrates, by name Mr. Michael Kagwa, appointed Registrar of the High Court with an enhanced status and a new nomenclature. The title was changed to the Chief Registrar with direction that he should take full charge of the administration of the court. There was also a few African Ugandan clerical staff, some of which were on temporary appointments. The other African magistrate was Mr. Kulubya. He was a practicing magistrate who was assigned a court of his own. He was efficient.

As in Nigeria, the legal profession is fused in Uganda. Lawyers practice both as barrister and solicitor. This is also true of East Africa as a whole. Unlike Nigeria, however, there was, during the period under review, a predominance of solicitors duly qualified in India and Great Britain over barristers so that, instead of a Bar Association in each of the three East African countries of Uganda, Tanzania and

Kenya as in Nigeria, there was to be found an organisation of lawyers which bore the appellation of "The Law Society". As already indicated, in 1963 when I assumed office as Chief Justice, there were parallel systems of courts. There was the High Court of Judicature besides which there were other judicial institutions known as subordinate courts, which comprised Magistrate's Courts and African and Native Courts. Moreover, the High Court and the Magistrate's Courts were not open to Africans in civil cases or matters. Wide jurisdiction in such cases or matters as well as in criminal matters was conferred on African and Native Courts. For instance, African and Native Courts, on convicting an African, had such an extensive jurisdiction to be able to impose, in an appropriate case, a sentence of life imprisonment and to order the deportation of the convict! The jurisdiction of African and Native Courts was, however, ousted in criminal cases of homicide, rapes, robbery and certain other heinous crimes including sedition, treason and treasonable felony.

As also stated before, in civil cases or matters, Africans had no access to the High Court and the various Magistrate's Courts established all over the country, whatever might be the amount claimed by a prospective African litigant. Africans, on the other hand, had access to the High Court and the Magistrate's Courts in the event of the occurrence of a dispute between an African and either a European or an Asian (Indian or Pakistani) so that it would be correct to state that, up to 1966, the High Courts and the Magistrate's Courts were truly outposts of the British Empire to which only Europeans and Indians had access in civil cases or matters. Indeed, as a matter of historical interest, it may be observed that even though the High Court was established in the constitution of 1962, its jurisdiction was still derived from an Order-in-Council of 1902 until the enactment of the Judicature Act by the Parliament of Uganda at my request and insistence.

In continuation of the comparison and contrasting of the systems of practice and administration of justice in Nigeria and Uganda, I consider that it would be interesting to note that, whereas civil cases or matters are commenced or originated by means of a writ of summons in the High Court in Nigeria, to be followed after service and return by statements of claim and defence where necessary and so ordered by the court, in Uganda on the other hand, such cases or matters are commenced by means of a plaint containing all the necessary particulars and circumstances of the suit, which may be regarded as another name for a statement of claim. After the service of the plaint, the prospective defendant named on the plaint must enter appearance within a given period, say 21 days, and thereafter file his defence to the action. Also, in Uganda in civil actions where damages were involved, the amount of damages claimed was not required to be stated in the plaint. As a rule, costs were usually taxed before the registrar of the court who, in that respect and for that purpose, would act in the capacity of the master and from whose orders appeals would lie to a judge in chambers.

It was interesting to observe that, as regards criminal matters, a judge, assisted by two assessors, conducted all trials in the High Court of Uganda. At the conclusion of the evidence in the case, the judge would address the assessors as if in the manner of addressing members of a jury and thereafter call upon the assessors to express their opinions and make recommendations individually, as their findings and conclusions, to the presiding judge, who was not bound to accept such opinions or recommendations in his judgment. The use of assessors, it must be pointed out, in criminal trials in the High Courts was a relic of the Indian system of administration of justice and, until independence in 1962, the Indian civil code was applicable to Uganda. It was also brought to my knowledge that, in the old days, appeals from the courts of East Africa used to lie to the Court of Appeal in India. Judges in the courts in East Africa originally closely followed the Indian Penal Code Practice and Procedure as well as its Civil Practice and Procedure. This association no longer obtained. East African countries no longer looked towards India for inspiration. For instance, the Penal Code of Uganda was inspired by and was adapted from the Nigerian Criminal Code which itself originated from the Queensland Code. A Court of Appeal for Eastern Africa had since been established with headquarters at Nairobi in Kenya and from which there was a right of appeal in certain important cases to the Privy Council.

On my assumption of duty, I found the system of administration somewhat confusing. There was the element of competition between the High Court of the judicature of Uganda and the Magistrate's Courts administering the received common law of England. Also, there were the statutory laws enacted by the legislature, on the one hand, and the African and Native Courts, on the other. Records of proceedings in African and Native Courts were kept in the vernacular languages and would only be translated into the English language by a bureau of translators attached to the various African and Native Courts when the matter was brought to the High Court by way of appeal. That practice used to lead to considerable delays and it was not unknown that, in some cases, by the time the matter reached the High Court, the appellant concerned in a criminal case might have completely served his sentence.

Such a system was not only unsatisfactory but also cried aloud to the high heavens for rectification and reform. Happily, the cry was not in vain for, between the years 1964 and 1966, those parallel and competing systems of administration of justice were abrogated. The courts were integrated. African and Native Courts were abolished and replaced by Magistrate's courts, which were graded as Chief Magistrate's courts and the courts of Magistrates Grades (I) to (III). Accordingly, Chief Magistrates and Magistrates Grade I were professional lawyers but Magistrates Grades II and III were experienced laymen of repute and appreciable standard of education and had further to be trained in the Law School established for the purpose especially as regards practice and procedure. What were before known as Long·Benches with respect to African and Native Courts were weeded away and in their places Magistrate's Grades II and III were substituted. Counsel was granted the right of audience in all the courts of the land. All customary offences were by implication abolished having regard to the famous provision contained in Chapter III Article 15(8) of the 1962 Constitution of Uganda, the terms of which were as hereunder set forth:-

"15(8)   No person shall be tried for a criminal offence unless that offence is defined and the penalty therefore is prescribed in a written law:

Provided that nothing in this clause shall prevent a court of record from punishing any person for contempt of itself, notwithstanding that the act or omission constituting the contempt is not defined in a written law and the penalty, therefore, is not prescribed."

Those offences not abolished, like adultery, which was still a recognised criminal offence in Uganda, were declared offences by Acts of Parliament and incorporated in the Penal Code.

Up to the time of my departure from Uganda in 1969, the establishment of the judiciary, apart from the Chief Justice, comprised 14 Puisne Judges, of whom 4 were Africans, and a large number of magistrates. The judges and magistrates were appointed on the recommendation of the Judicial Service Commission of which I was the chairman. The Magisterial Bench is predominantly African. The post of the registrar of the High Court changed its status and title to that of the Chief Registrar who was also a highly qualified African barrister-at-law of considerable administrative experience under whom also served one Deputy Chief Registrar, an Assistant Chief Registrar, and several registrars all of whom were qualified barristers-at-law and indigenes of Uganda. As Chief Justice, I was also, ex-officio, the Chairman of the Council of Legal Education. There was also established a Ugandan Law School. A faculty of law empowered to award the LLB degree was also created in Makerere University College, Uganda. On the festive occasion of the inauguration of the faculty in the University, I had the rare privilege of delivering the inaugural public lecture on "The Role of Lawyers in Developing Countries" on the invitation jointly addressed to me by the head of the new faculty of law and the head of the department of social sciences. The lecture was well received and given the widest possible publicity.

By an Act of Parliament, as Chief Justice, I was the president of the Constitutional Court, vested with the duty of interpreting the constitution exclusively. The Constitutional Court by law was made up of the Chief Justice as president and two other judges selected by him. The court must be constituted and empanelled by the Chief Justice whenever there was to be heard any case involving the interpretation of the constitution. Prior to the promulgation of the 1967 Constitution, appeals from the Constitutional Court used to lie directly to the Privy Council in Great Britain. The Court of Appeal for Eastern Africa was by-passed. Under the 1967 Constitution, the right of appeal to the Privy Council or to any other court was abrogated. The decision of the Constitutional Court in all constitutional cases or matters was final. But the right of appeal in other cases or matters to the Court of Appeal for Eastern Africa was preserved.

It may, perhaps, be of interest to mention that during the period of my tenure of the office of Chief Justice, the Constitutional Court was called upon from time to time to, and did, deal with many controversial matters of considerable constitutional importance to the country. One such matter was the celebrated case of Uganda vs. The Commissioner of Prisons Ex parte Matovu 1966 EALR Part IV PP 514 to 546, details of which appear as an Appendix of this book. It is a matter of pride for me to state that up to the abolition of the right of appeal in 1967, all appeals from our decisions on constitutional matters, with the exception of one case, had always suffered the fate which they deserved, namely, that of dismissal. In the one case constituting the exception our decision was merely modified on a point that was not contested before us and the Privy Council said as much in its judgment.

CHAPTER TWENTY - THREE

I Embark On A World Tour In 1965

"People and their endless creative powers were the most precious asset that any nation could have".

During my sojourn in Uganda as Chief Justice, I received an invitation to attend the 3rd Commonwealth and Empire Law Conference, which was scheduled to be held in Sydney, Australia from July 1 to August 15, 1965. Prior to that, however, as a member of the Association of World Judges - an organisation within World Peace Through Law Conference, I had already committed myself by accepting an invitation to attend that conference to be held in Washington, United States of America in September, 1965.

Having accepted both invitations, I undertook to visit a few places in South Eastern Asia, that is, in the Far East, including Japan and pos-sibly parts of China, as I was anxious to see the ancient walls of China about which I had read a lot. I was also keen on seeing the Emperor of Japan. I therefore set off early in June 1965, with the prior approval of the Prime Minister of Uganda, then Dr. Milton Obote, on a world tour, so to speak. By special arrangement, my wife, Grace, was to join me in Washington, United States of America.

According to arrangements made, I boarded an Air-India plane from Entebbe to Karachi; thence to Lebanon but could not get to Japan as we learnt that the route was stormy. I was able to spend two weeks at Lebanon. Thereafter I returned to Bombay, the then most cosmopolitan city in India, where I spent a pleasant two days' stay in a first class hotel with Sir Samuel Quashie-Idun, then the President of the Court of Appeal for Eastern Africa. We both visited the University of Bombay. We noticed that the outskirts or suburban areas of Bombay were not dissimilar to the outskirts of the ancient city of Ibadan in Nigeria at the time.

At the appointed time we took off by the Trans Australia Airline and landed at Ceylon, now known as Sri-Lanka. Taking off from

Katunayake in Ceylon, we flew across the Pacific Ocean into Broome International Airport in North-Western Australia, the airport being known and regarded as the main entry point in Australia. There, on landing, we were examined for appropriate inoculation and it was discovered that Sir Samuel Quashie-Idun was not inoculated against yellow fever. The vaccination was done there and then by medical officials belonging to the Australian government after which Sir Samuel Quashie-Idun was permitted entry into Australia. Thereafter and on completion of the usual entry formalities, including immigration and customs disembarkation formalities, we flew therefrom all night to Sydney observing, in the process and throughout the flight, night-fires ablaze at various centres. Very often, the pilot of the plane drew our attention to them. I was particularly fascinated by the sight of the fires and could therefore not sleep a wink all night long. We eventually successfully landed at Sydney airport in the early morning hours. It was a pleasant flight.

As arranged, we were met at the airport and conveyed to our various hotels. Fortunately, both Sir Samuel Quashie-Idun and I were lodged in the Queen Elizabeth hotel - a very distinguished and glamorous hotel where we had the good fortune of enjoying orchestral music in the dining hall during our meals. The management of the hotel was of the highest standard and it went out of its way to satisfy all the lodgers, especially those of us who were visitors from other lands.

At the appointed time according to schedule, the Commonwealth Law Conference took off under the leadership of the Lord High Chancellor of the United Kingdom of Great Britain and Northern Ireland. There were present Chief Justices, judges and law officers and ministers of law from all parts of the Commonwealth of Nations. There were judges with ancient robes, some of which were embroidered with emeralds and mother of pearls. There were robes with trains and other quite plain scarlet robes.

Sir Samuel Quashie-Idun who, as President of the Court of Appeal for Eastern Africa with permanent residence in Nairobi, Kenya, Eastern Africa, was unhappily not in the mood to enjoy it all because in addition to the heavy dose of inoculation pumped into him at the port of entry, he was, he told me, also suffering from gout. None-theless, it is only right and proper to mention that at the opening session of the conference he, Sir Samuel Quashie-Idun, as president of the

Court of Appeal for Eastern Africa, was one of the speakers. He spoke in terms of the woolsack and of sheep being reared in Kenya, that country bearing an abundance of wool, just as the Honourable Sir Hugh Wooding of Trinidad and Tobago spoke in reminiscence of cricket of which sport he used to be a batsman.

While the conference was still in progress at Sydney, it was decided that all Chief Justices from countries of the Commonwealth should proceed to Canberra, the capital of Australia, there to continue their separate conference as to the system of administration of justice as the conference at Sydney tended to be dominated by politics, especially in connection with the abolition of the right of appeal to the Privy Council by independent Commonwealth countries and because of the preponderance of law ministers. When the Chief Justices of the countries of the Commonwealth met at Canberra, it was considered to be the first meeting of national Chief Justices of the countries of the Commonwealth. The meeting took place on Thursday and Friday, that is on the 2nd and 3rd September, 1965. It was recorded that the conference had met at the invitation of the Australian government in the A. L. G. McDonald Room in the R. G. Menzies Building, in the Australian National University, Acton, Canberra.

Present at the conference at Canberra were the following:-

1. The Right Honourable Lord Parker of Waddington, Lord Chief Justice of England.
2. The Honourable Mr. Justice Ronald Hartland, Judge of the Supreme Court of Canada representing the Chief Justice of Canada.
3. The Right Honourable Sir. Harold Barrowclough, KCMG, CB, DSO, MC, ED, Chief Justice of New Zealand.
4. The Honourable P. B. Gajendragadhar, Chief Justice of India.
5. Mr. Justice A. R. Cornelius, Chief Justice of Pakistan.
6. The Honourable M. C. Sansoni, Chief Justice of Ceylon.
7. The Right Honourable Sir Adetokunbo Ademola, KBE, CFR, Chief Justice of Nigeria.
8. Mr. Justice F. K. Apaloo, Judge of the Supreme Court of Ghana, representing the Chief Justice of Ghana.
9. The Honourable Dato' Sir James Thomson, PMN, PJK, Chief Justice of Malaysia.
10. The Honourable Sir Hugh Wooding, CBE, Chief Justice of Trinidad and Tobago.

11. The Honourable Mr. Justice C. O. E. Cole, OBE, Judge of the Supreme Court of Sierra Leone, representing the Chief Justice of Sierra Leone.

12. The Honourable Sir Udo Udoma, Chief Justice of Uganda.

13. The Honourable Mr. Justice A. Saidi, Judge of the High Court of Tanzania, representing the Chief Justice of Tanzania.

14. The Honourable Sir Frederick Southworth, Chief Justice of Malawi.

15. The Honourable Mr. Justice Wee Chong Jin, Chief Justice of Singapore.

16. The Honourable Sir Samuel Quashie-Idun, President of the Court of Appeal for Eastern Africa.

The Conference took place at Canberra in a calm atmosphere and continued *de die in diem* until its termination when every-one dispersed after a date had been agreed for the next National Chief Justices Conference of the countries of the Commonwealth coupled with the consensus that, in future, national Chief Justices conferences of the countries of the Commonwealth should be held at intervals of every two-and-a-half years instead of the five years interval applicable to the Commonwealth Law Conference; that such meetings be confidential; that formal agenda should be determined by the host country on each occasion; and that papers should be prepared for delivery and general discussion upon selected topics. It was also tentatively agreed that, if the decision to hold the conference at intervals was accepted generally, the next conference should be held at Trinidad in the Caribbean where Sir Hugh Wooding was Chief Justice, the conference to take place some time in 1968.

At Canberra it was interesting to discover that the city was artificially created, that the government of Australia built it practically on no man's land in Northern Australia and that there were also artificial watercourses including canals present. There were artificially forested areas and, quite importantly, there was established a war museum on the walls of which there were plans illustrative of Australians in combat uniforms participating in some world wars of the past. There was also already established the houses of Parliament for Australia while the High Court of Australia - the highest court of appeal and a strong court for all Australians - was still located at Taylor Square, Darlinghurst, New South Wales, Australia. The city of Canberra was well planned in that there was a separate area set aside for civil servants with its own shopping centre. On the whole, Canberra, as a city, was quite interesting and attractive. It was clean and well maintained.While still engaged in the National Chief Justices' Conference, I received an invitation by the Australian government to attend a seminar for the drawing up of a constitution for Papua and New Guinea, then known to the government of Australia as "the Territory". I most readily and willingly accepted the invitation and attended what turned out to be a Seminar *cum* Constituent Assembly organised under the auspices of the government of Australia at Papua and New Guinea, for the administration of which a Governor-General was put in charge.

At the Seminar *cum* Constituent Assembly, we were engaged in drawing up a constitution for the independence and governance of Papua and New Guinea so as to enable the Territory to be free from direct administration by the government of Australia. As the guest of the Australian government, I had the good fortune of lodging with the Governor-General of the Territory at Government House at the latter's request. The constitution that was recommended was based on the Westminster model or pattern. In the course of the proceedings at the Seminar *cum* Constituent Assembly, I had the delicious pleasure of listening to my judgment, which I delivered in the famous constitutional case of Chief Obafemi Awolowo and Others vs. the Minister of Internal Affairs of Nigeria, already reported elsewhere in this book, being severely criticised by Geoffrey Sawer, the foundation chair in law in the Research School of Social Sciences at the Australian National University, in his opening address. The Professor, apparently unaware that I was among his audience, attacked my judgment severely. The mistake made by the Professor, I believe, was that because, when I delivered the judgment, I was plainly "Mr. Justice" in the High Court of the federal territory of Lagos, Nigeria, whereas in Australia, having since been knighted by Her Majesty the Queen, I was then addressed as the Honourable Sir Udo Udoma, Chief Justice of Uganda, Eastern Africa, he apparently was not aware that I was the same person.

Naturally, after his captious address, I was up on my feet and, having obtained permission from the chairman, I immediately opened up by defending my judgment after having indicated that the judgment criticised by the Professor was delivered by me when I was an ordinary High Court Judge in Lagos, Nigeria. I stated with emphasis that if I had to deal with that same case a second time, even in my capacity as Chief Justice, I would give the same judgment, amidst the applause and admiration of the people there gathered. I was, subsequently, the recipient of many pleasantries and courtesies from many distinguished Australians and scholars.

On completion of my assignment after a fortnight, I boarded my plane back to Sydney and thence to the United States of America; en route we flew past and across the date-line and subsequently landed at Haiti. There I spent two days prowling round and viewing and admiring the famous island - an island which is quite famous in Afro-Caribbean history. In due course, we took off once again by air heading for California in the United States of America. We successfully made it to California in the evening of the same day. There, some of us who were fond of the open air slept in tents. I found California to be very attractive and we all dined in a restaurant quite comfortably amidst candle light. The next morning we took off by air again and were soon flying across the great Mississippi river of the United States of America. Unfortunately, we flew into the tail end of hurricane Bessy, which brushed our plane and shook us up several times. We were then warned by the pilot to belt up, which we did. We finally successfully landed beautifully in safety in Washington, DC.

To my astonishment, I observed in Washington, DC that most of the storey buildings were all of the same height - none was taller than Lincoln's memorial! I was given to understand that the law of the United States' Congress regulated that. There was no skyscraper to be seen. I was very pleased at last to be joined by my wife, Grace, in Washington, DC. By the generosity of the World Peace Through Law Conference, we were both lodged in a private home as the guests of Mr. and Mrs. Friedman - Mr. Friedman being himself, I believe, a member of the World Peace Through Law Conference as an attorney employed by the American government. On the other hand, Mrs. Friedman was a magistrate in a juvenile court. During the conference, by the generosity again this time of our host and hostess, we were conveyed in their car to and from the conference and back to our residence. Incidentally, one day in the course of our conversation, Mr. Friedman, with pride informed me that he was a New Yorker and only lived in Washington because he was a government lawyer, which was quite interesting.

On the appointed day and at the appointed time, more precisely sometime in September 1965, I attended the World Peace

Through Law Conference organised by the World Peace Through Law Centre whose temporary address was at 400 Hill Buildings, Washington D. C. 2006 and whose permanent address was usually given as 75 Rue de Lyon, 1203 Geneva, Suisse. The conference was already in progress with Mr. Charles S. Rhyne, its founding President, presiding. Prior to that, however, there had taken place, in Washington D. C. too, the conference of the Association of World Judges which was presided over by the Honourable the Chief Justice of the Supreme Court of the United States of America, then Justice Earl Warren.

At the conference of World Peace Through Law, there were present several Chief Justices from several countries of the world including the Chief Justice of Nigeria, the Honourable Sir Adetokunbo Ademola, PC and Sir Samuel Quashie-Idun, President of the Court of Appeal for Eastern Africa. There were also many judges and practicing lawyers from several countries and among the lawyers present there was the then Attorney-General of Nigeria, Dr. T. O. Elias, PhD. The President of the United States of America, Mr. John Kennedy, having been assassinated at Dallas, Mr. Lyndon Johnson, as acting President, addressed the conference. He addressed the conference encased in a bulletproof glass cubicle to the astonishment of everyone.

At the close of the conference after one week, my wife, Grace, and I decided to go on sight seeing of part of North-Eastern America as tourists. In the execution of our decision, we were driven in an American limousine by road to the city of New York. On our way to New York we had to stop at every town and every hamlet whenever there was a tourist attraction; and as we approached the city of New York we were driven through an underground tunnel where we had to pay toll before being allowed to pass through to the famous city of New York. There in the city of New York we were greeted by a large number of skyscrapers.

I should have mentioned before that while we were in Washington D. C. during the conference, we were fortunate to run into Dr. and Mrs. Clement Nyong Isong of Nigeria who entertained us to lunch in their well furnished home in Washington D. C. It may be remembered that, at the inception of the Central Bank of Nigeria, Dr. Isong, who was then a well-known economist, was its first secretary, serving under an expatriate economist seconded to Nigeria from the Bank of England specifically for setting up the Nigerian Central Bank. The

Central Bank of Nigeria having been successfully established, Dr. Clement Nyong Isong was posted to the International Monetary Fund in Washington D. C., United States of America as an economist to serve at the World Bank. In Washington D. C., he and his wife appeared very happy and contented.

Now back to New York. During our sojourn in New York, apart from making time to attend shows in different Broadway theatres depending on what was being shown, we also attended the United Nations Assembly where, by a stroke of good fortune, we were able to witness the swearing in of a new President of the United Nations Assembly by the incumbent President and a Ghanaian member, Mr. Alex Quason-Sackey, himself the nineteenth (19th) President of the United Nations Assembly. Ghana had been granted independence under the leadership of Dr. Kwame Nkrumah as President since 1957 by the British Imperial government. At the precincts of the United Nations Assembly we were also lucky to meet Chief Simeon Adebo, a Nigerian who was employed there as a world public servant. He was graciously pleased to entertain us to lunch and to explain to us some of the intricate facets and procedures of the United Nations Assembly. We also visited the Statue of Liberty and the Empire State Building - being the tallest skyscraper in New York at the time.

After our workmanlike tour of America, we decided that it was time to return to Uganda - the pearl of Africa. We flew from Kennedy airport across the Atlantic Ocean to Heathrow airport in London. We spent the night in a hotel in London - indeed the hotel was no other than the famous St. Ermines hotel, the resort of a large number of members of the Conservative Party of Great Britain. Having retired to bed early, I woke up at midnight feeling like I had an attack of what I suspected was asphyxia in that, in waking up, I found it extremely difficult to breathe. I felt suffocated. I was panting for air just like the weaverbird panting for the water brook. With the assistance of my wife, we were able to open one of the windows of the room which was on the third floor of the hotel just to let in some fresh air, as it was already winter, being then November 1965. I sat on a chair by the opened window and took in fresh air with some difficulty. I could not understand what had come over me. At last, having sat there for a long time I suddenly felt like sleeping again. I then managed to retire to bed again and fell asleep only to wake up in the early hours of the morning refreshed. I felt as fit as a fiddle and ready for our flight from London to Entebbe in Uganda.

After breakfast at the hotel, we were driven by car to Heathrow airport, London where we boarded our plane and soon were airborne en route to Entebbe. We successfully landed at Entebbe airport towards the evening of that day. This was in November 1965 and it was also time for me to go home to Nigeria on furlough. Soon after arrival in Kampala, Uganda, arrangements were taken on hand preparatory to my leaving for home leave. By special arrangement, my wife, Grace, had to precede me as she had to travel by train from Uganda to Mombassa in Kenya, Eastern Africa there to board a mail boat to Nigeria via the Suez Canal in Egypt and Cadiz in Spain conveying my heavy luggage and of course also travelling accompanied by four of our children namely, Masters Udoma Udo Udoma, Ebong Udo Udoma, Edem Udo Udoma and Ekpo Udo Udoma. She left Uganda early in December 1965.

I remained alone in Uganda throughout the greater part of December 1965. Happily for me, I did not have any more attack of the kind of suffocation I had experienced in London during the night we spent there. I therefore thoughtfully concluded that what happened in London might have been a freak occurrence. I then began to prepare to leave for Nigeria on furlough. On or about 15 December 1965, with the prior approval of the Prime Minister of Uganda, Dr. A. Milton Obote, I flew from Entebbe airport by an American Airline plane direct to Nigeria. We successfully landed at Ikeja airport, Lagos, Nigeria after an uneventful flight that same evening. I felt most refreshed to be back in Nigeria after about two years of absence. On arrival, the Prime Minister of Nigeria, Alhaji the Honourable Sir Tafawa Balewa, was delighted to see me and, at my request, arranged for me to be accommodated in a VIP flat in Ikoyi, Lagos. I had to wait in Lagos for the arrival of my wife, Grace, and our four children by sea. Eventually she and the children arrived. I went to Apapa harbour to receive them and we returned happily to my flat at Ikoyi, Lagos.

Unhappily, during our short stay in Lagos, I had another attack of the feeling of being suffocated in the night. That was about 18 December 1965. As we retired to bed that night, as soon as all the doors and windows of my bedroom were shut, I found it extremely difficult to breathe. I was panting for air again. I found it impossible to remain indoors. I was compelled to leave my wife in bed and to come out into fresh air in the compound. I had to remain outside taking in fresh air for a long time. I was only able to go back to bed during the early hours of the morning when I managed somehow to sleep for a few hours. In the morning I felt disparately worried and therefore had to contact Dr. Moses Majekodunmi who was then Minister of Health of cabinet rank in the federal government of Nigeria, sited in the federal territory of Lagos. In response to my request, the Minister of Health, who was also a personal friend, instructed a government psychiatrist to attend to my needs. The psychiatrist, an American, after having questioned and examined me, explained that my condition was psychological and that it was brought about by my having to attend several conferences without a break. He therefore prescribed for me a drug called "Librium" and directed that I should also be taking plenty of water from time to time. I thereupon acquired a quantity of the drug and began to treat myself as directed. There was an immediate improvement, I thought, and I began also to prepare to leave for my hometown, Ikot Abasi, preparatory to the celebration of the feast of Christmas with my entire family.

As soon as I felt I could travel without any hazards as to my health, my immediate family and I took to the road by car travelling from Lagos to Ikot Abasi township. We were able to make it to Ikot Abasi township in the evening of the same day. As soon as I was able to step into my permanent residence, christened by me as "MFUT ITIAT ENIN" which by interpretation means "the shelter of the elephant rock", I breathed a sigh of relief. I felt I was safe among my people. By the grace of God, we were able to celebrate the feast of Christmas, which is a family feast, in the traditional manner with the singing of carols. In addition, I had the pleasurable duty of entertaining some members of my extended family after two years of absence in the service of Africa in Uganda, Eastern Africa as Chief Justice. It was a happy moment for me. There were then all my children namely, Ayanti, Inam, Udoma, Ebong, Edem and Ekpo, the youngest of them then. I will write more about my family in Chapter 25.

Then, early in January 1966, in response to an invitation by the Honourable Sir Louis N. Mbanefo, a personal and intimate friend, who was then the Chief Justice of the Eastern Region of Nigeria, I visited Enugu, then capital of the Eastern Region. I was to spend the weekend with him and his wife, Lady Elizabeth Mbanefo, and his children. As I sat with the Honourable Sir Louis and Lady Mbanefo in their exquisitely furnished parlour watching the television during the second night of my stay at Enugu, there was an announcement to the effect that there was to take place in Lagos, Nigeria a conference of the Prime Ministers of the Commonwealth under the leadership of Mr. Harold Wilson, then Prime Minister of Great Britain and Northern Ireland for the purpose of giving consideration to the unilateral declaration of independence by Southern Rhodesia under the leadership of her Prime Minister, Mr. Ian Smith, and that delegates for the conference had begun arriving in Lagos. Shortly after the announcement, still watching the television, I noticed that among the passengers disembarking from a plane from Eastern Africa at Ikeja, Lagos was Dr. A. Milton Obote, Prime Minister of Uganda, arriving for the purpose of participating in the Commonwealth Prime Ministers' Conference; and it was also so announced. I was completely taken aback because, before I left Uganda for home leave in December, 1965, on enquiry, Dr. A. Milton Obote, Prime Minister of Uganda had informed me that he was not likely to attend the conference but that instead he would send his Foreign Minister, Mr. Sam Udaka, to represent the government of Uganda. I was rather astonished and confused. Here was I at Enugu far away from Ikot Abasi township, my home town, where I had my permanent residence and where the whole of my family was waiting and expecting me to join them soon.

In the circumstance, I had no alternative but to bow to the exigencies of the moment. After a discussion with the Honourable Sir Louis N. Mbanefo, I decided that I must leave for Lagos by car the next morning, being Monday, so as to contact the Prime Minister of Uganda. It was a hurried move. The next morning, my driver and I left for Lagos after breakfast, and driving all day, arrived in Lagos in the evening. Fortunately I was able to reoccupy the flat at Ikoyi, Lagos that I had vacated in December 1965. The following morning I was able to contact the Prime Minister of Nigeria, who generously offered me his former residence at Marina, Lagos for the purpose of organising a hurried dinner party in honour of the Prime Minister of Uganda. I thanked him most profusely.

I immediately, thereafter, met the Prime Minister of Uganda, Dr. A. Milton Obote, and settled with him a date for the dinner; we both agreed that the dinner should take place on the night of 14 January 1966. I had to rush around to be able to personally contact the Nigerian invitees to the dinner. There was no time for any written invitation. Fortunately, in this connection, I was ably assisted by two great friends of mine, namely, the Honourable Mr. Justice Charles Dadi Onyeama, then Justice of the Supreme Court, Nigeria and the Honourable Mr. Jacob C. Obande, then Minister of Defence in the federal government of Nigeria. With the help of my two trusted friends, I was able to make contact with a good crop of distinguished Nigerians, all resident in Lagos, to attend the dinner party in honour of the Prime Minister of Uganda, Eastern Africa, Dr. A. Milton Obote. Unfortunately, at the last minute, the Prime Minister of Nigeria, the Honourable Alhaji Sir Tafawa Balewa, informed me that he would not be able to attend. The dinner took place in the evening of the day the Commonwealth Prime Ministers' Conference ended. Mr. Harold Wilson, Labour Party Prime Minister of Great Britain and Northern Ireland, departed from Nigeria the same day. I was happy to be successfully able to have entertained the Prime Minister of Uganda and his entourage that night. The dinner was over by midnight and thereafter, after exchange of pleasantries, the Prime Minister of Uganda's entourage boarded their belongings to the then Ethiopian Airline at Ikeja, Lagos airport and departed for Uganda leaving the Prime Minister of Uganda, Dr. A. Milton Obote, to join them later.

I was then seen home to my flat at Ikoyi, Lagos by the Honourable Mr. Justice Charles Dadi Onyeama of the Supreme Court of Nigeria. At my flat, the Honourable Mr. Justice Charles Dadi Onyeama bade me goodnight and departed to his residence. I then retired to bed happy in the knowledge that I had successfully prosecuted my ambition of playing host to Dr. A. Milton Obote, Prime Minister of Uganda, during his brief visit to Nigeria. Then at about 4 a. m. on the 15 January 1966, I noticed that my air conditioner had ceased to function and on looking out of the window of my flat I observed also that the streetlights had been extinguished. Shortly thereafter, I heard a report like an explosion from the direction of Ikoyi hotel which was opposite my flat in Ikoyi, Lagos. I decided to remain in bed and subsequently I was overtaken by sleep. I was still in bed at about 10 a. m. when I heard a knock at the outer door of my flat. Following upon the knock, there was a voice calling out my name. I recognised the voice to be that of the Honourable Mr. Justice Charles Dadi Onyeama, so I thereupon got out of bed and, having put on my morning gown, I opened the door and admitted the Honourable Mr. Justice Charles Dadi Onyeama into my flat.

With great excitement, the Honourable Mr. Justice Onyeama informed me that Nigeria was in great trouble and that the army, under the leadership of Major Nzeogu, assisted by Major Ifeajuna, had successfully staged a coup d'état against the Honourable Alhaji Tafawa

Balewa's government of Nigeria; that the Sardauna of Sokoto, the late Alhaji Sir Ahmadu Bello, the Premier of the Northern Region of Nigeria, and a large number of senior military officers of Northern origin had been killed; that Chief S. L. Akintola, Premier of the Western Region of Nigeria had also been murdered by military officers; and that what was worse, the Prime Minister of Nigeria, Alhaji Tafawa Balewa was missing having been, it was alleged, kidnapped by military officers. I was noticeably alarmed. I could not understand why Nigerian army officers should have staged a *coup d'état* against the government of Nigeria immediately after the conference of the Prime Ministers of the Commonwealth ended, although everyone was aware of the fact that Nigeria was then under a cloud. There was heavy tension in the country following upon law and order having broken down in the Western region of Nigeria that had resulted in the declaration of a state of emergency and the imposition of emergency laws in the region.

Thereupon, I having got dressed, both the Honourable Mr. Justice Onyeama and I decided to go out into the city of Lagos to do some scouting so as to be able to ascertain the reaction of the people of Lagos. Our first port of call was Ikoyi hotel in order to enquire into the cause of the explosion I had heard early in the morning and also to obtain my bill for their services in having catered for the dinner given by me in honour of the Prime Minister of Uganda. Having gained entry into the hotel some members of the staff appeared reluctant to communicate with us, giving the impression that they were being watched. I then shouted that I wanted to see the general manager, who, on hearing my voice, came out from his office to receive us.

The manager then took us to his office and, in confidence, explained to us how a colonel in the Nigerian Army, who was supposed to be the personal bodyguard of Chief S. L. Akintola, the Premier of the Western region of Nigeria at Ibadan, and had visited Lagos in connection with some army celebrations, was killed and his body dragged down the staircase in the early morning hours, while lodging in one of the rooms of the hotel. The perpetrators were members of the Nigerian army concerned with staging the coup d'état. He informed us that the incident had so instilled fear into members of the staff of the hotel that they were frightened to speak to anyone about the event as some soldiers had been molesting their lives since the morning. He then assured me that, as soon as my bill was ready, it would be sent to me.

We then left the hotel and went into Tinubu Square and there were informed that Chief Festus Okotie-Eboh, Minister of Finance in the cabinet, was also killed. There we also noticed that some people were rejoicing over the army take over from what they described as a corrupt government. We, thereupon, returned to Ikoyi, Lagos to the residence of the Honourable Mr. Justice Charles Dadi Onyeama and there, after a chat, I left for my flat. I remained in my flat throughout the day. Then it occurred to me to enquire as to the fate of the Prime Minister of Uganda, Dr. A. Milton Obote, my special guest at the dinner party. Later, I was assured that he had, early in the morning, been successfully escorted by an armed guard from the Federal Palace hotel, where he had been accommodated during the conference, to the Ikeja airport, Lagos where he emplaned for Entebbe airport in Uganda as prearranged. I received the information with considerable relief. I then met with some friends who were discussing the merits and demerits of the coup d'état. Some of the people were sorrow stricken while others were prejudicially rejoicing. I felt it was a sad day for Nigeria as an independent African country of great prominence that was on the eve of independence expected to be one of the leading countries in the continent of Africa.

Towards the evening, I was visited by Mr. J. C. Obande, the Minister of Defence in the federal government, who, with my permission, was able to telephone Kaduna for confirmation of the events that had occurred in the North. Thereafter, he confirmed that the Premier of the Northern region of Nigeria and the most senior army officers of Northern origin had been murdered. He then informed me that General Aguiyi-Ironsi, Officer Commanding Nigerian Army had successfully intervened to stop more killings in the army and had agreed to take over power from the cabinet in the absence of the Prime Minister of Nigeria who was believed to have been kidnapped, and that the ceremony for the take over had already been arranged to take place within a couple of days so as to stop any further blood shed and so as to enable him to maintain peace and order.

Subsequently as arranged, the ceremony of handing over power took place. In the absence of the President of Nigeria, Commander-in-Chief of the Armed Forces of Nigeria, Dr. Nnamdi Azikiwe, who was reportedly at the Caribbean enjoying sea breeze as a means of restoring his sagging health, the ceremony of handing over power had to be performed by Dr. Nwafor Orizu, President of the Senate and acting President of Nigeria standing in for the President. On taking over power with the consent of the remnant of the cabinet, the Federal Government of Nigeria was dissolved and the officer commanding the Nigerian Army, General Johnson Aguiyi-Ironsi was entrusted with the power and duty of dealing with the coup d'état plotters and of maintaining law and order. Thereafter, having taken over power as the new Head of State and Commander-in-Chief of the Armed Forces of Nigeria, General Johnson Aguiyi-Ironsi made his maiden broadcast to the nation and the world, promising among other things to honour all international agreements between Nigeria and other countries of the world. It was an impressive broadcast.

After the broadcast, I felt it was time to return home to join my family at Ikot Abasi. I was confident that peace had been restored in Nigeria. I therefore left Lagos in my car with my driver for Ikot Abasi, arriving there in safety as usual in the evening. The journey was uneventful. It was a happy reunion for me and my family, which was all the time kept informed of my movement.

Towards the end of January 1966 I decided that it was time for me to get ready to return to Uganda to resume work as Chief Justice since my period of leave had expired. I therefore once more visited Lagos, Nigeria, and while there I sought and obtained permission to pay my respects to the Head of State, General Johnson Aguiyi-Ironsi at the State House, Marina as we were both old friends. In the course of our conversation, I sought from him permission to return to Uganda to resume duty as Chief Justice since my period of leave had expired. He appeared at first most reluctant to grant me such permission explaining that, in the awkward circumstances which Nigeria had found itself, it would be considered unreasonable and unwise for a person of my stamp and status to be allowed to return to Uganda as Chief Justice since, at that point in time, all Nigerians of distinction and experience were required to remain in Nigeria to help in restoring peace. As a result of pressure from me and reminding him of his solemn promise made in his maiden broadcast to honour all international agreements entered into between Nigeria and foreign countries, he most reluctantly granted me permission to return to Uganda, subject to the condition that, while in Uganda, as soon as I received an order from him, I was unfailingly to return to Nigeria, as he felt that Nigeria stood more in need of my services than any foreign country. I accepted the condition without demur since, in any event, I had only three more years to serve the government and people of Uganda according to the terms of my assignment.

Accordingly, towards the end of February 1966 after having settled those of our children who had to school in Nigeria, my wife, Grace and I and three of our children in the persons of Ebong, Edem and Ekpo flew by air back to Uganda. On arrival, I found, to my astonishment, that Uganda was itself already on the boil. Five cabinet ministers were already under detention pending investigation and possible deportation following upon allegation of conspiracy against the government. That incident took place on 22 February 1966. As part of the event, the Prime Minister of Uganda also seized all powers of government and thereupon took upon himself to remove both the President and the Vice-President of Uganda from their respective offices contrary to the provisions of the constitution of Uganda on the ground that the President, Sir Edward Mutesa, who was until then the Supreme Head and Commander-in-Chief of the Armed Forces of Uganda, was plotting to overthrow the government of Uganda with the aid of foreign troops. The same day, the Prime Minister suspended the 1962 Constitution of Uganda. There then followed a series of events from time to time and in quick succession culminating in the adoption of a new constitution on April 15, 1966 whereby the Prime Minister of Uganda, by the operation of law, automatically became the President of Uganda and Commander-in-Chief of the Armed Forces of Uganda and the former President and the Kabaka of Buganda Kingdom, Sir Edward Mutesa, fled the country and was compelled by the situation to seek and obtain asylum in the United Kingdom.

While in Uganda on my return from home leave, I once more had an attack of asphyxia, that is to say, the feeling of suffocation as if I was short of breath at night. The following morning, I had to consult a psychiatrist at the specialist hospital in Uganda. Once more, after a thorough examination, he confirmed the findings of the psychiatrist who had treated me in Lagos but instead of "Librium" he prescribed for me "Valium", usually produced in the form of tablets, to be taken by me from time to time with plenty of fluid. He then suggested that it was his belief that the psychiatrist who treated me in Lagos might have been an American because, in his view, only Americans were fond of Librium, and that, under the British system of practice, Valium was preferred to Librium. I at once changed over from Librium to Valium and felt relieved from my traumatic experience. I continued in the treatment of myself with Valium from time to time. It took many years before I could feel that the experience might not occur again.

With my family in Uganda before my daughter was born

Introducing guests to Dr. Milton Obote, President of Uganda, at my
reception for him in Lagos, Nigeria in December 1966

Standing with Dr. Moses Majekodunmi, the guest-of-honour and Hon. Abdul
Razak at the reception for Dr. Milton Obote

Receiving the Uganda government's farewell gift to me from Attorney General,
Hon. Lameck Ubowa

Receiving the Uganda Law Society's gift to me from its President, Mr Akena Adoko, at my farewell party given by the Society

Sitting with Mr. Akena Adoko and His Excellency, Mr. M. J. Etuk, Nigeria's High Commissioner to Uganda at the farewell party

On a courtesy visit to General Yakubu Gowon, Military Head of State of Nigeria, at Dodan Barracks on my return to Nigeria in 1969

At reception for Grace and me by the communities of Ikot Abasi province on our return from Uganda

Wearing my gown, with Professor Ishaya Audu (the V.C.) looking on, before receiving my A. B. U. honorary LLD

As Justice of the Supreme Court

Receiving a gift at festivities commemorating my appointment as Vice President of the Methodist Church of Nigeria

Supreme Court Justices meet with the Supreme Military Council in 1972

My daughter, Enoabasi Iquo Udoma, cutting her birthday cake at age 3

With General Yakubu Gowon at my installation as Chancellor, Ahmadu Bello University, Zaria (A. B. U.) on December 1, 1972

As Chancellor standing with the Acting Registrar (far left), Chief J. C. Obande and another Council member outside the A.B.U. Council Chambers

With my wife, Grace, my son, Udoma, my daughter, Eno, Chief Dick Usen (far right) and others after convocation at A.B.U. in 1972

CHAPTER TWENTY-FOUR

I Leave Uganda Finally And Return To Nigeria

"We live our lives under the twin categories of time and space and when the two come into conflict we get the great moment". – John Bucham in "A Book of Escapes and Hurried Journeys".

Continuing with the events in Uganda, on February 2, 1967, the validity of the constitution of Uganda adopted on April 15, 1966 was put to the test in the famous and historic case of <u>Uganda vs. The Commissioner of Prisons Ex parte Matovu</u> (see Appendix C). And as already stated, the Constitutional Court of Uganda affirmed the validity of the new constitution and the affirmation was upheld and approved by the Privy Council in the United Kingdom.

In spite of the tremendous tension in which Uganda appeared to have been enveloped in consequence of the enormous and abrupt changes that had occurred, most people seemed to have gone about their normal businesses unperturbed. That, in effect, proved that the government of Uganda, under the new president, had a firm grip over the country and had everything under its full control. There appeared to have been no competing forces, at least on the surface. In the circumstances, I had felt free to accept an invitation from Mr. Charles S. Rhyne, President of the World Peace Through Law Centre to attend the World Peace Through Law Conference scheduled to take place in Geneva, Switzerland from 9 to 14 July 1967 as a full member of the World Peace Through Law Conference.

Before leaving for Geneva, Switzerland, on reflection, I felt that the news reaching me from Nigeria left a lot to be desired. There was the story of the assassination of the Head of State and Commander-in-Chief of the Armed Forces of Nigeria, General Johnson Aguiyi-Ironsi in a counter coup d'état, and the latter having been replaced by Colonel Yakubu Gowon, the most senior surviving army officer of Northern origin in the Armed Forces of Nigeria. Colonel Yakubu Gowon, having assumed power, was engaged in arranging a national constitutional conference, which resulted in Colonel Odumegwu Ojukwu thr-eatening secession from Nigeria of the Eastern region under the assumed name of Biafra. All along, I was being kept regularly informed of developments in Nigeria. Emissaries sent from time to time by Colonel Ojukwu to contact me in Uganda were constantly feeding me with information.

The first set of emissaries from Colonel Ojukwu in Enugu, Eastern Nigeria to meet me for consultation was led by Dr. Chike Obi, the founder and leader of the Dynamic Party - a political party in Nigeria. Dr. Chike Obi, an indigenous Eastern Nigerian, used to be a lecturer in the University of Ibadan, was later promoted Professor of Mathematics and then Dean, School of Mathematics and Physical Sciences of the University of Lagos. Professor Chike Obi used to boast to me that he was going to be the first dictator of Nigeria. However, on the occasion of their visit to me in Uganda, he, in particular, appeared full of praises for Colonel Ojukwu as an outstanding leader in the Eastern region of Nigeria who had suddenly emerged as the redeemer of the region having regard to the proposal to establish an entirely new country to be known as Biafra, which should remain separate and independent of the rest of Nigeria. The emissaries gave me to understand that they were sent to consult me on the proposal as it had become impossible for the Eastern region to continue to form an integral part of Nigeria. My opinion was also sought as to the possibility of establishing Nigeria as a confederation instead of a federation as existed then and as to whether it would be advantageous to reconstruct Nigeria as countries sharing common services as then existed in Eastern Africa as Kenya, Tanzania and Uganda were said to be then sharing common services.

In vain did I try to wriggle out of discussing the proposals raised by the emissaries, even though I was careful to point out to them that, as I was no longer in politics but a Chief Justice presiding over disputes in court, it would be incompatible with my office for me to indulge in political discussions. In the end, I had to yield by explaining that I could only consider the matter as purely constitutional issues since they insisted that, for Eastern Nigerians, it was a matter of survival. I then quickly dismissed, summarily firstly, the issue of common services as obtained in Eastern Africa by pointing out that the concept might appear beautiful on paper but in practice it was not a successful experiment even though the three countries of Kenya, Tanzania and Uganda that operated the concept were friendly, independent sovereign states. And secondly, on the issue of confederation, I observed that that was where the United States of America began and had to end up as a federation after the civil war during which President Abraham Lincoln was reported to have declared that you could not have a country the inhabitants of which were half free and half slaves. I then also pointed out with emphasis that Nigeria could not go back to being a confederation after having been established a federation, and further that, in my view, the solution to Nigeria's problem would appear to lie in the creation of states throughout the country for which we had campaigned unsuccessfully when I was in politics.

As a compliment to Professor Chike Obi, I observed that I was rather startled to note that he was full of praises for Colonel Odumegwu Ojukwu for championing the secession of the Eastern Region of Nigeria from Nigeria and constituting itself a brand new country under the nomenclature of Biafra. I observed that if the secession should become successful then it would appear that Professor Chike Obi had abandoned his ambition of becoming the first civilian dictator of Nigeria as a united country. As soon as I concluded my observation, Professor Chike Obi reacted by stating that he had in no way abandoned his ambition. That remark brought immediate reaction from his companions, who insisted that, as emissaries, they ought to stick to their mission and had to perform the same faithfully without any equivocation and that they had not come to Uganda to discuss Professor Chike Obi's ambition, whatever that was.

Then in March 1967, I was again honoured by the visit of emissaries purported to have been despatched to Uganda in East Africa by the Military Governor of the Eastern Region. The emissaries came this time under the leadership of Mr. (later Chief) E. U. Okon. It was then unfolded to me I that a firm decision had been taken that Biafra be established in the Eastern Region, that I be prevailed upon to accept that a brand new country free from the Federation of Nigeria was preferable to the mere creation of state, with which I was regarded as obsessed, and that the plan to declare Biafra was being pursued in collaboration with the Western Region who would declare the "Oduduwa" country simultaneously.

In the course of the discussion which ensued, I was assured that Chief Obafemi Awolowo was the exponent of the establishment of "Oduduwa" country, that since his release from prison he had been working in cooperation with the Military Governor of the Eastern Region and had been recruiting Yoruba soldiers from the Western Region and sending them to Enugu, Eastern Region to be trained there under the supervision of the Military Governor of the Eastern Region, and that what was required of me was to resign from my office of Chief Justice of Uganda and return home to the Eastern Region before it was too late.

I, in all sincerity, was grateful that I was still being remembered in the Eastern Region and expressed my gratitude to the Military Governor of the region. I observed that the fact that the creation of "Oduduwa" country was then being pursued in the Western Region had introduced a new dimension into the political concept of the struggle for survival in the Federation of Nigeria, but that I was doubtful as to the ability of Chief Obafemi Awolowo to carry the Western Region with him in his quest for new pastures. It was necessary to study carefully the popularity of the idea of "Oduduwa" country and also to discover what men of substance supported the proposal because most people in the Western Region were most conservative in their outlook.

When I drew the attention of the emissaries to the problems of resources, and of military personnel available to the Eastern Region in relation to paucity, the emissaries assured me that the Military Governor of the Eastern Region had received assurances from France that, provided the Military Governor could guarantee to secure for France only the monopoly control of the mineral oils in the region, France would undertake to prevail upon Francophone African countries and colonies to recognise in time the right of Biafra to exist as an *independent* country unmolested by Nigeria. The emissaries maintained that it would be quick, quick business for no European power would like to grant recognition to Biafra except to follow in the footsteps of African countries. If need be, French troops might fight on the side of Biafra as mercenaries.

Thus assured by France, the Military Governor of the Eastern Region and his advisers, despite the enormity of the problems to be encountered should the proposal to establish Biafra become a reality, feverishly and fanatically engaged themselves in a frantic preparation to bring it about. It was a struggle for survival.

Later, I received from Colonel Yakubu Gowon through Dr. Okoi Arikpo, who was then External Affairs Minister in Colonel Yakubu Gowon's newly constituted federal cabinet, an enquiry as to whether as a leader of the COR State Movement, I would insist that the whole area embracing Calabar, Ogoja and Rivers provinces (COR for short) should be carved out as a new state in the Eastern Region of Nigeria, as Colonel Yakubu Gowon was determined to create states in all regions of Nigeria. In reply, I advised that it had secretly been agreed by all supporters of the COR State Movement that, when states were to be created, the Rivers province should be created a separate state by itself while Calabar and the four divisions of Ogoja, Obudu, Obubra and Ikom in Ogoja province should also be together created a separate state - in other words, that there should be two separate states to be created out of the COR State area. Thereafter, to my delight, I received information from home in Nigeria that the Rivers province had been created a separate state by the name of Rivers state while Calabar province together with the four divisions of Ogoja, Obudu, Obubra and Ikom in Ogoja province had also by common consent of the people been created a separate state under the name of South Eastern state to the joy of the people. All together, Colonel Gowon created 12 states throughout Nigeria on 27ᵗʰ March 1967. Thus, Nigeria became a federation of states, no longer a federation of regions. The creation of states pre-empted the declaration of Biafra by Colonel Odumegwu Ojukwu.

The last emissaries from Enugu, Eastern Region of Nigeria who visited me in Uganda were under the leadership of a distinguished Nigerian in the person of the Honourable Sir Louis N. Mbanefo, then Chief Justice of the Eastern region of Nigeria and comprised of Mr. Christopher C. Mojekwu, Mr. E. U. Okon and Mr. B. C. Okwu. I successfully arranged hotel accommodation for the three gentlemen already named while I arranged to accommodate the Honourable Sir Louis N. Mbanefo, as a personal friend of many years standing, in my residence in Kampala. While lodging with me, the Honourable Sir Louis spent the whole night discussing with me the whole situation in Nigeria including the possibility of the secession of the whole of the Eastern region of Nigeria from Nigeria under the nomenclature of Biafra. He then mentioned that he had been sent purposely to ascertain from me whether I would raise any objection if he were appointed President of the Court of Appeal for the Eastern region of Nigeria, which had then been newly created. He explained further that Colonel Ojukwu was earnestly expecting me to return to join the courts in the Eastern region and that on that account only two of us, that is, himself and myself, were being considered for the post of the President of the Court of Appeal as the only other person qualified for consideration for the filling of the vacancy was the Honourable Mr. Justice Charles Dadi Onyeama, who was then already a member of the International Court of Justice at the Hague. I assured him of my support that he should be given the job since he was senior to me in any event. I also disclosed to him in confidence that there was no likelihood of my leaving Uganda for Biafra as I was not enamoured at all with the idea of Biafra as a separate country from Nigeria and that the whole concept of Biafra embracing the whole of the Eastern region of Nigeria was revolting and that it was difficult for me to appreciate why he himself, the Honourable Sir Louis N. Mbanefo, could support such a concept which, to my mind, was a recipe for disaster. The next morning the team left Entebbe by air back to Nigeria.

Then on July 7, 1967, I flew from Entebbe airport via Rome, Italy *en route* to Geneva, Switzerland to attend the World Peace Through Law Conference, scheduled to take place as already stated from 9 to 14 July, 1967. At the airport in Rome, I was received by the Nigerian Ambassador who drove me in his car to his Rome residence. There we were able to listen to Radio Nigeria in which we heard that Colonel Odumegwu Ojukwu having declared the secession of Eastern region from Nigeria under the name of Biafra, it had become necessary for the federal government of Nigeria under the leadership of Colonel Yakubu Gowon to undertake Police action against the so called Biafra. War had not actually been declared by the federal government but the boundaries separating the Eastern region of Nigeria from the rest of Nigeria as a united country were being policed as a warning that federal Nigeria would not tolerate any active secession. It turned out that, in fact and although I was not aware of it, the Nigerian Civil War, also known as the Biafran War, had actually started on July 6, 1967.

I then flew from Rome to Geneva, Switzerland on 8 July 1967. The conference opened on 9 July 1967 with the registration of members. I was happy to meet Mr. Charles S. Rhyne, President of World Peace Through Law Centre and many old friends. I also met some strange faces as well. There were in attendance a total of 2,500 persons from over 100 nations. There also took place the first Assembly of World Judges. World Law Day was also observed and there were World Law awards. Among the people there assembled were representatives of some oil companies in America who, on approaching me, informed me that, to show their great interest in the declaration and establishment of Biafra in Nigeria, five oil companies in the United States of America had formed a consortium and raised a large sum of money and transmitted the same to Biafra to assist in the prosecution of the war against Nigeria on terms that on the successful conclusion of the war, Biafra would grant the companies exclusive right of exploring and evacuating mineral oils from the swamps of Biafra. I was interested in learning of the intrigue. I felt that the scheme, although far sighted, was a miscalculated adventure because there was no guarantee that, in the event of a war breaking out between Nigeria and Biafra, the latter would win. My informants assured me that, should a war break out between Biafra and Nigeria, there was every reason to believe that Biafra would defeat Nigeria because, according to them, Biafra was fully prepared and even her womenfolk were trained already as soldiers and they bore arms without demur. My informants went even further. They accused me of withholding information from them since, as an indigene of the Eastern region of Nigeria, then Biafra, I ought to know the armed strength of Biafra and that even the French government had openly professed their support for Biafra. I concluded the discussion by making it clear to my informants that they ought to realise that it was impossible for me, as Chief Justice of Uganda, Eastern Africa, to obtain information from Nigeria as a whole as regards soldiering and the training of soldiers preparatory to the outbreak of war.

As soon as the World Peace Through Law Conference ended in Geneva, I boarded a Swiss Air plane on a flight to Lagos, Nigeria. At the Ikeja airport in Lagos, I was met by the liaison-officer representing the Military Governor of the South Eastern state and other members on the staff of the government of South Eastern state of Nigeria. I was then driven to and accommodated in a government flat at Ikoyi, Nigeria. I was delighted to be home again although on a flying visit. The Military Governor of the South Eastern state of Nigeria, Colonel U. J. Essuene, and many other old friends welcomed me home. The following day, I had to attend a grand reception arranged in my honour by the government of the South Eastern state, Nigeria. In the course of the proceedings, in my address I praised the federal military government for having created 12 states in the federation in its wisdom. I mentioned that, in my view, had Nigerian politicians been wise and liberally minded enough to have supported the campaigns for the creation of states in all the regions of Nigeria and had the states been created, probably, the *coup d'état*, which occurred on January 15, 1966, might not have taken place. I therefore congratulated Major-General Yakubu Gowon, as the head of the federal military government, for having been wise and far sighted enough to have created 12 states in the federation of Nigeria. As my contribution to the war effort, I donated sums of money to the federal troops comfort fund and to the fund for the rehabilitation of refugees - the donations were heavily applauded. The reception and the speeches were broadcast live both on the radio and television and were heard by Colonel Odumegwu Ojukwu - the Military Governor of the Eastern region.

Thereafter, I was introduced to Major-General Yakubu Gowon at his Dodan barrack's residence. The latter, after shaking my hands, congratulated me for my speech at the reception and my donations. The following morning, I took off by air back to Uganda and successfully landed at Entebbe airport the same day. I was met at the airport by my chauffer driving my official car with the letters C. J. distinctly marked by the front fender. The car was a Mercedes Benz. The following morning found me at my desk in my chambers in Kampala. The High Court was bubbling with action. The judges were glad to see me back. Each of them congratulated me for my excellent performance at the conference. Later, I reported in writing to the President of Uganda and Commander-in-Chief of the Armed Forces of Uganda who, in due course, acknowledged receipt of the letter reporting my return from World Peace Through Law Conference which was held in Geneva, Switzerland. I was happy to note that all was still peaceful in Uganda and that nothing untoward had happened during my absence. I then undertook an inspection tour of the various districts and was satisfied that all was peaceful. It was, however, reported to me that the only noticeable change in the country was that the President of Uganda, Dr. Milton Obote, had then adopted a novel practice of being accompanied by a large contingent of the army any time he had a political rally in any of the districts.

I then settled down to the task of administering justice in the country. As hitherto, I held sessions of the High Court of Uganda in

Kampala for the disposal of civil suits pending in the court. The mood of the generality of the people seemed to have changed considerably especially in the kingdom of Buganda with the departure to the United Kingdom of His Highness, Sir Edward Mutesa, the Kabaka of Buganda in search of asylum. The Kabaka was in compulsory exile in the United Kingdom. There was also the abolition by legislation of the other kingdoms of Bunyoro, Toro and Ankole. On the surface, life appeared peaceful and unruffled. Colonel Idi Amin, promoted General, had become the head of the Ugandan Army. The government appeared to have a firm grip of the whole country.

I was still brooding over the affairs of Uganda when I received a circular letter dated August 30, 1967 from Sir Hugh Wooding, Chief Justice of Trinidad and Tobago, reminding me of the decision taken at Canberra, Australia during the first of the conferences of the Chief Justices of the Commonwealth to the effect that the next conference of the Chief Justices of the Commonwealth be held at Trinidad and Tobago from April 17- 20 1968 and assigning to me the duty of reading a paper to be prepared by me on "Fundamental Human Rights and Freedoms - the East African experience". The theme of the conference was to be "The Judiciary and the State". It was indicated in the circular letter that the government of Trinidad and Tobago had generously offered to play host to the delegates to the conference. Subsequently, in his letter of December 18, 1967, the Honourable the Chief Justice of Trinidad and Tobago, Sir Hugh Wooding, convened the conference of the Chief Justices of the Commonwealth to take place at Port of Spain, Trinidad from April 17-20, 1968. By the generosity of the government of Trinidad and Tobago, under the leadership of Dr. Eric Williams as Prime Minister, delegates were booked to be accommodated at the Trinidad Hilton hotel. Accepting the invitation to attend the conference, I also undertook to prepare for delivery by me a paper entitled "Fundamental Human Rights and Freedoms - the East African Experience" at the conference.

Then on April 16, 1968, I left Entebbe by air for Trinidad arriving there in the evening. Accordingly, on April 17, 1968, the Conference of Chief Justices of the Commonwealth took place at Port-of-Spain, Trinidad with fanfare and in splendour, according to the programme already formulated. I was delighted to see the Rt. Honourable Sir Adetokunbo Ademola, CFR KBE PC, Chief Justice of Nigeria, in full regalia, which reassured me that the civil war in Nigeria had not assumed an alarming proportion. In the course of the proceedings, I delivered my paper on "Fundamental Human Rights and Freedoms - the East African Experience" which was well received, to my delight. There were other papers delivered on the occasion that included "- The English Experience" by the Rt. Honourable Lord Justice Widgery and "- The Indian Experience" by the Honourable Chief Justice Radayatullah, Chief Justice of India.

Participants at the conference included the Rt. Honourable Sir Garfield Barwick, GCMG - Chief Justice of Australia, the Honourable Mr. Justice Randolph Douglas - Chief Justice of Barbados, the Rt. Honourable Sir John Widgery, OBE TD, - Lord Justice representing the Lord Chief Justice of England, the Honourable Mr. Justice J.R. Cartwright - Chief Justice of Canada, the Honourable Mr. Justice J. S. Vassiliades - President of the Supreme Court of Cyprus, the Honourable Sir Charles Newbold, CMG - President of the Court of Appeal for Eastern Africa, the Honourable Mr. Justice E. Akufo-Addo Chief Justice of Ghana; the Honourable Sir Kenneth Stoby - Chancellor of the Supreme Court of Guyana, the Honourable Mr. Justice M. Radayatullah, Chief Justice of India, the Honourable Sir Herbert Duffus - Chief Justice of Jamaica, the Honourable Tan Sri Azini Mohammed - Chief Justice of West Malaysia representing the Lord President, the Rt. Honourable Sir Adetokunbo Ademola, KBE CFR - Chief Justice of Nigeria, the Honourable Sir Samuel Bankole Jones - President, the Court of Appeal of Sierra Leone, the Honourable Mr. Justice Wee Chong Jin - Chief Justice of Singapore, the Honourable Mr. Justice Telford George - Chief Justice of Tanzania, the Rt. Honourable Sir Hugh Wooding - Chief Justice Trinidad and Tobago, the Honourable Sir Allen Lewis - Chief Justice of the West Indies Associated States, the Honourable Mr. Justice J. R. Blagden OBE TD - Chief Justice of Zambia and myself as Chief Justice of Uganda.

As soon as the conference ended, I flew back to Uganda from Trinidad on April 20 arriving Entebbe by air on April 22, 1968 after we had an enjoyable time. I was glad to return to join my family in Uganda. I was delighted to find my wife and the children in good health. They were also enjoying themselves. On enquiry, I was informed that the President of Uganda and Commander-in-Chief of the Armed Forces was engaged on touring the whole country for the purpose of educating the masses as to the political situation in the country. Having rested for about one week, I forwarded to him my report of the Conference of Chief Justices of the Commonwealth which was held at Trinidad and Tobago in the Caribbean and expressed the opinion that the conference was a success and useful particularly in those days of unrest in African countries within the Commonwealth. I then resumed my activities.

Shortly after I had resumed duty, there came before the President a proposal by the Ford Foundation of America for the establishment of a law research centre at Kampala to be headed by Mr. Justice K. T. Fuad, one of the Judges of the High Court of Uganda, the proposal being that Mr. Justice K. T. Fuad should be seconded from the High Court to the new institution while still retaining his post as a judge of the High Court of Uganda. Furthermore, Mr. K. T. Fuad was also to combine his work as a judge of the High Court of Uganda with the function of a legal draftsman for the legal department, that is to say, the Department of the Solicitor-General of the Ministry of Justice of the executive government of Uganda. I raised a very strong objection to the proposal on the cogent ground that the situation to be created might be misleading and the general public might be confused to think that the Judiciary was no longer independent but had become an integral part of the Ministry of Justice and that such a situation might be dangerous. I pressed that, since Mr. Justice K. T. Fuad was assigned to the new research centre and would combine his work there with the function of a legal draftsman, the proper thing to do was for him to retire from the Judiciary so as to concentrate his attention on his new assignment. But the objection was brushed aside by the President on the advice of the Solicitor General, Mr. P. J. Nkambo Mugerwa, and that created a misunderstanding between the Judiciary and the Executive Department of State.

It was in the midst of the misunderstanding that I applied to the President of Uganda for permission, which was granted, for me to go home to Nigeria on furlough, considering that, during the Conference of the Chief Justices of the Commonwealth held at Trinidad, the Chief Justice of Nigeria, the Rt. Honourable Sir Adetokunbo Ademola, CFR KBE, had informed me that everyone in Nigeria was anxious that I should return from Uganda to Nigeria as there was a heavy shortage of judicial officers of experience in Nigeria as a result of the civil war. I therefore got myself and my family prepared to leave for Nigeria on home leave. My wife and the children, namely Ebong, Edem and Ekpo preceded me. They flew from Entebbe airport early in August 1968 by an American Airline plane and arrived in Lagos the same day; and with a brief stop in Lagos they flew the same day to Calabar where they were lodged in my Calabar house at No. 27 Wilkie Street, Calabar. I successfully joined them in Calabar early in September 1968. On the day I was to leave Kampala, there was an indication that the President of Uganda, Dr. Milton Obote, was reluctant to release me and therefore insisted that he was anxious that I must not keep too long on leave. There was held for me at Entebbe airport a parade by Uganda Airforce officers and men under the supervision of the Minister of Defence, Mr. Namma. I appreciated it very much and thanked the Airforce for their performance and assured them that I would not be away for long.

At my Calabar house, No. 27 Wilkie Street, I received instructions to visit Ikot Abasi township where I would meet with Colonel Benjamin Adekunle, the Commander of the Third Marine Commando of the Nigerian Armed Forces who were settled there after having cleared Ikot Abasi area of all Biafran forces. It was understood that, as a reaction to the speech I had made in Lagos at my reception in 1967 when I had flown in from Geneva, Switzerland, Colonel Ojukwu, the Commander-in-Chief of the Armed Forces of Biafra, had ordered that my school, Secondary Commercial School, Ibekwe be evacuated of the students and the same be occupied by Biafran troops. That, having been done, resulted in my own houses and property in Ikot Abasi township being exposed to the grave danger of looting and destruction. It was even rumoured that my personal house had been set on fire. Accordingly, I flew from Calabar by a helicopter across to Ikot Abasi township and successfully landed on the open field at the Consulate beach and thence I was conveyed in Colonel Adekunle's car, driven by him personally, to his office. From there, I was able to speak by radiotelephone to Colonel Yakubu Gowon, the Head of State at Dodan Barracks, Lagos. Thereafter, I was taken round Ikot Abasi township to identify some of my property.

At the Secondary Commercial School, Ibekwe I was struck by the sort of vandalism that had occurred. The only storey building in front of the premises and school compound, which had housed some classrooms as well as the library, was virtually destroyed. Some of the classroom blocks appeared already dilapidated. I was assured by Colonel Adekunle that, while it was true that Biafran troops were quartered in the premises of the Secondary Commercial School, it was also true that, as soon as Biafran troops were driven out of the compound, Nigerian troops also occupied the school compound and that Nigerian troops had no idea that the school was my private property. They had all thought it was a mission school. We then went over to my personal houses. We first viewed the newly completed house, which today constitutes my main residence. Thereafter, we inspected my old residence, which I now use as a library - *Ise Nwed*. There, we found that the bulk of the property that had been in the house had been looted. My safe was taken out into the bush near by and there broken up in search of cash, which apparently they thought I must have left behind when I left for Uganda, especially as I had left my cook, Benson, behind to take charge of the house. My rich carpet, crockery and cutlery sets were all looted - the cupboards into which most of the things were packed being opened with the keys. There was nothing damaged. The locks were opened with keys that I had left in the possession of my cook, Benson.

I then reported to Colonel Adekunle that I had received information prior to our visit that the looting of my property was organised by one Etim Usoro Ekitok, then the manager in charge of Opobo Boat Yard, formerly Eastern Region Production Development Board (ERPDB) Boat Yard, which was then being organised in Ikot Abasi township area of the then Opobo Division of Calabar province for the purpose of producing flying or speed boats for the use of the army. I requested that I would like Etim Usoro Ekitok to be produced by the army for me to be able to identify him, and that, thereafter, I would like the report I received to be investigated thoroughly before any action could be taken in that regard by the military authorities. My request was immediately granted and Etim Usoro Ekitok was produced and I not only identified him personally but also put certain questions to him. In interrogating him, I asked him specifically whether it was true that he had organised the looting of my property from my house with the aid of the Biafran army. I told him that I heard that, to do that successfully, he had removed Benson, my cook and his own half brother, from the house and posted him to the boat yard as a security man. That operation had given him free access into my residence. I told him that, feeling as disgusted as I was, my first impulse was to have him shot dead if I had a gun with me. I impressed upon him that I had commissioned the army to investigate the allegation thoroughly before taking the legitimate action the army was entitled to take if, in the end, the allegation should prove true and that I was shocked to learn that, in spite of all I had done to help him in life, he should have rewarded me by behaving towards me in such an ungrateful manner. I then requested that he be taken away from my presence. After the inspection, I returned to Calabar.

As Christmas approached and the Nigerian civil war was still raging on, the family and I decided to spend Christmas in Nigeria since there was the prospect that the war was progressing towards completion or termination. There were still areas of fierce fighting even though Port Harcourt had been captured by the Nigerian troops. Later, I gathered that President Milton Obote did not take kindly to the fact that I did not return to Uganda to celebrate the Christmas there. He then began to imagine that I might be unwilling to return to Uganda as Chief Justice. With that frame of mind, President Milton Obote fell into a trap that had been set for him by Biafran agents. On being approached with a cartload of offers by the same agents including the offer of free publicity by representatives of Biafra in Geneva, Switzerland, provided he would undertake to dispense with my services as Chief Justice, President Milton Obote fell into the trap. In the circumstance, President Milton Obote, behaving like an ungrateful idiot, undertook to write a letter informing me that, as it was unlikely that I would be returning to Uganda, he had decided to implement the scheme which he and I had floated while I was Chief Justice as to promoting certain Ugandans to higher judicial offices and that, in the event, he was promoting Mr. Oteng, who was then acting Chief Magistrate, as the new Chief Justice of Uganda as that would be in keeping with the Ugandanisation of the judicial offices.

At the material time in question, Dr. Okoi Arikpo was the External Affairs Minister of Nigeria and the letter intended for me from Uganda fell into the hands of one of the secretaries in the External Affairs Ministry. Unfortunately, the letter was not delivered to me. I then, in January 1969, decided to return to Uganda. On arrival at the Entebbe airport, I waited in vain for my official car and driver to meet me at the airport. Instead, it was the Nigerian High Commissioner for Uganda, Mr. M. J. Etuk, who came to the airport with his official car to receive me. I was astonished, yet the worst was yet to happen. Immediately on my arrival in Kampala, President Milton Obote issued a press release informing the world that he could not understand why, in spite of the fact that he had communicated to me that, since the terms of my services had expired, I should no longer return to Uganda, the government of Nigeria was still insisting on imposing me on Uganda; and that in so far as the government of Uganda was concerned, I was no longer the Chief Justice of Uganda as my services had been terminated. He went further to state that, because of the assurance given by the Nigerian military government that the civil war with Biafra would only last for 18 months, and since the war was still raging for a period of two years, he would not consider the government of Uganda bound not to recognise Biafra, as the government of Uganda considered itself absolved from its previous undertaking having regard to the effluxion of time. He said further that on no account would the government of Uganda be prepared to accept me as its Chief Justice.

All that happened came to me as a shock having regard to the fact that, when I left for home leave in September, 1968, there was a request directed to me by all and sundry in Uganda including members of the air force that I must not fail to return to Uganda on the expiration of my leave. Why the press release by President Milton Obote informing the whole world that my services were no longer required and calling upon the acting Chief Justice, the Honourable Mr. Justice Sheridan to sit tight in his post as Chief Justice regardless of the fact that I had returned from home leave? Thereafter, I received a note from the Honourable Mr. Justice Sheridan assuring me that he was not a party to whatever other arrangement President Milton Obote had made and that he was personally embarrassed by the situation. Information was then made available to me that, during my absence on leave, Dr. Michael Okpara and some other emissaries from Biafra had visited President Milton Obote with very tempting financial offers provided my services were dispensed with and recognition granted Biafra and that President Milton Obote had accepted the offer hence his violent reaction towards my return to resume service as Chief Justice of Uganda. For, to do otherwise, would have amounted to a breach of his undertaking and a consequent loss of revenue.

I then immediately began to arrange for my return to Nigeria and wrote a letter addressed to President Milton Obote informing him of my decision. In acknowledging the receipt of my letter, President Milton Obote of Uganda thanked me for my decision and drew my attention to a letter which he had addressed to me through the Ministry of External Affairs, Lagos, Nigeria, informing me of the changes which he had planned to introduce into the judicial system of Uganda as regards personnel with a view to the enhancement of the reputation of Ugandan judicial officers - a letter which I did not receive at all. I thereupon arranged and dispatched my wife to fly back to Nigeria, which she did during the second week of January 1969. On arrival in Lagos my wife was flown immediately to Calabar to my Calabar residence, No. 17 Wilkie Street. I was only able to join her in March 1969 after a farewell party arranged in my honour by the government of Uganda and members of the Law Society of Uganda, Eastern Africa.

I must conclude this aspect of my service in Uganda, Eastern Africa, that pearl of Africa, by observing that I had enjoyed every moment of my approximately six years sojourn in Uganda and, perhaps, what was more important from the point of view of the image of our dear country, Nigeria, I could claim with pride that up to the time of my departure I was blessed with the unique good fortune of successfully winning and enjoying the confidence and respect not only of the government and people of Uganda but also of the Bar and the profession as a whole. My judges and magistrates and, indeed, all members of staff, as far as could be ascertained, remained loyal and cooperative throughout. It was their loyalty and cooperation coupled with the wonderful encouragement accorded me by His Excellency, the President of the Republic of Uganda, Dr. A. Milton Obote and his cabinet which contributed in no small measure to whatever successes had attended my efforts. Indeed, it was such meaningful cooperation and support that sustained my endeavours all the while. To the entire judicial establishment and the government of the republic of Uganda, Eastern Africa, I must seize this opportunity to pay my humble tribute.

On the whole, I found the work as Chief Justice of the republic of Uganda most fascinating and challenging though sometimes most irksome, exacting and arduous. It was most challenging because I had all the while considered myself a pioneer as an African in that particular field of human endeavour. I must confess that, originally, it was indirectly the concept of African unity and the desire to place Nigeria on the Eastern African map in the field of law which had inspired every of my action. It should be remembered that that was the era when the concept of African unity was in vogue following upon the foundation establishment of the Organisation of African Unity (OAU) in Addis Ababa, Ethiopia as a world wide institution, which should exist as a parallel organisation of the United Nations Organisation in New York City of the United States of America. It came also to me as an inducement and an added impetus when, within two years of my services as Chief Justice of the Republic of Uganda, Eastern Africa, the government of Uganda demonstrably was pleased by an act of parliament to alter the terms and conditions of my service by means of enhancement to my great advantage and satisfaction, quite unexpectedly, which included a chauffeur driven limousine, soft furnishings of my residence and increased emolument for myself and entertainment allowances for my judges and the High Court of Uganda, which enabled me every year regularly to organise, after church service at the Namirembe Cathedral, a garden party for the entertainment of invited guests, and at which function the famous Uganda Police band was always in attendance to entertain guests and members of the public who cared to attend as spectators, with classical and other enjoyable music in celebration of the commencement of the Law year. The occasion was usually most enjoyable by members of the public. There was also the award to me of a knighthood by Her gracious Majesty, Queen Elizabeth II of Great Britain and Northern Ireland and head of the Commonwealth of Nations, the ceremony for which I had to attend as the guest of the British government at Buckingham Palace, London, there to be decorated personally with the accolade for the knighthood by Her Majesty, the Queen. All these were pointers to the fact that, while in Uganda, I was regarded by the government and the people of Uganda as a success, although, in normal circumstance, modesty dictates that I should admit that the proper assessment and judgment of my success must be reserved to posterity and in particular to African historians of the future.

In this connection, I consider it most expedient and a matter of considerable interest to quote passages from letters written by His Excellency Dr. A. Milton Obote, President of Uganda, concerning my work and performance at the time when I bowed out of the stage of the judiciary of Uganda. The first letter, which was addressed to me, was dated 25th April 1969 and was signed personally by His Excellency the President. The relevant passage of that letter reads as follows:

"I wish to seize this opportunity to express to you our appreciation for the outstanding work which you did as Chief Justice which work we fervently believe went a long way to promote respect for the Judiciary in Uganda and under-

standing of the rule of law by the general public. I, in particular, will never forget and will never underrate the period of your service in Uganda which period, as you will agree, was characterised by some of the most difficult changes that any developing country can experience. You assured smooth transition and I want to assure you immediately that the broad views you took and the correct interpretation of the facts and the law are very much appreciated by the people of Uganda and that you have already earned a most important place in the history of Uganda.

I end by assuring you of my personal confidence in you and wish once more to reaffirm the appreciation of the people of Uganda for the services you rendered to this country".

In his letter dated 14th June, 1969 addressed to His Excellency Major-General Yakubu Gowon, the head of the federal military government of Nigeria, His Excellency the President of Uganda, also said:-

"I am writing to convey to you my very sincere appreciation and thanks, together with those of the government of the republic of Uganda, for the services that have been rendered to this country by Sir Udo Udoma as Chief Justice for the last five years.

The services to Uganda of Sir Udo Udoma have covered a very exciting period in the history of our country and his services will for long be remembered in Uganda.

I would like to take this opportunity to express to you the very sincere appreciation and thanks of the government of the republic of Uganda, to the government of the federal republic of Nigeria, for having made the services of Sir Udo Udoma available to this country."

Finally I must state that when I bowed off the stage of Uganda after six years of hard work, I was satisfied that I had made a large measure of contribution to the main stream of the jurisprudence of East Africa. I also made enormous contribution to the field of sports and the encouragement of Christian religious worship and expansion of the Kingdom of God on earth as a patron of the Young Men's Christian Association (YMCA), which thrived tremendously in Uganda. I left Uganda a happy man, satisfied that I had served Uganda honestly and sincerely to the best of my ability and which had won for me the admiration of the people and respect and affection for me in their hearts.

It is impossible to forget that it was during the time of my sojourn in Uganda as Chief Justice in 1967 that, based on my humble suggestion and in an endeavour to bring about stability in Nigeria, General Gowon, on the eve of the civil war, made the first ever effort to create and successfully created 12 states including the Rivers and the South Eastern states of Nigeria and Nigeria thereby becoming a federation of states - a near perfect union. Thus it was certain that while in Uganda I did not cease to think about the future of my country, Nigeria, and to assist in the finding of solutions to some of her problems.

On arrival in Lagos, Nigeria, by the order of the head of the federal military government, Colonel Yakubu Gowon, I was immediately appointed Justice of the Supreme Court of Nigeria, Lagos, Nigeria. The federal military government rejected a request that I should be allowed to accept the offer of the post of the Chief Justice of the South Eastern state by the Military Governor of South Eastern state, Lt. Colonel U. J. Essuene. It was explained to Lt. Colonel U. J. Essuene that, prior to my positing to Uganda as Chief Justice, it was agreed that, on my return from Uganda on completion of my assignment there, I was to be appointed directly as Justice of the Supreme Court of Nigeria, Lagos. It was further explained that my appointment as Justice of the Supreme Court of Nigeria was also prompted by the fact that the Chief Justice of Nigeria, the Honourable Sir Adetokunbo Ademola CFR, was approaching his retirement period on the ground of age, making it therefore necessary to strengthen the Supreme Court of Nigeria by my appointment to the court. In any event, I left Uganda after 6 years of meritorious service as Chief Justice, having served the country from 1963 to 1969. I therefore became a member of the Supreme Court of Nigeria in about May 1969.

Then, in January 1970, the Nigerian civil war known as the Biafran secession war came to an abrupt end after Colonel Adekunle had been replaced by Colonel Olusegun Obasanjo as the Commander of the Third Marine Commando at Port Harcourt. Then, in 1971, General Idi Amin overthrew Dr. Milton Obote as President of Uganda and Commander-in-Chief of the Armed Forces of Uganda in a military coup d'état. Dr. Milton Obote had to seek asylum in Tanzania.

CHAPTER TWENTY-FIVE

My Mariages And My Family

"As a people our temperament is febrile and our society depends upon the natural continuity of the family".

When I was a student at school, it was drummed into me that any marriage, to be profitable, must be celebrated when the couple is young. Marriage by an old couple cannot be regarded as a true and worthy marriage, but rather a partnership. Therefore, for one to enjoy his marriage to the full, one must marry young. On the other hand, the spouses must not be immature, for then they cannot appreciate what marriage truly and really is and represents - a sacred bond between two matured people, a male and a female, which must be sustained through life. It is a sacred union between two families, never to be dis-united or separated, if possible, according to African tradition. According to custom, one marries into a family.

Acting on these teachings, my mother, who was a famous trader, and who, in the course of her trade, was fond of travelling far and wide throughout Calabar province of old, felt that I should marry young. Even as a school boy attending school regularly, I would observe my mother, from time to time in the course of her travels to different parts of Calabar province, bring back, on her return from her journey, a young girl intended to be married by her to me. On each such occasion I would decline to enter into marriage arrangement with such a strange girl. Later, I explained further to my anxious mother that I preferred to complete my education before contemplating any form of marriage with any one. I was able to get off with such an explanation because custom demands that I should only marry a woman of my choice.

Such was the position as regards the question of my marriage until the death by the gun fire of British soldiers of my beloved mother who, as one of the leading women, was a victim of the women's war of rebellion against the then British colonial administration, which took place in what was known as Opobo division, part of which is now Ikot Abasi local government area of Akwa Ibom state. As may be recalled, the women of Opobo division had risen in rebellion against the British colonial government when it sought to impose poll tax on women in the then Eastern provinces of Nigeria.

Despite my mother's sudden death as a result of violence perpetrated by the British colonial army, I was able to continue my education as my father virtually stepped into my mother's shoes and was willing and determined to see that I was properly educated by undertaking to fund my education. Spurred on by my father's willingness to finance my education, I remained at school and was able to pass my first school leaving certificate examination, known locally as the Standard VI examination in 1931. In January 1932, I was admitted into Class III Middle having sat and passed with flying colours the entrance examination into the institution then known as Uzuakoli Institute of the Methodist Mission in Bende division of Owerri province. On completion of my education in Uzuakoli Institute of the Methodist Mission in Nigeria, I was employed by Messrs G. B. Ollivant & Co. Limited in Opobo division, the agent of which was Mr. A. C. Butler, who was acknowledged as the worthy representative of Messrs G. B. Ollivant & Co. Ltd, on payment on my behalf of a sum of money by my beloved father by way of security. Shortly after I had secured employment by Messrs G. B. Ollivant & Co Limited as a security employee, my father then married for me Miss Lucy George Ubeng Ata Ekong of Ikot Aba, Ibekwe who was a product of Mary Hanney Memorial School for girls at Oron - also a Methodist institution. The marriage was solemnised according to custom and I was pleased to accept the young lady.

As husband and wife, Lucy George Ubeng and I cohabited at Port Harcourt and at old grand Bonny where I worked as a custom's officer. Then in 1938, having been awarded a scholarship by Ibibio Union, I together with other scholars set sail for the United Kingdom in search of the Golden Fleece. But before my departure for overseas, by special arrangement and by the grace of the Methodist Mission, my wife, Lucy George Ubeng, was accepted at Itu Mbang hospital to be there trained as a nurse and midwife during my absence in the United Kingdom and Ireland. After her training and having qualified professionally, she was employed by the mission as a nurse and midwife pending my return from overseas.

On completion of my studies overseas and after having been called to the Bar by Grays Inn in London, I returned to Nigeria in December 1945 as a Barrister-at-Law. On arrival in Nigeria, I was admitted and registered as a Barrister-at-Law and Solicitor of the Supreme Court of Nigeria in Lagos and therefore was entitled to practice as a legal practitioner in Nigeria. I, having arrived and settled down at Ikot Abasi, asked that the Methodist Mission release my wife, Lucy George Ubeng, and thereupon she in consequence joined me once more as her husband and we settled down together quite happily.

In 1946, I moved to Aba where I set up my practice as a legal practitioner and together we cohabited up to 1950 when because of unhappy events we were compelled to arrange for separation to be followed thereafter by divorce. Thus was brought to an unhappy end and without any issue my youthful marriage with Lucy George Ubeng to my utter regret.

Just before and in the course of the process of separation, by special arrangement, I got engaged to my present beloved wife, then Miss Grace Bassey - a product of Queen's College, Lagos, and subsequently a nurse in training in the government General Hospital, Aba. The engagement in due course ripened into full marriage according to custom organised under the auspices of her step father, Chief Inyang, at Ayadeghe village in Itu division and resulted in my cohabiting together with Grace Bassey the product of which by the grace of God was my first son by name Ayanti. The naming ceremony of Ayanti was conducted by my paternal cousin, Chief Martin A. Inam, as the head of *Ayanti compound* of Ikot Abasi village in the presence of the late Mr. E. U. Bassey, a certificated teacher and my brother-in-law and the guardian of my wife. My first son was named Ayanti in commemoration and perpetuation of the memory of Ayanti Umo Idonho Abasi Enin, the founder of *Ayanti compound*, and one of the sons of Abasi Akpan Enin, the founder of Ikot Abasi village, according to tradition. The arrival of Ayanti in 1950 signalled a most successful union and occasioned great rejoicing among the people of Ikot Abasi village and, indeed, of Ibibio Country, who had longed for many years since my return from the United Kingdom in 1945 for the occasion when I would be blessed with an issue, and, in particular, an heir. It should also be remembered that I was then also the National President of the Ibibio State Union.

My son, Ayanti, was blessed and christened in the old Ebenezer Methodist Church, Ibekwe. The arrival of Ayanti coincided with the occasion of the warming ceremony of my new house at No. 22 Park Road, Aba, in now Abia state and the dedication of my newspaper the "Eastern States Express" published at Aba by the Ikemesit Company Limited. It is worthy of note to state that the blessing of my house and the dedication of the newspaper, which was a daily, was performed the same day by his Grace, Bishop Dimeari of St. Michael's Church, Aba of the Anglican denomination on my invitation and at my request which he generously accepted. The performance and celebrations of the events took place at Aba in 1951 among a large concourse of people.

The occasion was celebrated in grand style in that participants, in response to my invitation, came from all corners of the Eastern provinces of Nigeria - some came from Calabar township and the Ibibio mainland of Calabar province; some from Onitsha and Enugu of Onitsha province; some from Owerri and Umuahia of Owerri province; and others from Buguma, Abonnema and Port Harcourt of the Rivers province. The Resident of Calabar province, Mr. C. J. Mayne, and the Resident, Rivers province, Major Allen, graced the functions with their attendance. But the Resident of Owerri province resident at Umuahia, Mr. J. S. Smith, was unavoidably absent. There was rejoicing everywhere and the celebrations lasted from Friday to Sunday morning when it became necessary to worship in St. Michael's Church, Aba, which we did. There were large canopies or awnings and tents spread in front of my compound for visitors.

Then in 1952, I became the lucky father of another bouncing baby boy by my beloved wife, Mrs. Grace Udoma. After the performance of ancient rituals by Chief Martin A. Inam, my second son was named Inam in accordance with custom in memory of my grandfather, Inam (Unwa Mfon) Ayanti (Umo Idonho) Abasi Akpan Enin. It should be noted that I have placed certain female names after Inam and Ayanti respectively in brackets. This action on my part is deliberate because, according to Ibibio custom, in the ancient days it was usual in daily life to call a son or daughter after the mother as a result of the practice of polygamy so that, even though Inam was the son of Ayanti in normal daily life, Inam would be called after or often referred to the mother and the practice served to identify that Inam was the son of a woman whose names were Unwa Mfon. And similarly that Ayanti's mother was Umo Idonho.

It may also be explained that, according to Ibibio custom, the practice of naming children was to perpetuate the names of the family going back to the original founder of the compound or settlement as the case may be. Sometimes also, the name in daily use may be different from the real name of the person concerned according to their family tree.

In 1954, by the grace of God, my third son was born. Again, in due course, he was brought to Ikot Abasi for the purpose of the customary naming ceremony. After the due performance of the usual rituals, according to custom, Chief Martin A. Inam, as the head of *Ayanti compound,* named him Udoma. He was given the name Udoma in perpetuation and commemoration of the memory of my father, Udoma Inam, then dead of course. It therefore became my duty always to refer to him as my father, which is represented by the Ibibio expression "Ete" or "Tete". My sister Adiaha'ma always addressed him as "Etuk Ete" (the small father). I was very proud of my third son, Udoma, for from the point of view of the ancient custom of the Ibibio people, it is regarded as a matter of great pride, an achievement for me to be able to have a son to be named after my own father, especially as I had lost my father by death since 1936.

Furthermore, it is a matter for which God had to be glorified by me, realising, as one must, that during his life time my beloved father, as was his conceived duty, had married for me a wife who, unfortunately, had no issue until her death and I was then a laughing stock to all and sundry particularly as a legal practitioner with a lucrative practice who had a reputation of being hospitable and always entertaining all visitors to my abode but was denied an issue of my own. Indeed, it was often the talk of the town and country that without an issue my wealth was worthless. In circumstance, to be blessed with a third son, who turned out to be most brilliant intellectually was indeed more than an achievement. It was the work of God. He heard my prayers and had done His wishes. Because of the wonderful work of God, my life had become a pleasure to me.

Then in 1957, there was born unto me, by the grace of God, another bouncing baby; a son. In the usual way he was brought to Ikot Abasi to go through the ritual of the traditional naming ceremony among a rejoicing assemblage of outstanding personalities like Mr. Harry A. Ekanem and Chief Dick E. Usen, both of Ikot Akpaden. He was given the name Ebong as my choice, in reverence to my wife's mother who exclaimed at his birth, "*Ebong Udoma nagha do!*" – "stop the 'Udoma' rants!" He was born to me during the period I was head and shoulder in politics as the founder, leader and champion of the COR State Movement, COR signifying Calabar, Ogoja and Rivers provinces. It was also the year in which the British colonial government set up a commission of inquiry to investigate the fears of minorities in Nigeria over the acquisition of independence by Nigeria, whether such fears were well or ill-founded, and to recommend the process such fears might be allayed including the creation of states as a last resort. Sir Henry Willink was the chairman of the commission.

During the conduct of the inquiry throughout Nigeria, I was privileged to appear both at Calabar, being then the headquarters of Calabar province, and at Port Harcourt as the headquarters of the then Rivers province. At Calabar, Dr. Okoi Arikpo and I testified as witnesses whilst at Port Harcourt I appeared as counsel for the COR State Movement. I really had a hectic time during the period in question. As a result of political activities connected with the struggle for the creation of states in Nigeria, I was initiated into the famous Ekpe Iyamba titled society of Calabar by the Obong of Calabar, that being the second time of my having been initiated into the Ekpe titled society; my first initiation into Ekpe titled society having taken place at Mbiakong. That first time, I was initiated into the powerful Ekpe Uruan titled society.

As a member of the Federal House of Representatives, the highest legislature in Nigeria, which legislature along with the Senate constituted the apex legislature in Nigeria, I moved a motion calling upon the federal government of Nigeria to reopen the sea port at Opobo (now Ikot Abasi), which had previously been closed down for no just cause, by having the bar at the estuary of the Ikot Abasi river dredged so as to enable ocean-going vessels to re-enter into the port for the purpose of unloading or discharging and reloading cargoes for transportation to lands beyond the seas. The motion succeeded and it was unanimously passed by the House of Representatives and accepted, not by the Minister for Transport but by the Prime Minister himself, the Honourable Alhaji Abubakar Tafawa Balewa of blessed memory. In accepting the motion on behalf of the federal government, the Honourable the Prime Minister spoke in glowing terms in praise of the mover of the motion whom he described as a man of vision. The motion having been accepted by the federal government, as an earnest to the acceptance of the motion aforesaid, money by way of a token sum was provided for the project in the estimates indicating that the federal government was intent on prosecuting the project consisting of the dredging of the bar and the construction of a befitting harbour where ships could be moored.

Perhaps it should be explained that Opobo port (now Ikot Abasi port), from the time of the establishment of the Oil Rivers Protectorate of 1891 by the British government, was an on going, prosperous and a well known port patronised by ocean going vessels for the discharging of commodities and manufactured goods from overseas in exchange for palm oil and palm kernel. For those purposes, there was established by British companies trading in the river a bulk oil plant for the purification and storage of palm oil before shipment in tankers to overseas markets. There was also established a Customs Department under the charge of a senior collector of customs and his staff.

As a result of the provision of such facilities, Opobo (now Ikot Abasi) port participated in the trade of the world and became a well known established port in Nigeria, blessed with prosperity. So famous and prosperous was the port all along until, unfortunately, during the period of the second world war (1939-45) when ships departing from the port became easy targets for German U-boats prowling along the Atlantic ocean with the result that some of the ships were attacked and made to sink, the port being naturally open to the Atlantic ocean into which the Ikot Abasi river empties itself. Consequently, in order to avoid sustaining heavy losses due to the activities of German U-boats as enemy, it was decided by the British government that ocean-going vessels should be forbidden from entering into and departing from the port since it was not fortified for security. Thereupon the port remained closed to ocean-going vessels.

In consequence of the port remaining unused during the period of the war, the bar became silted up so that, at the end of the war, it was considered unsafe for any ocean-going vessel to enter into the port. On proper and thorough examination, it was confirmed that the bar had silted up and that without proper dredging it would be dangerous for ocean-going vessels to be allowed to navigate into the port. Thereupon, the government declared the port closed and the Customs Department and marine officers stationed in the port area were removed and transferred elsewhere in the county, because the cost of dredging the bar and constructing a harbour was considered and placed at a very high figure of the order of twenty one million pounds (£21,000,000) at the time as estimated; that estimate was given by the Development department in the Nigerian Secretariat in or about 1947. Thus came to an unexpected end the port of Opobo (now Ikot Abasi port), which for many years had served Nigeria well and was considered one of the natural, useful and famous ports in Nigeria with a long history of connection with the British colonial system.

Unhappily, by reason of such closure, Nigerians were denied the use of their ancient port even up to 1959 when most of the active ports in the country were rather congested with ships forming queues in the Lagos harbour for instance, without a proper berth in the harbour for such ships to be moored - hence my motion in 1959.

Then in November 1959, following upon the dissolution of the House of Representatives, I contested the election with a view to be returned to the House of Representatives of which I had been a member since its inception in 1952. Unfortunately, I failed to be elected because of heavy rigging induced by the NCNC party, that being the party in government. I was then a member of the UNIP, that is, the United National Independence Party, which was in opposition in the Eastern regional House of Assembly as well as the House of Representatives in alliance with the Action Group party.

The result of my having failed in the elections of 1959 was disastrous. For the projected plan of having the bar in the Opobo river (now Ikot Abasi river) dredged as well as having the harbour constructed, as prayed for in my motion which, as already indicated, was accepted whole-heartedly by the federal government became a dead letter. The project was not prosecuted. Rather, the money voted for the project was diverted into the dredging and construction of Koko port in the Mid-Western region of Nigeria perhaps because of the influence of Mr. Festus Okotie-Eboh, then Minister of Finance in the federal cabinet at Lagos. All the same, there was a strong feeling abroad that if I had been returned to the House of Representatives after the election as a member, the federal government would have been bound to pursue the project concerning Opobo port (now Ikot Abasi port) according to their pledged word in accepting the motion.

Thus, in consequence of my having failed in the election, Opobo port (now Ikot Abasi port) was denied the privilege of being reopened because the federal government under the same Prime Minister, the Honourable Alhaji Sir Tafawa Balewa, had failed in its duty to dredge the bar, which was reported to have silted up, and construct the harbour for the mooring of ocean-going vessels. As it happened, my successor as member of the House of Representatives, because of inexperience, did not follow my lead. My motion, even though it had been passed unanimously in the House of Representatives and accepted by the federal government of the day, had remained a dead letter and Ikot Abasi port has remained still closed even today as I write these lines.

Then at the beginning of the next year, 1960, as a consolation, I had the distinct pleasure of welcoming into my family another bouncing baby boy by my wife, Grace. The baby was named by me Edem. After the observance and celebration of the usual ancient ritual according to custom at Ikot Abasi, my ancestral home, he was given the name after my beloved mother (deceased) whose names were Adiaha Edem and he grew to be a brilliant boy and successfully entered King's College, Lagos, Nigeria at the minimum age of 12 years.

In 1963 when I was appointed Chief Justice of Uganda, Edem was one of my children who accompanied my wife and me to Uganda. Indeed it was in Uganda that Edem proved to be asthmatic and subsequently died suddenly in 1983 after my retirement from serving as a Justice of the Supreme Court of Nigeria. He was buried in Lagos in the Ikoyi cemetery with great honour us usual among products of King's College, Lagos. There was a large concourse of people to mourn his loss.

Then late in 1961, my wife, Grace, was the happy recipient of good wishes in the form of a baby boy whom I later christened Ekpo. He was born after I had assumed appointment as a judge of the High Court of the federal territory of Lagos, Nigeria in May 1961. I named him Ekpo after my maternal grand mother whose names were Adiaha Ekpo Abia. He also accompanied us to Uganda on my appointment as Chief Justice of Uganda. He grew up to be a young man of extraordinary character. He does not understand what is meant by loneliness because even when alone he could always invent ways of enjoying himself. He is studious and artistic by nature. He has a cultivated spirit of endurance.

The last issue by my wife, Lady Grace, came in 1969 on our return from Uganda. By the grace of God she is a girl - our only daughter who was christened by me as Enoabasi and at the special request of my wife as Iquo, being named after my wife's mother, Madam Iquo Bassey. Enoabasi (Eno for short) means "God's gift" in Ibibio. Enoabasi Iquo Udoma was born at Calabar at the time we were sojourned there and I had just assumed appointment as a Justice of the Supreme Court of Nigeria at Lagos. It was just as well that she was not born in Uganda. All my children are Nigerians and therefore are Nigerian citizens by birth.

CHAPTER TWENTY-SIX

Serving On The Supreme Court Bench

"There are no certainties in human life or in the life of a state".
– Churchill

  As intimated before I digressed to present my family along with the events surrounding each significant milestone in its development, I left Uganda finally and returned home to Nigeria in 1969, the year my last child was born. On arrival in Lagos, I was given a tumultuous reception. Almost everyone was happy to have me back in Nigeria. I personally felt very much at home. I was glad to be home with my family at last. Soon thereafter, the government of the South Eastern state of Nigeria offered me the vacant post of the Chief Justice of the South Eastern state, which up till then had remained unfilled. I had to decline the offer because, having regard to the arrangement made on terms of which I had agreed to go to Uganda, I was to be appointed a Justice of the Supreme Court of Nigeria on my return to Nigeria on the conclusion of my assignment in Uganda.

  Consequently on my arrival in Lagos, the Federal Military Government of Nigeria through the Chief Justice of the Federation, the Honourable Sir Adetokunbo Ademola, CFR, KBE, wasted no time in intimating to me that my services were required in the Supreme Court as a Justice of the Supreme Court of Nigeria and that I should prepare myself for the assignment. Within two weeks of my arrival in Nigeria, I was appointed a Justice of the Supreme Court of Nigeria. I assumed duty at once amidst rumours that as the Honourable the Chief Justice of Nigeria, the Honourable Sir Adetokunbo Ademola, CFR, KBE was likely to retire within a short time thereafter, it was likely that I might be called upon to replace him in due course. Among those who had wished me well in that respect was Lt. Colonel Hassan Katsina, Chief of Staff, Nigerian Army.

  Having commenced sitting in court, I soon became absorbed in the work of the court, which work I found most interesting. Then rumours rent the air to the effect that the civil war, called Biafran War, was soon to end as Lt. Colonel Odumegwu Ojukwu had fled the country ostensibly in search of peace. Shortly thereafter, in January 1970, the Nigerian civil war came to an end abruptly with Biafran war leaders surrendering to the Nigerian war lords. There was rejoicing everywhere. Under the leadership of General Yakubu Gowon, the slogan then adopted was "No Victor! No Vanquished!" - the unity of federal Nigeria must be restored and kept intact.

In February 1970, there occurred a very serious railway accident at a place known as Langa-Langa in a part of the Northern region in which several passengers lost their lives and had to be buried in mass graves. As a result of such a serious accident, the celebration concerning the end of the civil war had to be curtailed because in many homes in the Northern region many innocent souls who were passengers on the train involved in the accident lost their lives. It was a sad blow to Nigeria as a whole and therefore necessitated the setting up of a commission of inquiry in response to the agitation of the populace into the causes of the accident just at the time when the civil war ended. On 25 March 1970, to my utter surprise, I was appointed by Major General Yakubu Gowon, head of the federal military government and Commander-in-Chief of the Armed Forces of the federal republic of Nigeria, as chairman of the Langa-Langa Train Accident Tribunal of Inquiry to inquire into the cause or causes of the accident and the circumstances in which the 156 Down-Mixed passengers train became involved in the accident at mile 379 ½ on the eastern line at approximately 17.15 hours in the evening of 16 February 1970 while travelling on the run from Kaduna Junction to Igumale station. Other members of the tribunal of inquiry were Mr. Bingignavle V. Seshadri, Mr. James A. Orshi, Alhaji Ali Akilu and Abdul M. A. Razaq.

The terms of reference according to which the tribunal of inquiry had to operate were as follows:

The tribunal shall, with all convenient speed –

(a)   inquire into the cause or causes of the accident, and the circumstances in which 156 Down-Mixed passenger train became involved in the accident, at mile 379 ½ on the eastern line, at approximately 17.15 hours on the evening of February, 1970 while travelling on the run from Kaduna Junction to Igunmale station, and determine whether the railway management, or any railway employee(s) by conduct or negligence, in any way caused or contributed to the accident;

(b) inquire into and report on any action taken for the restoration of traffic, the medical attention to the injured and police protection of property at the site of the accident; and

(c) make, in the light of the findings in paragraph (a) above, recommendations for improving conditions of track, rolling stock (including locomotives) and train working in the railway system for greater safety of the travelling public."

After due enquiry and on terms of our findings, appropriate recommendations were submitted to the Head of the federal military government for consideration and necessary action. On receiving the report, the Head of State of the federal military government spoke very highly of the work of the tribunal of inquiry and assured us that government would make a careful study of the report and recommendations and a white paper would be prepared, accordingly, in furtherance of whatever action government would take in the implementation of the recommendations subject to the availability of funds. The report and recommendations were submitted to the government on or about July 17, 1970.

Then, in 1972, there broke out three isolated trade disputes between (1) the Lagos State government medical doctors and the Lagos state government; (2) the Association of Medical Consultants, Lagos University Teaching Hospital coupled with the Board of Management of the Lagos University Teaching Hospital, and the University of Lagos; and (3) the Association of Clinical Teachers, University College Hospital, Ibadan coupled with the Board of Management of the University College Hospital, Ibadan, and the University of Ibadan, Nigeria.

Quite surprisingly, the Commissioner, Federal Ministry of Labour, informed me that a decision had been reached that I be appointed chairman of the three Trade Dispute Boards to be set up by the federal military government of Nigeria, the matter having been exhaustively discussed by the Supreme Military Council. Thereupon, by instruments dated 24 April 1972 and 31 May 1972, respectively, and subsequent amendments thereto issued by the Commissioner of Labour, Federal Ministry of Labour, under his hand and in the exercise of the powers conferred upon him by the Trade Disputes (Emergency Provisions) Decree, 1968, I, a Justice of the Supreme Court, as chairman, and Professor Kenneth R. Hill, Vice-Chancellor, the University of Benin; Mrs. F. A. David, a trained teacher, a qualified nurse and mid-wife, and a social worker; Mr. A. Mora, a retired permanent secretary in the federal public service; and Mr. M. O. Akinrele, a lecturer/consultant, Nigerian Institute of Management, Lagos as members were appointed and constituted into three separate and distinct Boards of Inquiry, namely:

(1) The Lagos State Doctors Trade Dispute Board;

(2) The Association of Consultants, Lagos University Teaching Hospital Trade Dispute Board; and

(3) The Association of Clinical Teachers of the University College Hospital, Ibadan Trade Dispute Board.

According to the instrument of our appointment and constitution, each of the boards was given separate and distinct terms of reference. Consequently, the three boards had to function in three separate and distinct capacities. Mr. R. Sappor, Senior Labour Officer, Federal Ministry of Labour was appointed Secretary to the Boards as constituted. The terms of reference of each board were separate and distinct, as already stated, having regard to the nature of the disputes, the subject matters in controversy for inquiry, and the organisations, institutions or even individuals concerned and involved in the disputes.

As was to be expected, some of the terms of reference of some of the boards differ considerably in some material respects from some of the terms of reference of the other boards. Therefore, in accordance with the order of sequence corresponding to the order in which the boards were constituted, I consider it necessary to, and I do herein and hereunder set out separately and for proper appreciation of the significant task called for by such inquiry, the terms of reference of each of the boards as hereunder appearing:-

Terms of References:-

A. The terms of reference of the Lagos State Doctors Trade Dispute Board were as follows –

"The board shall, with all convenient speed -

(a) inquire into the causes and circumstances of the dispute between the Lagos State government doctors and the Lagos State Ministry of Health and Social Welfare, and any other matter appearing to the board to be connected with or relevant to the said dispute, including the following issues, that is to say,

(i) whether or not there is need for the establishment of a hospital management board for government hospitals in Lagos state;

(ii) the existence or non-existence of differentials between the salaries payable to doctors in teaching hospitals and their counterparts in the Lagos state government hospitals, taking into account the qualifications, post qualification training, experience and the degree and weight of responsibility borne by the doctors in each case, and where such differentials exist the reasons and justification therefor, if any;

(iii) the existence or non-existence of differentials between the salaries of paramedical staff employed in Lagos state government hospitals and paramedical staff employed in the teaching hospitals, and between paramedical staff and doctors generally, and where such differentials exist the reasons and justification therefor, if any; and for the purposes of this paragraph "paramedical staff" means such staff as are mentioned in the schedule hereto;

(iv) whether or not any allowances or entitlements in the nature of "fringe benefits" should be payable to the doctors and, if so, the nature, amount and extent of such benefits;

(v) what promotion prospects there are for the doctors in the service of the Lagos state government;

(vi) the availability and adequacy or otherwise, of facilities, drugs and equipment in the hospitals;

(vii) the appropriateness or otherwise of the hours of duties of the doctors; and

(viii) whether or not the doctors should engage in private practice, and, if so, to what extent;

(b) submit a detailed statement of its findings as to the causes and circumstances of the said dispute; and

(c) make such recommendations, if any, as it may consider expedient and appropriate".

B. For the Association of Consultants, Lagos University Teaching Hospital Trade Dispute Board, the terms of reference were as hereunder set forth:-

"The board shall, with all convenient speed:-

(a) inquire into the causes and circumstances of the dispute between the Association of Consultants, Lagos University Teaching Hospital, the Board of Management of the Lagos University Teaching Hospital and the University of Lagos, and any other matter appearing to the board to be connected with or relevant to the said dispute, including the following issues, that is to say –

(i) the existence or non-existence of differentials between the salary payable to the consultants and the resident doctors of the Lagos University teaching hospitals taking into consideration the qualification, postqualification training, experience and the degree and weight of responsibility of the consultants and where such differentials exist, the reasons therefor, if any;

(ii) whether or not the consultants should be paid any honorarium, and, if so, the nature, amount and extent of such honorarium;

(iii) whether or not clinical consultants should be represented on the board of management of the hospital, and, if so, the proportion of such representation in relation to the constitution and powers of the board;

(b) submit a detailed statement of its findings as to the causes and circumstances of the said dispute; and

(c) make such recommendations, if any, as it may consider expedient and appropriate".

C. The Association of Clinical Teachers of the University College Hospital, Ibadan, Trade Dispute Board had the following terms of reference:-

"The board shall, with all convenient speed -

(a) inquire into the causes and circumstances of the dispute between the Association of Clinical Teachers of the University of Ibadan, and any other matter appearing to the board to be connected with or relevant to the said dispute, including the following issues, that is to say -

(i) the existence or non-existence of differentials between the salary payable to the clinical teachers and the resident doctors in the University College Hospital, Ibadan taking into consideration the qualifications, post-qualification training, experience and the degree and weight of responsibility of the clinical teachers and where such differentials exist, the reason therefor, if any; and

(ii) whether or not the clinical teachers should be paid salary supplementation or honorarium and, if so, the nature, amount and extent of such salary supplementation or honorarium;

(b)   submit a detailed statement of its findings as to the causes and circumstances of the said dispute; and

(c)   make such recommendations, if any, as it may consider expedient and appropriate".

In the conduct of the inquiries, the order of sequence was strictly adhered to, observed and maintained and was reflected in the report which the boards submitted to the federal military government of Nigeria through the Commissioner of Labour, Federal Ministry of Labour, Nigeria.

During the various inquiries the boards heard a total of 44 witnesses who testified on behalf of and as representing various interests. A total of 29 counsel appeared before the boards as representing certain institutions, organisations and groups. Although all the parties concerned in the various disputes took part in the proceedings, it would be considered fair to observe that the organisations, institutions, professional associations, paramedical groups and government departments and ministries, which not only submitted memoranda and were represented by counsel but also participated actively, directly and most effectively in the inquiries by giving evidence and other useful information and rendering invaluable assistance to the boards during the inquiries, included:-

(i)   The Medical Guild;

(ii)   The Nigerian Medical Association;

(iii) The Guild of Registered Nurses;

(iv)   The Professional Association of Trained Nurses;

(v)   The Nigerian Union of Pharmacists;

(vi)   The Occupational Therapists;

(vii) The Radiographers;

(viii) Dental Technologists;

(ix)   Medical Laboratory Technologists;

(x)   Catering Supervisors;

(xi)   Lagos State Government Ministry of Health and Social Welfare;

(xii) Federal Ministry of Health;

(xiii) The National Council on Establishment;

(xiv) The Association of Consultants, Lagos University Teaching Hospital;

(xv)   Lagos University Management Board;

(xvi) The University of Lagos;

(xvii) The Association of Clinical Teachers, University College Hospital, Ibadan;

(xviii) University College Hospital Management Board Ibadan and

(xix) The University of Ibadan.

For the purpose of checking and testing the evidence already given during the conduct of the various inquiries by witnesses, the boards visited, inspected and toured round the various hospitals listed hereunder according to dates indicated opposite each hospital:-

1. The General Hospital, Lagos	-	21 August 1972
2. Lagos Island Maternity Hospital	-	22 August 1972
3. University College Hospital, Ibadan	-	9 September 1972
4. Lagos University Teaching Hospital	-	26 September 1972
5. Children's Hospital, Massey Street, Lagos		27 September 1972
6. Royal Orthopaedic Hospital, Igbobi	-	27 September 1972
7. The General Hospital, Ikeja	-	27 September 1972

The proceedings of the boards were accorded wide publicity by the press and other national information media. They were recorded verbatim by stenographers and published in bound volumes daily.

The proceedings of the Lagos State Board were contained in 49 such bound volumes while there were 10 and 5 such bound volumes of the proceedings of the Association of Consultants, Lagos University Teaching Hospital Trade Dispute Board and of the Association of Clinical Teachers of University College Hospital, Ibadan Trade Dispute Board, respectively.

After due inquiries, reports were prepared in conformance with the terms of reference already indicated and submitted with the requisite recommendations to the federal military government of Nigeria.

Soon after the completion of these tedious assignments concerning the inquiries into the various disputes set out above, it was time for the Chief Justice of Nigeria, the Rt. Hon Sir Adetokunbo Ademola, KBE, PC to retire, and so it became necessary to look for a successor to the office. For the purpose, the Supreme Military Council had to meet. The names of five candidates consisting of Dr. T. O. S. Elias, Attorney General of the federation, the Hon Mr. Justice J. I. C. Taylor, then Chief Justice of the High Court of the federal territory of Lagos, the Hon Justice G. B. A. Coker, Justice, Supreme Court, Chief F. R. A. Williams, private legal practitioner, and myself, the Hon Sir Udo Udoma, formerly Chief Justice of Uganda and then Justice of the Supreme Court were submitted for consideration by the Supreme Military Council. Before the names were considered, it was alleged that, on the advice of the then incumbent Chief Justice, Sir Adetokunbo Ademola, the uncle of Dr. T. O. S. Elias through the auspices of the Muslim Association of Nigeria of which he was then vice-president serving under the then Sultan of Sokoto, now dead, who was the president of the association, had, on behalf of Dr. T. O. S. Elias, offered gratification to the Sultan of Sokoto as an inducement to enable the latter to exert pressure on the Head of State of Nigeria to favourably support the candidature of Dr. T. O. S. Elias and thereby to have him appointed Chief Justice of Nigeria.

To the surprise of everyone, the intrigue worked. For even though Dr. T. O. S. Elias' candidature was opposed by the majority of the military governors, on the third day of giving consideration to the matter, the Head of State, General Yakubu Gowon, in the application and exercise of the powers vested in him as Head of State and head of the federal military government and Commander-in-Chief of the Armed Forces of Nigeria, of his own volition appointed Dr. T. O. S. Elias Chief Justice of Nigeria by his own command and order and Dr. T. O. S. Elias was immediately sworn in as Chief Justice of Nigeria as successor to the Honourable Sir Adetokunbo Ademola to the disgust of most people, not the least the military governors of the Northern states under the leadership of Brigadier Abba Kyari in the absence of General Usman Katsina, who was then in the United Kingdom pursuing a course of study in military science at the request and on the order of General Yakubu Gowon, Head of the federal military government of Nigeria.

As a consolation and at the special request of all the military governors of the six Northern states comprising Brigadier Abba Kyari, Commissioner of Police J. D. Gomwalk, Brigadier Musa Usman, Commissioner of Police Alhaji Audu Bako, Col. D. L. Bamigboye and Assistant Commissioner Alhaji Usman Faruk, with the approval of the Council of Ahmadu Bello University, Zaria, I who had previously been tipped as the likely successor to the Rt. Honourable Sir Adetokunbo Ademola CFR, KBE, PC was offered the important but honorific post of the Chancellor of Ahmadu Bello University, Zaria. Having willingly and delightedly accepted the offer, I was on Friday, December 1, 1972 installed the third chancellor of the university since its foundation, during the annual convocation and the celebration of the tenth anniversary of the university at the University campus on Friday and Saturday, 1 and 2 December 1972. As the post of chancellor of a university is not a full time job, it was still possible for me with ease to continue to serve Nigeria as a Justice of the Supreme Court of Nigeria until retirement from that high office as prescribed by law.

I must confess that I very much enjoyed the period of my service as Chancellor of Ahmadu Bello University, Zaria, Nigeria. It was indeed a pleasant diversion from the tedious job of the administration of justice involving adjudication according to law and equity with equity prevailing some of the time. As far as the work of Chancellor was concerned, it was part of my duty to prepare with care and thought my addresses for delivery during convocation. I also assisted in revising the statutes of the university. Serving as Chancellor with a very active Vice-Chancellor such as Professor Ishaya S. Audu and a Chairman of the University Council in the person of Alhaji Umar Suleiman, the Emir of Bedde, both of who were distinguished and gifted university administrators of undoubted integrity and exemplary character, gave me great joy.

Unhappily, towards the end of my service as Chancellor, I took ill and had to be admitted for treatment. The treatment involved radiation which was ignorantly and negligently administered by Dr.

Duncan in the Lagos University Teaching Hospital which treatment proved unsuccessful and necessitated my having to be flown over to the United Kingdom on the generous order of General Yakubu Gowon for further and better medical treatment.

While I was undergoing treatment in a hospital in the United Kingdom, General Yakubu Gowon was overthrown by a *coup d'état* in 1975. General Murtala Mohammed assumed power and had to remove Dr. T. O. S. Elias from the office of Chief Justice of the Federation because of the allegations, among others, of the gift of gratification to the Sultan of Sokoto (deceased), already mentioned. The Honourable Justice Sir Darnley Alexander, who was until then the Chief Justice of the South Eastern state of Nigeria, replaced Dr. T. O. S. Elias. The Honourable Justice Sir Darnley Alexander was elevated to act as the Chief Justice of the federation until a substantive Chief Justice was appointed. Six months after General Murtala Mohammed assumed power, Lieutenant Colonel Bukar Sukar Dimka of the Nigeria Army Corps of Physical Education assassinated him in a failed coup attempt on February 13, 1976.

On my resumption of duty in the Supreme Court of Nigeria as a Justice of the Supreme Court of Nigeria, it came to me as a surprise beyond measure to find the Honourable Sir Darnley Alexander occupying the office of the Chief Justice of Nigeria whereas before my illness it was on my recommendation that the Honourable Justice Sir Darnley Alexander was appointed the Chief Justice of the South Eastern state of Nigeria. His appointment to that office was after I had been given the chance of first refusal. It has been necessary to mention this fact here because of certain events to follow.

Very shortly after my return from the United Kingdom to Nigeria as a Justice of the Supreme Court of Nigeria, I was appointed Chairman, Constituent Assembly for the drawing up and enacting of a new constitution for the governance of the Federal Republic of Nigeria based on the draft already prepared by the Constitution Drafting Committee which had previously been set up by General Murtala Mohammed before his death by assassination. The Constituent Assembly, operating in accordance with the terms and under the authority of the Constituent Assembly Decree of 1977, issued under the hand of Lieutenant General Olusegun Obasanjo as Head of State and head of the federal military government and approved by the Supreme Military Council, successfully produced the 1979 Constitution of the

Federal Republic of Nigeria. At the conclusion of that assignment, I was awarded the high order of the Commander of the Federal Republic (CFR for short).

Perhaps, at this juncture, I ought to mention an incident that occurred in the course of the production of the constitution by the Constituent Assembly. The incident was concerned with the dynamic issue of the creation of new states in Nigeria and happened in this way: While engaged in the discussion of the definition clause of the constitution, some members raised the issue concerning the number of states then created which had numbered nineteen (19), and contended that at least three (3) more states namely, Katsina, Awawa or Enugu and Akwa Ibom States, from whom petitions for their creation had been received, ought to be created so as to raise the number of states to twenty-two (22) from nineteen (19). The contention was unanimously accepted. But since the Constituent Assembly had no power to create new states, it became necessary for me as chairman to arrange to have a special meeting with the Supreme Military Council. The meeting was accordingly arranged with success.

Unfortunately, my meeting with the Supreme Military Council drew a blank because Brigadier Shehu Musa Yar'adua had rejected the proposal concerning the three states out of hand speaking on behalf of the Supreme Military Council. All the same, on completion of my duty as the chairman of the Constituent Assembly, I was satisfied that I had done my best for my country, Nigeria. It was indeed an outstanding achievement having regard to the fact particularly that I had survived negligent treatment with radiation.

In spite of my handicap, as Justice of the Supreme Court of Nigeria, I was engaged in the discharge of my responsibilities in the court with undiminished zeal and gusto not to mention vigour, fully encouraged by General Olusegun Obasanjo as head of the federal military government and Head of State who, on one occasion when I mentioned to him the fact of my being handicapped by reason of being an amputee, at once dismissed it by asking me: "do you think with your feet?" In other words, that my indisposition as an amputee could not prevent me from the use of my brains since the job of a judge is not like a football game. That was most encouraging to me. Shortly afterwards, I had to go to Germany for treatment for my other leg which had also been radiated by Dr. Duncan. Unfortunately, that too had to be amputated and consequently I was a double amputee and initially required two walking sticks in order to walk.

It should be clearly understood that, as successor to General Murtala Mohammed, General Olusegun Obasanjo was engaged in the execution of the transitional programme already set in motion by General Murtala Mohammed for the purpose of handing over power to a civilian regime. Then, after the formation of parties by politicians, general elections had to be conducted by the then National Electoral Commission throughout the country. Around that time, the Honourable Sir Darnley Alexander, who had been acting as Chief Justice of Nigeria, was appointed Chairman of the Law Reform Commission. The electoral provisions stipulated in the constitution allowed appeals from decisions of the Presidential Election Tribunal to lie in the Supreme Court and it became therefore necessary to appoint a new Chief Justice of Nigeria. The rumour then current in the country was that I was then seriously being considered for appointment as the Chief Justice of Nigeria having regard to my service in Uganda, Eastern Africa as Chief Justice, considered along with my meritorious service since my return to Nigeria as Justice of the Supreme Court. In the circumstances, Mr. Justice Fatayi-Williams, then also a Justice of the Supreme Court registered a solemn protest on the ground that he saw no reason why I should be given such a high post as the Chief Justice of Nigeria despite the fact that I was an amputee. He felt strongly that the Supreme Military Council, under the leadership of a Yoruba man like himself, would not be justified to ignore him who then had no handicap. He then contacted several Yoruba men including Chief S. L. Edu to contact General Olusegun Obasanjo as Head of State to plead his case.

According to Mr. Justice Fatayi-Williams in his book "Cases, Faces and Places", his intrigues succeeded and he was preferred to me because, in his representation, he was able to convince General Olusegun Obasanjo that since Alhaji Shehu Shagari as a Hausa-Fulani was contesting the office of President of Nigeria and had chosen Dr. Ekwueme, an Igbo man, as his running mate as Vice-President, both of whom were likely to win, then the office of Chief Justice of Nigeria ought to be filled by himself, a Yoruba man, especially as Chief Obafemi Awolowo was sure to lose the election. It is interesting to note that, in concluding this portion of his book, Mr. Justice Fatayi-Williams sadly observed that after he had been appointed Chief Justice of Nigeria, he was so overjoyed that he had to mention the matter to both his wife and his mother. But on receiving the news of his success, his wife appeared completely uninterested - which showed that his wife is a woman of very high moral principles because all along in the Supreme Court his charming wife knew that the Honourable Mr. Justice Fatayi-Williams was always boasting that both he and myself were great friends and his wife would not approve of his hitting me below the belt without crying foul.

However, on my return to Nigeria from Germany after treatment, General Olusegun Obasanjo had to break the news of my having been superseded gently to me in so far as the post of Chief Justice of Nigeria was concerned. He said to me that because of my disclosure to him in my letter that I had to undergo a second amputation by reason of which I had to be walking soon after the operation with the help of two walking sticks, the Supreme Military Council, being of the opinion that to appoint me Chief Justice of Nigeria would be to overburden me with heavy responsibility, had no alternative but to offer the post of Chief Justice of Nigeria to my friend, Mr. Justice Fatayi-Williams in the hope that I would not feel disappointed. Of course I felt extremely disappointed particularly having been informed that the Honourable Mr. Justice Fatayi-Williams had canvassed for the office at my expense. Indeed I had to raise the question of my being released to retire on the terms entrenched in the new constitution but it was refused by the Head of State.

The Head of State would not hear of releasing me to retire just as he would not hear of granting me permission to institute action against the Lagos University Teaching Hospital for negligence as regards the manner in which I was medically treated as a patient in the hospital. He drummed into me that I must appreciate that the Lagos University Teaching Hospital was a federal institution and that for the Federal Military Government to grant me permission to institute legal proceedings in the High Court against the hospital for damages for negligence would be tantamount to agreeing that the hospital be closed down.

Shortly thereafter, I was appointed Chairman and Director of Seminars for newly appointed judges throughout the federation, which I had to accept and the performance of which I had to combine with my duties as a Justice of the Supreme Court. On the issue of retirement, the Head of State assured me that on no account would the Supreme Military Council wish to dispense with my services. It was the policy of the Supreme Military Council to strengthen the Supreme Court for which purposes my services were indispensable having regard to my knowledge and experience.

CHAPTER TWENTY-SEVEN

I Retire From The Civil Service

"Remember that it is nothing to do your duty, that is demanded of you and is no more meritorious than to wash your hands when they are dirty; when love and duty are one then grace is in you and you will enjoy happiness which passes all understanding". – Sommerset Maughan in "The Painted Veil".

I continued to serve obediently and cooperatively throughout the period of my loyal service to my country, Nigeria, both as a Justice of the Supreme Court of Nigeria and Chairman and Director of Seminars for newly appointed judges throughout the federal republic of Nigeria and under the Chief Justiceship of Mr. Justice Fatayi Williams, until I retired in 1982. Although sometimes I used to feel depressed, yet I took it all in my stride. I enjoyed my work. I bore nobody malice. Even though my normal conversations and association with Mr. Fatayi Williams had to be curtailed having regard to his numerous engagements and his natural display of superiority as Chief Justice of Nigeria, all the same, from time to time, I felt it my duty to call upon him and pay him my respects, although normally as Chief Justice of Nigeria, he was regarded as *primus inter pares* among the Justices of the Supreme Court of Nigeria.

Then a time came and I had to inform, as was my duty, His Excellency, the President of the federal republic of Nigeria, Alhaji Shehu Shagari, that it was time I retired on full pension as regulated by law. To my surprise, on receiving my notice of retirement, His Excellency, the President of Nigeria invited me for a discussion in his office. I promptly accepted the invitation. I humbly and respectfully attended a meeting with His Excellency, Alhaji Shehu Shagari, at his office on the appointed day. In the course of our discussion, His Excellency, the President offered to me, on retirement as Justice, Supreme Court of Nigeria, the new and vacant post of Chairman, Declaration of Assets Tribunal soon then to be set up in Lagos to take charge of high officials and members of the Senate and the House of Representatives, especially having regard to my physical disability. I gently and politely declined the offer on the ground that I had already decided to move house from Lagos to Ikot Abasi in the then Cross River state but now Akwa Ibom state and there to settle until my grand old age and, of course, final demise as I was anxious that I be buried among the bones of my ancestors, although, according to an old adage, a man could only know where he was born but not where he would die. That decision constitutes a part of my last will and testament.

In vain did His Excellency attempt to prevail upon me. In consequence of his insistence that the new appointment would be only part time, I reacted by pointing out to him that I was certain members of the Senate and of the House of Representatives might consider me as often too strict in my approach to public affairs and therefore unsuitable for the post. I made clear to His Excellency that, in my old age after having fought hard to satisfy humanity, it was my wish to die peacefully and preferably in my sleep. I drew his attention to my performances in regard to the Langa-Langa train accident inquiry, the Doctors and Consultants Trade Dispute tribunals and, in deed, the Constituent Assembly for the drawing up of a new constitution for the governance of Nigeria: "All these and more; what was my reward?", I asked. And I told him that I felt I had done more than enough without any reward. I had therefore decided on a quiet life and exit having regard to my physical condition of health. On that note we parted company as old friends.

Thereafter, I moved house as quietly as I had decided I would. The month after my retirement found me already settled in my new house with a large compound, which home I named MFUT ITIAT ENIN at Ikot Abasi Township - MFUT ITIAT ENIN meaning "in the shelter of the elephant rock", ENIN being "an elephant" and the name of my ancestor who was also the founder of the original IKOT ABASI VILLAGE, according to tradition. For IKOT ABASI is a shortened form of IKOT ABASI AKPAN ENIN, which means "the people or followers of ABASI AKPAN ENIN". ABASI means God but was the name given to my ancestor.

I considered myself extremely lucky to have retired from the service in sound health, having regard to the fact that, in the course of my services, I felt so seriously ill that it was only by the grace of God and the help of the federal government of Nigeria that I had to be flown first to Great Britain and latterly to West Germany, where I had to be admitted into specialist hospitals for medical treatment. In each case, the treatment was surgery ultimately. The result is that I am now a double amputee. On each occasion I escaped death by the skin of my teeth and through the love of our Merciful God.

Having rested for over one year, I received an invitation from the Cross River state government to accept an offer of the post of Chairman, Law Reform Commission, then to be established by the state. Having considered the fact that Calabar, the headquarters of Cross River state government, was very close to my home at Ikot Abasi, I willingly accepted the offer. In response to an invitation by His Excellency, Dr. Clement Isong, the governor of the state, I went to Calabar for the purpose of being sworn in based on the assurance by the then Attorney-General, Dr. Ita Ekanem, that approval had been given by the state house of assembly for the establishment of the institution. His Excellency, Dr. Clement N. Isong, on the appointed day, in fact, swore me in. Then, on the following day, a debate on the issue was opened in the state house of assembly. I felt rather embarrassed, as the impression was abroad that I was at Calabar to exert pressure on the members of the house of assembly for a successful passage of the motion to create the institution of law reform for the state. I was angry.

Immediately, I got into touch with His Excellency, the governor, and registered a protest indicating that I was seriously embarrassed by the situation. For it was obvious that the house of assembly, as such, had not granted approval for the establishment of the institution of the Law Reform Commission for the state. His Excellency apologised for the situation and pleaded with me not to depart from Calabar. Shortly thereafter, I left Calabar and returned to Ikot Abasi township. I was disappointed with the manner in which the attorney general, Dr. Ita Ekanem, handled the whole matter.

The next I heard of the Law Reform Commission for Cross River state was after the *coup d'état* that overthrew Alhaji Shehu Shagari as President of the federal republic of Nigeria, which *coup d'état* took place after the general elections of 1983. The new Head of State of the federal military government was General Buhari with Col. Idiagbon as his deputy. The military governor of the Cross River state was then Lt. Col. Dan Archibong, who immediately having settled down, resuscitated the idea of establishing the Law Reform Commission in Cross River state. That was in about 1985.

As soon as the idea was revived, I was contacted by some members of the staff of the Ministry of Justice of the Cross River state at the request, I was told, of the new military governor of the state. There then followed a series of serious detail negotiations as to the terms and conditions of service if I should accept the offer. I had then felt that "once bitten twice shy" according to an old adage and therefore must leave no stone unturned. Finally, I accepted the offer and went down to Calabar and was sworn in a second time but this time by the military governor of the state, Lt. Col. Dan Archibong early in 1985. I, also, soon thereafter commenced work at Calabar relishing the wonderful assistance of Mrs. Otu, the solicitor general of the state, I believe, who spared no pains in arranging suitable accommodation for my family and me, and about whom I write with gratitude and the highest of respects.

I was fully engaged in law reform as the chairman of the commission when, happily in September 1987, Akwa Ibom state - the land of promise – was created by the generosity of General Buhari's successor, General Babangida, to the delight of the Ibibio people. With the creation of Akwa Ibom state, my interest in law reform for Cross River state began to flag and wane. Still encouraged by Commander Princewill, who succeeded Lt. Col. Dan Archibong as military governor, I had to devise a system whereby the Law Reform Commission could be extended to Akwa Ibom state so that it might turn out to be a joint enterprise for the two states since it started out that way when the two states were one. All the same, as a native of Akwa Ibom state, I had to move house back to Ikot Abasi township, my ancestral home and normal habitat.

At Akwa Ibom state, I endeavoured to initiate action in connection with the opening and establishing of an office to be occupied by the entire staff of the Law Reform Commission, which, with the consent of Commander Princewill, the military governor of Cross River state, would operate for both states. Luckily for me, at Ikot Abasi township and quite close to the location of the headquarters of the Ikot Abasi local government council hall, offices and secretariat, there was to be found an abandoned building, which was originally constructed to constitute a government guesthouse. It was uncompleted but abandoned. I at once picked on the uncompleted but abandoned government guest house and invited the military governor at Uyo, headquarters of Akwa Ibom state, to visit Ikot Abasi township for the purpose of inspecting and approving the uncompleted but abandoned government guest house as the office block for the accommodation of the proposed Law Reform Commission to be operated as joint enterprise for the Cross River and Akwa Ibom states. The governor of Akwa Ibom state accepted the invitation. He then appointed a day for the visit.

On the appointed day, Lt. Col. Ogbeha, the new military governor of Akwa Ibom state, promptly arrived. He visited the *locus in quo* and, in the course of conversation, enquired where at that particular point in time the staff of the Law Reform Commission was located. I explained that, ever since our departure from Calabar, the skeleton staff of the commission who agreed to leave with me usually assembled in my personal library in my large compound. There was nowhere else they could be accommodated, hence the search for office accommodation. During the inspection, there was also in attendance the loyal and faithful Mrs. Otu, now solicitor general of Akwa Ibom state. The solicitor general rendered useful service as usual and assisted the military governor in making up his mind which resulted in the approval of the uncompleted but abandoned government guest house as the appropriate building to house the Law Reform Commission at Ikot Abasi.

Immediately thereafter, Lt. Col. Ogbeha ordered that work should be resumed so as to have the uncompleted but abandoned government guest house completed with an altered plan to house the Law Reform Commission to be operated as a joint enterprise for the two states, namely, Akwa Ibom and Cross River. A new contractor was at once engaged. He was instructed to undertake in the completion of the uncompleted but abandoned government guesthouse under the supervision of the chairman of the local government council, Ikot Abasi.

In the mean time, the Law Reform Commission was approved to continue to operate in my library at Ikot Abasi. The Law Reform Commission was thus approved to operate as a joint enterprise for both the Cross River and Akwa Ibom states of Nigeria in Ikot Abasi township without recourse to Uyo as the capital of Akwa Ibom state. Any move on my part to Uyo in search of accommodation was thereby avoided as it became unnecessary. I remained in my house at Ikot Abasi to watch the progress of the work by the new contractor. I also engaged myself in the work of law reform since my personal secretary was with me at Ikot Abasi. I was heartily congratulated for my skill in being able to persuade the military governor, Lt. Col. Ogbeha, to allow me to remain in Ikot Abasi while engaged in law reform as the chairman of the commission. In addition, I also succeeded in getting both states to cooperate as far as law reform was concerned and to execute jointly a memorandum of understanding in that respect, the memorandum having been executed by the attorneys-general of both states as representatives of both military governors of the two states.

Eventually, the uncompleted but abandoned government guesthouse, as altered, was completed. It was ready for occupation. I was preparing to move from my library to occupy the completed block of offices at any time on being so commanded. Shortly thereafter and instead of receiving the word of command for me to move to occupy the block of offices, there was an announcement that Lt. Col. Ogbeha had proceeded on transfer and that he was to be succeeded by Lt. Col.

Abbey as the military governor of Akwa Ibom state. There upon, Lt. Col. Abbey took over from Lt. Col. Ogbeha and assumed the office of the military governor of Akwa Ibom state and Obong Etuk-Eyen was secretary to the military government of the state.

Within the month of the assumption of duty by Lt. Col. Abbey, I applied for permission to visit him at Uyo and there to pay him my respects as an officer serving under him. I then travelled to Uyo and visited Lt. Col. Abbey for the purpose of welcoming him to Akwa Ibom state. As soon as Lt. Col. Abbey saw me he asked what I wanted at Uyo and said that he had already heard so much about me. He mentioned that he was told that it was my plan to conduct the Law Reform Commission, of which I was chairman, as a joint enterprise for both Akwa Ibom and Cross River states and that I had already succeeded in prevailing upon Lt. Col. Ogbeha to accept my decision and that he could find no earthly reason to justify my decision why Akwa Ibom and Cross River states should operate the Law Reform Commission as a joint enterprise. In any case, he pointed out that it was quite competent for him to overrule my decision in that respect. Lt. Col. Abbey continued to rebuke me for having influenced his predecessor to support my decision. In vain did I endeavour to point out to him that it was not my decision but that of both Commander Princewill, military governor, Cross River state and Lt. Col. Ogbeha, military governor, Akwa Ibom state who took the view that the Law Reform Commission be operated as a joint enterprise by the two states. It was their considered opinion that to operate the Law Reform Commission as a joint enterprise would result in reducing the cost of operation. In vain did I endeavour to argue with him that the stand taken by the two governors was reasonable, in the circumstance.

I there and then mentioned to him that the governors of the two states had jointly executed a memorandum of understanding to the effect that the Law Reform Commission be operated as a joint enterprise under my chairmanship. I was completely flabbergasted by the behaviour of Lt. Col. Abbey towards me even at first sight. I was at a loss to understand and appreciate what had brought it about. We had never met before nor had we ever been in association. My name and presence before him seemed to carry a stink. I was dumb founded. I therefore decided to depart from his presence. I was convinced his behaviour was calculated. I decided to leave him at Uyo and return to Ikot Abasi when he told me that he himself had already decided that Akwa Ibom state should be detached from the Cross River state and must therefore have a Law Reform Commission of its own. He told me emphatically that he had already decided to set up an entirely new Law Reform Commission for Akwa Ibom state.

As I left him on my way to board my car, he got up from his seat and preceded me in an attempt to see me off. On reaching my car, he opened the door and invited me to board the car, which I did. As my driver drove off, I bade him farewell. As we drove away, I found myself in a state of confusion. I began to wonder what the officers, particularly the secretary to the government, Obong Etuk-Eyen, could have told Lt. Col. Abbey about me. At home at Ikot Abasi, I waited patiently but in vain to see whether I would receive any communication from the military governor or even from his office at Uyo. I continued to operate the Law Reform Commission in my library with the skeleton staff who had joined me from Calabar.

I then travelled to Calabar in an effort to contact Commander Princewill, the military governor of Cross River state, after having reported my experience with Lt. Col. Abbey to him in writing. At Calabar, I drew a blank because, on arrival, I was told that the military governor, Commander Princewill, was away on tour of the state. I returned to Ikot Abasi and continued to operate the Law Reform Commission the best I could. Then towards the end of the year 1987, I received, quite unexpectedly, the attorneys-generals of both Cross River and Akwa Ibom states on a visit of inspection. I was happy to receive them both, for at least, it was an indication that all was not lost. Both governments were conscious of our existence. Thereafter and early in the ensuing year, I applied for my salary and indicated to the Akwa Ibom state ministry of justice that, as usual, my salary should be paid into my current bank account as and when due. I then entertained some hope that Lt. Col. Abbey, military governor of Akwa Ibom state, would probably do the right thing concerning his decision to establish a separate Law Reform Commission for Akwa Ibom state. But nothing happened. Instead there was a stalemate. On reflection, I decided to resign from the Law Reform Commission and that was precisely what I did and with no regrets. At the end of the year, 1988, I tendered my resignation from the chairmanship of the commission.

On receiving my resignation, Lt. Col. Abbey refused to order that I be paid my hard earned salaries, which had accumulated for two years - 1987 to 1988. I wrote demanding the payment of my salaries for two years by Akwa Ibom state to which we in the service of Akwa Ibom state belonged and were posted since, in law, my salaries had become a charge against Akwa Ibom state. Because of the creation of Akwa Ibom state in 1987, those of us who belonged to Akwa Ibom were immediately transferred from the public service of Cross River state to the Public service of Akwa Ibom state, our services being continuous. We had moved *embloc* at the request and command of Akwa Ibom state from Calabar to Uyo in Akwa Ibom state. But in my case, on arrival at Uyo and finding that there was no accommodation to house the Law Reform Commission, I had decided, with the approval of the military governor, Lt. Col. Ogbeha, to move and did move on to Ikot Abasi, my ancestral home.

Finding that, on the order of Lt. Col. Abbey, I had been refused my two years salaries, I decided to ignore the situation, the alternative being an action in court to recover the debt. As a result of the situation, it also occurred to me that I had also lost the privilege of visiting the United Kingdom for medical treatment at the expense of Akwa Ibom state.

Now that the question of privilege has been mentioned, it is necessary to offer some explanation as to how it came about. After I had served as chairman, Law Reform Commission, under Lt. Col. Dan Archibong as the military governor of Cross River state, Lt. Col. Dan Archibong had to go on transfer. Commander Princewill succeeded him as military governor, Cross River state. During the first year of his service as military governor, I visited Government House on the invitation of Commander Princewill. In the course of conversation, the military governor informed me that he understood that because of my physical disability it was usually necessary for me to visit the United Kingdom once a year for medical treatment. I, at once, confirmed the information. The military governor then asked whether the federal government usually funded such visits. I replied in the negative and the military governor, who then appeared angry, told me that the story of my disability was well known to have been caused by the negligence of the Lagos University Teaching Hospital and its staff, and that it was unfair for me to be saddled with the burden of such expenses.

There and then, Commander Princewill, in a very generous manner undertook that, from then on, the funding of my visits to the United Kingdom every year must be borne by the Cross River state government. That undertaking was later confirmed in writing to the effect that, so long as my visit concerned medical treatment in the United Kingdom in relation to my disability, the expenses should be borne by the Cross River state government. I benefited from the undertaking only twice before the creation of Akwa Ibom state.

Curiously enough, on the day that Nigerian Telecommunications Limited (NITEL) was to be commissioned in Ikot Abasi in 1990,

Lt. Col. Abbey visited Ikot Abasi as one of the important guests of NITEL. At the commissioning of NITEL, I met Lt. Col. Abbey at the function in Ikot Abasi. On seeing me at the function, Lt. Col. Abbey came close and saluted me. He told me that he had decided to visit me in my house immediately after the function. I, again being flabbergasted, asked him: "What for?". He told me that the purpose of his visit to my house was a well-kept secret but that he was looking forward to seeing me at my residence. Immediately after the function, I left for my residence, there to await the arrival of Lt. Col. Abbey as my important though strange visitor. Arriving home, I went upstairs for a change of clothing so as to restore myself to my personal comfort. On my descending downstairs, I met Lt. Col. Abbey and his entourage already in my parlour. Lt. Col. Abbey was already seated in my cushion chair. I greeted him again and indicated that I was surprised to find him already seated. He blinked his eyes.

I then asked what had brought him to my house. However, in order to maintain my manners I greeted him cheerfully and asked him whether he would be kind enough to inform me the entertainment of his choice having regard to the manner of his visit to me. I then presented to his Aide camp a bottle of Haigh Dimple. But, before his Aide camp could stretch his hand to accept the gift, Lt. Col. Abbey himself swept aside his Aide camp and by himself received the bottle of whisky. He then spoke by way of address. He confessed that he had personally decided to visit me that day in order to atone for the injustice that I had to suffer in his hand. That he had come personally to apologise to me in front of his entourage for the offence which he had done to me because, on arrival in Akwa Ibom, he had listened to gossip about me by his own staff. He said that he had discovered that he had made a mistake by treating me the way he had done even to the extent of causing me to resign from the post of the chairmanship of the Law Reform Commission. He had discovered his mistake rather too late to mend.

On discovering that he had offended me unduly, he had found it difficult to approach me again, he said. But now that he was to proceed on transfer from Akwa Ibom, he felt that he must visit me and openly confess his fault. Otherwise, he might leave Akwa Ibom state with a heavy heart. In return, I told him that I did not bear him any grudge. As far as his behaviour was concerned, my feeling at the time was that he was carrying out his duty in the manner he knew best. He then asked whether I had forgiven him. In my answer I said, "Of course, yes". We then parted as good friends.

CHAPTER TWENTY-EIGHT

The Man Clocks 80

"All political scientists seem agreed that the hour when a democracy begins to collapse is when the people's demands exceed the country's resources, and refusing to face this fact, they begin to raid their own Treasury".

Dad's resignation as chairman of the joint Law Reform Commission for Akwa Ibom and Cross-River states marked the end of over five decades of his meritorious service to his fatherland and allowed him to settle into a full-fletched life of retirement. It also allowed him ample time to reflect on his life and his family and to smell the roses, so to say. Now an elder-statesman, he devoted much of his time to fearlessly critiquing the polity, educating the reading public and his guests on the history and politics of Nigeria and of the Ibibio Country, and to the continued documentation, in book form, of his experiences vis-à-vis these historical and political developments for posterity, which project he had started as soon as he left Lagos for Ikot Abasi. Having been in the forefront of the fight for the emancipation of the British colonies of Africa, having been active as an advocate of equality for and freedom of his people from the shackles of colonialism and ethnic suppression, having served as a High Court judge, a Supreme Court Justice, a Chief Justice of a nation, Chairman of the Constituent Assembly and several tribunals, and as Chancellor of Ahmadu Bello University, Zaria, he was seen as an authority on a slew of subjects. Accordingly, he often had to play host to visiting dignitaries to Akwa Ibom State and, of course, members of the press who often solicited his take on the matters of concern of the day pertaining to the government and the welfare of the country. He held no-hold-barred interviews with the press tracing the steady decline in Nigeria's social and moral fabric, including the decline and politicisation of the Judiciary. In November 1995, Policy Magazine quoted him as saying that "Nigeria has collapsed".

He now started work on his second book, this one on Nigerian constitutional law. Earlier, in 1985, on finishing work on documenting the background, emergence, aims, objectives and achievements of the Ibibio Union, he got Spectrum Books Ltd. to publish "The Story of The Ibibio Union" which was very well received and remains the sole reference material for the successful experiment at re-integration of a people - to use dad's words - the people being the Ibibios which include the Annangs. He hoped that "the present and future generations will be able to produce a better history of the Ibibio Union, which has now become a landmark in the history of the growth and development of the Nigerian nation". That same year, Mr. Dennis S. Udo-Inyang, who worked tirelessly along with Dr. Okoi Arikpo and a host of others in supporting dad in fighting the cause of the COR State Movement, released a small book dedicated to dad who the author described as "the great son of Africa who has made his indelible footprint in the African Continent and who is reckoned with the top jurists of this modern world". Dr. Okoi Arikpo, a one time Minister of External Affairs of Nigeria, in the foreword to that book, "The Man – Sir Justice Udo Udoma", said: "Udoma's generosity is proverbial. His courage is infectious. It is these great qualities of Sir Egbert Udo Udoma that Mr. Udo-Inyang has set out to portray in this book. He has chosen a few incidents in the life of the Man to show that Udoma was not only born great but earned greatness in everything he did – education, politics, law". Though dad was not one to delve on adulation or to expect a pat on the back for anything he did, and was used to rarely being shown appreciation by the very people he sacrificed so much for, to the extent that I personally thought that this, no doubt, heartfelt tribute by Mr. Udo-Inyang was too little too late, he must have appreciated the sincerity and devotion that attended Mr. Udo-Inyang's work. It must have taken a lot for Mr. Udo-Inyang to admit in that book to once being one of those ungrateful people who had criticised dad out of ignorance and from listening to dad's detractors. The book must also have helped to validate dad's decision to document his experiences and knowledge for posterity.

Dad continued to take his annual trips to the United Kingdom for his medical check-up, at which time he would spend a few transit days in Lagos. But, other than that, he rarely travelled anywhere far away from his residence at Ikot Abasi. Often, I would travel from the United States to London to spend some time with him and mum, at which time he would share tit-bits of "the Eagle's flight" with me. The beauty of listening to the detailed and passionate stories that dad told, is the combination of his heightened sense of recall of events of his past and the amazingly intuitive sense of direction he had for his life, even in his youth. Dad would tell me the exact address of the home of the person he was sent to deliver a letter to when he went to London for the first time. Dad remembered his nanny's name, the name of the person who married her, and what he did for a living at the time. Dad would talk of his insistence on doing the right thing - testifying at the Sir Stafford Foster-Sutton enquiry in 1956, or of contesting election in 1959, in spite of warnings from his well wishers, including the Sadauna of Sokoto, of imminent danger and of even death threats. He insisted that since the 1958 Nigeria Constitutional Conference held in London had decided that further consideration of the creation of states would be determined by the results of the federal election of December 1959, it was incumbent upon him to return to the House of Representatives to continue to shepherd the COR state movement. But, ironically, when he was "rigged" out of the House of Representatives, he completely ignored the pleading of his supporters who sorely needed him to join them in protesting against the rigged election and deman-ding re-election. Rather, seemingly unperturbed, he re-signed himself to his fate. I guess he knew that it was time to move on.

My tête-à-têtes with dad on those occasions revealed something that I do not think that many of those who idolised him even realised. He had a deep spirituality, and by that I mean a deep at-oneness with the Almighty, which fact accounts for his sharp sense of recall and intuition, I believe. That also explains his abhorrence of materialism in all of its ramifications. He was not interested in amassing money or property and wouldn't go to court to solicit recourse for whatever injustice was done to him or debt was owed him. He wouldn't even institute an action to recover the salaries owed him by the Akwa Ibom state government in 1987 and 1988. In 1950, as he recalled, Chief Bode Thomas, a thriving legal practitioner and businessman of the time, offered dad six plots of land on Ikorodu Road, Lagos for fifty pounds (£50) per plot but he rejected the offer. "If you are interested in litigation," he said, "go and acquire land in Lagos". Asked in 1995 what he thought about that decision in retrospect, he answered, "I still stand by that statement". He was the consummate humanist and saw himself as his proverbial brother's keeper and strove to lead by example. We, his children, have been immensely blessed by Providence to have had the best mentor any child can have in their formative years.

He finished his second book in 1995 and got Malthouse Press Limited to publish "History and the Law of the Constitution of Nigeria". He had developed interest in Constitutional Law and History while an undergraduate student of Law at Trinity College, Dublin where he manifested sound knowledge in these subjects as well as Criminal Law and the Law of Evidence. He also had the good fortune of attending every Constitutional Conference ever held for the formulation of constitutions for the governance of Nigeria prior to independence in October 1960. He included the judgment that he and his colleagues passed in the landmark Constitutional Law case Uganda vs. the Commissioner of Prisons, Ex Parte Matovu in this book (see Appendix C).

As he related in Chapter 26, he was the Chairman of the Constituent Assembly that prescribed Nigeria's 1979 Constitution and, so, it was befitting and pertinent for him to write an authoritative source of reference for students of Law as well as legal practitioners in Nigeria. The book was launched at the Institute of International Affairs in Victoria Island, Lagos. He returned home to Ikot Abasi after the launching and started work on what turned out to be his last book - this book, his autobiography.

Dad always looked forward to the end of year festivities because at that time he would assemble all members of his family at Ikot Abasi. Other than a few times when Ebong could not make it down, or Inam had to travel to London to be with his family, we all came down to spend the Christmas holidays with him and mum. In December 1996, I passed through Aba, as I usually did, on my way home and was told by the son of one of dad's friends and the contractor of his house at 22 Park Road, that many people had gone to him to enquire if dad wouldn't sell the house since they obviously noticed that dad's tenant was not taking good care of the house. He went on to say that someone had even offered a certain amount of money for it. I promised to pass on the message and did so as soon as I arrived at Ikot Abasi. Dad assured me that that was one house he had no intention of selling, as it was his first house and, for sentimental reasons, he would keep it. I relayed his message back to his friend at Aba. Lo and behold, a few months later, my brother, Udoma, called me up and said "Guess what!" "What is it?" I enquired. "You know, dad has gone and sold the Aba house without even saying a word to any of us?" I said, "Well, it's his house; at least this time he sold it instead of just giving it away as he did his houses in Port Harcourt and Enugu." Udoma asked, "Do you know how much he sold it for?" and then continued before I could even respond "For half of what you mentioned was even offered to his friend which amount is even a far cry from its market value!!". When I travelled to London in the early summer of that year to see dad, I brought up the subject of the house that "we were not going to sell, for sentimental reasons". Dad looked down and said, "Well, the man kept travelling down from Aba to bother me over the house, and so, to get him off my back, I decided to let him have it for what he was offering." He quickly changed the topic and that was that.

As dad's eightieth birthday approached, we, his children, huddled to discuss what plans we should make to mark the occasion – what form the celebration should take and where we should hold it. We resolved that, since the core of dad's life's work could be categorised as "work for country" and "struggle for his people", we should have two birthday parties, one in Lagos to allow his colleagues and friends as well as dignitaries at the federal level to attend, and the other in Ikot Abasi for the people of the state to come and celebrate with their hero. On communicating our plan to dad and receiving his approval, my brothers in consort with a committee of friends put a plan in place to put on a show for him, and so they did. Mum and dad made plans to arrive in Lagos from their annual trip to London a few days before the Lagos luncheon reception commenced. My brother Ebong and I arrived just before the festivities from our stations in the USA as well.

So, on Saturday, June 14, 1997, we held a befitting reception at the Metropolitan Club in Victoria Island for dad, under the chairmanship of the then Chief Justice of Nigeria, the Honourable Justice Mohammed Lawal Uwais. It was very well attended and dad got to see some of his friends again - Chief Moses Majekodunmi, Chief T. O. S. Benson, Chief Rotimi Williams, who proposed the toast to dad, and Chief Ayo Rosiji, to mention a few. Music diva Christie Essien and her band provided the music and dad was happy and I couldn't be happier for him. I, however, had mixed feelings when Chief Rotimi Williams, in lamenting the fact that dad was not made Chief Justice ostensibly because he was a double amputee, unwittingly compared dad to FDR (Franklin D. Roosevelt) who served as the President of the United States of America in spite of the polio that crippled him from the age of 39. In fact, I was so perturbed by it that I had an emotional breakdown while making my own remarks in tribute to dad on behalf of my siblings and myself. My displeasure was as to the fact that such an analogy gave the impression that dad's medical demise was an act of God, which is what polio is. Now, when the son of man radiates someone's feet with enough radium to kill him, in treating varicose veins on one foot, that cannot translate to an act of God. Secondly, even though dad had this done to him over twenty years before his 80th birthday, the matter hadn't had much publicity and even in 1997 very few people knew anything about it. And yet, an enquiry had been set up by General Gowon's government and the panel had recommended that Dr. Duncan's license to practice medicine be revoked after St. Bartholomew's hospital sent a report to the effect that he should not be practicing medicine since he had administered enough radium into dad to kill him. My recollection of the events surrounding the matter is that there was not only a concerted effort to get Duncan a less severe punishment but to hush the matter entirely as well. It was all I could do at the time not to think that the act was wilful and orchestrated to prevent dad from being Chief Justice of Nigeria. And so, those who had seen dad on a wheel chair were thinking that perhaps complications of diabetes or something like that had caused him to be wheel chair ridden. I, therefore, felt that Chief Rotimi William's statement further propagated that myth. Further, out of respect for the Chief, (he obviously meant well) I couldn't explain my emotional conflict to the august audience either; getting it off my chest would certainly have helped to relax me. Gladly, dad understood and that was the only thing that mattered.

On Tuesday, June 17, 1997 at the Lecture Hall of the Nigerian Institute for International Affairs in Victoria Island, Lagos, there was a public presentation of a book on dad derived from the manuscript of this book and other of dad's publications, and which book was written by Barrister Ekong Samson and published by Patrioni Books. It is titled "Law And Statesmanship: The Legacy Of Sir Udo Udoma". The chairman of the occasion was Chief Rotimi Williams, the guest lecturer was the Honourable Justice Mamman Nasir, then the chairman of the Transition Implementation Committee; the book reviewer was the Honourable Justice Kayode Eso; and the special guest of honour was Air Vice Marshall Nsikak Eduok who was then the Chief of Air Staff of Nigeria. Some others in attendance included Chief T. O. S. Benson, a first republic Minister, Chief M. D. Yusuf, former Inspector-General of Police, Brigadier Mobolaji Johnson, first Military Governor of Lagos State, Commodore Ebitu Ukiwe, former Chief of General Staff, Nigerian Armed Forces and Justice Bola Ajibola, former Attorney General of the Federation and former World Court Judge. "This Day" reported that: "It was a harvest of tributes at the book launch, and the subject-matter, Sir Udo Udoma, shone like a million stars as he basked in the encomiums that poured forth from one speaker after another ..". That says it all.

The second party a week later on his actual 80th birthday, June 21, 1997, involved a thanksgiving service at the Ebenezer Methodist Cathedral in Ikot Abasi followed by a reception at the Ikot Abasi Government Hall. The service was conducted by the then Prelate of the Methodist Church, His Highness Sunday Mbang, while Air Vice Marshall Nsikak Eduok chaired the reception. Chief N. U. Akpan gave a toast to the Federal Republic of Nigeria while Mr. Dennis S. Udo-Inyang gave one to the celebrant. Dad was extremely elated and savoured this great moment. At the conclusion of the official portion of the programme, lunch was served next door at the Greenstar Guest House.

Since dad needed to use the conveniences before going for lunch, he, mum and I returned to the house driven by dad's driver. Unbeknownst to us, while we were at the reception dad's driver had joined in the festivities, so to say, and got intoxicated. By the grace of God, we managed to get to the house uneventfully. When we were ready to return to the reception for lunch, I noticed that the car was not in the porch and went to call the driver to bring back the car since we were returning to the reception. Apparently, the driver thought that he was done for the day and had probably gone to continue with his binging. As the driver backed the car towards the porch I realised that something was wrong. He was driving too fast and heading straight for the sidewall of the house. I screamed at him and he managed to stop the car just before hitting the wall. I was livid. I asked him to get out of the car and scolded him but to my surprise, my dad did not say one word. Madam Emma Brown, a celebrated activist and daughter of dad's "Godfather", Chief John King Usoro, who was travelling with us asked me to leave the driver alone, "after all, we are celebrating!", she said. I replied, "I see; we are in celebration and so it is ok for the driver to go and get my dad killed". I sent the driver away and took the wheel myself and as we drove back to the reception that day, I couldn't help reflecting on the times I used to drive my father to the Lagos University Teaching Hospital for treatment not knowing that I was taking him there to receive a death sentence.

Having observed the 80th anniversary of dad's birth - complete with fan and pageantry - and all festivities over, my siblings left the next day for their respective stations. I spent a couple of days more with mum and dad. Dad was really excited at turning 80 and I must say that I was really thankful to the Almighty to see him in such high spirits and enjoying such good health. Coverage of his birthday week was extensive – on TV, on the radio and in the newspapers. There were publications galore as several media houses had sent people to interview him. "This Day Magazine" started dad's birthday feature article with the caption "The Military Cannot Plan Nigeria's Future". In that report, one of the questions asked was: "What will be your message to General Abacha (General Sani Abacha, the then Military Head of State of Nigeria), because there is rumour that he may succeed himself in 1998?" To that dad answered, "How could he do that? I have not heard that from him. He said he would hand over power. ….". To the next question: "So you are saying that Abacha should not succumb to the pressure being mounted on him to run for President?" dad calmly answered: "I think that the people who want him to be President are misadvised". When I read that I reminisced about dad. Here was an erudite and zealous advocate for the independence of the Nigerian nation who had since witnessed his dear country go from being seen as the advertised "Lion of Africa" to what dad termed "no better than scum in the lily pond"! Here was a retired Supreme Court Judge who now could not survive even for a month on his annual pension because of the inflation that had attended Nigeria's economy since his retirement!! Here he was suffering under the heat and humidity of Southern Nigeria thanks to only sporadic availability of electricity and apparent incompetent maintenance of his generators. There was so much poverty, so much discontent, so much mistrust and yet so much greed abounding – so much to disillusion any visionary; but apparently not this one. Dad was still full of hope for Nigeria and very happy with himself and his lot – he seemed contented, in spite of the abysmal political climate! He was heartbroken but not spirit broken – was this not a contradiction in terms? Why was his spirit not broken? Anyway, yes, another lion was prowling but the eagle sat perched atop the oil palm unperturbed. I said a silent prayer for dad, as I could not help reflecting on Psalms 90:10,

The days of our years are threescore years and ten; and if by reason of strength they be fourscore years, yet is their strength labour and sorrow; for it is soon cut off, and we fly away.

We enjoyed the two days together and then I had to bid mum and dad farewell as I returned to the USA via Lagos, bearing in mind that in six months the family would have to reconvene at home for my dear mother's 70th birthday and my sister's wedding.

CHAPTER TWENTY-NINE

The Eagle Glides Down Gracefully And Lands

"Finally, Brethren, Whatsoever things are true;
Whatsoever things are honest;
Whatsoever things are just; Whatsoever things are pure;
Whatsoever things are lovely; Whatsoever things are of good report;
If there be any virtue And there be any praise,
*Think on these things". - **Philippians 4:8***

I returned to Nigeria on December 21 and arrived in Ikot Abasi on December 23, 1997. The *Mbup* ceremony for the hands of my sister, Enoabasi, in marriage was to be conducted on Friday, December 26 while her marriage ceremony, according to native laws and customs, was to take place on Saturday, December 27. We had our mum's 70th birthday thanksgiving service scheduled for Sunday, the 28th. It was going to be a glorious weekend and the entire family was going to be together again. Dad was delighted to see me and seemed to be in high spirits and looking forward to the celebrations. One of the things I discussed with dad during my first couple of days at home was my observation that the Methodist Church of Nigeria seemed to be taking a leaf from the Pentecostal Churches and "carnivalising" church services. I felt that the Church was moving away from Wesleyan Methodism, which endorsed revivalism – an attempt to reawaken the evangelical faith. My query to dad was predicated on what I perceived to be the circularisation of the church as evidenced by all the dancing through the pews, the excessive number of collections, and the honorary awards given to the rank and file of the church, including Knighthood - activities I saw as being counter productive to evangelicalism which stresses the importance of personal conversion and faith as the means of salvation. Dad had been the Vice President of the Methodist Church of Nigeria until his retirement from active service and later was made a Knight of John Wesley by the church and so my enquiry was more than cursory. He said to me that John Wesley himself, along with his colleagues, cut away from the mainstream of the Church of England because they realised that systems must evolve as the society evolves. He further said that God sees what is in each person's heart and on their mind and hence a person's mode of worship is secondary. *Touché!*

By Thursday, Christmas day, every member of the family had arrived and Ikot Abasi was buzzing as much in response to the spirit of the season as in anticipation of the forthcoming celebrations. At lunch that Thursday, after church service, dad asked me to say the grace and I thanked our Creator for all His kind mercies to us as a family including travelling mercies, our continued good health and welfare, the invaluable leadership of our family head, and the food that we had in front of us. I asked that the Lord allowed us his Grace through the weekend's festivities and going forward kept us all constantly attuned with His mind so that we may be more readily inspired to do His will for us.

The young man who was marrying into our family was not completely unknown to me or to our family but I was not really that familiar with him. I had interacted with his elder siblings in the past and so knew of him. His parents were known to mine and, in fact, used to come to our house to visit dad and mum when we were living in Ikoyi in Lagos. I was told that the young man was a pastor in a Pentecostal Church in Accra, Ghana. Knowing dad to be quite intuitive and blunt about his impressions of people, I saw the fact that both my mum and dad were looking forward to the marriage ceremony to mean that all due diligence had been done and our sister's suitor was acceptable to the family. I know dad expressed delight at the fact that our sister, Eno, was marrying an Ibibio man but I wondered at the time if that was not just an over reaction, or at least a sensitivity, to his relatives' musings about the fact that my brothers Inam and Udoma had married Egba women and my brother Ebong a Jewish woman – a Jewess, as dad preferred to say. Anyway, as a consequence, I let down my guard concerning the young man and concentrated on giving my utmost to preparing for the celebration and welcoming the young man's family to Ikot Abasi. Dad, according to tradition, had invited the top surviving members of the *Ayanti quarter*, including the oldest two, to join our family in receiving our prospective in-laws and their entourage and in carrying out our traditional obligations as related to the occasion. The two senior members are Princewill Abraham Udoma, first son of dad's elder brother Abraham Udoma and the present head of the quarter, and Mfon Martin Inam, first son of his late cousin Martin A. Inam. Of course all the womenfolk and children of the *Ayanti quarter* were not going to miss this rare spectacle for anything in the world.

As traditional as dad was, there hadn't been any traditional or cultural ceremony that he had officiated in that I had witnessed myself and so this was a rare spectacle even for me. I thought it would be nice to see dad in his cultural elements, so to say, since his official and social demeanour was well known to me and was much advertised. Both Lt-General Olusegun Obasanjo in his citation during the award to dad of the Commander of the Order of the Federal Republic, and Mr. Dennis Udo-Inyang, the author of the book "The Man – Sir Justice Udo Udoma", used the same words to describe dad thus: "A stickler for precision and accuracy, a passionate exponent of form and protocol"; they must have attended the same English class in school. We rolled out the red carpet for our visitors and the *Mbup* (Asking) ceremony commenced. The traditional breaking of the kola, prayers, libations, and the mutual accounting of the "bride price", including accompanying domestic goods, were all done, but not without a fair share of drama. I will, however, acquaint you with the goings on that evening in the light of three distinctive observations I made of my dad's handling of his role in the ceremony, which along with the marriage ceremony the next day, constituted the last affair that he presided over.

As with most activities in Nigeria, the *Asking* ceremony started late as our visitors arrived late, but arrive eventually they did. Despite the fact that the young man's parents were both present at the function, his father presented a woman unknown to us as head of their delegation, which fact seemed to annoy dad. He expected the young man's father, whom he thought to be the oldest surviving male of his lineage, or else, some male elder in their extended family, to lead the delegation. He could not understand why a family such as theirs would break tradition in this manner, especially since dad was someone they knew pretty well. The ceremony started on the wrong foot, I thought.

Next, reports filtered to dad that there were irregularities concerning the reconciliation of the bride price list. Mfon Martin Inam had been assigned the responsibility of doing that in consort with the prospective groom's delegation leader. Thirdly, Princewill Abraham Udoma and some of the womenfolk had complained that the proper procedure was not being adopted in connection with the bride price. The price should be haggled rather than us just accepting their offer. Knowing that dad was even embarrassed to accept anything at all on the head of his daughter and was only allowing the process to go on because of his reverence for tradition, I was not surprised when he vetoed their submission and ruled that there would be no haggling. As regarded the disparity in the quantities and quality of items submitted, he said that a copy of the reconciliation statement should be given to me and that I should see to it that I collected the items due when we returned to Lagos. Yes, he had passed the buck and postponed the inevitable to a time that it would become inconsequential, or so it would seem; but he had done his duty. So, my conclusion was that when it came to tradition and culture, the "stickler for precision and accuracy" thing could be thrown out the window but it was imperative that "form and protocol" still be observed; but were they observed in this instance?

Well, let's give him a break. He did complain about form and protocol not being duly observed and, besides, love does conquer all, doesn't it? His only daughter was getting married and he was not going to let his insistence on the observance of form and protocol stand in the way. I was learning. I, however, also felt like he was telling us something and that something, on reflection, was in fact quite consistent with his belief system and practice. Rules are guidelines and should not be broken as much as possible, but if there is a higher question of fairness and equity involved, then one can break that rule, especially if no one else is hurt by it. He even exercised this prerogative in the matter of <u>Uganda v. The Commissioner of Prisons, Uganda Ex parte Michael Matovu</u> where he wrote as part of the judgment of the Constitutional Court as follows:

> "On reflection, however, bearing in mind the facts that the application as presented in the first instance was not objected to by counsel who had appeared for the state; that the liberty of

a citizen of Uganda was involved; and that considerable importance was attached to the questions of law under reference since they involved the interpretation of the Constitution of Uganda; we decided, in the interests of justice, to jettison formalism to the winds and overlook the several deficiencies in the application, and thereupon proceeded to the determination of the issues referred to us."

Dad jettisoned formalism to the winds in the interest of justice. Anyway, coming back to the *Asking* ceremony, not withstanding his irritation over some of the goings on, dad was most magnanimous and welcomed our guests very warmly. He seemed to be happy once the drama and speeches were done with. The festivities went on successfully and I believe everyone was delighted when it was all over.

The next morning, Saturday, the compound was transformed into a celebration venue. Canopies were erected and tables and chairs were arranged and decorations in purple and white – the wedding theme - including balloons and banners, were hoisted everywhere. Before the official commencement of the event, there was already a lot of activity in the compound. Caterers had come to arrange themselves appropriately for their task ahead and *Ayanti quarter* women had been cooking in the backyard almost all day for themselves and members of the quarter. Traditional dancers, a church choir group, extended family members from around the country, and friends of my sister had arrived and familiarised themselves with what was expected of them once the ceremony started. Dad appeared in traditional regalia specially prepared for the occasion by the groom's family. This was my first time of seeing my dad wearing anything but European clothing, except of course when he was in a Judge's or an academic robe, which clothing I daresay is also European. He was wearing flowery and shiny regalia complete with a black bowler hat and, dunning his usual walking stick, looked every inch the Father-of-the-day that he was. Soon, the compound was filled with all cadres of people including some very important personalities. There were representatives of the Akwa Ibom state government and the expatriate management of the Aluminium Smelting Company of Nigeria (ALSCON) in attendance and dad was very pleased to see them all. The celebration started with a prayer by Rt. Rev. B. N. Enyeting of the Ebenezer Methodist Church, Ikot Abasi and then there was entertainment of all kinds. There was a lot to eat and drink and various traditional dancers and masquerades did their thing. Then there were speeches galore followed by the groom's dance procession as the groom and his entourage came amidst singing and music to join the ceremony. Then followed the bridal train as young ladies – Eno's friends and females of *Ayanti* quarter – escorted Eno, singing and dancing, to the ceremonial table. My loving sister, Eno, was looking pretty and happy and was very much in her elements as she went through the ritual of giving a sip of the ceremonial drink of choice to significant members of both families and then finally to her suitor. Dad just sat expressionless, apparently soaking it all in, and I suspect with pride and delight.

The next day, Sunday, I drove in dad's car with him and mum to church for mum's birthday thanksgiving service. Dad was smartly dressed in a striped grey suit, a striped pink shirt and a fancy tie. Mum's 70th birthday had occurred on December 9 but the thanksgiving service was moved to the festive season to allow the whole family to attend. As it turned out, all her relatives who had come from around the country for Eno's marriage ceremony, including mum's cousin Akpabio Ikpaha, affectionately called Ukpa, were also able to attend. The service, which was well attended, was officiated by Rt. Rev. B. N. Enyeting, the Methodist bishop of the Diocese of Ikot Abasi. After the service, we returned to the family house for the cutting of the cake and refreshments. Mum's nephew, James Obong Bassey (Sonny), proposed a toast to mum and, after responding to the toast, mum cut her birthday cake. Dad, having changed into more comfortable clothing, sat back relaxed but attentive in support of his soul mate.

Late that night, the family having gathered in dad's recreation room upstairs by way of us bidding him farewell, dad gave us instructions on how to handle Eno's church wedding in Lagos the following Saturday, January 3, 1998. Since the plan was for us all to leave early the following morning for Lagos and as it was unlikely that we would see dad in the morning before we left, we thought we should say our goodbyes before he retired for the night. In addition to other instructions, he directed me to represent him at Eno's wedding, as he would be unable to travel to Lagos. Overnight, on reflection, I decided that I would spend one more day with dad so that we could

have another *tête-à-tête* since there was not any urgency for me to return to Lagos that Monday. However, in the morning, on my way back
to the family house from the ALSCON estate where I spent the night,
I met the motorcade taking my siblings and other family members to
the airport as it was coming to the estate to pick me up. For some
reason, it had become necessary to leave earlier than was planned the
night before. On speaking to my brother Udoma, I decided to go with
my siblings after all, a decision I regret until this day because I never
got to see dad again. Dad for some years had tried to impress upon me
the necessity for me to return home from the USA. He had been nurs-
ing the proposition of me returning to work for ALSCON since I am
an engineer but at the time I just thought that he was just being needy
and suggested that perhaps we should encourage my brother Ekpo,
who is an Art Historian, to move to Uyo as a lecturer so as to be close
to dad. I reminded dad that ALSCON had still not outlived its image
as a white elephant. As time went by though, I had begun to think that
perhaps his desire to have me home was not unconnected with his
efforts to set his house in order before going back to his maker.

Back in Lagos, I carried out dad's orders and Eno's church
wedding went very well. I reported to dad and mum accordingly before leaving the country on January 6, 1998 to return to the USA.

Sometime in January 1998, a situation arose in dad's compound concerning his power generator. Since electricity service supplied by the Nigeria Electric Power Authority (NEPA) had become a
rare commodity, dad like most Nigerians found it necessary to rely
more on generator power for electricity. And since generators were
constructed for standby use as opposed to a source of perennial power,
there was frequent breakdown of the generator and it did not help
that the only people who could repair generators were auto mechanics who were not very reliable. When the generator broke down this
time, dad was told that it was necessary to replace a certain part, which
unfortunately was not available to buy in Ikot Abasi. The driver was
sent to Aba to buy the part but he returned to say that the part was
said to be available only in Lagos. My brother Inam was then contacted in Lagos to procure the required part. Since he could not get a
proper description of the part, he had to travel from Lagos to Ikot Abasi
to pick up the defective module and return to Lagos to try to get a
replacement for it. Well, when it rains it pours! Inam discovered that

the defective module could only be ordered from abroad. The good news was that the entire module did not have to be replaced, as the only thing that was defective was a smaller part, which was an insert of the module. The part was ordered for but, in the meantime, dad had to struggle to bear the heat at home. He was very uncomfortable in the muggy weather. Eventually, towards the end of the month, the part arrived and arrangements were made to have it transported home to be reinstalled. Dad happily looked forward to its arrival and to finally being able to have the use of his air conditioners and fans again. Well, the ordered part did get to Ikot Abasi all right but the module of which it was a part was left behind in Lagos! Dad couldn't be more disappointed.

The next day, Sunday, February 1, 1998, as I later learnt from mum, dad who hadn't gone anywhere since his wife's birthday thanksgiving service, got dressed and told mum that he was coming to church with her. His loving wife was going to be honoured by the church and he was not going to miss the occasion. So dad went for church service that morning with mum and witnessed the presentation to mum of the title of *Eka Ibed Idem Iban* – the women's patron - for her contributions to the Ebenezer Methodist Cathedral and the community. She felt very highly honoured and dad was very happy for and proud of her. The next morning when she woke up, she found that dad was already out of bed and sitting in an armchair on the adjacent balcony, as he was wont to do because of the extreme heat. She then went to make the bath for him, as that usually would help him feel a little better. The bath made, she returned to tell him and then turned to go away. However, she realised that he had not responded and so turned again to look at him. She then knew that something was wrong as she only got a blank stare back and a gesticulation with his hands falling on his laps as if in bewilderment or perhaps, as if to say, like the Apostle Paul:

> *"For I am now ready to be offered, and the time of my departure is at hand. I have fought a good fight, I have finished my course, I have kept the faith:"* - **2 Timothy 4: 6-7**

Mum sent for a doctor. Doctors came from the nearby Enebong Clinic and the farther ALSCON Medical Centre. Not very long after the last of the doctors left, dad gave up the ghost.

APPENDIX A

The Lion and the Oil Palm

**(Being my address on the occasion of my installation
as President of the University PhilosophicalSociety at
Trinity College, Dublin, Eire for the 1942-1943 session.)**

*Tacitus once observed about human appetite for the
goods of this world: "There is no such thing as enough".*

      In choosing this title for the subject of my address tonight, I
have endeavoured to keep within the bounds of the ancient traditions of the University Philosophical Society. While I can assure you
that I shall not be so dramatic as to produce for your inspection a
palm tree, whose natural home is sunny Africa, I think you will all
agree with me when I say that I have produced here for you four live
lions, one of whom is unique in being at once a lion and a lion tamer;
so that, even to this extent, my choice of this title is not without significance. And, so, I beseech you to bear with me patiently while we,
together, unravel this mystery.

      It is needless to mention that, in my opinion, one and, per-
haps, the most important contributive factor towards the present international catastrophe is the question of a "place under the sun". Before the outbreak of the present conflict, the world was divided into
two main groups - the "haves" and the "have-nots". The various con-
stituents of these groups are well known to any student of international politics.

      I have chosen to address the House on colonial policy, not be-
cause I am an expert in the game, but because, in spite of being a
victim of this policy, I can claim, like Addison, "that the bystander, as a
rule, can more easily discover the flaws in any organisation which
are apt to escape the eyes of the expert of the game," or, to put it in
another way, makers of tight shoes don't know where they pinch, whilst
the wearers have no say in how they are made or altered. This essay of

mine is reminiscent of a story told of an Irish soldier who knocked down a person who made a disparaging remark about the late Queen Victoria. On being asked for an explanation, he replied, "She is my Queen and I can say what I like about her, but it isn't for the likes of you".

Now to my subject: Africa, that great and ancient continent which has excited heroism, greed, pity, political passion, and the scramble of control, was to Western Europeans, even in the early nineteenth century, a "dark continent" inhabited by naked savages, and to the early Greek and Roman writers, the home of gods and giants. Very little was made of the great part that Africa – that vast continent stretching from the Suez to the Cape - had played in European politics. Even in those "dark days", Africa had her own glories, her compact civilisation, her unique culture, and her arts. Her present art of sculpture, the art of music, the art of dancing, and the art of song and poetry point eloquently to a distant past. These are things which must have firm roots in the minds and hearts of a people who have trodden their path of well-established traditions.

West Africa had its own indigenous form of government. Authority was vested in the natural rulers of the people, subject to this, that such authority was only exercisable after consultation with the communal council, consisting of selected leading men learned in native laws and customs. The council also discussed matters of defence in the face of threatened attacks by external foes, made rules regarding the taking of title and the control of fairs, and passed laws regarding criminal offences. These councils, composed of heads of families, young, able-bodied and intelligent men, were usually presided over by the king or chief, and officered by warriors or titled men selected from each village. The importance of this kinship grouping can hardly be over-emphasised, for this sort of organisation, which had as its anchorage the extended kindred, formed the fundamental unit of law and authority. The kinship or family organisation is therefore the cradle of morality, the basis of the political structure and the mainstay of the good ordering of the entire community.

Indeed, the village group was the highest unit of government, being the association of people bound together by the closest bonds of common interest, sharing the same lands, the same markets, the same cult and traditions, and with its own parliament and judiciary. This, of course, does not mean that West Africa, before the advent of Europeans, knew a golden age of law and order. There is hardly a

scintilla of doubt that it is quite possible that an individual of considerable wealth and ability might have, occasionally in his own village,
acted the village idiot by wielding autocratic powers. It is quite con-
ceivable also that the kings heading these super-democracies were not
all upright men. Nevertheless, to an African, his king or chief was
paramount leader in time of war and a symbol of unity in times of
peace. These councils of elders used to operate somewhat as a symbol
of checks and balances, restraining the power of the chiefs and thus
producing equilibrium in the whole community.

        Authorities on Africa are agreed that the government of vil-
lages and towns was the business of the whole community, that it was
based on the family organisation, and that authority was, in consequence, widely distributed. West Africa was in such a state when there
came the voyages of the notorious Bristol men who broke the Papal
Bull. I refer, gentlemen, to John Tintam, William Fabian and Sir John
Hawkins, whose work of exploration was later intensified by the in-
trepid adventures of Mungo Park, Dr. David Livingstone, and Henry
Morton Stanley.

        With the opening up of the then New World, there began the
greatest scramble the world had ever known – a scramble which was
neither for gold, nor for diamonds, nor even for the oil-palm with
which West Africa is abundantly blessed, but most regrettably to relate, this notorious scramble was for human beings. The demand for
tropical labour in America as a source of wealth led to the transportation of Africans as slaves across the Atlantic to a continent to which
they were helpless strangers and in which they were ever, afterwards,
to be doomed to eternal servitude.

        It is not the purpose of this essay to deal with this iniquitous
trade, with which Queen Elizabeth had to reprove old Sir John Hawkins
with these words: "If any of the Negroes should be carried off without
their consent, it would be detestable, and I would be compelled to
call down the vengeance of heaven upon you". We must here give
thanks for the efforts of William Wilberforce who, in the face of great
odds and bitter opposition but with the able support of some enlightened men like Dr. R. R. Madden, fought fearlessly for the suppression
of the cursed trade. The echo of William Wilberforce's voice was later
caught by a young barrister, Abraham Lincoln, on the other side of
the Atlantic. These far-sighted but lonely fighters against inhumanity
have had their names enshrined forever in the hearts, not only of Africans but of all mankind.

After the Franco-Prussian war, crippled by her defeat, France proclaimed that it was to greater France beyond the seas that she must look for rehabilitation. Germany, with a desire to create naval bases, raise black armies, and acquire raw materials, longed for a place under the sun. And Great Britain, seemingly prompted by a humanitarian motive, namely the suppression of the slave trade, became lured into the acquisition of African territories. With the collision of the interests of these great powers, there followed a second scramble, this time for a place under the sun – a scramble without any parallel in human history, which subsequently led to the development of the policy of the "spheres of influence".

In 1874, Great Britain decided that the organised power of the Ashanti people was incompatible with the purpose of the Empire. General Wolseley then began the destruction of the military strength of the Ashanti kingdom. This destruction was completed only after eight campaigns, the last of which was caused by the dispute over the Golden Stool, which was regarded by the Ashantis as a symbol of religious and political leadership. According to Governor Hadgson, the Golden Stool was the greatest obstacle in the way of bringing the whole of the Gold Coast into the Empire fold, and with its capture, King Prempeh was exiled and the work of colonisation was complete.

The story of Nigeria, the most populous and largest British African territory, is a different one. The foundation of the British Empire in Nigeria was laid by Sir George Goldie - the Cecil Rhodes of West Africa.

Some Europeans, after the last Great War, came to appreciate the immense contribution which Africans had made towards the suppression of what then was recognised as a world tyranny. The Treaty of Versailles attempted, in a rather vague and Utopian way, to provide for the protection of African interests. The African Mandate system was born out of this treaty, but born, like all creatures of warfare, an orphan even at its birth. As humanitarian as the aim of the creators of this semblance of a perfect institution might have been, it is indeed difficult to reconcile such an aim with the fact that the native people whose interests were said to be protected had no direct representative of the commission.

Article 22 of the League Covenant speaks of the Dual Mandate or Trusteeship, terms that were of British invention. It maintained that the well-being and development of colonial people form a "sacred trust of civilisation". Edmund Burke, that eminent and humane thinker, whose views and ideas were as progressive as those of the leader under whom he had to serve and against whom he had to wage a vocal war were conservative, remarked in his speech on Fox's India Bill, 1782, that "rights and privileges derived from political power were all in the strictest sense of trust" and that, in the last resort, the British people were to exercise that trust in the case of India. This idea was strongly emphasised by Great Britain on behalf of the colonies at the Peace Conference.

Lord Lugard calls this principle by various names. At one time it is the "white man's burden", at another it is the "Dual Mandate", and yet at another it is either "Trusteeship" or "Indirect Rule". What is indirect rule? According to certain authorities, indirect rule is the opposite of direct rule, and direct rule implies centralisation of the functions of government in a Suzerain power, which controls its subjects by means of its own staff of civil servants".

Sir Donald Cameron maintains that the "aim of indirect rule is to graft our higher civilisation (meaning British) upon the soundly rooted native stock, stock that had its foundation in the minds and hearts and thoughts of the people and therefore one on which we can build".

Analysing these definitions, we find, perhaps a little to our amazement, that indirect rule is a weak thing – a mere superimposition based on the presumption of a pre-existing system of native government. It thus gives the lie to the old uninformed, biased belief that there was not organised system of government in Africa before the coming of the Whiteman. In this connection, Dr. Meek says, "when indirect rule was introduced in Northern Nigeria, the British government found in existence a highly developed system of government, including a Fulah Sultanate composed of numerous provinces, each administered by a native governor with his own council, executive, army, police, treasury, and judiciary. The object of indirect rule was to provide a bridge by which the people might pass safely from the old culture to the new".

Lord Lugard, the chief exponent of the system of trusteeship, maintains that it is devoid of the cankerworm of monopoly and exploitation, but that its aims are assistance, education, production, and co-operation. This statement is, in my opinion, absolutely wide of the mark of the truth. What of the privileged class's vested interests in

Africa? What of free labour and the big combines that are engaged in life and death war to strangle and stifle every African business enterprise for fear of competition? Here I can do no better than quote from a famous speech made during the debate in the British House of Commons on Italy's determination to attack Abyssinia. Sir Edward Grigg, at one time Governor of Kenya, said, "When we hear of other people coveting colonies, let us remember what we get out of ours. That is an extremely valuable asset, which we can understand other people envying. We have this fact, that on the average, out of the total revenue of the African colonies, seventy-five per cent is spent in a manner that inures directly to our benefit every year. We, unquestionably, do very well out of these colonies".

What does this statement mean? It means, as applied to the theory of trusteeship, that of the profit made out of the estate of the ward, the trustee takes seventy-five per cent (75%) and reluctantly gives twenty-five (25%) to the ward. This is indeed a serious indictment – a flagrant breech of the trust and confidence of the ward, the result of which is an appalling financial poverty. The native people, thus deprived of their natural God-given wealth and resources, are in consequence compelled to work for bare subsistence and to look to their overlords for their daily bread. Is it any wonder that such a situation of things should occasionally give rise to an outburst against the Government?

As regards education, I need only mention that, for the past ten years, the people have been clamouring, but in vain, for compulsory education for the masses. The reason for refusing such a legitimate demand is not far to seek. There is hardly any doubt that the "Powers that be" realise that it is far easier to control, repress, oppress, and rule over an uneducated people. Today, West Africa hungers and thirsts, as never before, for education – a form of education that necessarily must be vocational, social, and humane. Hitherto, European education had concentrated purely on teaching Africans what Europe, and not what Africa, is. The new African education that this paper envisages must be such as would teach the people not what, but how to think for themselves. The feeling about the present state of education in Africa is best expressed in a poem by Ida Proctor, in which she says,

> *"The thought I think, I think is not my thought,*
> *But is the thought of one who thought that I ought*
> *To think his thought".*

At this juncture, I think it is but proper that I should express my deep appreciation of the work many missionaries have done in battling, often single-handedly and with very little financial assistance from the government, against mass ignorance. Africans, in general, are indebted to these missionaries.

If Great Britain had conscientiously applied this principle of trusteeship, it could be argued that it would literally be true that she has no colonies. It seems to me that, in the light of present practice, there exists an almost unbridgeable gap between realism and idealism. We are still running after phantoms. To many, the sense of domination is sweet and to have others produce wealth, even with slave labour, is indeed convenient. The paradox of domination is not that men prefer the state of masters to that of slaves; it is rather that the masters come to believe, often quite genuinely, that their mastery is beneficial to the slaves. And what is more, that very idea can, with an effective propaganda machine, be instilled into the minds of the slaves themselves. Jay Gould, you may remember, once said that he could always hire half the working class to shoot down the other half.

In supporting the principle of trusteeship, Sir Donald Cameron pointed out that there was no other way by which the obligations implied in the Mandate system to encourage such an evolution of people "not yet able to stand by themselves" could be carried out. I know that Sir Donald, during his administration in Nigeria, had won the admiration and sincere respect of all Nigerians, but I am tempted here to question what he means by the phrase "people not yet able to stand by themselves" and also to question the right of any nation to say to another "thus far shalt thou go and no further". This is indeed the crux of the matter, "who has the right to determine when a particular nation shall be able to stand by itself?".

Although the principle of trusteeship was first enunciated by Sir George Goldie in 1877, its adoption as a policy is a matter of recent history. At first, it was customary for European officials, often young headstrong and not invariably gifted with sympathy and understanding, to trample underfoot African customs which do not bear the stamp of London, oblivious of the fact that every custom is the outgrowth of the spirit of the people and, therefore, full of rich meaning. African indigenous customs were uprooted by the European civil servants, not because these customs were bad in themselves but, rather, because these perfect creatures, called civil servants, believed that to encourage these customs would be to give the African confidence in his own institutions. Such uprooted customs might be replaced by so-called imported civilised ones, the importation of which, more often than not, meant the importation of disease and misery. The African fez, turban, and straw-hat must give place to silk top-hats, no matter whether the temperature is over a hundred-and-fifty degrees (150°) in the shade. This method of destroying what you never built, of reaping what you never sowed, and of compulsorily creating markets for European goods came to a head when the British Government met with fierce opposition from the native people.

One writer has said that "the government (of Nigeria) has been strengthened by the criticism of African politicians in the legislative council and African journalists. Some of these have been men of intelligence and public spirit who can challenge comparison with the political representatives of any other country. The conclusion is not that the political energies of men like these should be repressed, but that they should be given a proper sphere in which to develop. In the services performed by the central government, we should press forward the policy of employing more Africans in positions of trust. There is, however, one branch into which, I believe, Africans should not enter, and that is the administrative service. We should be prepared to defend, against African and European critics, the policy of gradual development. We have lately come to value our representative democracy ... Africa is not a ready soil for democracy". What contradictory statements to be made by a person who claims to be a democrat! These statements, to say the least, reveal a deep-rooted prejudice and arrant ignorance of African anthropology and aim at creating an intentional agrarian grievance. It has been well said that a man, who speaks or preaches to one generation only, is dead; but I say this, that a man who not only preaches but writes to one generation only, that is to say, a man who in his writings says "peace in my time and after that bother if I care", is buried alive.

Anglo-African relationship would have been a very poor one indeed if it were based on such conflicting and ill-conceived statements as I have quoted above. But, thank God, we can still find consolation in the warm, sincere, and glowing words of Miss Mary Kingsley, who was the first to advocate, as a student of science, the study of African anthropology and complete co-operation between the Englishman and the African for their mutual benefit. Would to God that more of her type were given even to our generation!

By way of contrast to the British system, under the French system – a system that had done so much to remove ill feelings between the governing and the governed – there were both the principles of equality of status and opportunity, and a system of "Inspectorate". The Inspectorate Department was charged with the function of sending out colonial inspectors to the colonies from time to time. The inspectors must submit their reports within a reasonable time. The old France, that France that will never die in the hearts of her colonial peoples, regarded herself as the guardian and partner of her colonies. The colonies used to form an integral part of France, mutually inter-dependent and sufficing. On the other hand, in Great Britain, we have a body of persons who claim to be colonial experts and advisers to the colonial office. The tragedy of it all is not that there is anything sinful in the mere offer of advice, but that, more often than not, these self-styled experts are without any colonial experience except, perhaps, that they had paid a visit to be feted by a colonial governor and on their return had written the inevitable book of colonial administration.

These experts are often persons with vested interests in the colonies and whose sole interest is the protection of their investment. It is interesting here to note that a recent suggestion by Lord Hailey for the creation of a Colonial Advisory Council was rejected in a House of Lords' debate.

To Englishmen, with very few exceptions, British Africa is a dust heap of the Empire - a land, though flowing with milk and honey, is inhabited by cannibals – ideas which, even today, many text books and novels still teach.

Sometime ago, after the fiasco in Munich, a sensational rumour was current in the English press of a British intention to transfer certain West African territories to Germany as a European peace settlement. The deal was in fact being planned without the consultation of the native inhabitants concerned. "Slavery", said Edmund Burke, "is a weed that grows in every soil". The assumption that Africans would have allowed their God-given country to be used as a pawn in an international game of chess was indeed fantastic. Any such attempt would have led to complete revolution.

When Dr. W. B. Mumford pointed out the obvious fact that the colonies belong to the inhabitants and that the colonial peoples should be helped to self-government by the so-called trustees, so that they might enter as free peoples into a world-wide Commonwealth of Nations, Lord Lugard retorted by saying that the inhabitants of these colonies were not yet ripe to take their place as equals in a world state. In reply to such a retort, I can only say that it seems to me, in the words of Edmund Burke, "there will always be those whose instinct, when they are brought face to face with some crisis, is to coerce rather than reconcile, to punish the disturber rather than seek out the cause of disturbance, who imagine that their souls are cooped and cabined in unless they have some men or body of men dependent upon their mercy. Is it not true to facts that magnanimity in politics is not seldom the truest wisdom, and that a great Empire and little minds go ill together?".

Returning to Dr. Mumford's statement, if by a "world-wide Commonwealth of Nations" he was thinking of the British Commonwealth of Nations, then I have no hesitation in stating that I am in total agreement with his views.

As regards the question of the internationalisation of colonies, which at present seems to be the view of certain sections in Great Britain, I am compelled to protest with all the emphasis at my command against any such proposal. Internationalisation, I believe, would be tantamount to a grievous breach of faith, a betrayal of the principle of trusteeship. It would mean the break-up of an age partnership, an achievement and a process that scarcely has a parallel in history. We believe in the sanctity of the given pledge. We believe in the three fine elements of our common constitution, namely, the element of liberty for all men to develop all that is good and to battle down all that is evil; the element of justice to all men; and the element of representative government for which West African Congress petitioned the colonial office in 1923. Internalisation would probably mean the end of all that some of our outstanding administrators and missionaries with a sense of vocation have struggled these many years to build up. Of these administrators and missionaries it may be said, "their story is not only graven in stone over their native earth, but lives on far away, without visible symbols, woven into the stuff of other men's lives". Such an association, as these men and women have helped to build up, surely deserves a certain amount of respect.

At the present day, it is not only the danger of internationisation which threatens West Africa. I see ominous signs in the distant sky. I see on the horizon a new horde with stars and stripes looking with longing eyes to the West Coast. This new threat is far greater than what West Africa has ever known. I have read of "Jim Crowism" and the societies of the "Ku-Klux-Klan". Hitherto, the feeling among West Africans was exemplified in the following saying: "When you are a West Coast African, you are one of two things: under a British or a French rule. If you are under the British, don't worry; you are one of two things: in the government service, and comparatively well paid, or you are out of a job. If you are out of a job, don't worry; you are one of two things: related to a man in a job who will provide for you, or the owner of a bit of productive soil. If you are the owner of a bit of soil, you are one of two things: able to get enough out of it for a living, or on the starvation line. If you are on the starvation line, you are one of two things: well enough to carry on or ill enough for free attendance in hospital. If you are in hospital, don't worry; you are one of two things: going to get well or to die. If you are going to die, don't worry, for there is always a heaven to which all God's children go".

I do hope that the meaning behind this saying will be intensified at the end of the present conflict, and if indeed a foreign power is to be introduced in the West Coast (and I am saying this, I hope, with the greatest caution), that that power will realise Africa is not a new but an old world whose civilisation is not built up on new forms of slavery. We strongly believe that West Africa cannot afford to have freedom for half its population whilst the other half is in perpetual bondage.

I have endeavoured throughout this paper to show that the Dual Mandate, excellent in itself as a doctrine, is nothing more than a mere counsel of perfection. It is, at best, a paper form of government and therefore unreal. It is anachronistic, for, although it may have served a particular purpose during the early days of colonisation, there is no doubt that it has outlived its usefulness. It is extremely unprogressive and essentially un-African – un-African in that it is chained to the mock Legislative Council, the majority of whose members are the nominees of the governor himself. It is therefore a denial of the principle of representation. Over the Legislative Council, the governor, unless he be wise and sympathetic, is a virtual dictator. The existence of this extraordinary delegation of powers often tempts the governor to exercise them to the full and sometimes in the wrong direction, for neither the governor nor the administrative machinery is anywhere called to account. Here we find the real bureaucracy in great triumph. Parliament is itself being lulled to sleep in an armchair before a warm fire. Criticism by the colonial people themselves is considered seditious, for, in the words of a great authority on African affairs, "the British genius for colonisation is an article of faith".

I have also endeavoured to emphasise the need for education and for an objectively planned system of government. The days of juggling between laissez faire and repression are now over. Of planning, a distinction must be drawn between planning against the people, planning for the people, and planning with the people. In West Africa, there must be a combination of planning with the people to the exclusion of planning against the people; and it is this combination that would be conducive to the founding of a common Ethos for a world state. The practice hitherto has been to do all planning in Whitehall and then to superimpose such plans on the native population. This practice must go, and if Whitehall should insist, it is sufficient to point out that the old belief in the myth of an ever stable and approximately unalterable world – in effect, a child's world – is gone and gone for ever.

The type of planning which this paper emphasises would ensure, to the African, a part in the shaping of his future. It would mean the substitution of action for the usual empty platitude, so as to convince the colonial peoples of Britain's sincerity. In short, it would amount to an assurance that, within a limited number of years, the colonial people would be entitled to take their place as equals within the British Commonwealth of Nations.

Now we see this great lion of freedom, this "lion whose tail", according to Harold Nicholson, "has been so twisted and twisted that there are only about two hairs left", has successfully, whether by accident or by design, wound its twisted tail so tightly round the oil-palm that they are from henceforth inseparable. Separation is not only undesirable, it is unthinkable.

If this paper has stimulated sympathetic and intelligent thought as distinct from mere emotional pity, which is not what we Africans need; if this paper has successfully communicated to you my own feelings on the subject, then I shall feel satisfied that my duty is done, and will return to my "native jungle" realising that I may have given as well as derived some benefit from the best part of my youth, which I have spent in this land of saints and scholars and, above all, in a Christian university.

Congratulating Gen. Gowon after his official installation as Visitor to A. B. U.

With participants of my Seminar for Judges of January 28 – February 1, 1980

At the valedictory session of the Supreme Court held in my honour

Sitting with Dr. Okoi Arikpo at the launching of Mr. Dennis Udo-Inyang's
book, "The Man – Sir Justice Udo Udoma"

Addressing the audience at the launching of my book "History and the Law of the Constitution of Nigeria" in 1995

Cutting my 80th birthday cake, assisted by my wife, Grace, at the Lagos luncheon

With the Chief Justice of Nigeria, Mr. Mohammed Bello, at the book launch

With the author, Ekong Samson, at the launching of "Law And Statesmanship, The Legacy Of Sir Udo Udoma"

Addressing the congregation at my 80th birthday thanksgiving service in Ikot Abasi

Later, at the reception, cutting my birthday cake with the assistance of my wife Grace

Ayanti quarter men were in attendance at my daughter's *Mbup* (Asking) ceremony including an unhappy Monday, (Princewill Udoma), my oldest surviving relative

Ayanti quarter women were a happier looking bunch at Eno's Asking ceremony

Arriving for Eno's marriage ceremony on December 27, 1997

Watching intently as our daughter's marriage ceremony proceeds in earnest
and my cousin's son, Mfon Martin Inam, addresses her

At my wife Grace's 70th birthday thanksgiving service

With *Eka Ibed Idem Iban* at her title conferment

The Clash of Cultures

(Being my prize essay for which the University Philosophical Society at Trinity College, Dublin, Eire awarded me a silver medal.)

"I thought for a time of being a man of letters then I remembered Sir Walter Scott saying that literature was a good staff but a bad crutch".

I believe my first duty this evening is to ask your pardon for the ambiguity of title under which the subject of my essay has been announced, and for my endeavour, as you may ultimately think, to obtain your audience under false pretences. Indeed, my object is not to discuss principally the various degrees of culture, but merely to indicate rather dispassionately the flood of human activities.

So little is really definitely known, and what is more, among those supposed to know, opinions vary, as to what constitutes culture that to go into the subject itself in its abstract form in any essay of this type would be to undertake, within a limited time and space, a most difficult investigation entirely beyond the competence of your essayist.

According to Professor A. H. R. Fairchild, "the most distinct mark of a cultured mind is the ability to take another's point of view. To be willing to test a new idea; to be able to live on the edge of difference in all matters intellectual; to examine without heat the burning questions of the day; to have imaginative sympathy, openness and flexibility of mind, steadiness and poise of feeling, and cool calmness of judgment: to have all these is to have culture".

Arthur Bryant, the now famous author of "Samuel Pepys" and "Macaulay", in his "The National Character" writes: "Our culture – to use a terrifying and much misused word - is a country culture. We have not as yet built up a civil culture to take its place". "By culture", he continues, "I mean that part of man's needs which is explained by the phrase 'man does not live by bread alone'". But yet another writer of equal repute considers the arts, the wisdom, and the learning of the people as the manifestations of culture. So we see, on that score, there is a conflict of views.

Culture, I believe, is not the hammer but the spark struck from the anvil. It is recognised when it exhibits itself in the external acts of individuals as well as nations. Consequently, I shall devote a good portion of this paper when considering that vast continent from which I hail, not to its learning and wisdom, but to its arts and religion. I may point out that the scope of this essay will not by any means be limited to Africa.

In considering British culture, Bryant writes, "Our industrial discontent, the restless, dissatisfied state of our family life, the discomfort, ugliness, and overcrowding of our towns, in part spring from the fact that every Englishman is so certain that the only lasting Utopia for him is a rose garden and a cottage in the country that he can never settle down seriously to make himself comfortable in a town. He, as it were, squats there and puts up with sordid surroundings, second-rate amusements, and a general 'higgledy-pigglediness' quite surprising in the institutions of such a civilised orderly people. An English cottage garden is one of the most beautiful things in the world, and the English industrial town certainly one of the ugliest". It has been suggested that the fact of English culture being a country one may be explained by its history. Once, it is true, a great city civilisation flourished in Britain – that of imperial Rome and its colonists. But it never took real root, except in London, where there are probably still traces of Roman organisation and habit, and when the legions were withdrawn, that civilisation vanished as though it never existed. It is quite safe to imagine here that if British armies were withdrawn from India, followed by a systematic termination of occupation, Western civilisation would disappear in the same manner.

Stanley Baldwin has put all that an Englishman feels about his country culture in words that can never be bettered: "The sounds of England, the tinkle of the hammer on the anvil in the country smithy, the corncrake on a dewy morning, the sound of the scythe against the whetstone, and the sight of a plough team coming over the brow of a hill, the sight that has been seen in England long after the kingdom has perished and every work in England has ceased to function, for centuries the one eternal sight of England. The wild anemones in the woods in April, the last load at night of hay being drawn down a lane as the twilight comes on, when you can scarcely distinguish the figures of the horses as they take it home to the farm, and, above all, most subtle, most penetrating, and most moving, the smell of wood smoke coming up in an autumn evening, or the smell of the scratch fire – these things strike down into the very depths of our nature, and touch chords that go back to the beginning of time and the human race, but they are chords that with every year of our life sound a deeper note in our innermost being".

Another noble example of how such feelings haunt the thought and literature of an Englishman after a century and a half of city life is to be found in Miss Sackville West's "Saxon Song":

> *"Tools with the comely names,*
> *Mattock and scythe and spade,*
> *Couth and bitter as flames,*
> *Clean, and bowed in the blade –*
> *A man and his tools make a man and his trade.*
> *Leisurely flocks and herds,*
> *Cool-eyed cattle that come*
> *Mildly to wonted words,*
> *Swine that in orchards roam –*
> *A man and his beasts make a man and his home.*
> *Children sturdy and flaxen*
> *Shouting in brotherly strife,*
> *Like the land they are Saxon,*
> *Sons of a man and his wife –*
> *For a man and his loves make a man and his life".*

English poetry, agriculture, and music are all founded on this country model. These very themes have inspired composers like Gustav Holst, Hubert Parry, Peter Warlock, and Percy Grainger.

But leaving English culture severely alone, let us turn our attention to the wide world, and imagine ourselves armed with binoculars going on a journey in an aeroplane. We can then see the world in its true perspective. We are looking down from our plane – an American clipper – Look! There are startled faces!! My! What colours!! First, while in Europe, the brown, yellow, and darker brown; in Asia, yet deeper and deeper brown, turning to black in Africa. What contrast of races partly based on colour! The white European, the bearded olive-face Jew, the swarthy desert Arab, the teeming brown myriads of

India, the yellow Chinese and Japanese, the Red Indians of America, the Black Negroes of Africa – a most fascinating picture.

As we look across the world everywhere we see the rise, and hear the murmur and fret of the stupendous tide of humanity. And looking afresh then at the scene as a whole and trying to envisage it from the elevated and detached position of a scientist on the moon, we see a broad fluttering tide of human beings flowing over the world.

We may ask the question: "What are they all saying and doing?" That question can only be adequately answered by taking a look at the leading paper of each country. A map of the world does not exhibit a more distinct view of the boundaries and situations of any country than does its newspaper. The newspaper is considered to be the mirror of the activities, of the genii, and of the morals of the inhabitants of the country that it represents. It is indeed the "Fourth Estate of the Realm". He who would read it with a philosophical eye might perceive in every paragraph something characteristic of the nation to which it belongs – the militaristic and inventive spirit of Germany, the pride of England, the superstitious and philosophical outlook of Africa, the humour of Ireland, the resistance of Spain, and the callousness of America.

Perhaps it may interest you to hear excerpts from the "World Mirror" whose editor is Lucifer. The "World Mirror", you may not know, is a magazine composed by men of very great mental calibre drawn from all classes and from all corners of the universe. Its editorials and articles are usually of fabulous quality. One only needs to glance at its pages in order to gather a store of information that contributes to make the world go round; and therein, with no effort at all, one can distinguish the characters of the various nations that are united in its composition.

An issue of the World Mirror" of the 31ˢᵗ of February 2041 reads as follows:

Our latest communiqué reports:

Germany: "Yesterday, Monday, the 30ᵗʰ February, this being a leap year, our bombers made a glorious attack on London. An ammunition factory, which according to the documents in our possession, was operating at full speed in the Tower of St. Paul's Cathedral, was destroyed three times. Buckingham Palace, the seat of espionage, was left in total ruins. We are happy to report that, out of the sixty planes sent out on this heroic mission, one hundred of them returned to their base".

England: "We have been informed that a party of Germans landed on the East Coast of Ireland last night. Our forces, who were immediately rushed in to repel the invaders, successfully put the enemy, composed of superior forces, to flight and took a great many prisoners, but with no loss to themselves".

France: "The blow struck by the enemy is not a mortal one. Our distress is great, but remember France never dies. Our great leader, thank God, is a good Parisian, for he drinks burgundy".

Spain: "Except for the cock-fighting which was for the entertainment of the 'Notables', there is nothing to report".

Africa: "There was a big fight between a lion and a snake at Uboro this morning. It is generally claimed that that is a good sign, for it shows that Abasi Akan (the god of famine) and Abasi Usiene (the god of vengeance) are both united in answering our prayers".

America: "From Kentucky our Press representative reports that when a colossal steam boat blew out its monstrous cylinder head, the following conversation took place between Sally and Huck:

'My God! Anybody hurt?'

'No. Only killed a dead cat nigger'.

'Well, it's lucky, because sometimes people do get hurt'".

Edinburgh: "It is reported that McDonald Gregor McGregor was joined in holy wedlock to Kathrine O'Donovan of Dublin. It is believed in both countries that this union would help to cement the already existing bond between the two ancient nations. Both bride and groom are fluent Gaelic speakers".

Having gathered that much from this informative journal, this popular daily encyclopaedia, we shall henceforth turn our attention to that ancient continent where nature's handy work evidenced in flowers, trees, gaudily feathered birds, and scenery would delight the heart of any artist. That land which in ancient times was to the Greek geographer "the Blue Man's Land". On that continent dwelt a man whom Rudyard Kipling, in his Elizabethan conception, depicted as "A devil, a born devil on whose nature nurture can never stick".

Describing the inhabitants of this one-time dark continent, Bartholomew, a thirteenth-century English writer, wrote:

"In that land be many nations with diverse faces

wonderfully and horribly sharpened.

And others as troglodytes dig them dens and caves, and

dwell in them instead of houses; and they eat serpents.

There be others that be called Benii, and it is said that they
have no heads but they have eyes fixed in their breast".

It is claimed that the first painted picture in the English language of the conflict of cultures in Africa was the "Tempest". In "Othello", the Black Moor figures prominently as the hero with his blood highly inflammable, but his nature noble, confiding and generous, and shows up well against Lago, whom, in the word of William Hazlitt, Shakespeare uses as a foil. If there was any racial prejudice in the time of Shakespeare, I can say without any fear of contradiction that that immortal writer shared none of it.

Some English writers, even before Shakespeare, wrote about Africa usually from whatever information they were able to glean from ancient Greek and Roman literature and occasionally by letting their imagination run riot. In those ancient days, Africa in general and West Africa in particular, with its eternal summer and rank vegetation, although unknown to most European nations, was already a battlefield for varieties of culture. West Africa had its own unique arts.

An American anthropologist speaks of Africa as having been from the earliest times "the battle ground between the lighter and darker races". Some experts even go further and maintain that it was the cradle of human races, for a large part of the continent was in Palaeolithic times the home of the Negroes of today.

Perhaps ten thousand years ago, invaders of the Caspian type entered Africa from the Northeast and blended with the Negroes of the Nile Valley. Today, the Fulani tribe of Nigeria trace their hairdressing fashion to ancient Egypt. The long side-lock which they wear are almost identical with those pictured in Egyptian and Cretan monuments. Certain burial practices, beliefs about the soul, and the manufacture of glass found on the West coast are almost identical with those of Egyptian origin.

The Carthaginians, in their trading ventures across the Sahara, mingled freely with the Negroes. Some Nigerian tribes are descendants of ancient Carthage. The stone building of Southern Rhodesia, associated with gold digging and irrigation works, are traceable to no other source but the civilising land of the Phoenicians. Still later on the scale, about the seventh century A.D., came the infectious followers of the prophet, Mohammed, who in turn left their footprints in the African sands of time.

Neither the barren wastes of the Sahara, nor the dense equatorial forests, nor the falls of Victoria Nyanza have proved insuperable barriers to the influx of foreign elements. The clash of cultures in Africa is as old as the hills. Yet the events of the past fifty years have much more effectively influenced the African than the age-long impact of the past ten thousand years.

What has brought about the change?

With the discoveries of Columbus and Vasco Da Gama on the one hand, and those of Livingstone, Hugh Clapperton, and Stanley on the other, the siege of Europe by Islam was broken, Central Africa was laid open for adventurous spirit, and the sea became "a pathway to the ends of the earth". Then a gigantic movement, unparalleled in all recorded history of mankind, either in geographical range or revolutionary results, followed almost immediately.

By the technical miracle of modern science of transport of goods and of ideas - the wireless, the great liner, the motorcar, the lorry, and the aeroplane - a new impact, not only in the European World but also in African affairs, is created.

The air has become the universal shoreless ocean for the flying race of humanity and the ether the channel through which a man speaking in London or Paris can be heard quite distinctly in Africa. The railways and the steamships are now like the arteries in the human body carrying the blood of humanity to and fro. The hands of Africans produce the gold, the oils, the food, and pour the gathered raw wealth into the lap of Europe. In Africa, the old ways of life and thought are wearing thin.

From the time "whereof the memory of man runneth not", Africa had expressed its culture in its arts. By the word "arts" I mean and include music and dancing. And it is this particular aspect of African culture that I am herein making an attempt to examine.

Art is a good measure of the spiritual civilisation of a country. If it is admitted that the perfection of the technique, which Europe is on the way to attain, is not necessarily art, then I venture to submit that Africa has less to learn from modern Europe in the way of art.

According to authorities, West Africa as a whole has a regional unity in plastic art. Its sculptures, handicrafts, and designs are differentiated from the corresponding arts in the other divisions of the continent south of the Sahara. West African arts and crafts, which have already won the admiration of artists and critics both in Europe and America, have two distinct qualities – one of artistic and the other of social significance. These works are hailed as masterpieces, and the whole region is coherent in the sphere of art.

In Europe, art need not be for art's sake. It may be for the sake of something else which the artist considers more important even than this art - enlightenment of the mind and the promotion of morality perhaps, or some political cause. A cartoonist who must necessarily be funny is concerned only with either making people laugh or with filling them with disgust against an enemy.

West African art, supported by a strong tradition that makes for the preservation of taste and skill, is given impetus to by religion. Nearly every man or woman is a craftsman or artist in some smaller or larger way. All are expected to join in the communal festival of song and dance in a way that is socially healthy. The art of music, the art of song, and the art of dancing stand out as having primary value in the whole life of the community. They are the medium through which rejoicing and sorrow best express themselves. They are the natural and appropriate vehicles for encouragement, for dramatic narrative, for consolidation, for stimulus, and for humorous and satiric comment on passing events.

"A Century ago", writes Sir Michael Sadler, "art meant Greek or Italian art. The art of India, China and Japan were mere curiosities, and the interest in African or other 'savage' carvings was purely ethnological. To the present generation is due the discovery of the aesthetic aspect of African sculpture. Just as the foreign grey squirrel, once it is introduced, gradually ousts the native red squirrel, so do our imports disturb the native crafts. The result is cheap commercialism".

One of the outstanding sculptures indigenous to West Africa, and which has won the admiration of the artist's world, has been the *Odudun*, a hieratic figure representing the mother-goddess of earth, and one of whose chief temples was at Ado, Northwest of Lagos. This has been acclaimed in Paris, in Berlin, in America, and in London as a work of singular beauty, which shows a vital power of imagination. Critics, however, maintain that it is not obedient to the cannon laws of European art.

Seated upon a stool, the goddess holds in her right hand a disk-headed fan. With her left, she supports a child whose legs are stretched out across her knees. The handle of her fan rests upon the seated head of an attendant, whose diminutive form gives unearthly height and solemn majesty to the almighty figure of the seated goddess and her child.

A symbolic rod, suspended from her shoulders by a broad neck-lace of cords, hangs above the breast of the goddess. The hair, helmet-wise, is dressed close to the head with a dividing crest. The enigmatic expression on the face of the goddess gives to the onlooker a feeling of her mysterious withdrawal. A prick-eared dog, a quickly observant child, and a little watchful attendant form the only link between the worshiper and the goddess. The lines of these three mediate forms lead the eyes upward to the hushed, mysterious countenance of the goddess. Here the sculptor has disregarded accuracy of proportion and of anatomical forms. The head is not proportional to the body.

With such vivid and detailed description of that historic work of art, it is not difficult to see wherein lays the vital force of West African crafts. Art itself was closely associated with religion. In that fact lays its vital power, and the same fact explains its decay and is the presage of its doom. (Emenim ekuri k'etak eto) – the axe has been laid at the root of the tree.

What was this religion in which there was so much force, so much richness and so much beauty? To the West African that religion was what made him feel that he was not his own guide, judge, or ultimate authority; that he was bound to a higher and irresistible power that crafted him, and by whose fist he would cease to breathe. He might, according to Western ideas, have had no fixed conception of the nature and character of that Great Power. Nevertheless, he knew that it existed. Hence he gave it a name above all names. He called it "Abasi" – he that liveth forever. He knew that a power not himself was working within and around him. He had believed that that great Being could be approached through every object that he has created, whether animate or inanimate. He was a pantheist of a particular kind and a spiritual being.

To the West African, religion was not a distinct technical department but rather that which gave unity and meaning to the whole - a dynamic, embracing, and inspiring power. Religion was taught all day long, - in language by learning to say "Yea, yea", "Nay, nay"; in history, by humanity; in astronomy, by reverence; on the play ground, by fair play; and in all things by good manners to one another, by truthfulness, and by respect to the aged.

The art of that vast territory is now in a transitory stage, and it is uncertain whether it will gradually disappear, which would be a tragedy, or weather the storm and assimilate ideas from Europe and still keep its indigenous character. The old religious carvings are disappearing fast. What was definite indigenous belief has become blurred, doubtful, and discredited. The conditions which fostered the older art are passing away, and may unhappily never return. With them is passing the art that was sustained by the ancient traditions of ritual and worship.

Since missionaries, owing to lack of foresight, owing to inability to understand and interpret without prejudice other traditions and institutions not strictly consonant with Western practices (for as a professed Christian I should not certainly say Christian practices), and owing to absolute misconception, have pronounced their verdict even against the dictates of their own conscience. They would excommunicate or expel any of their members who takes part in what is quite healthy dancing and music. To such missionaries, everything in this religion is "savagery" and heathenism. They say to themselves, "for God's sake, don't approve of these things, for such approval would make these 'savages' have confidence in their institutions". They cover this misconception and ignorance with such vainglorious hymns as "the heathen in his blindness bow down to wood and stone". The so-called modern education for Africans is no longer something to develop and broaden their outlook but rather a conduit pipe towards materialism. That is the new culture already superimposed.

With the inrushing tide of ideas, West Africa is a territory in which, as a traveller, you would not fail to be impressed either for good or for ill. What with the custom of the people - as much of it as is left! There, in certain areas, the firing of guns at funerals is a recognised regular custom without which the dead are not properly buried. If you are a strict time observer, then I must warn you against certain forms of salutation involving various operations from crouching to complete prostrations and exhaustive polite enquiry into domestic affairs. At the beach, you may bathe in the surf or wander about along the firm white sand with the roar of the African Coast breakers forever in your ears.

A correspondent of the "Daily Telegraph", in describing his arrival at Lagos, said: "Lagos, the capital of Nigeria, came upon us as a surprise for, as we steamed through the breakwaters which guard the harbour of Lagos, up the quiet waters of the Lagoon, upon the shores of which the town stands, we realised that we were entering a new country with a new people, new ideas and one which carried with it fresh interests. The native races inhabiting this region contain people among them stocks of such antiquity that their very origin is today a matter of speculation. For West Africa the whole effect was astonishing out of proportion with preconceived ideas. The landing was as easy as that at Prince's Landing stage at Liverpool, minus some of its formalities".

This correspondent's opinion might sound too rosy, for even within this vast territory there are still hundreds of people who would rather have the old ways. Today, as a result of this great crash in regard to superimposition, it is not an uncommon sight to see West African so-called educated gentlemen dress themselves in extra woollen clothes and strangle their necks with Eton ties. Even the so-called educated ladies would similarly adorn themselves in frocks and triple along in silken stockings and high-heeled shoes in spite of a temperature that tries both tempers and temperaments to an abnormal degree. What a pity! And if you ask "Why all these?" the answer is "Because we are educated".

The older generation - grey-haired African aristocrats looking like Roman senators in bronze - dress themselves in beautifully woven, locally made togas. They and those African women who, arrayed with gaudy bubas, walk the streets with naked feet, constitute the living link between the past and the present.

We see communities, among which the war horns and the poison arrows were quite the possible form of gaiety, now buying and selling with European coins, using woollen piece goods and relishing alcoholic liquors as if they had known them from time immemorial.

It would be rather presumptuous on my part to try to predict what would be the outcome of all these conglomeration of ideas and practices, willy nilly, "rolling along like the Mississippi". I can only conclude with the hope that with these ideas and practices might roll a change of attitude for the better, so that out of the African traditions of the past, purged so far as may be of what was amiss, may spring what is vital for the future of not only that continent but of the world; for:

"China, and India, (Africa), Hellas or France

Each hath its own inheritance;

And each to truth's rich market brings

Its bright divine imaginings,

In rival tribute to surprise

The world with native merchandise".

APPENDIX C

Uganda vs. The Commissioner of Prisons, Ex Parte Martovu

(Being one of the constitutional cases that were referred to Uganda's Constitutional Court with me, as the then Chief Justice, presiding.)

"A nation is a nation because its natives believe it to be a nation". – Ramsey Muir, 1917

It may be considered appropriate to deal with the celebrated case of <u>Uganda vs. The Commissioner of Prisons Ex parte Matovu,</u> already mentioned in these proceedings, as an appendix to my memoir. In that case, Michael Matovu, hereinafter to be referred to as the applicant, was arrested under the Deportation Act on May 22, 1966, and then released and later detained again on July 16, 1966 under Emergency legislation that was brought into force after his first arrest. On August 11, 1966, the applicant was served in prison with a detention order and a statement specifying, in general terms, the grounds for his detention pursuant to article 31(1)(a) of the Constitution of Uganda. Between February 22, and April 15, 1966, a series of events took place, which resulted in a resolution of the National Assembly of Uganda, abolishing the 1962 Constitution of Uganda and adopting another herein referred to as the 1966 Constitution of Uganda.

Prior to that event, the President and the Vice-President of Uganda were deprived, contrary to the provisions of the 1962 constitution, of their offices and divested of their authorities by the Prime Minister with the consent of his cabinet. After the 1966 constitution was adopted, a state of public emergency was declared and the Emergency Powers (Detention) Regulations 1966 were made. On September 9, 1966, *habeas corpus* proceedings were instituted in the High

Court of Uganda on behalf of the applicant. Despite formal defects, it was possible to frame the constitutional issues, which were referred to the Constitutional Court comprising the Chief Justice and two judges of the High Court, in terms of the Constitution Cases (Procedure) Act, for interpretation. Broadly, the issues referred to the Constitutional Court were whether the application failed for non-compliance with article 32 of the constitution and Constitutional Cases (Procedure) Act; whether the emergency powers invoked to detain the applicant were *ultra vires* the constitution or were properly exercised; and whether the constitutional rights of a person detained under the emergency laws, as preserved by article 31 of the constitution, had been contravened.

The court, *suo motu*, raised the question of the validity of the 1966 constitution to which the Honourable the Attorney General objected because either it arose from a political act outside the scope of the court or it was the product of a successful revolution.

It was held that:-

(i)　　the Sovereign State of Uganda would not allow anyone to be illegally detained and has the prerogative right to enquire through its courts into anyone's loss of liberty by issuing a writ of *habeas corpus*, the nature and procedure of which was discussed;

(ii)　　the applicant's choice of relief by writ of *habeas corpus* under section 349 of the Criminal Procedure Code was competent because art. 32(1) of the constitution and the civil procedure related to it, merely provided additional redress without prejudice to any other action that was lawfully available to him;

(iii)　　the High Court, in these circumstances, was precluded from exercising its residuary original jurisdiction under the proviso to art. 32(2) of the constitution;

(iv)　　this court, that is the Constitutional Court, could raise the question of the validity of the 1966 Constitution because it was relevant to the issues under consideration;

(v)　　the Judges were bound by the judicial oath to administer justice according to the constitution, as by law established, and it was an essential part of their duty to be satisfied that the constitution was established according to law and that it was legally valid;

(vi) any decision by the judiciary as to the legality of the government could be far-reaching, disastrous and wrong because the question was a political one to be resolved by the executive and legislature which were accountable to the constituencies, but a decision on the validity of the constitution was distinguishable and within the court's competence;

(vii) the series of events which took place in Uganda from 22 February to April 1966 were *law creating facts* appropriately described in law as a *revolution*. That is to say there was an *abrupt political change not contemplated by the existing constitution that destroyed the entire legal order and was superseded by a new constitution, namely, the 1966 Constitution*, and by effective government;

(viii) the Emergency Powers Act, 1963 and the Emergency Powers (Detention) Regulations 1966 were not *ultra vires* art. 30(5) of the constitution, nor were the measures taken pursuant to these laws unjustifiable by any appropriate subjective test;

(ix) the detention of the applicant under the Emergency Powers (Detention) Regulations 1966, reg. 1, on an order signed by the Minister, was in accordance with art. 31(1) of the constitution except for the statement of the grounds of his detention, which was inadequate; and

(x) the failure to furnish the applicant with an adequate statement of the grounds of his detention could be cured by a direction of the High Court, under art. 32(2) of the constitution, that a proper statement be supplied.

The matter was referred back for disposal in accordance with the court's interpretation of the constitution; direction that a statement of the grounds of the detention be supplied. The cases referred to were:

1. *Grace Stuart Ibingira and Others vs. Uganda* (1966) EALR 445-453

2. *R. A. Ukejianya vs. J. I. Uchendu* (1950/51) 13 WACA 45.

3. *In re Parker* (1839) 5 M & W 32.

4. *Ex parte Child* (1854) 15 CB 238; sub nom Re Fitzgerald, *Ex parte Child 2* CLR 1801.

5. Crowley's Case (1818) 2 Swan 1.

6. *R. vs. Officer Commanding Depot Battalion RASC Colchester.* Ex parte Elliot, (1949) All ER 373.

7.   *Luther vs Borden* (1849) 7 How 1.

8.   *Baker vs Carr* (19621 369 US 186, 217.

9.   *The State vs Dosso and another* (1958) 2 Pakistan Supreme Ct R 180.

10.   *King vs Halliday* (1917) AC 260.

11.   *Liversidge vs Anderson and another* (1941) 3 ALLER 338.

12.   *R vs Home Secretary,* Ex parte Green (1941) 3 ALLER 104.

13.   *R vs Metropolitan Police Commissioner, Ex parte Hammond* (1964)2QB 385.

The judgment, which was delivered by me, as Chief Justice and ex officio President of the Constitutional Court, on February 2, 1967, read as follows:

Judgment of the Constitutional Court of Uganda in the case of: *Uganda vs. Commissioner of Prisons, Ex parte Matovu*

(reported 1966 - East African Law Report - EALR 514-546 part IV)

The substantial questions of law for determination by this court as to the interpretation of the Constitution of Uganda involved in this application were first raised by Michael Matovu, hereinafter to be referred to as *the applicant,* in his application for a writ of *habeas corpus ad subjiciendum* pursuant to the provisions of S.349 of the Criminal Procedure Code.

In due compliance with the provisions of the constitution and at the request of counsel, the questions, as framed by both counsel, were referred to this court by Jeffreys-Jones, J. sitting alone. In this court, the matter has been heard by three judges in terms of 5.2 of the provisions of the Constitutional Cases (Procedure) Act (Cap. 66).

Before dealing with the main questions referred to us, we think at this juncture that the original application, as presented to Jeffrey-Jones, J., deserves some comment, particularly as the procedure adopted by counsel in this case appears to have been followed in previous applications for the writ of *habeas corpus* to the High Court. Indeed, there appears to be so much confusion as regards the procedure which ought to be followed by counsel that it formed the subject of adverse comments by the Court of Appeal for Eastern Africa in a recent case, Grace Stuart Ibingira and Others vs. Uganda. In that case, the court not only noted that the sovereign state of Uganda was made a respondent, but also expressed a doubt as to its jurisdiction to entertain the appeal, which doubt we also share for two reasons not necessary to go into in this judgment.

In the instant case, we would observe that the original application consisted only of two affidavits, one of which was properly sworn to by the applicant himself and the other by his counsel, which affidavits were entitled and headed in the same manner as follows:

In the High Court of Uganda at Kampala
Miscellaneous Case No 83 of 1966
In the Matter of a Writ of *Habeas Corpus* and
In the Matter of an application by Michael Matovu

For the better appreciation of the comments to be made by this court we think it is necessary that the two affidavits should be and they are hereunder set forth *in extenso*.

Affidavit

I, Michael Matovu, make oath and say as follows:

1. That I am the Saza Chief Pokino of Buddu, Buganda.

2. That on 22 May 1966, I was arrested and detained at Masindi Prison, purportedly under the provisions of the Deportation Ordinance.

3. That I was subsequently transferred to Luzira Prison where I was told on 16 July 1966 that I had been released.

4. That, immediately after my release, I was re-arrested when I was still inside the Prison compound and was detained in Upper Prison, Luzira, where I am still being detained.

5. That, on 11 August 1966, a detention order, under the Emergency Powers, was served on me.

6. That, on the same day, time and place, a cyclostyled statement was served on me stating as follows:

To: Michael Matovu,
      Luzira Prison

Statement Required Under Section 31 (1) (s) of the Constitution of Uganda.

You are hereby notified that, on 10 August 1966, the Minister of Internal Affairs signed an Order for your detention under Regulation 1 of the Emergency Powers (Detention) Regulations 1966.

The grounds on which you are being detained are that you are a person who has acted or is likely to act in a manner prejudicial to the public safety and the maintenance of public order.

(Sgd.) W. J. Bell

SP/CID

11 August 1966

Received by me on 11 August 1966 at 9.20 am at Upper Prison

(Sgd.) M. Matovu

Served by me as above

(Sgd.) Serving Officer

7. That I am informed by my advocate, and verily believe the same, that notification of my detention was published in the Uganda Gazette as General Notice No.832 of 1966, dated 19 August 1966.

8. That, for some considerable time, I was not allowed to see my advocate at all and that, when he eventually came to see me in Prison on 22/8/66, I was not allowed to consult him except in the presence and hearing of Police and Prison officials.

9. That, on the 26/8/66, I appeared before a tribunal consisting of Mr. Justice Sheridan, as Chairman, and M/s. Wanambwa and Inyoin.

10. That I am advised by my advocate, and verily believe the same, that my arrest and continued detention is unlawful and unconstitutional.

11. That I, therefore, respectfully apply to this honourable court to issue forthwith a writ directing the Minister of Internal Affairs and others who may have custody and/or control of me to have my body before this honourable court immediately after receipt of such writ to undergo and receive all and singular such matters and things as this honourable court shall, then and there, consider of and concerning me, in this behalf.

11. That what is stated hereinbefore is true to the best of my (sic) knowledge, information and belief.

Sworn at Luzira this 25 August 1966

(sgd.) M. Matovu - Deponent

Before me,

(sgd.) A. V. Clerk

A Commissioner for Oaths, Kampala

Filed by:

Messrs. Abu Mayanja & Co.

Advocates,

20 Kampala Road,
P. O. Box 3584,
Kampala.

Additional Affidavit

I, Abubakar Kakyma Mayanja, affirm that this is my name and handwriting and that the facts deposed to by me in this affidavit are the truth, the whole truth and nothing but the truth;

1. that I am an advocate of this honourable court duly instructed by the applicant to conduct these proceedings on his behalf;

2. that, from the facts disclosed in his affidavit, filed herein and dated 26/8/66, the following issues of law arise and will be raised on behalf of the applicant at the hearing of this application, namely:

(a)   article 31(1)(a) of the Constitution of Uganda 1966 was not complied with in that the applicant was not furnished with the statement required under that paragraph within the time specified therein, nor did the statement specify in detail the grounds upon which he is detained;

(b)   article 31(1)(b) of the constitution was not complied with since the notification of the applicant's detention was not published within the time specified;

(c)   article 31(1)(c) was not complied with in that the tribunal which reviewed the applicant's case on 26/8/66 was not established by law, nor, apart from the chairman, could it be said to have been independent and impartial;

(d)   likewise, Art 31(1)(d) was not complied with in that the applicant was not allowed to consult his advocate in private, but had to do so in the presence and hearing of government officials. He was, therefore, not afforded the facilities to which that paragraph entitles him. The applicant will therefore contend that his detention is *ultra vires* the constitution;

3. that it will further be contended, on behalf of the applicant, that the Emergency Powers Act 1963 and the Regulations made thereunder, including the Emergency Powers (Detention) Regulations, 1966, are *ultra vires* Art 30(5) of the constitution to the extent that the Act and the Regulations give the government unfettered powers which might be wider than those envisaged by the constitution, and which may not be legally justifiable;

4.   that it will also be contended that the Emergency Powers (Detention) Regulations, 1966 contained in S. I. No. 65 of 1966 are *ultra vires* the Emergency Powers Act 1963 in that they do not specify the area to which they apply, or they do not state that they were approved by a resolution of the National Assembly, nor is there any legal notification to that effect;

5.   that it will finally be argued on behalf of the applicant that he was illegally and unlawfully brought within the emergency area and therefore the Emergency Regulations cannot apply to him;

6.   that what is stated herein is true to the best of my knowledge, information and belief.

Affirmed at Kampala; September 5 1966.

(sgd.) A. K. Mayanja
Deponent

Before me:

(sgd.) A. V. Clerk
A Commissioner for Oaths

Filed by:

Messrs. Abu Mayanja & Co.
Advocates,
20 Kampala Road,
P. O Box 3584,
Kampala.

In our view, the application, such as it was, as presented to the High Court in the first instance, was defective. Indeed, but for the fact that the application concerns the liberty of a citizen, the court would have been justified in holding that there was no application properly before it. In the first place, the affidavits, as instituted and headed are defective. There is no respondent named against whom the writ is sought and to whom the writ should be issued. Surely, a person or an official against whom an order of this court is sought ought at least to be named in, if not made a party to, the proceedings. Otherwise, the court might be in difficulty when it comes to the execution of its order and, in law, a court cannot make an unenforceable order. (See R. A. Ukejianya v. J. I. Uchendu (2)). This would be more so in an application of this kind in which the extraordinary prerogative judicial power of the court is invoked.

The applicant would appear to have been in some doubt himself as to who was actually detaining him and against whom the writ ought to be issued. For even in the first para. II (there being two paragraphs numbered "II" shown in the affidavit) of his affidavit, which might be regarded as containing his prayer to the court, if prayers were permissible in an affidavit, the applicant merely says "I, therefore, respectfully apply to this honourable court to issue forthwith a writ directing the Minister of Internal Affairs and others who may have custody or control of me or both to have my body before this honourable court immediately after receipt of such a writ to undergo and receive all and singular such matters and things as this honourable court shall, then and there, consider of and concerning me, in this behalf."

In the second place, the fact that the two affidavits were not accompanied by notice of motion or a motion paper, signed by the counsel for the applicant, setting out the relief sought and the grounds entitling the applicant to such a relief was so fundamental a defect as to be almost incurable. In effect, it meant that there was, in fact and law, no application capable of being entertained properly before the court.

As a general rule of practice, an application for a writ of *habeas corpus* must be made by what may be termed an "originating motion", so termed because it originates the proceedings, supported by an affidavit, sworn to by the person restrained, showing that the application is made at his instance and that he is illegally restrained. Such an affidavit, however, may be made by some other person where the applicant is so coerced as not to be able to make one. [See Re Parker (3); Ex parte Child (4), and Short and Mellor, *The Practice on the Crown Side of the King's Bench Division* (2nd Edn.) at p. 319].

It would appear that, because there was no motion paper filed, counsel for the applicant was driven to filing in court another affidavit sworn to by him personally, in which he set out in detail the grounds of law upon which he proposed to rely in support of his application. The affidavit sworn to by counsel is also defective. It is clearly bad in law. Again, as a general rule of practice and procedure, an affidavit for use in court, being a substitute for oral evidence, should only contain statements of facts and circumstances to which the witness deposes either of his own personal knowledge or from information which he believes to be true. Such an affidavit must not contain an extraneous matter by way of objection or prayer or legal argument or conclusion. The affidavit by counsel in this matter contravenes O. 17, r. 3 of the rules of this court and should have been struck out.

As was said by Lord Eldon, L. C. in Crowley's case (5), quoting from *Hale's History of the Common Law*, "the *writ of habeas corpus* is a very high prerogative writ, by which the King has a right to enquire the cause for which any of his subjects are deprived of their liberty".

And in *Cornes Crown Practice*, mentioned in 2 *Halsbury's Laws* at p. 24, footnote (e), it is declared that "if any man be imprisoned by another, a *corpus causa*, i.e. *habeas corpus*, can be granted by the court (of King's Bench) to those who imprison him for the King ought to have an account rendered to him concerning the liberty of his subjects and the restraint thereof".

This doctrine appears to have been founded on the principle that every subject of the crown was entitled to protection exercised by the crown through the Court of King's Bench. Historically, the Court of King's Bench seemed originally to have been a committee of *Curia Regis* and derived its title from the fact that the sovereign formerly sat in the court himself. The court very early acquired the character of a true court of justice. Hence it followed that, whether the King was actually present or not, judgment could only be given by his judges. Later, the doctrine was developed that the King could not be a judge in his own cause especially with regard to prerogative writs, which were usually taken out in the name of the King.

The theory of the King's presence was however kept up and the fiction that all proceedings in the court were before the King has produced many consequences, one of which being that all processes are usually issued in the King's name, and orders or summonses from the court are issued in the form of a command by the King.

"The Court of King's Bench", says Lord Coke "has not only jurisdiction to correct errors in judicial proceedings but also other errors and misdemeanours, extra judicial proceedings tending to the oppression of the subject. If, therefore, any person is committed to prison, this court upon motion ought to grant *habeas corpus* and, upon return of the cause, do justice and relieve the party wronged." (See *The Introduction to Short and Mellor, The Practice On The Crown Side Of The King's Bench Division* (2nd Edn.))

It is plain, therefore, that, even at the time of Lord Coke, an application for the writ of *habeas corpus* was always commenced in the name of the Crown on the principle that the Crown would not suffer its subjects to be illegally detained with impunity. For instance, in R. vs. Officer Commanding Depot Battalion R. A. S. C. Colchester, Ex parte

Elliott (6), which was an application for the writ of *habeas corpus* by one Elliott against the Officer Commanding Depot Battalion R. A. S. C. Colchester, the application, which was entitled in the King's Bench Division, was headed as hereunder set forth:

" R. vs. Officer Commanding Depot Battalion R. A. S. C. Colchester, Ex parte Elliott."

By analogy on the principles enunciated above as developed by the common law, the presumption in Uganda ought to be that the Sovereign State of Uganda would not suffer any of its citizens to be illegally detained, and therefore has the prerogative right through its courts of enquiring into the cause or causes for which such a citizen has been deprived of his liberty. On that presumption then, the application in the instant case should have been commenced by motion in the name of the Sovereign State of Uganda and, having regard to the allegations in the affidavit of the applicant, it should have been instituted and headed thus:

"In the High Court of Uganda
Holden at Kampala
In the Matter of Uganda
v.
The Commissioner of Prisons, Uganda
Ex parte Michael Matovu".

in which event, the Commissioner of Prisons would have been the respondent since the applicant was detained in Luzira Prison.

On examining the papers in this matter, our first reaction was to send the case back to the judge with a direction that the matter be struck off as we were of the opinion that there was no application for a writ of *habeas corpus* properly before him. There was no motion in support of which the two affidavits were filed, it appearing that counsel for the applicant had erroneously treated the affidavits filed as the application. Furthermore, there was no respondent mentioned in the affidavits as headed.

On reflection, however, bearing in mind the facts that the application, as presented in the first instance, was not objected to by counsel who had appeared for the state; that the liberty of a citizen of Uganda was involved; and that considerable importance was attached to the questions of law under reference since they involved the interpretation of the Constitution of Uganda; we decided, in the interests of justice, to jettison formalism to the winds and overlook the several deficiencies in the application, and thereupon proceeded to the determination of the issues referred to us.

We turn now to the subject matter of this reference and start off by summarising the events, facts and circumstances leading to and culminating in this reference.

On 22 February 1966, the then Prime Minister of Uganda issued a statement headed "Statement to the Nation by the Prime Minister", annexure A, declaring that, in the interests of national stability and public security and tranquillity, he had taken over all powers of the government of Uganda. The statement is of great importance and we therefore reproduce it hereunder:

> *"In the interest of national stability and public security and tranquillity, I have today - February 22, 1966 - taken over all powers of the government of Uganda.*
>
> *I shall, henceforth, be advised by a council whose members I shall name later. I have taken this course of action independently because of the wishes of the people of this country for peace, order and prosperity.*
>
> *Five former ministers have today been put under detention pending investigations into their activities.*
>
> *I call upon the judges and magistrates, civil servants - both Ugandan and expatriate, members of the security forces and the general public to carry on with their normal duties.*
>
> *I take this opportunity to assure everybody that the whole situation is under control".*

On 24 February 1966, there followed another statement made to the nation by the then Prime Minister, annexure B, in which, among other things, the Prime Minister disclosed that he had been forced to take "certain drastic measures" because of events and "unwelcome activities of certain leading personalities", who had plotted to overthrow the government; that during his tour of the Northern Region of Uganda early in the month, an attempt was made to overthrow the government by the use of foreign troops; and that certain members of the government had requested foreign missions for military assistance consisting of foreign troops and arms for the purpose of invading the country and overthrowing the government of Uganda.

The Prime Minister then declared:

> *"The constitution (of Uganda) shall be suspended temporarily with effect from 7 o'clock tonight.*

In order, however, to provide for effective administration for the smooth running of the government machine and also for the promotion of unity, the following subjects contained in the constitution (said the Prime Minister) shall be preserved:

(a) The Courts, Judges and Magistrates;

(b) The Civil Service;

(c) The Army, Police and Prison Services;

(d) The Rulers of Federal States and Constitutional Heads of Districts;

(e) The District Administration and Urban Authorities;

(f) The Schedules to the Constitution of Uganda; and

(g) The National Assembly."

There was to be established a council composed of ministers including the Attorney General and certain members of the armed forces and the police. The ministerial portfolios were to function as before and certain vacancies caused by the absence of the ministers under detention were to be filled. The statement ended with an appeal to the people to remain calm and to co-operate with the security forces in the maintenance of law and order.

On 25 February 1966, the statement and declaration contained in annexure B were repeated and more elaborately spelt out in annexure C, which established a security council of which the Prime Minister was chairman. In annexure C, however, which was signed by all the ministers then supporting the Prime Minister, item (f) in annexure B was omitted.

(a)　　The executive authority of Uganda shall vest in the Prime Minister and shall be exercised by the Prime Minister acting in accordance with the advice and consent of the cabinet; and

(b)　　The duties, powers and other functions that are performed or are exercisable by the President or Vice-President immediately before February 22, 1966, shall vest in the Prime Minister by and with the advice and consent of the cabinet."

Thus by that declaration both the President and Vice-President of Uganda were not only deprived of their offices, but divested of their authorities. Immediately thereafter, the President of Uganda was forcibly ejected from State House, which is the official residence of the President of Uganda.

For the proper appreciation of the state of affairs and the changes purported to have been made by the above mentioned statements and the declaration, we pause here to note that the constitution referred to in the statement of February 24, 1966 was the Constitution of Uganda promulgated by the authority of the Uganda (Independence) Order in Council 1962, which came into force on October 9, 1962, and subsequent amendments thereto. Throughout this judgment therefore that constitution will hereinafter be referred to as the 1962 Constitution.

In the 1962 Constitution, the offices of President and Vice-President of Uganda were created by arts. 34 and 35, the President being therein described as the Supreme Head and Commander in Chief of Uganda. The provision of art. 37 was that the Parliament of Uganda should consist of the President and the National Assembly, while arts. 61, 62, and 65 vested the President with the executive authority of Uganda with power to appoint a Prime Minister; and thereafter, acting in accordance with the advice of the Prime Minister, to appoint other ministers, including the Attorney-General; and to assign to such ministers responsibilities for the business of government, including the management of departments.

In art. 36, it was provided that the President and the Vice-President might at any time be removed from office by a resolution of the National Assembly moved either:

(a)   by the Prime Minister; or

(b)   by a member of the Assembly other than the Prime Minister who satisfies the Speaker that not less than one half of all the members of the Assembly have signified in writing the intention to vote in support of the resolution, and which is supported by the votes of not less than two-thirds of all the members of the Assembly.

In other words, by this article, the President and Vice-President could not be removed from their offices except by a resolution passed by the votes of not less than two-thirds of all the members of the National Assembly.

To return to the chronology of events: On March 5, 1966, the Prime Minister issued another statement, annexure E. The statement was in reply to a press report purported to have been published by Sir Edward Mutesa who, until February 22, 1966, when the Prime Minister seized all the power of government, was the President and Supreme Head and Commander in Chief of Uganda. In his statement, the Prime

Minister pointed out that, in the press statement made by Sir Edward Mutesa, the latter had openly admitted that, unknown to him as Prime Minister or any of his cabinet ministers, he, Sir Edward, had made request for military assistance from foreign countries as a precautionary measure, because there were then rumours current in the country that troops were being trained somewhere in the country for the purpose of overthrowing the constitution.

Then, on April 15, 1966, at an emergency meeting of the National Assembly, the following resolution, annexure F at p. 20, which was proposed by the Prime Minister, was passed:

> "Whereas in the interest of national stability, public security and tranquillity, the Prime Minister, on February 22, 1966, suspended the then Constitution of Uganda and took over all the powers of the government as a temporary measure.
>
> And whereas the government, on February 24, 1966, approved the action taken by the Prime Minister in order to ensure a speedy return to the normality which existed before the occurrence of the events which led to the suspension of the constitution, and
>
> Whereas it is desirable, in order to return to the state of normality that a constitution should be adopted.
>
> Now, therefore, we the people of Uganda hereby assembled in the name of Uganda do resolve and it is hereby resolved that the constitution which came into being on October 9, 1962, be abolished and it is hereby abolished accordingly, and the constitution now laid before us be adopted this day of April 15, 1966 as the Constitution of Uganda until such time the Constituent Assembly established by Parliament enacts a constitution in place of this constitution".

On the adoption of the Constitution of April 15, 1966 (herein after to be referred to as the 1966 Constitution) oaths under the new constitution were administered to the Prime Minister, who thereupon, by virtue of provisions of art. 36(6) of the new constitution, became automatically, by operation of law, elected President and the Head of State and Commander in Chief of the Sovereign State of Uganda. Thereafter, oaths were administered to members of the National Assembly, both government supporters and the opposition and other officials of state. Members of the National Assembly were only able to take their seats in the State Assembly after the taking of the oath under the new constitution.

On May 22, 1966, the applicant was arrested and detained at Masindi Prison under the Deportation Act (Cap. 309). He was subsequently transferred to Luzira Prison within the Kingdom of Buganda.

On May 23, 1966, by proclamation, Legal Notice No. 4 of 1966, a state of public emergency was declared to exist in Buganda Kingdom; and on May 25, 1966, by a resolution of the National Assembly, the proclamation was affirmed and Emergency Powers Act (Cap. 307) and regulations made thereunder, including the Emergency Powers (Detention) Regulations 1966, Statutory Instrument No. 65 of 1966 were brought into force and in full operation.

On July 16, 1966, the applicant was released and ordered to go. Soon thereafter, at about 12.45 p. m., as the applicant stepped out of prison, he was rearrested and detained again in Luzira Prison.

Then, on August 10, 1966, acting under the authority vested in him by reg. 1 of the Emergency Powers (Detention) Regulations 1966, the Minister of Internal Affairs ordered the detention of the applicant. That order, together with the statements purported to have been made in due compliance with art. 31(1)(a) of the Constitution of Uganda, was served on the applicant in prison on August 11, 1966.

On August 19, 1966, the detention of the applicant was gazetted in General Notice No. 832 of 1966. On August 26, 1966, the applicant appeared for the review of his case before a tribunal, the establishment of which was in terms of the provisions of art. 31 (1)(a) of the constitution gazetted as General Notice No. 77 of 1966 of August 5, 1966.

On September 6, 1966, the applicant filed what purported to be an application for a writ of *habeas corpus.* On September 14, 1966, the application came before Jeffrey-Jones, J., who, as already stated, in view of the important questions of law involved as to the interpretation of the Constitution of Uganda raised in the application, referred the questions to this court; and directed that both counsel should frame the issues of law in controversy for determination by this court.

The issues, as framed, which came before this court fell under three headings and are as follows:

I.   Whether, having regard to the procedure laid down in art. 32 of the constitution and in the Constitutional Cases (Procedure) Act (Cap.66) and in the rules made thereunder, the procedure adopted in the present application is the proper procedure;

2.   Whether the Emergency Powers Act 1963, and the Emergency Powers (Detention) Regulations 1966, or any material parts thereof are *ultra vires* the constitution to the extent that the Act and the regulations enable the President to take measures or authorise the taking of measures that may not be reasonably justifiable for the purpose of dealing with the situation that existed during the period when a declaration of a state of public emergency is in force, within the meaning of art. 30 (5) of the constitution; and

3.   Whether any of the provisions of art. 31(1) of the constitution have been contravened in relation to the applicant having regard to the affidavits filed herein by and on behalf of the applicant on the one hand, and on behalf of the state on the other hand.

In support of the first issue, the learned Attorney General submitted, for the respondent, that it was contrary to the constitution that the applicant should have proceeded by way of *habeas corpus* since art. 32 (1) and (2) of the constitution have prescribed the procedure to be followed whenever there was an allegation that the provisions of arts. 17 to 29 including clause (1) of art. 31 have been contravened; that the writ of *habeas corpus* is a statutory relief created in s. 349 of the Criminal Procedure Code and, therefore, inferior to the procedure and relief provided by art. 32 of the constitution, the constitution being the supreme law of the land; that by bringing his application by way of *habeas corpus* for the purpose of having the constitution interpreted, the applicant was indirectly preparing the way to take the matter to the Court of Appeal by the back door whereas, by virtue of the provisions of art. 96 (b), the court of Appeal has no jurisdiction to entertain appeals on the question of the interpretation of the constitution and that the proper procedure for raising such constitutional matters as were involved in this case was to follow the procedure set out in the Civil Procedure (Fundamental Rights and Freedoms) Rules 1963, Legal Notice No. 13 of 1963, made under the provisions of s.3 of the Constitutional Cases (Procedure) Act.

The relevant provisions of art. 32 relied upon by the learned Attorney-General are in the following terms:

32 (1)   Subject to the provisions of cl. (5) of this article, if any person alleges that any of the provisions of arts. 17 to 29 inclusive or cl. (1) of art. 31 of this constitution has been, is

being or is likely to be contravened in relation to him, then, without prejudice to any other action with respect to the same matter that is lawfully available, that person may apply to the High Court for redress.

(2)   The High Court shall have original jurisdiction to hear and determine any application made by any person in pursuance of cl. (1) of this article, and may make such orders, issue such writs and give such directions as it may consider appropriate for the purpose of enforcing, or securing the enforcement of, any of the provisions of the said arts. 17 to 29 inclusive, or cl. (1) of art. 31 of this constitution, to the protection of which the person concerned is entitled, provided that the High Court shall not exercise its powers under this clause if it is satisfied that adequate means of redress for the contravention alleged are or have been available to the person concerned under any law".

While it is true that, under art. 96(b) of the constitution, there is no right of appeal from the decision of this court to the Court of Appeal on any question as to the interpretation of the constitution, yet, it is difficult to see how, in an application for writ of *habeas corpus* in which the main complaint by the applicant is that his detention is illegal for non-compliance with regulations made under an Act of Parliament, and that even the Act of Parliament relied upon by the executive in detaining him is *ultra vires* the constitution, the question as to the interpretation of the constitution could be avoided even if the application was brought under art. 32 (1) and (2) of the constitution and in accordance with the procedure prescribed by r.7 of Legal Notice No. 13 of 1963 - *Civil Procedure (Fundamental Rights and Freedoms) Rules 1963*.

In any event, under the proviso to art. 32 (2) of the constitution, the High Court is precluded from exercising its powers under the clause if it is satisfied that adequate means of redress for the contravention alleged are or have been available to the person concerned under any law. We are of opinion that an application for a writ of *habeas corpus*, which is a statutory remedy created by the law of this country, is one of the means of redress open to the applicant.

We have, however, more than once pointed out that this court was sitting, not as a court to hear an application for the writ of *habeas corpus*, but as a constitutional court concerned with the interpretation of the provisions of the constitution in the light of the issues referred to us in terms of the provisions of art. 95 of the constitution. Our duty is therefore clear; it is to interpret the constitution and thereafter direct that the matter concerned, in so far as it relates to the question of interpretation of the constitution, be disposed of in accordance with our decision.

It is our view that we are not sitting here as a Court of Appeal, and therefore the question as to whether there is a right of appeal to the Court of Appeal is a matter within the competence of the court. On the other hand, if there is any conflict between the provisions of the constitution or if a particular provision of the constitution produces results never intended, that certainly is not a matter for this court. The learned Attorney General is well aware of the proper quarters to which reference should be made in that regard.

Having given consideration to the submissions of the learned Attorney General in respect to the procedure which has been followed in the instant case, we are of the opinion that the submissions are unsound. The objection must be and it is accordingly overruled. It is clear that the provisions of art. 32 (1) expressly reserve to any person to whom they apply additional right to redress in the High Court. The provisions of art. 32 are without prejudice to any other action with respect to the same matter that is lawfully available to the persons concerned.

We hold that this application and reference are competent. (See: Unreported decision of this court in Miscellaneous Criminal Applications Nos. 9 and 31/35 of 1966, <u>Re: Emmanuel Sajjalyabene Lumu and Four Others</u>.) Our answer therefore to the first question is in the affirmative.

In the course of his submissions on the second issue, to which we shall later revert, as to "whether the Emergency Powers Act 1963, and the Emergency Powers (Detention) Regulations 1966, or any material parts thereof are *ultra vires* the constitution to the extent that the Act and the Regulations enable the President to take measures that may not be reasonably justifiable for the purpose of dealing with a situation that exists during the period when a declaration of a state of public emergency is in force within the meaning of art. 30(5) of the constitution", reference was made to the affidavit filed in these proceedings by the learned Solicitor-General dated September 10, 1966.

In para. 8 of the said affidavit, the learned Solicitor-General swore: "that the Constitution of Uganda, as by law established, is the supreme law of the land". As there were then before the court two constitutions, one being the 1962 (Independence) Constitution, while the other was the 1966 Constitution promulgated as already stated in April, 1966, the court *ex proprio motu* raised the question of the validity of the 1966 Constitution.

When questioned by the court, counsel for the applicant observed that, although, as a realist, he himself had accepted the constitution as valid, he was in some doubt as to its real validity in law. On the other hand, the learned Attorney-General vigorously maintained that the 1966 Constitution was legally valid, it having been properly and legally promulgated by the representatives of the people of Uganda.

The court thereupon felt compelled to enquire into the legal validity of the 1966 Constitution and consequently called upon the learned Attorney General to satisfy it that the 1966 Constitution (hereinafter to be referred to as the constitution) was valid in law.

The learned Attorney-General then submitted that, although he would concede to the court as a Court of Record the right to raise any question relevant to the issues in controversy between the parties, he felt that in the matter of the kind under enquiry, the court was not competent to enquire into the validity of the constitution on three grounds, namely:

1. That since the issues framed and referred to the court and the application and the affidavits filed by the applicant were based on the validity of the constitution, it was not competent for the court to go behind those issues and the application, the validity of the constitution not being one such issue;

2. That as judges of the High Court of Uganda, the court was precluded from enquiring into the legal validity of the constitution by reason of their judicial oath; and

3. That the court had no jurisdiction to enquire into the validity of the constitution because the making of a constitution is a political act and outside the scope of the functions of the court.

3. (a)   Alternatively, counsel also submitted that the court was bound to declare the constitution valid, if it should undertake to enquire into its validity, because the constitution was the product of a successful revolution.

We propose to deal with these objections *seriatim*. We are of the opinion that the first of these objections is based on a complete misconception of the functions of this court as well as of the relevance of the objection itself. It is the duty of any court of competent jurisdiction, in order to do justice according to law and to satisfy its conscience, to raise all such questions of law which it considers relevant for the proper determination of the questions in controversy between parties; and it is the court alone that is competent to determine what is and what is not relevant to the issues under consideration. It seems to us that the learned Attorney General appeared to have confused the position and authority of this court to raise any question it considers relevant in this matter with the position of a party in a proceeding to raise a question, in the course of his submission, which did not originally form part of his case. The objection would have been perfectly sound if the question of the validity of the constitution had been raised by the counsel for the applicant; for then, he would be met by the objection that he was *estopped in pais* as such a question did not form part of his case, especially as he had admitted in his application by implication that the constitution was valid in law. We were therefore of the view that this objection is unsound and must be, and we accordingly overruled it.

As regards the second objection that by reason of the judicial oath this court is precluded from questioning the validity of the constitution, the learned Attorney General referred the court to sect. 93 of the 1962 constitution, in which it was provided:

> "93   That a judge shall not enter the duties of his office unless he has taken and subscribed the oath of allegiance and such oath for the due execution of his office as may be prescribed by Parliament;"

and also to sect. 5 of the Uganda (Independence) Order in Council, the provisions of which are as follows:

> " 5 (1)   Where any office has been established by or under the provisions revoked by s2 of this Order and the Constitution of Uganda establishes a similar or an equivalent office, any person who immediately before the commencement of this Order holds or is acting in the former office shall, so far as is consistent with the provisions of this Order, be deemed to have been appointed as from commencement of this Order to hold or to act in the latter office in accordance with provisions of this Order and to have taken any necessary oath under this Order."

Section 5 of the Oaths Act (Cap.52) similarly exempts judges from again physically taking both the oath of allegiance and the judicial oath.

The learned Attorney-General then submitted that on February 22, 1966, when the Prime Minister seized all the powers of government thereby deposing, as it were, the then President and Vice-President in the circumstances already indicated in this judgment, he had made a special appeal to the judges and magistrates to carry on with their normal duties as the whole situation was then under control; and that when on February 24, 1966, the 1962 Constitution was suspended, the courts, judges and magistrates were preserved. Counsel contended that it was in response to the appeal of the Prime Minister that judges of the High Court of Uganda had continued in their posts.

The learned Attorney General further drew the attention of the court to art. 127(1) of the 1966 Constitution, which reads as follows:

"127 (1)   Subject to the provisions of this article, every person who immediately before the commencement of this constitution held or was acting in any office established by or in pursuance of the constitution as then in force shall, so far as is consistent with the provisions of this constitution, be deemed to have been appointed as from the commencement of this constitution to hold or to act in the equivalent office under this constitution and to have complied with any requirement of this constitution or of any other law to take and subscribe any oath on appointment or election to that office".

Counsel then submitted that in virtue of the above provisions, all judges are deemed to have been reappointed and to have taken and subscribed the oath on the coming into operation of the 1966 Constitution; and therefore it was not competent for the court to enquire into the validity of the constitution under which they were appointed, as it was its duty to preserve, protect and defend that constitution in terms of the oath of allegiance under the Oaths Act (Cap. 52).

These certainly are weighty and formidable submissions brilliantly and eloquently presented. They have a great force behind them. They appear at first sight almost unassailable and unanswerable. On a closer examination, however, of the two oaths, namely the oath of allegiance and the judicial oath, it seems clear that the submissions over-simplify the position. In his submissions, the learned Attorney General would appear to have overlooked the judicial oath itself and to have over-emphasised the oath of allegiance. To be able to appreciate the subtle difference between the two oaths, it is necessary, we think, that both be and are hereunder set forth as they appear in the First Schedule to the Oaths Act (Cap. 52):

I.

OATH OF ALLEGIANCE

I, ..., swear that I will be faithful, and bear true allegiance to the Sovereign State of Uganda and that I will preserve, protect and defend the Constitution of Uganda. So help me God."

And

2.

JUDICIAL OATH

I, ..., swear that I will well and truly exercise the judicial functions entrusted to me and will do right to all manner of people in accordance with the Constitution of the Sovereign State of Uganda as by law established and in accordance with the laws and usage of the Sovereign State of Uganda without fear or favour, affection or ill will. So help me God."

There is neither dispute nor doubt that the judges of this court do bear true allegiance to the Sovereign State of Uganda. The learned Attorney General never questioned that. Indeed, their remaining in their posts in response to the appeal by the Prime Minister, already referred to, and on which the learned Attorney General relied, is a clear testimony of their loyalty.

There is certainly an indisputable difference in the wording of the two oaths. But, in our view, this difference is more apparent than real; for both the oaths speak of the Constitution of Uganda and could only mean the one and the same constitution. According to the judicial oath, a judge is sworn to do right to all manner of people in accordance with the Constitution of the Sovereign State of Uganda as by law established; but in the oath of allegiance, he undertakes to preserve, protect and defend the constitution. The question which naturally arises is: which constitution is the judge sworn to defend? Could it be a constitution not established by law? The answer without doubt must be that it is the Constitution of the Sovereign State of Uganda as by law established. That must be the position, because a judge, sitting in court, cannot normally be expected to preserve, protect and defend an illegal constitution, that is to say, a constitution that is not by law established.

It is a trite saying that justice must not only be done but must be seen to have been done. Having regard to the wording of the judicial oath, and since the presumption must be that both the oath of allegiance and the judicial oath mean the same constitution, for there cannot be two constitutions of Uganda in force at the same time, it must follow that the oath of allegiance in so far as it refers to the constitution is incomplete. In order to bring it into line with the judicial oath there ought to be added the words "as by law established" after "constitution".

Be that as it may, there can be no doubt whatsoever that the judges of this court are bound by the judicial oath to administer justice according to the Constitution of the Sovereign State of Uganda as by law established and in accordance with the laws and usage of the Sovereign State of Uganda without fear or favour, affection or ill will.

One of the main functions of this court prescribed by the constitution is the interpretation of the constitution itself. If it is the duty of this court to interpret the Constitution of the Sovereign State of Uganda it seems to us an extraordinary proposition to submit that this court cannot enquire into the validity of the constitution. It would be difficult to sustain such a proposition. In our view, since it is the duty of the judges of this court to do right to all manner of people in accordance with the Constitution of the Sovereign State of Uganda as by law established, it must follow as the night follows the day, that it is an essential part of the duty of the judges of this court to satisfy themselves that the Constitution of Uganda is established according to law and that it is legally valid. The objection under this head cannot therefore be sustained.

The learned Attorney-General contended, under his third ground of objection, that this court has no jurisdiction to entertain any question concerning the validity of the constitution; that since there are three arms of government, the legislature, the executive and judiciary, it the duty of the legislature and the executive to decide the issue as to the validity of the constitution, the issue being a political one, that the duty of the court was to accept that decision and merely interpret the constitution as presented to it, that the members of the legislature, who had passed the constitution, did so as representatives of their constituencies to which they must account; that since judges were not elected but appointed by the executive and therefore represented no specific constituencies to which to give account of their stewardship, the court would be usurping the function of the legislature, and, indeed, of the people of Uganda as represented in the legislature, if it undertook to enquire into and to pronounce on the validity or otherwise of the constitution; and that the court, if by any chance, should come to the conclusion that the constitution was invalid, the effect of such a decision would be far-reaching and disastrous and would even affect the position of the judges themselves, because the old constitution having been annulled, all the judges are now operating the new constitution from which their post derived.

In the course of his submission, the court was referred to the 1963 revised and annotated edition of the Constitution of the United States of America, art. III, s. 2 at p. 611; and to the case of <u>Luther v. Borden</u> (7). The passage of the American Constitution to which we were referred reads as follows:

> "The rule has been long established that the courts have no general supervisory power over the executive or administrate branches of Government."

The concept of "political question" is an old one. As early as <u>Marbury v. Madison</u>, Marshall, C.J., stated:

> "The province of the court is, solely, to decide on the rights of individuals, not to enquire how the executive, or executive officers, perform duties in which they have discretion. Questions in their nature political, or which are, by the constitution and laws, submitted to the executive, can never be made in this court. The concept, as distinguished from that of interference with executive functions, was first elaborated in <u>Luther v. Borden</u> (7), which involved the meaning of 'a republican form of government' and the question of the lawful government of Rhode Island between two competing groups purporting to act as the lawful authority."

> Tanex, C. J. also declared that "it is the province of the court to expound the law, not to make it.".

It may be observed that this exposition of legal principles cannot be faulted. It is a sound doctrine if one may say so with respect, but the question which must be asked is: What is a political question in terms of this doctrine? And the answer is not far to seek. It is set out at p. 612 of the same constitution based, it is suggested, on the decision in <u>Luther v. Borden</u> (7), and more particularly elaborated upon in <u>Baker v. Carr</u> (8). In <u>Luther v. Borden</u> (7) a political question is defined as " a question relating to the possession of political power, of sovereignty, of government, determination of which is based on Congress and the President, whose decisions are conclusive on the courts".

The constitution goes on to state that the more common classifications of cases involving political questions are:

1. Those which raise the issue of what proof is required that a Statute has been enacted, or a constitutional amendment ratified;
2. Questions arising out of the conduct of foreign relations;
3. The termination of wars of rebellion;
4. The question of what constitutes a republican form of government, and the right of a State to protection from invasion or domestic violence; questions arising out of political actions of a State in determining the mode of choosing presidential electors, and reapportionment of district for congressional representation; and suits brought by States to test their so-called sovereign rights.

It is noteworthy that the question of the validity of a constitution is not included in this somewhat exhaustive and formidable list.

A Photostat copy of the judgment of the Supreme Court in <u>Luther v. Borden</u> (7) relied upon by the learned Attorney General was kindly supplied to us. The facts of the case were briefly that, at the time of the American Revolution, Rhode Island did not, like other states, adopt a new constitution, but was content to continue with the form of government established by the Charter granted to it by Charles II in 1663, but making only such alterations, by Acts of the Legislature, as were necessary to adapt it to their condition and rights as an independent state. But no mode of proceedings was pointed out by which amendments might be made.

In 1841, a portion of the people held meetings and formed associations, which resulted in the election of a convention to form a new constitution to be submitted to the people for their adoption or rejection. The convention framed a constitution, directed a vote to be taken on it, declared afterwards that it had been adopted and ratified by a majority of the people of the state and that it was the paramount law and Constitution of Rhode Island.

Under the constitution, elections were held for the post of Governor, members of the legislature and other officers, who assembled together in May 1842, and proceeded to organise the new government.

But the Charter government, which had been governing the Island since 1663, did not admit the validity of or acquiesce in these proceedings. On the contrary, it passed stringent laws, and finally passed an act declaring the state under martial law and, since the new government established by the voluntary convention refused to yield, the Charter government proceeded to call out the militia to repel the threatened attack by the new government and those who were engaged in it whom it treated as rebels.

In May 1843, a new constitution, which had been promulgated by a convention called together by the Charter government, went into operation and since then remained in office as the established and effective government of Rhode Island.

During the operation of the Martial Law declared by the Charter government, a large number of people, including the plaintiff, Martin Luther, who belonged to the government which had been established by the voluntary convention in 1841, rose in opposition to the Charter government, and with a view to overthrowing it by military force, actually levied war upon the state under the effective control of the Charter government.

The defendant, Luther M. Borden, with other supporters of the Charter government, was then in the military service of the state and, by the command of his superior officer, broke and entered into the house and conducted a search of the rooms of the plaintiff, who was then supposed to be in hiding, for the purpose of having him arrested.

Subsequently, the plaintiff brought an action of trespass against the defendant in the Circuit Court of Rhode Island. In his defence, the defendant pleaded that, in breaking into the plaintiff's house, he had done so for the purpose of suppressing insurrection against the legitimate government of Rhode Island, which was the Charter government.

The question for decision by the court was therefore "which of the two opposing governments was the legitimate government of Rhode Island?" which in effect meant that the existence and authority of the Charter government under which the defendant acted was being called to question. The Circuit Court of Rhode Island decided that the lawful and effective government of Rhode Island at the material time was the Charter government, which had ruled the Island since 1663, and, therefore, that the defendant was justified in the measure which he took in suppressing the insurrection by the government established by the voluntary convention of 1841. The plaintiff's action therefore failed.

On appeal by way of error to the Supreme Court of the United States of America, after an exhaustive review of the facts, the judgment of the Circuit Court was affirmed in these words:

"The question relates, altogether, to the constitution and laws of the state, and the well settled rule in this court is that the courts of the United States adopt and follow the decisions of the State Courts in questions which concern merely the constitution and laws of that State.

Upon the whole, we see no reason for disturbing the judgment of the Circuit Court and we must therefore regard the Charter government as the lawful and established government of the Island during the time of this contest".

It is true of course that, before arriving at that decision, the Supreme Court pointed out that "the Constitution of the United States treated the subject (i.e. the question whether or not a majority of those persons entitled to suffrage voted to adopt a constitution cannot be settled in a judicial proceeding) as political in nature and placed the power of recognising a state government in the hands of the Congress. Under the existing legislation of Congress, the exercise of this power by courts would be entirely inconsistent with that legislation".

In its strictures, the Supreme Court, quite properly, refused to be drawn into political questions in regard to the issue of suffrage and the number of votes. It observed finally that grave consequences would result if it were to reverse the decision of the Circuit Court by holding that the Charter government which had governed the Island since 1663 was not the legitimate government of the island. It also pointed out, in what one may not be far wrong to describe, with respect, as counsels of perfection, that it was undesirable for courts to embark on enquiries bordering on the political.

We are of opinion that, however useful and instructive the observations of the Supreme Court on the several matters discussed in that case may be, the learned Attorney-General was in error in relying on it as supporting the proposition that the issue as to the validity of the Constitution of 1966 was purely a political matter outside the scope of the jurisdiction of this court.

In any case, <u>Luther v. Borden</u> (7) is distinguishable from, and is irrelevant to, the circumstances of the instant case. In the first place in <u>Luther v. Borden</u> (7) there was a contest between two competing groups as to which should control the government of Rhode Island. There is no such contest in Uganda. The Government of Uganda is well established and has no rival. The question that was raised by the court was not as to the legality of the government but as to the validity of the constitution.

In the second place, <u>Luther v. Borden</u> (7) raised all sorts of political questions, including the right to vote and the qualification of such voters. There were two rival governors appointed and the rivalry between the two governments produced a situation which was tantamount to a state of civil war. In fact, insurrection had occurred and war was levied upon the state. There was also the question as to whether the government was republican or not, which is a political question reserved for the decision of the Congress under the Constitution of the United States of America.

Then there is the recent case of <u>Baker v. Carr</u> (8) which was an appeal from the decision of the United States District Court for the Middle District of Tennessee to the Supreme Court of the United States. There, the appellants were persons allegedly qualified to vote for the members of the General Assembly of Tennessee representing the counties in which they resided. They brought a suit in a Federal District Court in Tennessee under 42 U.S.C. pares. 1983 and 1988 on behalf of themselves and others similarly situated, to redress the alleged deprivation of their federal constitutional rights by legislation classifying voters with respect to representation in the General Assembly.

They alleged that arbitrarily and capriciously apportioning the seats in the General Assembly among the state's 95 counties, by means of a 1901 Statute of Tennessee, and failing to reapportion them subsequently, notwithstanding substantial growth and redistribution of the state's population, they suffered a "debasement of their votes" and were thereby denied the equal protection of the laws guaranteed them by the Fourteenth Amendment.

They sought, *inter alia*, a declaratory judgment that the 1901 Statute was unconstitutional and an injunction restraining certain state officers from conducting any further elections under it. The District Court dismissed the complaint on the grounds that it lacked jurisdiction of the subject-matter, and that no claim was stated upon which relief could be granted, because the claim, as presented, raised a "question of the distribution of the political strength for legislative purpose". For, to quote the conclusion reached by the court, "from a review of (numerous Supreme Courts) decisions, there can be no doubt that the federal rule, as enunciated and applied by the Supreme Court, is that the federal courts, whether from a lack of jurisdiction or from the appropriateness of the subject-matter for judicial consideration, will not intervene in cases of this type to compel legislative reapportionment".

On appeal to the Supreme Court, in the judgment of the court delivered by Brennan, J., it was held:

(1) That the District Court had jurisdiction to entertain the claim because the complaint asserted in the suit was the subject-matter of the federal constitutional claim;

(2) That the appellants had standing to maintain the suit; and

(3) That the complaint's allegations of a denial of equal protection presented a justifiable constitutional cause of action upon which the appellants were entitled to a trial and decision.

The decision of the District Court was therefore reversed and the case was sent back for retrial.

In a concurring judgment, Clark, J., said:

"It is well for this court to practice self-restraint and discipline in constitutional adjudication, but never in its history have those principles received sanction where the national rights of so many have been so clearly infringed for so long a time. National respect for the courts is more enhanced through the forthright enforcement of those rights rather than by rendering them nugatory through interposition of subterfuges. In my view, the ultimate decision today is in the greatest tradition of this court".

In his alternative submission, namely, that the 1966 Constitution is a valid constitution in law because it came into existence as a result of a revolution or a *coup d'état*, the learned Attorney General would appear to be on firm ground.

The learned Attorney General urged the court to hold that the incidents which finally culminated in the promulgation of the 1966 constitution had taken place abruptly. Most people were taken unawares. What happened then was a *coup d'état*. And *coups d'état* are recognised in international law as a proper and effective legal means of changing governments or constitutions in a country like Uganda, which is politically and completely independent and sovereign. In his attractive and impressive submission, the learned Attorney General contended that the four cardinal requirements in international law to give the 1966 Constitution and Government of Uganda validity in law have clearly been fulfilled. These requirements are:

1. That there must be an abrupt political change, i. e., a *coup d'état* or a revolution.

2. That change must not have been within the contemplation of an existing constitution.

3. The change must destroy the entire legal order except what is preserved; and

4. The new constitution and government must be effective.

Developing his argument on these requirements, counsel submitted that the declaration by the Prime Minister on February 22, 1966, annexure A, followed by the statement of February 24, 1966, in which the 1962 constitution was suspended; the seizure of all powers of government by the Prime Minister; the setting up of the Security Council for Uganda; the forcible ejection of the President and Head of State and Commander-in Chief from the state House, in consequence of which the latter ultimately fled the country; the abolition of the 1962 constitution, followed immediately by the promulgation of the 1966 constitution by a resolution of the National Assembly; the removal from the 1966 Constitution of the Order in Council by the authority of which the 1962 constitution was established; the automatic assumption of office by operation of law by the then Prime Minister as the Executive President of Uganda with the power to appoint anyone Vice-President of Uganda; the abolition of appeals to the Privy Council; the abolition of the federal system of government and the High Court of Buganda; and the enfranchisement of the people of Buganda who had been, since 1962, disenfranchised - all these were not only abrupt but such fundamental changes were not within the contemplation of the 1962 constitution and were therefore revolutionary in character. The end result was, in law, a revolution.

Counsel further contended that the 1966 Constitution was not only valid but legal, it being a constitution adopted by the people's representatives in a National Assembly for their people of Uganda; that since its adoption the people have accepted it with acclamation, and have unanimously given obedience to it as the best constitution for Uganda; and, finally, that by reason of the effectiveness of the constitution, the machinery of government has been functioning smoothly ever since. All taxes have been collected without resistance. Counsel then referred the court to Kelsen's *General Theory of Law and State* (1961 Edn,) at pp. 117 to 118, and the Pakistan case of The State v. Dosso and Another (9), as his authorities for the submission that the 1966 constitution is legally valid and that the court should so hold.

These submissions are doubtless irresistible and unassailable. On the theory of law and state propounded by the positivist school of

jurisprudence represented by the famous Professor Kelsen, it is beyond question, and we hold, that the series of events which took place
in Uganda from February 22 to April 1966, when the 1962 constitution was abolished in the National Assembly and the 1966 constitution adopted in its place, as a result of which the then Prime Minister
was installed as Executive President with power to appoint a Vice-
President, could only appropriately be described in law as a revolution. These changes had occurred not in accordance with the principle of legitimacy. But deliberately contrary to it. There were no pre-
tensions on the part of the Prime Minister to follow the procedure
prescribed by the 1962 Constitution in particular for the removal of
the President and the Vice-President from office.

Power was seized by force from both the President and the Vice-
President on the grounds mentioned in the early part of this judgment. There were even charges, to use the word in its popular sense,
of treason having been committed by the then President.

The learned Attorney-General's contention was that the seizure
of power in the manner in which it was done by the then Prime Minister was consistent with the principles of international law, although
not based on the principle of legitimacy. In support of this proposition, the attention of the court was drawn to the Kelsenian principles
to be found in his *General Theory of Law and State* at various pages
commencing from p. 117. The various passages to which we were referred are headed (c) The principle of Legitimacy, (d) Change of the
Basic Norm and (3) Birth and Death of the state as Legal Problems,
which we now reproduce hereunder.

(c) The Principle of Legitimacy, p. 117-118:

"The validity of legal norms may be limited in time, and it
is important to notice that the end as well as the beginning of
this validity is determined only by the order to which they belong. They remain valid as long as they have not been invali-
dated in the way in which the legal order itself determines.
This is the principle of legitimacy.

This principle, however, holds only under certain conditions. It fails to hold in the case of a revolution, this word understood in the most general sense, so that it also covers the so-called *coup d'état*. **A revolution, in this wide sense, occurs whenever the legal order of a community is nullified and replaced by a new order in an illegitimate way, that is, in a way
not prescribed by the first order itself. It is in this context**

irrelevant whether or not this replacement is effected through a violent uprising against those individuals who so far have been the legitimate organs competent to create and amend the legal order. It is equally irrelevant whether the replacement is effected through a movement emanating from the mass of the people, or through the action from those in government positions. From a juristic point of view, the decisive criterion of a revolution is that the order in force is overthrown and replaced by a new order in a way which the former had not itself anticipated. Usually, the new men whom a revolution brings to power annul only the constitution and certain laws of paramount political significance, putting other norms in their place. A great part of the old legal order 'remains' valid also within the frame of the new order. But the phrase 'they remain valid' does not give adequate description of the phenomenon. It is only the contents of these norms that remain the same, not the reason of their validity. They are no longer valid by virtue of having been created in the way the old constitution prescribed. That constitution is no longer in force; it is replaced by a new constitution which is not the result of a constitutional alteration of the former. If laws which were introduced under the old constitution 'continue to be valid' under the new constitution, it is possible only because the validity has expressly or tacitly been vested in them by the new constitution. The phenomenon is a case of reception (similar to the reception of Roman Law). The new order 'received', i. e. adopts norms from the old order; this means that the new order gives validity to (puts into force) norms which have the same content as norms of the old order. 'Reception' is an abbreviated procedure of law creation. The laws which, in the ordinary inaccurate parlance, continue to be valid are, from a juristic viewpoint, new laws whose import coincides with that of the old laws. They are not identical with the old laws because the reason for their validity is different. The reason for their validity is the new, not the old, constitution and, between the two, continuity holds neither from the point of view of the one nor from that of the other. Thus it is never the constitution merely but always the entire legal order that is changed by a revolution.

This shows that all norms of the old order have been deprived of their validity by a revolution and not according to the principle of legitimacy. And they have been so deprived not only *de facto* but also *de jury*. No jurist would maintain that even after a successful revolution the old constitution and the laws based thereupon remain in force, on the ground that they have not been nullified in a manner anticipated by the old order itself. Every jurist will presume that the old order - to which no political reality any longer corresponds - has ceased to be valid, and that all norms, which are valid within the new order, receive their validity exclusively from the new constitution. It follows that, from this juristic point of view, the norms of the old order can no longer be recognised as valid norms."

(d) Change of the basic norm, p. 118:

"It is just the phenomenon of revolution which clearly shows the significance of the basic norm. Suppose that a group of individuals attempt to seize power by force, in order to remove the legitimate government in a hitherto monarchic system, and to introduce a republican form of government. If they succeed, if the old order ceases and the new order begins to be efficacious because the individuals, whose behaviour the new order regulates, actually behave, by and large, in conformity with the new order, then this order is considered as a valid order. It is now according to this new order that the actual behaviour of individuals is interpreted as legal or illegal. But this means that a new basic norm is presupposed. It is no longer the norm according to which the old monarchical system is valid, but a norm endowing the revolutionary government with legal authority. If the revolutionaries fail - if the order they have tried to establish remains inefficacious, then on the other hand, their undertaking interpreted, not as legal, a law creating act, as the establishment of a constitution, but as an illegal act, as the crime of treason, and this according to the old monarchic constitution and its specific basic norm."

(3) Birth and Death of the state as Legal Problems: p.220:

"The problem as to the beginning and ending of the existence of a state is a legal problem only if we assume that international law really embodies some such principle as indicated in the foregoing chapter. Even though some authors advocate the opposite view, the whole problem, as usually formulated, has a specifically juristic character. It amounts to the question: under what circumstances does a national legal order begin or cease to be valid? The answer, given by international law, is that a national legal order begins to be valid as soon as it loses this efficacy. The legal order remains the same as long as its territorial sphere of validity remains essentially the same, even if the order should be changed in another way than that prescribed by the constitution, in the way of a revolution or *coup d'état*. A victorious revolution or a successful *coup d'état* does not destroy the identity of the legal order which it changes. The order established by revolution or *coup d'état* has to be considered as a modification of the old order, not as a new order, if this order is valid for the same territory. The government brought into permanent power by a revolution or *coup d'état* is, according to international law, the legitimate government of the state, whose identity is not affected by these events. Hence, according to international law, victorious revolutions or successful *coups d'état* are to be interpreted as procedures by which a national legal order can be changed. Both events are, viewed in the light of international law, law creating fact. Again *injuria jus oritur* and it is again the principle of effectiveness that is applied."

The effect of these submissions and references to the Kelsenian principles quoted above on this aspect of the case is that the 1966 Constitution was the product of a revolution. Of that there can be no doubt. The constitution had extra legal origin and therefore created a new legal order. Although the product of a revolution, the constitution is none-the-less valid in law because, in international law, revolutions and *coups d'état* are the recognised methods of changing governments and constitutions in sovereign states. For, in the language of James Bryce in his *Studies in History and Jurisprudence*, Vol. 2 (1904 Edn.) at p.107:

> "Knots which the law cannot untie may have to be cut by the sword."

According to *Salmond on Jurisprudence* (11th Edn.) by Granville Williams, at p. 101:

> "Every constitution has an extra legal origin, the best illustration being the United States of America which in open and

forcible defiance of English law broke away from England and set up new states and constitution, the origin of which was not merely extra legal but was illegal.

Yet, no sooner than those constitutions succeeded in obtaining *de facto* establishment in the rebellious colonies, they received recognition as legally valid from the courts of the colonies. Constitutional law followed hard upon the heels of constitutional facts. Courts, legislatures and therefore the constitution cannot derive its origin from them. So also with every constitution that is altered by way of illegal revolution. By what legal authority was the Bill of Rights 1686 passed, and by what legal title did William III assume the crown?"

In <u>The State v. Dosso and Another (9)</u> on October 7, 1958, the then President of Pakistan, feeling himself unable to cope with the problems of Pakistan and to maintain peace and order, declared martial law by proclamation throughout Pakistan; annulled the Constitution of Pakistan of March 23, 1956; dismissed the central cabinet as well as the provincial cabinets; dissolved both the national and provincial assemblies; and appointed General Ayub Khan Commander-in Chief of the Army, as the Chief Martial Law Administrator.

Three days later, the President promulgated the Laws (Continuance in Force) Order, the general effect of which was the validation of laws, other than the annulled constitution, which were in force before the proclamation, and restoration of the jurisdiction of all courts including the Supreme Court and the High Courts.

It was also directed in the order that, thereafter, the country was to be known as Pakistan and not the Islamic Republic of Pakistan; the order also declared all orders and judgments made or given by the Supreme Court between the proclamation and the promulgation of the order to be valid and binding but, saving such orders, no writ or order for a writ issued or made after the proclamation was to have effect, unless it was provided for in that order, and all applications and proceedings in respect of any writ not so provided for were to abate forthwith.

There were four appeals brought before the Supreme Court, and they involved the question whether the writs issued by the High Court in respect of orders of release to a Council of Elders, or convictions under s.II of the Frontier Crimes Regulations 1901, on the ground of repugnancy to art. 5 of the Constitution of 1956 had abated by reason of cl. 7, art 2 of the Laws (Continuance in Force) Order. The court was to determine the effect of the proclamation and the order on the writ jurisdiction of the High Court, including pending applications for writs and writs already issued which were subject of appeals in the Supreme Court.

It was held by the majority of the court, Muhammad Munir, C. J. (Shahabaddin and Amiruddin Ahmad, JJ.) that the President's proclamation of October 7, 1958, by which the Constitution of 1956 was annulled and martial law was proclaimed constituted an "abrupt political change", not within the contemplation of the said constitution, i. e., a revolution. A victorious revolution is an internationally recognised legal method of changing a constitution.

Such a revolution constitutes a new law-creating organ, by virtue of having become a basic law creating fact. Laws which derive from the *old order* may remain valid under the *new order* only because validity has expressly or tacitly been vested in them by the new constitution and it is only the contents of these norms that remain the same, not the reason of the validity. Further, no jurist would maintain that, even after a successful revolution, the old constitution and the laws based thereupon remain in force, on the ground that they have not been nullified in a manner anticipated by the old order itself. It was also held that the Laws (Continuance in Force) Order was a new legal order, and that it was in accordance with that order that the validity of laws and the correctness of judicial decisions had to be determined.

On the point of the survival of the fundamental rights, it was held unanimously that they were no longer a part of the new legal order, as the Constitution of 1959 had been expressly excluded from the list of laws in art. 4 of that order which were continued in force by the regime. Moreover, it was further held, the President had assumed full power to make adaptations in any such laws, thus overriding the prohibitions, contained in art. 4 of the Constitution of 1956, against laws contravening the fundamental rights. Further still, it was held that the appeals, being pending proceedings in relation to a writ sought on the ground that fundamental right had been contravened, must abate forthwith under art. 2(7) of the Laws (Continuance in Force) Order.

Applying the Kelsenian principles, which incidentally form the basis of the judgment of the Supreme Court of Pakistan in the above case, our deliberate and considered view is that the 1966 Constitution is a legally valid constitution and the supreme law of Uganda and that the 1962 Constitution, having been abolished as a result of a victorious revolution in law, does no longer exist nor does it now form part of the Laws of Uganda, it having been deprived of its *de facto* and *de jure* validity. The 1966 Constitution, we hold, is a new legal order and has been effective since April 14, 1966, when it first came into force.

We have before us a large number of affidavits sworn to by a large number of officials, the purpose of which is to prove to the satisfaction of the court that the new constitution is efficacious and that it has been accepted by the people since it came into force in April 1966. However, we need only mention eight of these affidavits, which we consider of considerable importance, as we are of the opinion that it was unnecessary to file such a large number of affidavits merely for the purpose of establishing that the new 1966 Constitution has been accepted without opposition and that, since its inception, the machinery of government has been functioning smoothly. The affidavits which we would like to mention are those sworn to by Mr. Francis Kalemera Kalimuzo, the Cabinet Secretary since 1962; Godfrey Lukongwa Binaisa, Esq., the learned Attorney-General since 1962; Mr. Erenayo Wilson Oryema, Inspector General of Police since 1964; Mr. Valerian Assa Pvonji, Permanent Secretary to the Ministry of Public Service; Mr. David Oyite Ojok, Deputy Assistant Adjutant and Quartermaster-General of the Uganda Armed Forces including the Uganda Air Force; Mr. Wilson Okumu Lutara, Permanent Secretary, Ministry of Defence; Mr. Zerubaberi Hosea Kwamya Bigirwenkya, Permanent Secretary, Ministry of Foreign Affairs; and Mr. Alfred Mubanda, Permanent Secretary, Ministry of Regional Administrations.

After a perusal of these affidavits, the contents of which have not been in any way challenged or contradicted, we are satisfied and find as a fact that the new constitution has been accepted by the people of Uganda and that it has been firmly established throughout the country, the changes introduced therein having been implemented without opposition, as there is not before us any evidence to the contrary.

We would however like to refer, in particular, to the affidavit sworn to by Mr. Bigirwenkya, Permanent Secretary of Foreign Affairs, the substance of which is that, ever since the coming into force of the new constitution and the installation of the new Executive President and new government, recognition has been accorded to the new government by all foreign countries with which Uganda deals. We would like to point out that Uganda, being a well-established independent state, the question of its recognition since the installation of the new Head of State by other nations is of considerable importance. As was said by L. Oppenheim in his *Treatise on International Law* (8th Edn.) Vol. I, at p. 129:

> "Recognition of a new State must not be confused with recognition of a new head of government of an old State. Recognition of the change in the headship of a State, is a matter of importance. But the granting or refusing of this recognition has nothing to do with the recognition of the state itself. If a foreign State refused to recognise a new head or a change in the form of the government of an old state, the latter does not thereby lose its recognition as an international personality, although no official intercourse is henceforth possible between the two States as long as recognition is not given either expressly or tacitly. If recognition of a new title of an old State is refused, the only consequence is that the latter cannot claim any privileges connected with the new title".

We would like to emphasise, however, that the question of the recognition of the new Head of State of Uganda by foreign nations is not strictly within the scope of this enquiry. For, in our view, it is not within the province of this court, nor is it within its competence to accord recognition to the government or international status of the government of this country which is our own country. Courts, legislatures and the law derive their origins from the constitution, and, therefore, the constitution cannot derive its origin from them, because there can be no law unless there is already a state whose law it is, and there can be no state without a constitution.

We now return to consider the second question of this reference, namely:

> "Whether the Emergency Powers Act, 1963, and the Emergency Powers (Detention) Regulations 1966, or any material part thereof are *ultra vires* the constitution to the extent that the Act and the Regulations enable the President to take measures or authorise the taking of measures that may not be reasonably justifiable for the purpose of dealing with the situation that exists during the period when a declaration of a state of republic emergency is in force, within the meaning of art. 30 (5) of the constitution."

Counsel for the applicant, in presenting the case of the applicant, prefaced his submissions with quoting the provisions of art. 1 of the constitution, which declares the constitution "to be the supreme law of Uganda." He pointed out that any law which was inconsistent therewith must be declared void to the extent of such inconsistency. He drew the attention of the court to art. 30 (5) of the constitution, the provisions of which are in the following terms:

> "30(5) Nothing contained in or done under the authority of an Act of Parliament shall be held to be inconsistent with or in contravention of arts. 19, 24 or 29 of this constitution to the extent that the Act authorised the taking, during any period when Uganda is at war or any period when a declaration of a state of public emergency under this article is in force, of measures that are reasonably justifiable for the purpose of dealing with the situation that exists during that period."

Counsel submitted that the important words in the clause are "reasonably justifiable" and that the words "reasonably justifiable" are the key words in the clause and may be described as words of limitation - limiting the type of measures that may be authorised by Parliament to be taken in dealing with a state of public emergency. He further submitted that it was within the power of this court to examine such measures authorised by Parliament in order to see whether they were reasonably justifiable in the present state of emergency in Uganda and that any act of Parliament, which authorised measures not reasonably justifiable, must be held by the court to be *ultra vires* art. 30(5) of the constitution, and that in examining such measures the court must apply an objective test.

Counsel then referred the court to the provisions of s. 3(1) (2) (a) of the Emergency Powers Act (Cap. 307), and reg. 1 of the Emergency Powers (Detention) Regulations 1966, Statutory Instrument No. 65 of 1966, and contended that they were *ultra vires* art. 30 (5) of the constitution in that under the Emergency Powers Act the minister is made the sole judge as to whether or not the measures taken by him are reasonably justifiable; and that under reg.1 the minister alone is to be satisfied.

The relevant section of the Emergency Powers Act 1963 and of the Emergency Powers (Detention) Regulations 1966 - the subject matters of this complaint - are as hereunder set forth:

> 3(1) Whenever an emergency proclamation is in force, the President may make such regulations as appear to him to be

necessary or expedient for securing the public safety, the defence of Uganda, the maintenance of public order and the suppression of mutiny, rebellion and riot, and for maintaining supplies and services essential to the life of the community.

(2) Without prejudice to the generality of the powers conferred by subsection (1) of this Section, emergency regulations may so far as appear to the President to be necessary or expedient for any of the purposes mentioned in that subsection:

    (a) make provision for the detention of persons or the restriction of their movements, and for the deportation and exclusion from Uganda of persons who are not citizens of Uganda.

Regulation 1 (1) of the Emergency Powers (Detention) Regulations 1966, made pursuant to s. 3 of the Emergency Powers Act, reads as follows:

1(1) Whenever the Minister is satisfied that, for the purpose of maintaining public order, it is necessary to exercise control over any person, the Minister may make an order against such person directing that he be detained and, thereupon, such person shall be arrested and detained.

(2) At any time after a detention order has been made against any person under this regulation, the Minister may revoke or vary the order, or may direct that the operation of the order be suspended subject to such condition:

    (a) ...
    (b) ...
    (c) ...
    (d) ...
    (e) ...

as the Minister thinks fit, and the Minister may revoke or vary any such direction whenever he thinks fit.

Counsel submitted that, since Uganda is governed under a written constitution, the National Assembly is not as supreme a legislature as the United Kingdom Parliament; that the power of the National Assembly is well defined in the Constitution of Uganda; and that the power which the National Assembly could confer on a minister is equally restricted, as it is subject to the rule of inconsistency with the constitution. That being so, the power which the National

Assembly could confer on a minister is not comparable to the power which Parliament in the United Kingdom could confer on ministers or, in particular, on the Home Secretary under the Defence Regulations.

Counsel for the applicant then contended that the powers given to the Minister of Internal Affairs by the Parliament of Uganda under s.3 (1) of the Emergency Powers Act 1963, as well as those conferred on him under reg.1 of the Emergency Powers (Detention) Regulations 1966, are too wide. They are not subject to any condition or limitation. In particular, under reg.1 of the Emergency Powers (Detention) Regulations, counsel submitted, the only person to be satisfied before invoking these powers is the Minister of Internal Affairs. In this contention, therefore, the Emergency Powers Act 1963 and the Emergency Powers (Detention) Regulations 1966, by giving such unfettered powers to the Minister of Internal Affairs, were *ultra vires* art. 30(5) of the constitution and that they should be so declared by the court.

The learned Attorney-General, in his submission contended that, while he agreed that the powers of the Parliament of Uganda were controlled and regulated by the Constitution of Uganda and that the Emergency Powers Act 1963 and the Emergency Powers (Detention) Regulations 1966 made thereunder must be considered in the light of the provisions of art. 30(5) of the constitution, the burden was upon the counsel for the applicant to show the respect in, and the extent to which, the Act and the Regulations are said to be *ultra vires* art. 30(5) of the constitution, and that counsel has failed to discharge that burden.

On the authorities of <u>King v. Halliday</u> (10); <u>Liversidge v. Anderson and Another</u> (11); <u>R. v. Home Secretary, Ex parte Green</u> (12), and <u>R. v. Metropolitan Police Commissioner, Ex parte Hammond</u> (13), counsel submitted that no government would embark on proclaiming a state of emergency unless the situation was really grave and warranted it, and that, in the grave situation which had developed in this country, Parliament was competent to give to the Minister of Internal Affairs discretion in the exercise of his most difficult office of maintaining law and order.

We may, at the risk of repetition here, recapitulate the events already described by us in the early part of this judgment in connection with the declaration of a state of emergency. A state of public emergency was declared on May 23, 1966, and approved on May 25,

1966, by the National Assembly. A number of Emergency Powers Regulations, including the Emergency Powers (Detention) Regulations, the subject-matter of this complaint, which were made by the Minister of Internal Affairs in virtue of the powers vested in him by the Transfer of Powers and Duties (No.2) Order 1965, Statutory Instrument No.91 of 1965, were all approved and affirmed by a resolution of the National Assembly in due compliance with provisions of s. 5 of the Emergency Powers Act 1963 on May 25, 1966. That resolution was moved by the Minister of Internal Affairs. The regulations were immediately brought into force (see annexure I, p. 52- official report of the proceedings of the National Assembly).

It is noteworthy that these regulations were debated and passed by the National Assembly, the membership of which is in the neighbourhood of over eighty. It is difficult to see how this court can, by the application of an objective test, which is an operation in the abstract, hold that the powers which over eighty citizens of Uganda, members of Parliament, had considered reasonably justifiable to be granted to the minister to enable him to deal with a serious situation in the country, was not reasonably justifiable in the existing situation.

The minister concerned is responsible to Parliament for his conduct and therefore not free from control. His activities are subject to constant check by members of Parliament. Indeed, his task is an invidious one for the burden of his responsibility is great.

Now, counsel for the applicant has requested this court to apply an objective test in the interpretation of the words "measures that are reasonably justifiable", and that it is the duty of this court to interpret the phrase within the context of the constitution.

We must confess that it was difficult to appreciate counsel's submission that the test to be applied must be an objective one. Indeed, to apply an objective test to the interpretation of the phrase "reasonably justifiable" would be tantamount to importing into the provisions of the constitution what was never intended; and that might do untold damage to the provisions as a whole. A careful examination of the whole of the provisions of art. 30(5) which, incidentally, must be read as a whole, clearly shows that the phrase "reasonably justifiable" is qualified by the sentence which follows it.

The article provides that an Act of Parliament may authorise the taking, during any period when Uganda is at war or any period when a declaration of a state of public emergency is in force, of measures that are reasonably justifiable for the purpose of dealing with the situation that exists during that period. The test applicable, therefore, must be subjective. Such measures must be reasonably justifiable for the purpose of dealing with the situation that exists at any particular time, and therefore whatever measures are adopted must depend upon how grave the situation is at that given time.

We think it unsound for counsel for the applicant to complain that Parliament exceeded its powers by passing or approving reg.1 of the Emergency Powers (Detention) Regulations, which imposed on the Minister of Internal Affairs the onerous duty of being personally satisfied before he could make an order of detention against any person. We do not think that the performance of his duty and the exercise of his discretion, in the circumstance of the instant case, can be the subject of a judicial review.

It was not clear whether counsel for the applicant would rather that every case of detention should go to Parliament and that the minister should only issue his order for the detention of a person concerned if Parliament had debated the case and been satisfied that the prospective detainee should be detained. That, of course, would be absurd and would certainly defeat the whole object of the exercise as the minister has to act on secret information supplied to him from various sources. In any case, such a practice would be inconsistent with and would render the ministerial system of government a farce. It would give the impression that a minister could not be entrusted with responsibility and be expected to exercise his discretion and satisfy his conscience before making an order so grave as that of detention.

As was said in <u>Liversidge v. Anderson and Another</u> (11), by Lord Macmillan (1941) 3 All E. R. at p. 363:

> "Is the standard of reasonableness, which must be satisfied, an impersonal standard independent of the Secretary of State's own mind, or is it the personal standard of what the Secretary of State himself deems reasonable? Between these two readings, there is a fundamental difference in legal effect. In the former case, the reasonableness of the cause which the Secretary of State had for his belief may, if challenged, be examined by a Court of Law in order to determine whether he had such cause of belief as would satisfy the ordinary reasonable man, and, to enable the court to adjudicate upon this question, there

must be disclosed to it the facts and circumstances which the Secretary of State had before him in arriving at his belief. In the latter case, it is for the Secretary of State alone to decide in the forum of his own conscience whether he has a reasonable cause of belief, and he cannot, if he has acted in good faith, be called upon to disclose to anyone the facts and circumstances which have induced his belief, or to satisfy anyone but himself that those facts and circumstance constituted a reasonable cause of belief."

These remarks, which are pertinent to the point under consideration raised by the counsel for the applicant, were made by Lord Macmillan in the course of his judgment on the interpretation of certain words contained in the Defence (General) Regulations, 1939, reg. 18b(1). By that regulation, the Secretary of State was empowered to make an order for the detention of any person if he has "reasonable cause to believe any person to be of hostile origin or associations or to have been recently concerned in acts prejudicial to the public safety …".

Having given careful consideration to the submissions of counsel, we are of the opinion that the counsel for the applicant has failed to satisfy us that the Emergency Powers Act, 1963 and the Emergency Powers (Detention) Regulations 1966 in so far as they relate to the case under consideration are *ultra vires* art. 30 (5) of the Constitution of Uganda. Our answer to the second question therefore is in the negative as we are satisfied that both the Act and the Regulation are *intra vires* and in due conformity with the provisions of the constitution.

It was contended by counsel for the applicant, in respect of the third question of this reference, namely:

"Whether any of the provisions of art. 31(1) of the constitution has been contravened in relation to the applicant having regard to the affidavits filed herein by and on behalf of the applicant on the one hand, and on behalf of the state on the other hand",

that the provisions of arts. 31(1)(a), 31(1)(b) and 31 (1)(c) were not complied with because, respectively,:

(1) The applicant was not furnished within five days of his detention with a statement in writing specifying in detail the grounds for his detention as required by art. 31(1)(a) of the constitution;

(2) The detention of the applicant was not published within fourteen days after the commencement of his detention as required by art. 31(1)(b) of the constitution; and

(3) The review of the applicant's case was done by a tribunal not established by law; and that the composition of the tribunal, apart from the Chairman appointed by the Chief Justice, were not independent as required by art. 31(1)(c) of the constitution.

In elaborating his contention on this point, counsel referred the court to the affidavit filed by the applicant, details of which we have set out at the early part of this judgment. In that affidavit, the applicant, in substance, swore that he was rearrested after having been released on July 16,1966 and detained at Luzira Prison; that it was only on August 11, 1966 that a detention order was served on him together with a piece of paper headed: "Statement required under s. 31(1)(a) of the Constitution of Uganda". The contents of the paper read as follows:

"You are hereby notified that, on August 10, 1966, the Minister of Internal Affairs signed an order for your detention under reg.1 of the Emergency Powers (Detention) Regulations 1966.

The grounds on which you are being detained are that you are a person who has acted or is likely to act in a manner prejudicial to the public safety and maintenance of public order."

The affidavit of the applicant continued to the effect that the notification of his detention was only published as General Notice No. 832 of 1966 in the Uganda Gazette on August 19, 1966 and that, on August 26, 1966, he appeared before a tribunal comprising the Hon. Mr. Justice Sheridan, as Chairman, and Mr. Wanambwa and Mr. Inyoin, as members.

The contention of counsel on this aspect of the case was that the only independent member of the tribunal was Sheridan, J., and that, although he did not entertain any doubt as to the impartiality of Mr. Wanambwa and Mr. Inyoin, but, because they are District Commissioners, they could not be regarded as independent; and that the presumption must be that they were not free from the influence of the executive. It was also submitted by counsel that the tribunal had not been established by law.

We think that counsel for the applicant was under misapprehension in asserting that the detention of the applicant commenced on July 16, 1966, when he was apprehended by the Police, and that the tribunal for the review of the case of the detainee was not properly established by law. Under reg. 3 of the Emergency Powers (Detention) Regulations 1966 which, as already stated, was approved and affirmed by Parliament, the Police are empowered to arrest and detain any person reasonably suspected to be a person who had acted, is about to act or likely to act in a manner prejudicial to the public safety and maintenance of public order for a period not exceeding twenty-eight days. Such detention is not a detention by the order of the minister.

It may be that the Police, in detaining such a person, may do so for the purpose of making enquiries to enable them to submit to the minister a report for consideration as to whether a detention order should be made. To constitute a detention under reg.1 of the Emergency Powers (Detention) Regulations 1966, an order signed by the minister authorising such a detention must be served on the detainee and it is after such service that it could be said that the person was detained by the minister in the exercise of his powers under the Regulation, and it is only then that the time prescribed under the constitution would begin to run.

In the instant case, therefore, on the affidavit of the applicant himself and of the Minister of Internal Affairs, the applicant was detained only as from August 11, 1966, when he was served with the order of detention signed by the minister. It is clear that the statement which he was furnished with on August 11, 1966 was within the time prescribed under art. 31(1)(a) of the constitution. It should also be noted that the actual order of detention was issued by the Minister of Internal Affairs on August 10, 1966 and that must be regarded as the day in which the Minister of Internal Affairs felt satisfied that the applicant ought to be detained.

The tribunal was established by law under reg. 5 of the Emergency Powers (Detention) Regulations 1966. As already stated, those regulations were approved and affirmed by a resolution of Parliament on May 25, 1966. The appointment of the members of the tribunal was gazetted on August 5, 1966, as General Notice No. 776 of 1966. The applicant's case was reviewed on August 26, 1966 by the tribunal, that is to say, within a period of less than one month in terms of art. 31 (1)(c) of the constitution.

Although, in his submission, counsel for the applicant was at pains to impress upon the court that there was no imputation of partiality directed against the other two members of the tribunal, we regard with disfavour the imputation that the other two members of the tribunal were not independent of executive influence. There was not a shred of evidence produced before us in support of such a serious allegation.

One would have thought that the two men concerned, who undoubtedly must have done well in the public service of Uganda to have risen to the senior posts of District Commissioners, and who owed their appointment to the Public Service Commission, ought to be regarded as men of integrity and high reputation with independent minds. It would be wrong and unjustified to assume otherwise. As the learned Attorney General rightly pointed out in his submission, the question of impartiality and independence are questions of fact. It is of some significance that the applicant did not depose in his affidavit that the tribunal which reviewed his case was not independent and impartial.

We would, however, observe, not necessarily because of the complaint made by the counsel for the applicant in the present case, that it is desirable wherever and whenever possible and practicable that the Minister of Internal Affairs should consider replacing government administrative officers with non-government employees as members of the tribunal. Such a change, we believe, would be all to the good and might serve to place the membership of the tribunal, like Caesar's wife, above suspicion.

We are not satisfied that the paper headed "Statement required under s. 31(1)(a) of the constitution" to which we have already referred, contains sufficient detail of the grounds for the detention of the applicant. The statement appears to be in a stereotype form. The applicant was therefore justified in complaining that the statement served on him on August 11, 1966 did not furnish him with sufficient details of the reason for his detention.

From the point of view of this court, this is a very difficult question. It is not clear to us why art. 31(1)(a) of the constitution should have required the Minister to furnish a detainee with a statement in writing specifying in detail the grounds upon which he is detained. One wonders the extent to which the minister could go in the specification of the grounds for detaining a person. The Minister of Internal Affairs, in virtue of his position, must of necessity obtain his information through secret and confidential sources. It might not be in the interest of public security that such sources be disclosed.

However that may be, we think that, under art. 31(1)(a) of the constitution, it is the duty of the Minister of Internal Affairs to supply the applicant with a statement in writing setting out the grounds upon which his detention was ordered. We do not think that the mere specification of the grounds would necessarily involve the disclosure of the source or sources of information. To that extent, our decision on this particular issue of the third question is that art. 31 (1)(a) has not been satisfactorily complied with by the minister.

Insufficiency of the statement of the grounds of detention served on the applicant is a mere matter of procedure. It is not a condition precedent but a condition subsequent. We hold therefore that it is not fatal to the order of detention made by the minister. It is curable because the High Court under art. 32(2) of the constitution has the power to give such directions as it may consider proper for the purpose of enforcing or securing the enforcement of any of the provisions of arts. 17 to 29 inclusive or cl. (1) of art. 31 of the constitution.

Our answer on the third question of this reference is in the affirmative but only to the extent of our observation that the statement furnished to the applicant was, in our view, not sufficient to enable him to prepare his defence for the review of his case before the tribunal. Our order, therefore, is that this matter be sent back to the judge who had referred the same to us, to dispose of it in accordance with our decision in so far as the issues of the interpretation of the constitution are concerned, and that, before such disposal, the judge do direct that art. 31 (1)(a) of the constitution be complied with by the Minister of Internal Affairs by serving the applicant with a statement specifying in detail the grounds upon which he is under detention.

In concluding this judgment, we would like to express our indebtedness to the learned Attorney General who was good enough to make available to us all the relevant public papers and proceedings concerning this case as well as Photostat copies of the judgments of foreign cases, which are not available in the library of this court. We also would like to express publicly our appreciation of the assistance given to us by both counsel in this difficult case. Both sides had fought the case with outstanding ability.

Matter referred back for disposal in accordance with the court's interpretation of the constitution; direction that a statement of grounds of detention be supplied.

The State Movement - How It Started

*"He who has something secret in the womb of his bundle of firewood
always struggles to put down the bundle from his head without the aid of
another person"*
- Ibibio Book of Wisdom

Ibibio Union Constitution

As regards the issue of the creation of states in Nigeria and as
to how it all began, I was elected General President, Ibibio Union in
succession to Mr. James Udo Affia in 1947. On assumption of office, I
discovered that the Ibibio Union had no written constitution. At the
Ibibio Union conference held that year at Uyo, I submitted, for study
and criticism, a draft constitution to a select committee, the chairman
of which was Mr. O. Bassey of the then Government Treasury Department at Enugu. One of the principal clauses of the constitution was
that changing the name of the union from Ibibio Union to Ibibio
State Union. In due course, the whole constitution was discussed by
the entire conference in session. In particular, the clause changing
the name of the union was explained to the satisfaction of the conference.

I explained that from the indication contained in the provisions
of Sir Arthur Richard's Constitution of 1945, which came into operation
in 1946 and which divided Nigeria into three regions of the Northern,
Western and Eastern Regions, it was clear that the British government,
after world War II of 1939-45, had abandoned the idea of developing
Nigeria as a unitary state and was, therefore, aiming at developing
Nigeria as a federation. In the light of that development, it was necessary that Nigerians, instead of waiting for the British colonial power
to direct the development of the federation, should start straight away
to engage themselves in directing the course of the federation; that

for that purpose it was necessary for Ibibio people to start to campaign for the creation of Ibibio State; and that, by changing the name Ibibio Union to Ibibio State Union, the Ibibio people would have been seen to have served notice on the whole of Nigeria, as a country, of their intention to have Ibibio State created.

The change immediately attracted publicity and press commentary to the extent that the Ibibio Union, Port Harcourt Branch, queried the necessity for the change. I was invited to Port Harcourt to answer the query on the principal reason that Ibibio elements in Port Harcourt were the objects of ridicule on the ground that the Ibibio people were considered too few to desire the creation of a state for themselves. That criticism was silent when, in 1949, the Ibo Union also changed its nomenclature to Ibo State Union.

Zik's Civilian Coup D'état

Then in 1953, Dr. Nnamdi Azikiwe, having been defeated in his bid to be Leader of Government Business of Western Nigeria at Ibadan by Mr. Obafemi Awolowo and his Action Group party, returned to Eastern Nigeria and successfully overthrew Professor Eyo Ita, who was Leader of Government Business of Eastern Nigeria, merely because the latter was a minority man from Calabar Province and the only reason for the success of Dr. Nnamdi Azikiwe being that he claimed himself to be a member of the Igbo ethnic group, which constituted the majority ethnic group in Eastern Nigeria.

In addition to Eyo Ita being overthrown from his office as Leader of Government Business of Eastern Nigeria, he was expelled from the NCNC party and a curse was also invoked on him and his race whereupon the minorities from Calabar, Ogoja and Rivers Provinces invited me to be their leader in the Eastern Regional House of Assembly at Enugu. I accepted the invitation on condition that they should pull together and form a separate state from the Eastern Region. This was accepted. As a result, we resigned en bloc from the NCNC and formed another party called NIP which later became United Independence Party of Nigeria (UNIP for short).

A constitutional conference was held in London subsequently in 1953 at the invitation of the Secretary of State for the Colonies at which, at the insistence of the Northern Peoples Congress (NPC for short), the regionalisation of Nigeria was reinforced and strengthened. The conference for the review of the Constitution of Nigeria resumed in January 1954 at Lagos for the purpose of completing some of the uncompleted tasks, including the sharing and distribution of revenue. In preparation for the resumed conference, I convened a conference of the people of Rivers, Ogoja and Calabar Provinces for the purpose of determining their future in view of the strengthening of the regionalisation of Nigeria.

COR Provinces Conference

The conference decided at Uyo in December 1953 that a memorandum be presented by a delegation to the Secretary of State, Mr. Oliver Lyttleton, at the resumed conference at Lagos demanding that, by the consent of the people concerned, the provinces of Calabar, Ogoja (without Abakiliki and Afikpo) and Rivers be constituted into a state, to be known as Calabar, Ogoja, Rivers (COR) State, separate from and independent of the Igbo ethnic sector of the Eastern Region. A memorandum of the kind, in order that it might be considered authoritative and given due weight, must bear the stamp and *imprimatur* of the peoples of Calabar, Ogoja and Rivers Provinces, which could only be given at a conference. The conference decided that a copy of the memorandum be forwarded through the usual official channel to Her Majesty, the Queen of England, Queen Elizabeth II, Head of the British Commonwealth and Empire. Members of the delegation were appointed at the conference and I was elected leader of the delegation having been earlier in Enugu elected Chairman of the COR State Movement then inaugurated.

Mr. Harold Wilcox (later Chief Biriye) was unanimously selected Honorary Secretary, he being regarded as an outstanding political activist. Chief Bishop D. Davies-Manuel was selected the Honorary Treasurer. The Executive Committee, as constituted at Enugu, consisted of Mr. D. D. Tom-George, Mr. Robert U. Umoinyang, Mr. A. U. A. Inyang, Mr. Akpan J. Ekpe, Mr. D. U. Assam and Mr. J. E. Ubom. It was agreed that the new organisation should be considered a movement for the creation of a new state as distinct from a new region in Eastern Nigeria, and therefore not a political party.

COR State Memorandum Submitted

Accordingly, I and Dr. Arikpo, who was elected Deputy Secretary General to me as Leader and Secretary General, duly in January 1954 presented the memorandum to the Secretary of State in Lagos. While accepting the memorandum, the Secretary of State for the Colonies advised that the issue of the creation of states be appropriately raised at the conference to be held in London in 1956 for the review of the constitution, for then "no holds would be barred" and that we should get ourselves organised properly. We left the conference rejoicing. Thereafter, we were engaged in the organisation of the COR State Movement and campaigning for the creation of the state. As a result of our campaign, the Midwest State Movement and the United Middle Belt State Congress (UMBC) surfaced.

Consequent upon our persistence in demanding the creation of the COR State and the emergence of the Midwest State Movement and the UMBC, the minority commission was appointed to consider the matter in 1957. The commission failed to recommend the creation of states as a means of allaying the fears of minorities and of protecting and safe guarding their interests in an independent Nigeria but merely recommended the creation of a Minority Council for the people of Calabar Province. This recommendation we rejected.

Immediately after the 1962 General Elections into the Eastern House of Assembly and the installation of Dr. Michael Iheonukara Okpara, as the Premier of the Eastern Region of Nigeria, the coalition federal government began to make preparations for the creation of what was termed the Mid-Western Region of Nigeria by the passing of the Mid-Western Region Act No. 6 of 1962. The move was said to be motivated by spite against the Action Group (A.G.) party, led by Chief Obafemi Awolowo who was said to have refused to join the coalition government under the leadership of Sir Abubakar Tafawa Balewa. Balewa, it was said, was anxious to form a national government of all the three political parties of N.P.C., N.C.N.C. and A.G..

Midwestern Region Formed

Then in 1963, with the passing of the Constitution of the Federation Act No. 20 of 1963 by the House of Representatives, Nigeria was declared the Federal Republic of Nigeria, and Dr. Nnamdi Azikiwe, as

Governor General of Nigeria, slid smoothly into the office of President of the Federal Republic of Nigeria. With this occurrence, the establishment of Benin Province, including Akoko Edo District in Afenmai Division, and Delta Province, including Warri Division and Warri Urban Township area, as the Mid-Western Region and the fourth region of Nigeria became a *fait accompli*. A new dimension was thus created in the political situation. A new concept had emerged in the Nigerian political horizon which raised fresh hopes in the breasts of those determined to see that states were also created in the Northern and the Eastern Regions of Nigeria. It was argued forcefully that, if the Western Region could be broken into two, there was no justification for refusing to split the Northern and the Eastern Regions, the Northern being the largest of the original three regions.

States Created In Nigeria

It was left for Nigerians to create states and this was initiated by Lt. Col. Yakubu Gowon who, on the eve of the declaration of Biafra, created 12 states among which were the Rivers State and the South Eastern State comprising Calabar and Ogoja Provinces less Abakiliki and Afikpo in Ogoja Province.[1] Then finally, on the 3rd of February 1976, the States (Creation and Transitional Provisions) Decree No. 12 of 1976 was promulgated, which raised the total number of states created in the whole of Nigeria to nineteen (19), each of which was specifically named and defined.[2]

Then on 27th August 1991, on the occasion of the celebration of the 6th anniversary of the assumption of power by the General Babangida led military government, he as President of the Federal Republic of Nigeria and Commander-in-Chief of the Armed Forces of Nigeria, Mr. President announced, in the course of his broadcast to the nation, the creation of nine (9) new states.[3]

The Armed Forces Ruling Council on 3rd September 1991 promulgated Decree No. 37 (States Creation and Transitional Provisions) of 1991. The opportunity was seized to amend section 3(1) of the 1979 constitution by the substitution of thirty (30) states for twenty-one (21), that is to say instead of twenty-one there were thirty (30) states in Nigeria.[4]

It should be observed that, prior to the creation of the nine (9) states, in September 1987 two (2) states, Akwa Ibom and Katsina States, were created and the existence of the two states was reflected in section 3(1) of the Constitution of the Federal Republic of Nigeria of 1989 which is in an inchoate state until 1st October 1992.[5]

On October 1, 1996, six states were added to the existing thirty states bringing the total number of states to thirty six (36).

Between Agitation for States & their Viabilty

Currently, the Senate Committee on the Review of the 1999 Constitution has received, for consideration in the amendment exercise, 56 requests for the creation of states. According to the Chairman of the SCRC, the demands for state creation have endured and proponents hinge their demands on the need for equity, justice, and speedy development. While memoranda and presentations for and against state creation were admitted at the just concluded National Public Hearing in Abuja, all memoranda and presentations proposing state creation, he said, are better handled and hence would be taken at the Public Hearing in the zones holding on November 15-16, 2013.

In contrast, Senator Olubunmi Adetumbi in October last year spoke on the state of bankruptcy of most of the states of the federation. Adetumbi said that most states had become social employers of labour with unsustainable high work force that does not reflect in improved service delivery to the people. He said, "In most states, the private sector is weak and unable to generate economic growth and jobs, thereby making the states and local governments the largest employers of labour with attendant fiscal imbalance. The bulk of the revenue of these states is currently financing the pay roll of the civil service, which constitutes less than 4% of the total population in those states. Under this development, six states are approaching distress. Kano will spend 127 %, Sokoto 62 %, Niger 56 %, Zamfara 54 %, Katsina 50 %, Osun 50 % of their gross annual revenue on civil service personnel."

According to him, most of the state governments now rush to the capital market to raise long term bonds to finance development projects, adding that without an appropriate framework, misuse of such funds could spell doom for the future of the states. He also revealed that the financial situation facing the states calls for urgent review of the revenue sharing structure amongst the Federal Government, the states and the local governments.[6]

Index

B

D

E

F

M

P

T

U

OTHER BOOKS BY THE AUTHOR

THE LION AND THE OIL PALM AND ANOTHER ESSAY
By Egbert Udo Udoma

In July 1943 the Council of the University Philosophical Society at Trinity College, Dublin decided to publish in booklet form two essays written and delivered by the author while a member of the society. "The Lion and the Oil Palm", which was a critique of the British colonial policy, was the inaugural address delivered by the author at the opening meeting of the Philosophical Society for the session 1942-43 when he was sworn in as the President of the society.

The essay is preceded in the booklet by a foreword by A. Creech Jones M.P. "The Clash of Cultures" was the author's prize essay that was delivered a few years earlier before a general public meeting of the Philosophical Society and for which he was awarded a silver medal by the society. It put in review how cultural differences may have affected Britain's administration of her colonies.

The booklet was printed at the University Press, Dublin by Ponsonby and Gibbs.

THE STORY OF THE IBIBIO UNION
By Sir Udo Udoma
ISBN: *978-0-9819192-3-2 (PB); 978-0-9819192-5-6 (HC)*

This book lays down the history of the Ibibio Union, as written by a pioneer, and it is the story of how it all began. It is the story of its imaginative beginning, its inspiring formation, its steady growth and wonderful expansion, its versatility and progress as a national institution, its dynamic flexibility, its arrested evolutionary development in the process of growth, and its untimely proscription as an active, virile and prolific association of a forward-looking, God-fearing, creative, dedicated and self-sacrificing Nigerian minority group in the old Eastern Region of Nigeria. The author hoped that present and future generations would be able to produce a better history of the Ibibio Union, which has become a landmark in the history of the growth and development of the Nigerian nation. The book was first published by Spectrum Books Limited in 1987 while an unabridged edition is being released by Amazing Grace Publishers this year (2018).

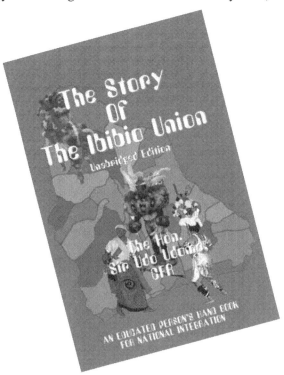

HISTORY AND THE LAW OF THE CONSTITUTION OF NIGERIA

By Sir Udo Udoma

ISBN: *978-0-9819192-2-5 (PB); 978-0-9819192-4-9 (HC)*

In writing this book, the author realised an ambition, which he had developed when he was a Reid's Professor's Prizeman of the Law School of the University of Dublin, Trinity College, Dublin, Ireland, to one day write a book on Constitutional Law. As an undergraduate student of Law, he manifested sound knowledge and keen interest in the study of Constitutional Law and History, Criminal Law, and the Law of Evidence and studied the Constitution of Eire, 1937 and later compared and contrasted the English Constitution and the constitutions of the Swiss Cantons and of the United States of America. Later on, he attended every constitutional conference ever held for the formulation of constitutions for the governance of Nigeria, presided over the Constitutional Court of Uganda when he was the Chief Justice of Uganda, and in 1977 chaired the Constituent Assembly that prescribed Nigeria's 1979 Constitution and, so, it was befitting and pertinent for him to have written an authoritative source of reference for students of Law as well as legal practitioners in Nigeria and elsewhere. The book was first published by Malthouse Press Limited in 1994 while an unabridged edition is being released by Amazing Grace Publishers this year (2011).

MUSINGS FROM THE SHELTER OF THE ELEPHANT ROCK
By Sir Udo Udoma
ISBN: 978-0-9819192-4-9 (HC)

     This book is a mosaic of excerpts from the different writings of the Hon. Sir Udo Udoma that relate to his heritage - the Ibibio people (including the Annang, the Obolo, the Oron and the Efik speaking people) and, in particular, the inhabitants of the village, township, river and local government area that bear the name of his ancestor, Abasi Akpan Enin, the lead founding father of Ikot Abasi in Akwa Ibom State of Nigeria, as compiled by the publisher.

     In this book, Sir Udoma also extrapolates on the circums-tances and events that necessitated and informed the agitation of minorities for states creation in Nigeria, as well as the injustice that was perpe-trated by the colonial government in allowing the people of Ikot Abasi to bear the foreign and unmeaning name of "Opobo" for so long in spite of the people's continuous agitation for a name change back to an indigenous one.

Printed in Great Britain
by Amazon